West Virginia State Archives, Kenna Collection

TALE
of the
ELK

TALE
of the
ELK

W. E. R. BYRNE

quarrier
press

CHARLESTON, WV

Quarrier Press
Charleston, WV

©1996, 2020 by Quarrier Press

Originally published in 1940 by the
West Virginia Publishing Co.

First Quarrier Press paperback edition, 1996

First Quarrier Press hardback edition, 2007

10 9 8 7 6 5 4 3 2

Printed in the United States of America

Library of Congress Control Number: 95-71152
ISBN-13: 978-0-9646197-2-2
ISBN-10: 0-9646197-2-5

Cover design: Mark S. Phillips

Distributed by:

West Virginia Book Company
1125 Central Avenue
Charleston, WV 25302
www.wvbookco.com

Contents

Contents

PREFACE

The Elk has a common mountain origin with other well known West Virginia rivers—the Greenbrier, the Gauley, the Tygarts Valley, the Cheat, the Little Kanawha, the Buckhannon, and the West Fork of the Monongahela. It flows south for 180 miles to join the Great Kanawha at Charleston, approximately 37 miles below the mouth of the Gauley. In another direction, the Tygarts Valley, the Cheat, and the West Fork make the Monongahela which flows north 250 miles to join the Ohio at Pittsburgh. The waters of the latter, be it noted, travel another 300 miles before they are swelled by the Great Kanawha at Point Pleasant.

Geologists declare that the Elk is many years "older" than the Gauley, just across the ridge to the south. The canyon of the Elk at Webster Springs is about 1500 feet deep and a small cut at the top of the ridge would turn the Gauley into the Elk Valley. At Camden-on-Gauley, the Gauley is over 500 feet higher than the Elk at Webster Springs and almost 1600 feet above the Elk at Sutton. The name Elk River antedates the Revolution. It was known to the Shawnee tribe of Indians as the Tis-chil-waugh, or river of "plenty fat elk." To the Miami Indians, it was, however, the Walnut River.

To write a story of the Elk River Valley and its people, one must keep in mind at all times human values, the author must indeed be a bred-in-the-bone lover of of the great outdoors. One must know the soul of the deep, unspoiled valleys and he must feel the roaring water pound the great rocks as he rests beside a mountain torrent. He must understand the song of the old mill wheel where man had harnessed the power of the stream; he must have an eye for the beauty of the hills and mountains that reach down to the water's edge and the trees and flowers that live upon the hills; and above all must crave time for reflection and cherish the good things that come from communing with nature. All of this, the author, William Eston Randolph Byrne, possessed to a remarkable degree.

Had it not always been so? Simon Kenton, Daniel Boone, Adam Yeager, the first Carpenter in the upper valley during the Indian wars—all had sampled the wares of the Elk and found them unusually good. Those who desire more prosaic evidence should turn to the elegant prospectus of the "West Virginia Iron Mining and Manufacturing Company," a little volume of some 29 pages, published in Richmond, March 15, 1837—one hundred and three years ago. The greatest of praise is given to the land along the Elk but the greatest of all inducements was that, "the pike measure from four to five feet in length and weighing from 30 to 40 pounds. The catfish measuring five feet and weighing 120 pounds." So let no reader of this story doubt a single word as to fish, be it weight, length, caught with a plug, snake, or in a hollow log, or perchance parade before a jury in the little courthouse at Clay.

If a little ray of reverence for the Elk shines through this preface the reader need not be surprised. Born on the West Fork of the Monongahela, at the little town of Roanoke, ten miles south of Weston, the writer watched the building of the West Virginia and Pittsburgh Railroad, so often mentioned in the text. The year was 1891-92 while the county of Lewis was proud of her own stories and fishing. The new railroad crossed to the Little Kanawha, rode over the crest and along the valley of the Elk for several miles and then followed the "Big Ditch" into Lane's Bottom, on the Gauley River. Over this new line came great timbers for the World's Fair, at Chicago in 1893, millions of feet of lumber for Eastern markets. Stories of game and fish far superior to the Monongahela came out of the same great wilderness.

In May, 1907, the writer, with other young men, journeyed down to Clarksburg to a meeting of the old

West Virginia Fish and Game Protective Association. There we heard from the lips of the late Andrew Price, and others, most marvelous "yarns." Then came the "thrill of a lifetime" when we were permitted to ride at public expense to the mouth of Holly and turn out in new homes, some ten large containers filled with some species of bass sent from a government hatchery. The year before the Point Lookout Camping Club had gotten under way, just below the mouth of Holly River, with Ed Ralston, Sr., as "President" and the writer as Secretary and "kitchen police." The spell of the Elk had intrigued "fishermen" and "laymen" alike, just as it had intrigued the author of the "tales" that follow.

The author was an able lawyer, a talented engineer, a philosopher and some alleged, a West Virginia politician. People and things and the law interested him every day. A little journal for the year 1899, starts the New Year off with a "talk with John Holt over the political situation." This done, he "made some maps" and checked a "four-inch snow." March 6 comes and with it a great flood with "two-thirds of Charleston under water." A law case calls him to Sutton and Webster Springs, the first about ninety miles away, but then, miles and miles away. A train to Huntington, thence to Parkersburg, a bus across town and a train to Clarksburg, thence to Weston, and on into Sutton. Two days on the way and all along stopped to see friends. Back into that country on April 22, he "received a pass good on the B. and O." from (Rand) Stalnaker, which so pleased him that he "went fishing with Charlie and Ed Bland and Shelt Carpenter to Dog Falls." In spite of Carpenter's reputation as a fisherman, he landed only two to Byrne's seven. On May 3 he was in Weston communing with kindred spirits and a little later Judge (Henry) Brannon assured him it always rained "on 10th of May." And believe it or not, he set down, "June 1. I sat in my office and watched it snow."

The month of July found the journalist back in court along the upper Elk, and by August 26 he left camp on Cranberry and "went to rattlesnake dens, caught 14 rattlers." Fall came and with it the Centennial at Parkersburg, where on Thursday, October 5, he assisted in "laying cornerstone of new Court House" and took "in the fire works" and started to Grafton. News came of a rich oil strike on the Camden farm at Weston, which caused "great excitement." The next day men along the Glenville road, leading into Weston, stopped some small boys and searched pockets for matches. The excitement noted by Mr. Byrne became so acute schools were dismissed and among the group mentioned was the writer. The year is brought to a close in the general practice of the law, on December 18, when "left for home at noon (from Clay C. H.), on a SPECIAL TRAIN with Gov. MacCorkle, Joe Chilton, McDermott and Sam Burdette." So all in all, the passing days were busy days but always with some time out for mental and physical refreshment along the Elk.

The series of stories here published is brought together from the files of the *West Virginia Wildlife,* official publication of the Wild Life League of West Virginia and the *Braxton Democrat* of Sutton, with one addition. A contributing editor of the first named publication, Mr. Byrne, during the summer of 1927, wrote a couple of stories for the magazine, which attracted attention from the public press. The result was that in the December, 1927, issue, he started the *Tale of the Elk* in some regular form, one "part" being published each month to December, 1931, inclusive. These parts were collected, arranged in order by the author and with some slight changes here and there, reprinted in the *Braxton Democrat,* at Sutton, in 1933. Some additions were made, and there the printed story ends.

It had been intended originally to run at least three more "parts." One had to do with "Bill Paxton's Baptism and the Straw Stack," a story that only the author could tell. Paxton was a noted character "who got religion," then after taking refuge in a straw stack to rest until the end of the world, the hand of fate struck with fire, transferred him (so he thought) to another world instead of the "good land," but all ended happily. Another had to do with the "town at the mouth of Elk" and the erection of the first capitol building at Charleston. In the material was a letter written by Collis P. Huntington, on stationery of the Willard Hotel, Washington, D. C., which proved that the sum of $40,-000 had been advanced on the building by the builder of the C. and O. railroad. A history-making document. Unfortunately the manuscripts (if completed) for these two proposed chapters were lost. One, which the author had marked "Part L," was never published and is here printed for the first time as Chapter 49. "Part 42," a long poem having to do with the law in general and lawyers in particular, and a short poem by J. L. Cole, (October, 1931), have been omitted.

In connection with the original publication several illustrations were used which are not here reproduced. Some of a general nature having to do with beauty spots along the river; others are more specialized. Among these may be mentioned the "headsprings and split rock" head of Elk; old Cowger's Mill; flood at Sutton; town of Henry (Clay) in 1896; and H. B. Davenport with his famous twenty-four pound pike. In the June, 1930, number was reproduced the original plat of two land surveys indicating change of names of streams along the Elk. The original is recorded in Map Book I, at Charleston.

Acknowledgments are due for assistance in this undertaking to H. B. Davenport, R. Carl Andrews, R. G. Kelly, D. N. Mohler, and Judge Fred L. Fox.

Charleston   Roy Bird Cook

INTRODUCTION

By Judge Fred L. Fox

A reading of the *Tale of the Elk* will vividly disclose that side of the author's character which attests his love of field, woods, and stream, and his fond associations with those of a kindred spirit; but it seems fitting that something be said of the man and his achievements in the world at large.

William Eston Randolph Byrne was born October 26, 1862, at Fort Defiance, in the Valley of Virginia, in the dark days of the war between the states. His ancestry was most distinguished. His father, Benjamin W. Byrne, was a leader of the bar in Braxton County at the outbreak of the war, and afterwards became a prominent figure in the early history of this State. His mother Mary (Holt) Byrne, was a sister of Homer A. Holt, a distinguished lawyer and for many years a circuit judge, and a member of the Supreme Court of Appeals of West Virginia. His parents, on returning to this State after the war, first lived at Clay Court House in the Elk Valley, and shortly thereafter removed to Charleston, where, with brief intermissions, he spent the formative years of his youth and was educated. Under the guidance of gifted parents he became deeply versed in history, biography, and the classics. He was a surveyor and engineer of no mean ability. When he attained manhood, he studied law under the tutorship of Judge Holt. He was licensed to practice in October, 1884; located at Sutton, in Braxton County, also in the Elk Valley, in April, 1885, where he remained for twelve years, and there laid the ground work of his success at the bar. He served one term as Prosecuting Attorney of Braxton County, and practiced his profession in the counties of Braxton, Clay, Nicholas and Webster. While living in that section, he had many opportunities to make the acquaintance of the early settlers and their descendants, and to indulge his fondness for outdoor life.

On June 12, 1891, he married Miss Amanda Austin of Lewisburg, and to this union were born the following children: George Austin; Marie Louise (Mrs. L. L. Sheets); Barbara Linn (Mrs. D. N. Mohler); Charlotte Virginia (Mrs. R. B. Mesmer); and William Eston Randolph, Jr.

He returned to Charleston in the year 1897, and was, for forty years, an honored and respected member of the Kanawha County bar, with a practice which extended widely throughout the State. From early manhood until his death, he was an active and trusted leader in the Democratic Party and held a high place in its councils. At different periods, he served as Clerk of both the Senate (1893) and the House of Delegates of his State (1899), and as Speaker of the House of Delegates in the session of 1923. In 1935 he was selected Chairman of the Workmen's Compensation Appeal Board, which position he held until his appointment as Clerk of the Supreme Court of Appeals on August 1, 1937, in which capacity he served until his death on December 11, 1937, at the age of seventy-five years.

These achievements may be recorded: A long and successful career at the bar; an honorable record of public service; a leader and a loyal servant of the political party of his choice; the respect and confidence of all with whom he came in contact during a full and busy life.

His chief characteristics were a high sense of honor in every relation of life, public and private; a devotion to the things he believed in, which was impregnable against attack; a disposition to uphold his beliefs, where principle was involved, against any appeal of personal gain or advantage to himself; pride in the family from which he sprang, and zeal that its record should not be tarnished by one ignoble act on his part; loyalty to friends, many times at the expense of personal sacrifice; constant adherence to lofty principles in public affairs by whomsoever administered; and a tender and fervent love for his family, unceasing to the end of his days, and from which there was no shadow of turning.

With this background of high principles, culture, and a busy and exacting life, he never lost the common touch. He had the rare faculty not only to adjust himself to any environment, but to make all associated with him feel at ease in his presence. By men and women of high station, and in the most select circles, he was looked upon as an equal, and to the native hunter and fisherman of his favorite stream, the Elk, he was a boon companion and with whom he loved to match wits and spend his periods of leisure. To everyone he was approachable and considerate, and he numbered his friends in all walks of life. He delighted in gathering his friends around the campfire at night and there relating the choice stories, gleaned from his rich experiences, many of which are, fortunately, preserved for the future in this volume. From them we learn how well-rounded a life he lived, and understand how genuine was the regret felt by the inhabitants of the Valley of the Elk and elsewhere, when the Fisherman of Souls called him home.

> "Home is the sailor, home from the sea,
> And the hunter home from the hill."

To those who knew him best this volume will, as the years come and go, preserve a most pleasant and ever-increasing appreciation of a unique and interesting man, and assist in holding in fond remembrance stories of days that are gone.

I

THE HEADWATERS

A SHORT TIME AGO (1927), my friend G. A. (Gus) Bolden, editor and general manager of *West Virginia Wild Life Magazine,* asked me if it were not true that I had traversed Elk River and had fished all the way from its headspring to the mouth. In an unguarded moment and with no thought of consequences, I admitted the impeachment or distinction, whichever it may be regarded: and was then and there by him commissioned and commanded to proceed to write this Tale or these Tales of the Elk, on the installment plan, for his magazine.

There being no conditions imposed, no rules or regulations prescribed, I propose to tell the story in my own way, make it long or short, as I please, leave the main stream and wander up the creeks, ravines, or mountain sides, whenever the notion strikes me, seek to vitalize in passing, lingering or loitering, the inanimate, and feel free to draw on the imagination when necessary for vitality or embellishment — in fact, using free hand in both warp and woof, for foreground, background, perspective, setting, and color — endeavoring always, however, to keep at least within the watershed of the main stream — and also of the main truth.

As it is always easier going — though often more perilous—down than upstream—floating with, rather than bucking the current, let us begin at the head and drift downward by easy stages, though sometimes difficult portages, to the mouth — or so far in that direction as we are fortunate enough to avoid shipwreck or other disaster.

The Elk is formed by the junction of the Big Spring Fork and the Old Field Fork, in Pocahontas County, 166 miles above its mouth at Charleston, at an elevation above sea level of 2,670 feet, or 2,070 feet above the Capital City.

It has its fountain source in the famous Greenbrier limestone belt of West Virginia, which embraces portions of the counties of Monroe, Greenbrier, Pocahontas, Webster, Randolph, Tucker, Hardy, and Grant, greater in extent than the far-famed Blue Grass region of Kentucky. The valleys of both Big Spring Fork and Old Field extend about nine miles above the Forks and though gashed deep in the strata and walled high by those great mountains forming the watershed between the Elk and Greenbrier on the east, the Tygarts Valley to the north and the Gauley and the Williams to the west and south, nevertheless their beds are devoid of water running above the ground, but for short stretches here and there, except during freshet seasons, the channel and outlet being subterranean. One of these mountains, dividing the waters of Elk from those of the Middle Fork of Gauley at an elevation of 4500 feet, I shall always remember from one memorable night's experience in limping the nine miles across, with a busted knee. But, as I am getting off the watershed, so much for that at this time.

The Big Spring Fork is usually held to be the main head of Elk, although the Old Field Fork is fully as large. Big Spring Fork takes its name from one or the other of two large springs, the lower of which gushes from the ground about one-half mile above the junction of the forks, affording sufficient water to operate a fair-sized gristmill, and the other about seven miles above, on the old Colonel Gatewood place. Which of these two big springs in fact furnished the name for the fork, would seem to depend on whether the fellow who applied it was traveling upstream or down. Ascending the narrow valley of this watercourse for about three miles above the lower big spring — two and a half miles of the distance being over a perfectly dry bed — you reach the split rock, which is sometimes spoken of, although erroneously, as the fountainhead of Elk; for, regardless of whether it was the upper or the lower of the two big springs for which the stream was named, the upper, or Gatewood spring, is in fact the fountain source.

I shall never forget my first introduction to the Split Rock. About a dozen years ago I visited it with my old friend and fishing partner, "Bear-Skin Bill" Hamrick, now a merchant at Webster Springs, who at that time lived at the mouth of Leatherwood on Elk (Bergoo post office), ten miles above Webster Springs, and eighteen miles below the forks. He and I had previously made numerous trips to the "Upper River," as it is called, but had always found trout so plentiful at, about, and below the forks, that we did not have need to go in search of pastures new. On this occasion, however, which, by the way, was the first summer after the railroad was completed from the Forks down to Leatherwood, Bill and I made the trip from his home to the Upper River on a railroad speeder, and found the stream a little flush and somewhat milky — not at all suitable for fly-fishing. We spent a day or so with rather indifferent success; we tried bait-fishing, which neither cared much for, and the third day Bill suggested that we go up to the Split Rock, stating that a man by the name of Varner owned the land on which the Split Rock Spring was located; that he was acquainted with Varner, and although that gentleman did not allow much fishing on his premises, no doubt he would favor us. I had heard my father speak of the Split Rock, and since boyhood had a strong desire to visit it; so we took the road for a three-mile jaunt up the creek along the dry bed, to the residence of Mr. Varner. We found him at the stile in front of his house, and Hamrick introduced me. I told him of the bad fishing conditions below, and of my lifelong desire to see and catch trout in the very fountainhead of Elk — the far-famed Split Rock Spring, of which I had heard so much — and requested that he confer a great favor by granting us permission to fish on his premises.

"Now, gentlemen," said he, in the most deprecating tone imaginable, "I have only a few trout left here on my place. Everybody wanted to fish, and I let them, until they pretty near ruined me, so finally I had to shut down on it altogether and let nobody fish. I haven't allowed a soul to fish there for a month — turned down neighbors and strangers alike — and, although I am sorry, you see it wouldn't be right for me to let you gentlemen fish when I won't let my neighbors."

And that was that.

After this knockout blow he turned to me and said: "However, I would be glad for you to see the Split Rock, and will take the pleasure in showing it to you; it is up the road just a little way."

I expressed gratitude for his offer and my keen desire to see the spring; so we wended our way in the direction indicated, Hamrick, rather sullen, bringing up the rear. Three or four hundred yards above the house and only a few steps from the road as it then was — the new state road is now (1927) under construction on the other side of the narrow valley — we stepped out upon a flat limestone ledge, and there, suddenly disclosed to view, I beheld the wonderful spring, hedged in on three sides by a perpendicular limestone wall, the water apparently coming from nowhere, forming a beautiful basin of about fifteen hundred feet in area, the depth varying from two to four feet — and then hastening away through a rock-cut channel to form a larger pool below.

Standing there entranced, I gazed upon the pure limpid water, its surface smooth and glassy, except here and there shot with arrows of sheen and shimmer left by the delicate kiss of a passing zephyr — a dazzling jewel, sparkling and scintillating there in its somber setting, encircled by majestic mountains rising step by step and peak on peak as far as vision carried, giving back to the eye in reflex the glories of a perfect midsummer sky — a purest gem of ray serene, hidden away in the unfrequented fastnesses of wildest Appalachia — and beneath, disporting themselves in the shallows, or idly lounging in the deeper parts, countless speckled beauties, challenging the admiration and wonder of the beholder and appealing to the keen desire of the angler. But— Thou Shalt Not! My feelings in that beautific yet distracting moment were doubtless akin to those of Apollo when/if he surprised the chaste and elusive Daphne at her morning ablutions in the crystal clear fountain; or of the ravenous Tantalus when he beheld the delicious but ever vanishing grapes spread mockingly before him; or of the first citizens of Eden when they spied for the first time the bidding but forbidden fruit, and called to mind the interdiction, "Touch not, taste not!" But, "stolen waters are sweet, and bread eaten in secret is pleasant"—and I was conscious of a furtive glance at my conductor, a rebellious, involuntary, and almost imperceptible movement of my hand and arm, but was restrained as is the despoiler, who, his guilty hand upon the gate latch, beholds the good man standing upon the threshold, and resignedly thinks to bide his time for a more propitious season. Then surged through my brain and almost into speech the thought: Good God, turn back the Universe and give me the good old days when the right of piscary was common to all people, and not a privilege to be bestowed or withheld by the lord of the manor!

I was startled by words falling from the lips of Varner, like a benediction from Heaven or the answer to prayer:

"S'pose you try your luck on those big fellows over on the far side!"

Turning to my partner and seeing him empty handed, I yelled: "Bill, where's your rod?"

"I left it down at the stile," said Bill, but he was well "on his way" before the reply was completed.

Hoglike, I unlimbered my tackle immediately without awaiting the return of my friend, but had not made many casts before Bill returned with his rod, but without his breath.

I tried the big ones on the far side, the medium ones in the middle, and the smaller ones in the shallows, and when Bill got his tackle ready, he did likewise. I changed my flies and Bill changed his. We tried them with Queen of Waters, Black Gnat, Parmachence Belle, Grizzly King, Brown Palmer, Black Palmer, Professor, Yellow May, Jungle Cock, Willow, Stone, Rube Wood, White Miller, all the hackles, and Cow Dungs of every shade and pattern. I borrowed flies from Bill and Bill borrowed flies from me. Neither got a strike! I had a new hatch of dry flies which both used with no better success. Sometimes a trout would deign to take scant notice of the lure and saunter leisurely in its direction, but invariably he changed his mind — if a trout has a mind — and had a mind to strike.

One fine fellow, standing full sixteen inches in his stocking feet, actually followed my flies clear across the pool, acting like he really might mean business, but stopped in shallow water within ten feet of where I was standing. I was watching him closely, saw him suddenly stop and look up at me, wiggle his fins and laugh! That is, I thought he laughed. I may have been mistaken, however, because Bill was standing near me looking at the trout, and was in every whit as good position to see, and when I said, "Did you see that trout laugh?" he replied: "No, I didn't see him laugh — but I wasn't noticing him very close." Bill is a fine chap and always tries to help a fellow out when he can do so conscientiously; and I know very well if that trout had laughed, Bill would have seen it, and if he had seen it, he would have said so — consequently, I am going to withdraw the assertion that I actually saw that trout laugh; but I still insist that I know darn well it did.

When we had been fishing about half an hour, Mr. Varner, who had eagerly watched the proceedings throughout with ever-increasing interest, remarked apologetically: "Gentlemen, I can't understand these trout. Usually they bite very freely, and for that reason I was reluctant to let you fish, for fear you would depopulate the pool. I am awfully sorry. You may have better luck in that next pool."

We repaired to the pool indicated, a long deep hole four times as large as the first, but much more difficult to negotiate, owing to the undergrowth along the bank on either side. Here we fished with flies and fished with worms and with crickets, grasshoppers and crawfish which Mr. Varner most generously provided for us; but neither strike nor bite rewarded our efforts. We then dropped downstream, whipping the smaller pools and shallows to and beyond Varner's residence, where the water sinks and for two and one-half miles or more traverses the labyrinthine limestone caverns and crevasses, before it again seeks daylight at the Big Spring above described. Not a bite!

I never saw a man give evidence of greater mortification and chagrin than did our host Varner. When once warm compassion, generated by the entreaty of our yearning and dejected gaze at the objects of our desire, had melted his frigid resolve, and he had yielded, he did so most graciously, wholeheartedly, and unreservedly. He wanted us to catch those trout and wouldn't have cared — but would have been delighted — if we had caught every "goldarned" one of them; and when the measly things balked and sulked and took the studs and refused to go through their paces, he was hurt to his bosom's core.

When we had wasted three hours of our time and his, in futile and unrequited effort, and were ready to throw up the sponge, Varner insisted that we be his guests for the night, and that we fish a few hours by moonlight and again at the first streak of dawn next morning.

We were forced, however, to decline his generous offer, owing to Bill's having an appointment to meet a man that evening down at "Bill" Gibson's at the mouth of Glady; so, reluctantly and crestfallen, we retreated from our Waterloo. I never saw my friend Varner again; I learned that he was gathered to his fathers several years ago, and sure I am that "flights of angels hymned him to his rest."

Last July my law partner, John Hamilton Linn, and I visited the head of Elk, driving over the Midland Trail to Lewisburg, thence by the Seneca Trail via Frankford, over Droop Mountain to Hillsboro, to Marlinton, and over the mountain between the Greenbrier and the Elk, to Glady Fork, the post office name of Forks of Elk. We took photographs of several points which may fit into this yarn, the first of which being "Split Rock." The image here presented is a poor counterpart of the real. You do not get the impression as eye would get it, owing to the fact that because of surrounding walls of stone the camera had to be too close up in order to show the water and at the same time the proper perspective. It will serve, however, to convey a general idea of the spring.

"If thou wouldst view fair Melrose aright" — go view it for yourself; don't take anybody's word or picture for it.

II

THE DRY BED

THE ELK having been duly constituted, organized, and declared ready to proceed to business in the first installment of this history, narrative tale, or what you may choose to call it, we will attempt to follow its wayward, devious, and distinctly freakish meanderings with such fidelity and accuracy as might be expected on the part of a fellow forced as to much that will be dealt with, to depend solely upon a recollection never infallible and sometimes most treacherous, of and concerning experiences and happenings extending from dates quite recent to those of twenty, thirty, forty, and fifty years ago. Due to the fact that my knowledge with respect to the stream was for the most part acquired as incidental to my indulgence in the piscatorial pastime, most naturally it is from that angle (not a pun — which I despise), that the subject should be treated, largely though not exclusively.

It was, I believe, in the year 1908, that I first saw the junction of the Big Spring and Old Field Forks. Bill Hamrick and I left his residence at the mouth of Leatherwood, bound for the head of Elk, crossing the mountain between Elk and Gauley, coming to the latter stream at the mouth of Straight Creek, just above "Pole" Barb's; thence up Gauley to the Three Forks, and nine miles over the mountain to the Forks of Elk, at the Harmon Sharp place. We spent some time fishing in Gauley as we passed along, reaching the Three Forks about sundown, the second or third day out, and decided to cross the mountain that night. Just as we were about to leave the stream and take the trail across the mountain, in jumping from rock to rock in the bed of the Middle Fork, I got a terrible fall, sustaining a severe injury to my right knee, the pain from which was so intense as to make me deathly sick for the space of about fifteen minutes, and a fit subject for the ambulance and hospital, had any such been available. Being miles from any habitation, and fearing inaction and resulting stiffness would be the worst thing possible, I decided to try to make the trip across that night — six miles up to the top of the mountain on the Gauley side and three miles down the other side to Elk. Every step up the mountain was painful, but when I started downgrade and changed gears, the pain was much more acute, and when we reached the Elk at the Harmon Sharp place about 10 o'clock p.m., I was "all in," and no mistake. Bill built a campfire and soon had ready a good supper of trout, bread, and coffee, which we disposed of promptly. By this time the moon was riding high in the heavens and Bill hurried away to the river, after inquiring if I would join him. But for the first and only time in my life I was compelled to renege. "No, thank you, Bill," said I, weakly, "I'd better go to bed." Getting to bed consisted of smoothing off a place before the fire — that is, picking up the rocks and sticks and tramping down the rough places, weeds and briers, such as chanced to encumber the ground at the chosen spot, and there depositing myself, with head upon the lap of Earth and the starry dome for a "coverlid." Having selected a rather concave or scooped-out place for my bed, I tucked myself snugly in, and almost instantly was dead to the world — sleeping a sleep the depth of which no man knoweth who never slept under like provocation. About 4 o'clock in the morning I was rudely awakened by a violent shake and a voice —

"Get up, I say — man, you'll drown!"

When I realized what all the fuss was about, the rain was pouring down in torrents in my upturned face, my body half submerged in the water which had filled the trough-like place in which I was lying, and Bill was standing over me with a fine string of brook trout. We hastened over to an old straw stack near by, under which we burrowed for shelter until the rain, heavy but short of duration, had ceased, when we rekindled the fire, before which we both lay down in wet clothes and slept for several hours.

And here let me take occasion to remark that a fellow will not take cold on a fishing trip, although he wear wet clothing all day and sleep in wet clothing all night.

Next day and night we fished about the Forks and up the Big Spring Fork as far as the water extended, and a short distance up the Slaty Fork, which empties into Old Field about one-half mile above the junction. The water was very low and clear, the dashing rain of the night before having no visible effect either to swell or color the streams. Our daylight catch was nothing to be proud of. That night, however, we waited for the moon to rise and then covered the same ground with much better luck as to both size and number.

About noon the following day we left the Forks and started down the river. From the Forks down there was a succession of pools and shallows, swifts and eddies, extending for a distance of about three miles, which, to my mind, surpasses anything in the way of trout water it has ever been my good fortune to visit, excepting only, but always, the three miles of the same stream, between Cowger's Mill and Whittaker Falls, which we will come to later.

Just above the mouth of Big Run, which comes in at the lower end of the Harmon Sharp place, there are two splendid holes, which now, since the advent of the Rainbow, are generally supposed to have yielded a larger catch of that variety than any other pools of the Upper River, as formerly they did of the speckled breed. From the mouth of Big Run down for several hundred yards, the water is quite swift, and, except in very low water, this is one of the best and sportiest stretches for fly-fishing anywhere to be found, the sporty feature being to wade and cast upstream and experience the thrill of a good strike when your fly touches the rushing water and

the trout whizzes down past you with thirty or forty feet
of line out, or darts off to one side, seeking refuge under
or alongside of a large boulder or rock cliff. To handle
your rod, slack of the line, your feet, your head — and
the trout — all at one and the same time, will give any
angler the thrill of his life. If you are lucky enough
to snag your trout and land him as well, then you get
both the thrill and the trout; but if you snag him and
then lose him, all you have lost is the trout,. which is *de
minimum* as compared with that which remains.

Right at this point I am reminded of what John L.
Dickinson, one of Charleston's and Elk River's most
devoted and successful bass fishermen, told me a short
time ago: "If I can hang a good bass and he will give
me a real fight and I can whip him and make him come
up and surrender, then I am ready to turn him loose for
the next fellow." I wish we had more sportsmen of the
same kidney.

The swift water dashes around a long curve and
against the base of a cliff on the left, turning suddenly
to the left at right angles into a splendid, long, deep pool
extending along the base of a limestone cliff for several
hundred feet. But in ordinary low water stages, instead
of swift water around this curve, there are a number of
small pools and swifts. I speak of this place in particular, because it was here in this curve that I first used
the dry fly in swift water. At the place where I started
in wading upstream, the overhanging branches on either
side made it necessary to wade in the middle of the stream
where the water was deep and swift — that is, about
knee-deep, which is deep wading against swift water. I
put out about thirty feet of line and, on the return,
stripped it rapidly with my left hand. Nothing happened. The next cast I let out about forty feet, and as
the fly was settling down, a brook trout met it at the
surface of the water and made a straight dive for me.
Not quick enough in stripping the line so as to use the
spring of the rod in my defense, the pesky thing was

right on me and had me completely surrounded, before I could get out of its way — surrounded with about twenty feet of tangled, gnarled, and knotted fishing line. As I did not attain sufficiently intimate acquaintance with that particular trout to ascertain his exact proportions, I'll just guess him off at twelve inches. After hobbling to shore, disengaging myself from the line, cutting off several yards, too badly messed up for untangling, I tried it again. Getting several rises before I got a real strike, I was becoming somewhat more dexterous in retrieving the line, and was congratulating myself that I was becoming quite an expert, when "bang!" a full-grown trout struck the fly as the fly struck the water, with forty feet of line out, and I never knew what had happened until the fine fellow broke water away over to my right next to a cliff, and spit out the fly. I hadn't even felt the tug. Then I realized that the novice in upstream swift water fly-fishing should not employ more line than he is able to handle. After that, I used about twenty to twenty-five feet of line and finally succeeded in landing two nice fellows, ten and twelve inches, respectively, but this did not happen until I had lost two or three times as many, one of them being a dandy, which I snagged and successfully steered downstream past where I was standing, but, checking him too suddenly in the swift current, the gut to the fly parted and he kept on going.

Bill and I put in the afternoon fishing down the river in a desultory sort of way for about a mile and a half and there built our campfire and waited for the moon to rise, whereupon we started in for real business. As it was my first visit to that section, and being therefore unfamiliar with the lay of the land, we fished together for the most part, Bill selecting the most likely pools below our campfire. We would quietly approach and quietly remain at the chosen point until the trout began "jumping," that is, feeding on the night-flies hovering about the surface of the water, the splash or ripple thus made being distinctly visible in the moonlight, and frequently the gulp, or whatever sound it is the trout makes when he smacks his lips on a fly, being quite audible. This was our invitation to begin fishing — and many old fishermen will sit out the moonlight hours and never wet line until and unless the invitation is extended with due form and ceremony.

It was by moonlight that I first saw the "Boiling Hole," which is referred to in my yarn about catching the bat which appeared in an earlier number of *Wild Life*. The bubbles caused by the water disappearing in the underlying strata and seeking its subterranean channel, were almost as fully perceptible as by sunlight. It is the better part of a mile from the Boiling Hole down to the Black Hole, where the water is supposed to finally disappear and the Dry Bed to begin, but I have seen the Black Hole as dry as a powder horn and not a drop of running water in the channel for at least a quarter of a mile above.

We made a fairly good haul that night, but, as I was still feeling the effects of my busted knee, when we had gotten back up the river as far as our campfire, I decided to hang up for the night. Bill, however, never wastes a minute of the "fishing moon," and there being fully thirty minutes left, betook himself to a pool a hundred yards or so above the campfire. I built up a roaring fire and was reposing peacefully when Bill roused me by touching my face with something cold and clammy. Opening my eyes, I beheld the largest brook trout I have ever seen. As Bill held it up between me and the bright fire, the thing looked uncanny, and my first exclamation was, "I don't believe it!" When I tell you that trout was only fifteen inches from tip to fork, yet weighed two and one-half pounds, you will appreciate my bewilderment.

In answering my question as to how he caught it, etc., Bill declared, "Partly with a hook and partly with my foot"; which being interpreted meant that it struck his fly in deep water, and that after quite a fight he had reeled it into shallow water between him and dry land and just as he was about to lead it out on a smooth sand bar, it gave a sudden flounce, spit out the hook and started for deep water, but by a lucky kick he landed it high and dry. The eggs in that trout made a double handful and must have weighed almost, if not fully, a pound.

After fishing out the Upper River, we proceeded downstream over the six miles of Dry Bed, past the mouth of the Dry Fork of Elk, which empties — when it has anything to empty — on the northern side opposite the old Bradshaw place. While I never negotiated the Dry Fork, my information is that it is just what and all that its name implies.

To describe the Dry Bed of Elk, extending a distance of six miles from the Upper River down to Cowger's Mill, where the water again comes to the surface, would be impossible, unless it be to some extent, by comparison with a stream with which the reader may be familiar.

The New River Gorge on a smaller scale, the mountains less high and steep; the Roughs of Gauley, toned down by half; the upper rough and rugged branches of the Cheat — take a six-mile section from these, and imagine the same to be wholly barren of running water, and you may have some slight conception of the Dry Bed of Elk. But there are some very marked features that none of these can supply, even by way of comparison. A large portion of this six miles shows the channel cut in limestone, here neatly and regularly chiseled as though by the hand of man, there rough, jagged, irregular, and bristling with jutting points and sharp angles, pitted, pock-marked and honey-combed; here a deep narrow chasm over which a man may leap, there a wide, deep abyss, eaten out of the solid rock, by erosion and the externally pounding floods of the ages; caverns extending far back under the overlying strata, huge rocks and boulders, everywhere in and along and adjacent to

the channel, and at one notable point, the river bed a
level flat rock two hundred and fifty feet in width and
twice as long, smooth as a flatiron and flat as a smoothing iron, used, by the way, by the people round about for
Fourth of July picnics, dances and like diversions; while
a short distance below, at the mouth of Chimney Rock
Branch, is a perennial ice house and cold storage plant,
where the winter snows, driven and packed in among the
rocks along the hillside, shaded through the spring and
summer months by dense foliage, are preserved for
Fourth of July ice cream and lemonade. In fact, I have
found ice at that place as late as August.

The Dry Bed extends to Cowger's Mill, where the
water gushes forth in two great springs, one of which
is within less than one hundred feet of the Old Cowger
Mill which was first installed almost one hundred years
ago. This spring is not affected by flood or drought,
but produces an even volume of water the year round —
that volume being sufficient to keep the mill in constant
operation — although for many years the mill has not
been so kept. The other spring, some two hundred yards
away, is largely affected by flood and drought, and at
times goes completely dry.

Before leaving the Dry Bed entirely, I cannot refrain
from a weak attempt to describe what was to me a most
impressive incident in connection therewith. On the
occasion of my first visit to Split Rock, as related in
the first installment of this tale, and the next day after
our lamentable experience as there related, Bill and I
decided to try our luck in Laurel Branch, a rather small
stream that comes in at the upper end of the Harmon
Sharp place. While fishing about a quarter of a mile up
the branch, it began to rain, and we concluded to quit
fishing altogether, get dinner at the boarding house,
return home on the speeder that afternoon and try for
bass down about Leatherwood. Before we got down to
the mouth of the branch, however, the rain so increased
that we felt compelled to take shelter under a tree. While

there, we were startled by the most terrific crash on crash and roar and roar, away off in the direction of the head of Old Field Fork. The sound was unlike the ordinary peals of thunder or any disturbances I had ever heard. It sounded more like a continuous crash such as would be made by all the trees in the forest falling at the same time, some being timed a little slower than the others, followed by a roar and alternating crash and roar, crash and roar, extending over ten minutes' time.

"Cloudburst up Old Field Fork," said Bill; "let's go."

We hastened to the boarding house, found dinner ready, which we ate quickly, and, coming out on the porch, where we could hear distinctly the roar of the coming flood, and in less than five minutes saw its advance guard a quarter of a mile away. To get to the railroad where our speeder was parked we had to cross the Old Field Fork on a footbridge, well above high water, and walk over some low ground between the bridge and the railroad. Fast as we traveled, we were caught in this low place by the water knee-deep, which means about four feet in the channel which two minutes before had been perfectly dry. Our first thought was to take the speeder and get away as fast as possible; but it occurred to me what a wonderful sight it would be to see that flood as it poured into and traversed the Dry Bed; and, having suggested this to Bill, he said we would give it a little time and then start out on our speeder and overtake it about the lower end of the Bradshaw place, where we could have a good view from the railroad. We waited half an hour or more, by which time there was over six feet of water in Old Field and four feet in Big Spring Fork, and then set forth to overtake the head of the flood, which we did just about the appointed place. At a point two or three hundred feet ahead, we stopped, and looking back, beheld the head and front of the rapidly oncoming yellow flood, lashing and buffeting its rock-bound confines, seeking out

and obliterating the voids in its pathway, ruthlessly
tossing aside the unfixed and spurning the fixed ob-
stacles to its progress, gathering the while from each
obstruction new impetus and greater volume; huge rocks,
half the size of a railroad car, trembled from the impact,
boulders of a ton in weight were displaced and buffeted
from side to side like so much cork; roll on roll, fold on
fold, and wave on wave — gliding, leaping, crashing,
dashing, hissing, roaring, it came — a vital, sentient
thing, not unlikeable to a mammoth steed, wild, infuri-
ated, free and unfettered, plunging headlong down the
rugged canyon, its high-held crest, its billowing mane
far flung to the breeze, charging, stumbling, vaulting,
staggering, pressing ever on and on with wild abandon,
unchecked, and unrestrained, when! suddenly reaching
the brink of a yawning gulf athwart its path, and seeming to sense that it was too late to wholly check its own
break-neck pace, halting momentarily as though to summon new strength and force for a mighty bound which
would clear the chasm — with a despairing hiss —
almost a shriek, and with the effort born of that despair,
leaped blindly into space! only to crash hopelessly
against the rocks beneath — the spray and froth and
foam from its agonized flanks, cruelly galled by the
impact, mounting in clouds and descending in dews
that thoroughly saturated us where we stood full one
hundred feet away. Once, twice, thrice, with demonia-
cal fury it assaulted and sought to demolish the imped-
ing wall of stone, and as often was thrown back upon its
haunches, broken and beaten; at length, reinforced by
ever-increasing volume and force and fury, by a last
supreme and frantic effort, the barrier that could not be
destroyed was cleared with a bound, and away sped the
liberated demon, cruel, ravaging, and relentless as
before. Time after time we witnessed a repetition of
the wild ride, varied only by the changing conditions of
its course, as we moved forward, always a little in advance, where we could see the approach, until finally,

the seething torrent poured out its turbid strength upon
and defiled the placid bosom of the broad and beautiful
pool at Cowger's Mill.

My thought, oft recurring during this thrilling experience, was: Oh, for a camera! A motion picture outfit would have been worth a movie queen's salary for a
whole month, and even a pocket Kodak might have been
cheap at a king's ransom — that a likeness might have
been preserved of a scene which none who did not witness
can imagine, nor one who did, find words to adequately
describe.

III

COWGER'S MILL AND WHITTAKER FALLS

THE POOL at Cowger's Mill is 2300 feet above sea level, which means that between this point and the junction of Big Spring and Old Field Forks, a distance of nine miles, there is a fall of 370 feet or 41 feet per mile. I do not think best to emphasize too much the attractiveness of that section of Elk River extending for three miles from Cowger's Mill down to Whittaker Falls, so far as concerns its merits as fishing ground, for the reason that the State Game and Fish Commission has set the same apart as breeding grounds for both brook and rainbow trout and has closed it against the fisherman; and I should be loth to say or do aught which might tempt any one to "set but one foot within that sacred ground." In fact, I cannot say as a matter of fact that in that proscribed section there is today a single trout of any breed, size, or description, for the reason that I had not been there for several years, until last summer, when Jack Linn and I visited that locality, on which occasion we piously refrained from even looking in the direction of the stream, much less wetting a line, until we passed through those hallowed precincts and reached the pool at the Falls, just below the dead line. But I guess it would be no harm to speak as of years gone by, when this stretch of water was the fisherman's paradise. By the way, it strikes me as a very wise move to close this three-mile section and probably to keep it closed for another season or two, until it shall have become well stocked with trout; after which time it might be well to open the upper mile for one season, keeping the lower two miles closed, and for the next season open the lower mile and keep the upper two miles closed, and so alternating year after year, keeping the middle section always closed as a City of Refuge. To open the entire three miles would result in the depopulation of the whole section in thirty days; and to keep the entire three miles eternally closed would result in no great good, unless to seine the larger trout and transport them elsewhere for stocking purposes — a process, it seems to me, much less practical than to plant fingerlings from a hatchery. Give the fishermen a chance — but not too much chance.

Less than half a mile below Cowger's Mill the Valley Fork empties from the north side. This is quite a sizable stream, probably six or seven miles in length, and takes its name from the fact that it heads back against the waters of the Tygarts Valley River, and seems to be an exchange of compliments for the name Elkwater given to a tributary of the Valley River, adjacent to, running parallel with, but flowing in the opposite direction from, the Valley Fork. There used to be good fishing for at least a mile or two up the Valley Fork. Here is where I had a fine opportunity to catch, with my bare hands—but had sense enough not to—a mink, which took me for a stump and ran up my leg and body above my waist, before discovering its error. A mink is the quickest and bitenest varmint in or out of captivity, and if I had followed the natural impulse to grab the pesky little brute, my hand would not have made good shoe strings.

There are many wonderful pools in the stretch of river covered by the three miles above Whittaker Falls —one, if not the finest, being the pool at Cowger's Mill. Deep at the head, where large rocks jut from the north bank, it extends for 200 or 300 feet before the shallows set in. Not so good, however, for daylight fishing as some other places, as there is no cover for the angler and the trout sees him in plain view. You know it is said no trout will strike when it sees the angler. I have seen this theory so often exploded, that it has entirely lost caste with me. I readily grant, however, that a trout is not so likely, as a general thing, to strike, when it can, as when it cannot, see a human being; but I have waded out in clear water in full view of every trout in the pool, and caught half a dozen without moving out of my tracks—and with all the splashing and hubbub incident thereto. My experience is that when a trout really needs food, he will come out on dry land and tackle a buzz saw. The trouble is, you do not often find them in this famished condition.

The largest trout it was ever my luck to bag, I caught in "Samp" Conrad's canoe hole, about halfway between Cowger's Mill and Whittaker Falls. Calvin Hamrick, about whom there will be more later on, and I, were fishing there one beautiful moonlight night about the year 1910. My recollection is that Calvin, who was a first-class fly-fisherman, had caught just about two to my one, and we were almost ready to quit. My line had gotten "Bird's nest" on the reel, and I had despaired of unraveling the tangle, so that I had not more than 25 feet from the tip of the rod. I was standing on the sand bar at the upper end, casting straight across the pool to the base of the cliff jutting out on the north bank. I got a beautiful strike from what I knew to be a dandy trout—I struck, and could tell I had him well snagged—tried to strip the line with my left hand to ease the tension a little, but the trout struck out down the river into deep water, and would not give me back an inch of line. As he was hooked with a No. 10 fly, and I had no more line to give him, my only hope was to let him have his way, wade in and follow him, until he was fagged out. In a few seconds I was out in water so deep I had to tiptoe to keep from strangling, and when just about to give up in despair, I succeeded in turning him slightly to my left, which allowed me to gradually work my way backward to the shore and guide him down to where the water was not so deep on my side of the river. It was a pretty fight, but finally I was able to reel him in slowly toward Calvin, who stood there ready with the landing net; but when he had given back only about half my line, out of the water he came, and took upstream again to the deep water; trying to check him but not too suddenly, I again waded out in the water, giving him as little line off the reel as possible, but before long I was again tiptoeing for breath and my line was all out. Finally I got him turned to my right and was able to inch it back to shore, and this time succeeded in steering him around where Calvin netted him. Whereupon Calvin Hamrick and I threw ourselves down on that sand bar, I from sheer exhaustion, and Calvin to roll and kick up his heels and laugh until he was black in the face. It was a 16½-inch brook trout weighing 1¾ pounds.

The canoe of the upper Elk, unlike the graceful, symmetrical craft so long in use, but now, alas, a thing of the past, on the lower part of the river, was nothing more nor less than a glorified hog-trough. A short, heavy, clubby dugout, made from a poplar log, only sixteen to twenty feet in length, the sides and bottom thick and roughly hewn, ill-shaped, both bow and stern, suitable and usable for the sole and only purpose of crossing the river when too deep for wading, and incapable of accommodating safely more than two or three persons. A dweller along the banks of the upper, rough, and rugged sections of the river was fortunate if near his residence there was a pool of sufficient length and width that in stages of ordinary high water he could safely ferry himself or members of his family —a neighbor or stranger—from side to side—"set him across," as the expression goes. When we get farther along down the river, I expect to have something more to say of the real Elk River canoe, those ships of commerce which for three-quarters of a century plied regularly between Charleston and Sutton and all way stations, and occasionally as much as fifteen miles farther up.

You see, it is hard for a fellow to "stick to his knittin'," when treating a subject such as that assigned to me, as "that reminds me" is constantly bobbing up and

provoking digression—you start out to discuss kings
and get sidetracked onto cabbages; but you will recall
that this was a right reserved when I accepted the assignment.

In the wild, picturesque, and naturally wonderful
sections of West Virginia, there are many, many points
of supreme delight and interest to the eye, the ear, the
fancy—to the fisherman, the hunter, to the general outdoorsman, and to the lover of nature in all its varied,
various, and varying forms and phases, but to me, that
which bears the name Whittaker Falls, is pre-eminently
the beauty of the scenic world, the paragon of the picturesque, and the last word in all those things which
combine to make up in composite the wild life delectable.
Situated in the very heart of the Big Game region
where deer and bear and wild turkey abound—if anywhere—practically the border line between the trout
and the bass fishing grounds of the Elk, surrounded
on all sides by mountains towering seventeen hundred
feet above, their respective precipitous sides garbed in
forest primeval, made up of every form and species of
tree life indigenous to West Virginia, from the laurel
and the ivy-laurel festooning the river banks, to the
yew pine, fringing the summits to the southward—this,
by the way, being the only trout point on Elk River
from which may be seen part of our once vast, but now
rapidly disappearing yew pine (black spruce) forest;
and, to the imagination, what a prolific incubator. The
outdoorsman who sees only with the eye, hears only
with the ear, and enjoys only with his sensory equipment, gets not one-tenth of one poor tithe from his environment. If he cannot thrill and abound at things
that are not, but are merely suggested by the things
that are; if he cannot so indulge and give free rein to
his fancy as to people void spaces with living actors,
perfect silence with delightful music, barren wastes
with tree and vine and verdure; see and hear and taste
and smell and FEEL from mere imagination, recollec-

tion, or anticipation; if he cannot snap an empty or imaginary gun at empty space and see the feathered quarry flutter and fall in the imaginary brake; if he cannot find keen pleasure in mimic angling and see the trout or bass or blue pike rise to his lure — if he cannot see with his mind's eye, smell with his mind's nose, and hear with his mind's ear, in January, the buds of spring, the perfume of the violet, the twitter of the thrush, and in April, the glorious autumn colorings, the odor of fresh fallen leaves, the call of the Bob White; if he cannot be present in spirit though absent in the flesh, and enjoy these diversions from sordid toil which make endurable the off season necessarily wasted between four smudgy, dingy walls— then the little Red Gods have failed "to get a good scald" on that chap — have inoculated him against, rather than infected him with, the genuine contagion.

To appreciate Whittaker Falls one must see and know, study, and so to speak—digest it and its environment. For instance, all the fisherman would see at first sight would be a huge rock ledge extending from one side of the river to the other, backed up by terraces of solid rock, extending a thousand feet up the river, the water pouring over these falls ten or fifteen feet, into a basin sixty by one hundred feet and ten or fifteen feet deep at points up near the rock, pronounce it "a darned good place for trout," and "go to it." If he be not of the imaginative kind he would be likely to get his greatest and most lasting impression of the place from the trout he got or did not get. Like the little boy who had just returned home from a short trip to Washington City, on being asked if he saw the Washington Monument and to describe it, said, "Yes, it is a great high thing sticking up in the air painted white—oh, higher than any telephone pole—yes, twice as high. I didn't pay much attention to that—but gee! you do get good ice cream at them hotels."

But to the real outdoorsman and nature lover who

can go out alone and find congenial companionship with stream and forest, field, rocks, trees, and flowers and all things wild—where spirit unto spirit speaks in language of the universe—this spot will not only carry its full appeal and lasting impression, but awaken, elevate, and expand the fancy to the furthest borders of its realm.

How easy for the imagination to perceive that this wonderful amphitheatre here, chiseled in the bedrock, walled by the massive monolith, as shown in the accompanying picture, filled to the brim with clear, sparkling water, was especially designed, constructed, and arranged to house the synod of the water gods; to picture old Neptune, if it so be that he ever stretched his arm of conquest so far inland as to include in his dominions this particular locality, presiding over the deliberations of the assembled deities, he, seated in state upon the throne carved in the top ledge of the rock, high and dry, he presides over, not under water, while the assembled gods and goddesses, nymphs, naiads, mermaids, and water sprites, all rigged out in one-piece, demitasse bathing suits— disport or dispose themselves in orderly assemblage in the ample spaces below—the three-pronged gig clutched firmly in his right hand, forked end down, ready to prod any recalcitrant deity who might dare to disturb the peace, dignity, or tranquillity of the conclave. My early mythological education having been somewhat neglected, you will kindly overlook my omission to state just how the deities above mentioned were provided for—that is, whether they sat down, stood up, or swam around during the meeting. However, there is ample room for any or all.

In years gone by I have caught and seen caught many beautiful trout at Whittaker Falls, but the largest I ever saw, or heard of, was caught on or about the Fourth of July last year (1927). Jack Linn and I went down there from Glady Fork on a log train early in July, and found a boy sitting on the fall rock, bait-fishing. We inquired what luck he was having and he replied, "None, but my brother caught a twenty-five-inch Rainbow here yesterday." We asked what became of the fish and he said it had been eaten, but added, "A Charleston man camping down the road had his picture taken with it." Jack and I fished there for a while, catching only a few medium-sized trout, and made our campfire on the island immediately below the Falls, down in the timber about 200 feet below the pool. Being the dark of the moon, we did not resume fishing until the first streak of dawn next morning—which, by the way, is one of the choice hours for fly-fishing. After fishing some time at the Falls, we decided to go down the river about a mile, to the "Ball Alley Cliffs," and fish back upstream to the Falls. Along the road we came to the campers indicated by the boy, who, instead of being from Charleston, turned out to be a gentleman and his family from Morgantown, by the name of Simpson. I said to Mr. Simpson, "So you are the chap who had his picture taken with the big Rainbow." He assented, and I declared, "Now you write the story and have it published with the picture in *Wild Life Magazine,* or I will write it myself." He said, "Well, maybe."

As Jack and I were returning two or three hours later, wading up and shipping the stream, when we got to a point opposite our campfire on the island, I stepped over to get my camera in order to take a picture of the Falls. Just as I got the camera, I heard voices up at the Falls, "Hold him! hold him!! hold him!!!" I rushed up through the timber and out on the rock bar, and spied my friend Simpson standing on the steep, rock-bound shore, reeling in a fish which was putting up such a fight as to assure me that he was a big one; Simpson yanked him out among the rocks, and suddenly threw down his rod and grabbed the fish about the middle and yelled to me "For God's sake, grab him!" I was but a step away by that time, and promptly went to the rescue, without knowing just what the trouble was except that which was obvious from the fact that the fish was between Simpson and the water only three feet away, secured only by a slippery hand hold about his middle—and stepping forward I quickly inserted in his gill my index finger, clinching it with my thumb in his mouth, whereupon Simpson relaxed his hold and said, "Don't you see! the hook came out." I looked, and saw that instead, the line had broken right at the hook, but the hook itself was still firmly embedded in the bony rim of the mouth. When I raised up with the fish, holding it with a sure and deathlike grip, my friend Simpson, and Jackson Linn, who had tardily appeared on the scene, formed in solid phalanx behind me and hustled me off up the steep rock bar and thirty yards out into the brush, to prevent all possibility of escape—by the trout. A beautiful Rainbow it was, indeed, measuring 19 inches from tip to fork, and to have lost him would indeed have been a pity. I took a picture of Mr. Simpson standing on the Falls with his splendid catch.

IV

A WHITTAKER FALLS FISH YARN

W HEN THE third or February (1928) installment of this tale was finished I intended, in the
succeeding one, to leave the Falls and proceed down the
river. But the story was scarcely in type when there
came a letter from Mr. H. H. Fish, of Richwood, West
Virginia, saying, "I have read with interest your articles, 'The Tale of the Elk,' and thought you might be interested in the enclosed snapshots taken last summer at
Whittaker Falls." The letter proceeded to state that
the pictures were taken on the third day of July, 1927,
and that the trout shown was caught by Grover Beckwith, a fourteen-year-old boy, living in the neighborhood, in Whittaker Falls, crawfish tail being the bait
used, length of the trout 25 inches from fork to tip, esti-
mated weight 6 pounds; "the day was dark and rainy
and the pictures do not show the trout or the boy to advantage; however, one can note the length of the trout
by comparison with the lady in the picture." Hence it
is fair to assume that the decapitated picture shown in
one of the accompanying photographs, is that of a lady,
to-wit, Mrs. Simpson, who was engaged in the laudable
pastime of making flapjacks for a very appreciative
family disposed about the breakfast table, when Jack
Linn and I invaded their camp on the occasion of our
first meeting the Simpsons, as already recounted.

There is nothing in these pictures to identify the place
where they were taken; but on examining them closely,
I was reminded that when Jack Linn and I visited the
Simpson camp, just below the Falls, as mentioned in
February *Wild Life*, we noticed an automobile parked
near by. You will observe the number on the automobile license plate, shown in the picture, is 140-161. Calling up the State Road Commission the information was

obtained that the owner of that license number for the year 1927, was W. T. Simpson, Morgantown, W. Va. So it would seem that we have finally got the two sections of the story pretty well hooked up, and the identities fairly well established. I am sorry the picture of Grover Beckwith, who caught this splendid Rainbow, does not show up better in the picture.

Fortunate indeed is the spinner of a fish yarn — or any other sort of yarn, for that matter — when he can furnish corroborating evidence; and I will surely feel supremely blest, if the yarns which I am expected to spin in succeeding numbers shall be so strongly buttressed by corroboration, as in the present instance.

Here at Whittaker Falls, the county line between Randolph and Webster counties crosses Elk River at right angles, and here we enter the domain of the Hamricks, a very prolific family, scions of the old stock of hardy pioneers who took up their abode in the fastnesses of an unbroken wilderness, when civilization west of the Alleghenies was in its embryonic stage, and the chief dependence for sustenance was the wild game then abounding, supplemented by a modest corn crop. Their habitat was at first confined to the narrow bottoms along the river for several miles down toward Fork Lick, the original name of the present town of Webster Springs, but, in time, as the families grew and multiplied, they extended back from the river, and into the mountains on both sides, but principally the northerly side, on Point Mountain, which divides the waters of Main Elk from those of the Back Fork and the Tygarts Valley, where they builded their homes and cleared out their farms and have grown and prospered and multiplied until this day.

The first house below Whittaker Falls is about a quarter of a mile distant, on the north side of the river, and was probably built by "Uncle John" Hamrick, who lived and died there many years ago, and whose son Calvin lived there when I first became acquainted with the place.

From the Falls down to Walter Hamrick's, a distance of about two miles, both trout and bass are found, although the trout seem to greatly predominate for at least the first mile; but from Walter Hamrick's down, it is rather rare to find a brook trout in the main river, although in the side streams they are quite plentiful. I have never seen a bass taken out of the pool at the Falls; but a quarter of a mile below, at Calvin's canoe hole, I have taken a nice string of bass on several occasions. This is a wonderful pool for both trout and bass; there is a flat rock ledge, broken in places, extending irregularly from one side of the river to the other, and at one place, a wide deep chasm between the upper and lower sections of the broken ledge, affording ample passage for a canoe or boat to cross the river. Between, and back under these broken ledges, is a splendid resort and refuge for the trout and the bass. One thing which I have never quite understood, is the fact that the trout and bass at this place never seem to be biting or striking at the same time. I remember on one occasion Calvin Hamrick and I were fishing at the Ball Alley Cliffs about three-quarters of a mile below, catching trout and bass in about equal numbers — now a trout and then a bass. Calvin said that this rarely happened at his canoe hole; that up there when you set in and caught trout, you caught no bass, and vice versa, although your initial catch was as apt to be the one as the other. Several times afterward I saw this demonstrated, and the catch was all trout or all bass. One day Calvin and I fished there in the morning and caught nothing but trout. In the afternoon we got all bass and no trout; while the next morning, about the same hour, we got nothing but bass, and that afternoon, about the same hour, we got nothing but trout. It must be that there obtains a sort of gentlemen's agreement that when one species is feeding the other will keep off the grass; although I have never known of its observance elsewhere.

A mile below Calvin's, and on the opposite side of the

river, empties a stream called Big Run. Why the name, might be somewhat of a puzzle to the uninitiated. You will find a great many small tributaries of Elk, especially the upper section, bearing the name "Big Run." A "drain" is a depression from which water runs during the wet season only; a "branch" is the smallest of the streams which usually afford water; the next in size is the "run," and the next is the "creek." In directing the stranger up or down the river, the native tells him to follow the river until he crosses the mouth of a drain and then a branch and then a run, and keep on to the first big run — and follow a path leading up this big run, et cetera. The stranger knows just what the direction means and has no difficulty in following. The creeks were given names quite early in the settlement of the country, but for many years later the smaller tributaries remained without particular designation, until they took names from someone who came to live near by, or from some local or comparatively recent event; and some of them never took a name more distinctive than Big Run. The Big Run in question extends from the river about one mile back into a deep gash in the mountain side, to the base of a cliff and waterfall of about 20 feet. The basin, into which the water pours, evidently was once a smooth flat rock, but is now saucer-like in shape, and about 20 feet across from side to side. Near the middle there is in the solid rock, a cavity about the size and shape of an oil barrel, which the constant pour of water, from the funnel-like spout above, has carved in the ages past. When there is an ordinary supply of water, the pool extends back and covers the broken base of the cliff, and the trout have numerous hiding places; but in extreme drought, the water draws away from these hiding places and leaves no refuge except this barrel-shaped hole in the center. At the approach of the fisherman in such dry season, every trout in the pool will take refuge in the "barrel" and it is "easy pickin'" to drop in a cricket or a crawfish tail, and take the whole tribe.

Once when I was at Calvin's and we had been fishing in the river from Walter Hamrick's to Cowger's Mill, the water became milky from a heavy rain up river, and Calvin took me to Big Run. We found it full of trout and took a nice lot. The hole up at the waterfall was brimful of water and we lured several nice trout from their hiding places back under the rocks. I was back there once or twice after that and always found plenty of water in this pool. On my last visit, Calvin was with me, and the water was very low. When we got up to the waterfall, we found the pool full of trout with nowhere to hide except in the "barrel," where they promptly scurried to refuge at our approach. We waited a few minutes for the excitement to subside, and then each quietly slipped a skinned crawfish tail down amongst them. In a jiffy each landed an eight or nine-inch trout. Before either had removed the speckled beauty from the hook, Calvin said, "I don't know how you feel about it, but that's too much like shootin' fish to suit me." And at the word, he unhooked his trout and turned him loose. Of course, I was forced to follow his splendid example, whether I wanted to or not, and the balance of our fishing was back down the stream, where the trout had a better run for their money.

Calvin Hamrick was one of the most splendid sportsmen I ever knew — and one of the most successful, too — fisherman, hunter, and trapper. I was hunting with him only once, at which time we went to a camp on the headwaters of Leatherwood, opposite and within about two miles from his home. It was a pleasant November evening when we reached camp, expecting to be joined the next day by two or three other fellows for a week's deer and bear hunt. But lo and behold, the next morning there was a six-inch blanket of snow on the ground. which by later afternoon had increased to 18 inches, with no sign of a letup; consequently, we pulled out for home, after leaving a note for our expected companions, to the effect that if they got in and it quit snowing and they wanted us to come back, they should shoot three times in quick succession. I stayed at Calvin's all the next day, and although the snowfall ceased, we never heard the signal, and on the day following I rode Calvin's mule to Webster Springs and sent it back by the mail carrier.

But many a day and night I have spent with Calvin at his home and out on fishing trips — and it is out in the wilds and around the campfire that you learn to really know a fellow — and it was there I found Calvin Hamrick to be one of nature's true noblemen, in every sense of the word; and it was with a profound feeling of personal loss that I learned a few years ago, that he had been summoned forth from the old haunts of stream and forest, by him so much loved and enjoyed, to the Elysian fields of the Great Beyond.

The nine-mile stretch of the Elk from Whittaker Falls down to the mouth of Leatherwood presents rare attractions, both from the standpoint of scenic beauty and piscatorial possibilities. Its freakish, serpentine course, with irregular changes from shoals and shallows to deep short pools, beset throughout with massive rocks in and alongside the stream, render it ideal for bass; and the high, steep, and rugged mountains on either side — and usually on four sides — garbed in virgin forest, is ever a delight to the eye and a challenge to instinctive admiration of the grand and of the sublime.

It is a man's job to negotiate this course with a fly-rod. The bait-fisherman has no trouble, for the reason that he can select his points of vantage and fish from the bank, or from an accommodating rock on or near the bank; but the fly-fisherman must avoid the bank with its overhanging trees and bushes and keep always a clear space behind; and, as a boat is impossible, there is nothing to do but wade, sometimes ankle-deep, frequently knee-deep, and sometimes waist-deep and even more.

And there is never a dull moment for the aggressive angler throughout the entire nine-mile stretch. Usually, the cast is so made that the fly will settle down near the edge of a rock or in some particularly likely looking place, in the pools; but not infrequently you get a strike in the swifts or in the shallows. Consequently, it is customary to whip every part of the stream, pool, shoal, and shallow, alike. It becomes a sort of habit to let no chance escape.

My first fishing in Elk River, above Leatherwood, was about forty years ago. I had gone from Webster Springs up to the home of "Kelly Ben" Hamrick, who then lived at the mouth of Leatherwood, expecting to fish for trout in Leatherwood and Bergoo. There had been a hard local rain which rendered these creeks unfit for fishing, but, on investigation, I found that the river above had not been affected; so I put in a day or two after bass, covering a stretch of about three miles of river up to the ford, where the road crosses from the south to the north side. Bass were plentiful in those days, and it was no trouble to catch from twenty to thirty a day; they were usually small, however, as compared with the average farther down the river, it being rather rare to get one larger than a pound. On this occasion I was fishing near the mouth of a small stream which empties from the north side, a short distance below the ford, the name of which is "Grand Daddy's" Run. A young man by the name of Hamrick, it is needless to say—as everybody in that section is named Hamrick—one of "Trigger Ben's" boys, I believe, was with me, and I was fortunate enough to land a three and one-half pound bass, very near the mouth of the run aforesaid. After admiring my catch, Hamrick declared, "Well, I have often wondered why they called this "Grand Daddy's" Run, and now I know — this "peerch" is sure the granddaddy of them all." I learned later that young Hamrick was mistaken, as the stream took its name from the fact that one of the earliest of the Hamrick

generation in that region had lived near that place almost a century before, and that he was the granddaddy
of the older Hamricks then living. I do not now recall
his name.

People these days are so careless about preserving
history and tradition, that it would not surprise me a
particle, if I should go back there now and ask how
that run got its name, someone would promptly reply,
"Oh, about forty-nine years ago one of 'Trigger Ben'
Hamrick's boys and another fellow caught a powerful
big bass right there at the mouth of the run. It was so
big that they 'lowed it was the granddaddy of all the
fish, so they just named the run for the fish—it weighed
eleven pounds."

Bergoo—accent on the "goo"—is a fine trout stream
flowing from the south side into Elk, about one and
one-half miles above Leatherwood. On this creek "Trigger Ben" Hamrick, so called to distinguish him from
"Kelly Ben" Hamrick before mentioned, lived for many
years and reared quite a large family. He was drowned
about forty-five years ago, in undertaking to cross Elk
River at the rough and rocky ford down at what is
known as Bernardstown about three miles below Leatherwood.

One of the largest boundaries of virgin forest yet
standing in West Virginia is the 32,000-acre tract
known as the Pratt lands, lying along Elk River
from a point a short distance below the Whittaker
Falls, well down toward Webster Springs, a distance
of fifteen miles or more. This land was purchased about
45 years ago by the late William Seymour Edwards
for C. M. Pratt, the Standard Oil magnate. Ten or fifteen years ago General George W. Curtin, the grand-
father of the gentleman of the same name who is now
(1928) chairman of the West Virginia Game and
Fish Commission, purchased the tract for Pardee &
Curtin Lumber Company, which for the last forty
years has been one of the most extensive hardwood lum-

ber manufacturers in this state. I am informed that this concern now (1928) has in process of construction a mammoth band mill and equipment for manufacturing this timber. The mill is to be located on the Elk immediately opposite the mouth of Leatherwood Creek. In a few short years this magnificent forest will be only a memory, and many of us will feel as did my old friend Pete Hammons—old Pete—who lived over on Williams River, on a large boundary of land known as the Caperton tract, now a part of the Cherry River Boom and Lumber Company holdings. The late Wesley Mollohan, of Charleston, far famed as a land lawyer, was attorney for Johnson N. Camden and his associates, the then owners of the Caperton lands, and two or three times each year, for many years, visited Webster Springs on business connected therewith. He knew everybody in that country, was frequently on the land, and was well acquainted with all the squatters, whom he soon converted into tenants. "Old Pete" Hammons was one of these tenants. About the year 1895 it was "norated around" that a railroad was to be built from Camden-on-Gauley up the Gauley and thence up Williams River to an eastern connection. The next time Mr. Mollohan visited Webster Springs, Old Pete came all the way over from his home in Williams to see him, in great perturbation. He said, "Mr. Molly-hawn, they tell me they are goin' to run a railroad up Williams right by my place, an' I come over to see if you couldn't let me have a place furder back—over on the head of Cherry, maybe — er Cranberry — somewhere that no railroad can't go to. I'll tell you, Mr. Molly-hawn, if things keeps on like this, this kentry won't be no fitten place fer men like me an' you to live in."

V

BIG CREEKS AND LITTLE CREEKS

HERE I have gotten myself in a terrible mess, likely to lose all my old friends and in imminent danger of being lynched, if I should ever venture back in the neighborhood of Whittaker Falls or Cowger's Mill. It seems that my very enthusiasm in endeavoring to portray the glories of that section as trout fishing grounds has caused all the trouble.

Since the publication of the February and March numbers (1928) of *Wild Life,* I have run across several prominent citizens of Webster Springs, who have been in the habit of trout fishing up about the Falls and Cowger's Mill, and they jumped on me with both feet about the last two installments of the Tale. "Why," said one, "don't you know that all of this stuff you have been writing will make people believe that Whittaker and Cowger's Mill is the greatest trout territory in the world, and that every trout fisherman in the state will flock in there the very first day of the open season, especially since the Game and Fish Commission has opened the three miles from Whittaker up to Cowger's Mill, and there won't be anything left for the people living around there? And besides, you have made it appear that there are no trout in the river below Walter Hamrick's. While this was true a few years back, since the rainbow has gotten a firm foothold up there, you find lots of trout in Elk River well down to Webster Springs."

I assured my friend that I would do my best to repair the damage done by pointing out other localities where trout abound in West Virginia, and to somewhat relieve the tension by calling attention to the fact above mentioned, that rainbow trout are found as far down as Webster Springs.

In the old days when most of my trout fishing was done—that is, from 1886 to 1915—I found splendid fishing in many different waters. That was before the days of the rainbow, with the exception of the head of Elk, which was the only place, except Mann's Creek, in Fayette County, where I ever saw a rainbow trout, until recent years. Consequently, when I undertake to locate the habitat of the trout in these other streams, you will understand that I refer to the brook trout; and also that wherever rainbow trout have been introduced and become thoroughly established they may be found much farther down the stream, as well as up among the brook trout.

Main Gauley River and its side streams, beginning at Turkey Creek, which is about six miles above the state road at Bolair—and extending up to the forks and for several miles up each fork—is hard to beat. Both Turkey Creek and Straight Creek, which is three or four miles above, are sizeable streams and full of trout. Bolair is on the road from Summersville to Webster Springs, about thirty miles from the former and four miles from the latter place.

Williams River, from the "Governor" Sawyer's place to its headwaters, with its larger streams, including the far-famed Tea Creek, where Judge George W. McClintic has been holding forth as camp cook—too lazy to fish—for so many years, is a veritable fisherman's paradise.

Next comes Cranberry River, which empties into Gauley at Woodbine, about six miles below Camden-on-Gauley and one and one-half miles above the mouth of Cherry. From about six miles up this river, and up Fox Tree, Bear Branch, Hanging Rock Branch, Dogway, and other side streams, the names of which I have forgotten, on up to its headwaters and into the Cranberry Glades, trout have always abounded.

The North and South Forks, which form Cherry River at Richwood, are both splendid trout streams, and so also is Laurel Creek, which empties about two miles below the forks. Of the two forks of Cherry, I have always regarded the North Fork as the better, probably because I have fished there a great deal and very little in the South Fork; but others say they are equally good. My first visit to that locality was in 1895, when the present site of the proud city of Richwood was called Cherry Tree Bottoms and contained just two buildings, to-wit, the log cabin and log barn of Abe Spencer. I will guarantee that if the North Fork of Cherry is anything like it was between twenty-five and thirty-three years ago, from its mouth for fifteen miles up to the foot of Little Briery Knob, where it is a tiny stream winding its way through glade grass and bulrushes, the jolly angler will find all the sport he is looking for.

Hominy Creek, another tributary of Gauley, from Hominy Falls up to its headwaters, is a fairly good trout stream. The state road, from Quinwood to Nettie and Summersville, reaches Hominy and about three miles from Quinwood, and will be open for travel in a few months.

Angling's Creek, which flows into Meadow River about two miles below Nallen, and Young's Creek, the mouth of which is at Nallen, have long been noted trout streams.

Surbaugh's Branch and Laurel Creek, tributaries of Meadow River, between Nallen and Rainelle, above "The Loop," are both good trout streams, although rather small.

Everybody knows of the famous Big and Little Clear Creeks, near Rupert, Greenbrier County. The lower section of Big Clear Creek, as well as Brown's Creek, a large tributary of Big Clear Creek, from the Baller McClung ford down, will be open this season, although Little Clear Creek and the upper reach of Big Clear Creek and Brown's Creek will be closed.

I have found good trout fishing on the waters of

Shaver's Fork of Cheat, especially Fishing Hawk, near
Montes, which is across the mountain and about seventeen miles distant from Elkins. Here the Pond Lick
and several small streams dash down the mountain sides
and pour into Fishing Hawk near the town of Montes.
Following these streams up the steep slope you will find
little pools scarcely larger than a washing tub, and will
surprise yourself by catching brook trout as large as ten
inches. I have never fished on other waters of Cheat,
nor have I ever visited the splendid trout waters of the
Upper Greenbrier nor the South Branch of the Potomac.
As I am only to name the points with which I am familiar, I hope some one else will, before the season opens,
tell *Wild Life* readers the virtues of other trout fishing
grounds, in order that Upper Elk will not attract all
the anglers, in one fell swoop.

But returning to the watershed of the Elk, from which
I have been forced far afield in order to correct the
erroneous impression supposed to have been by me created, that the places mentioned in the preceding installments were the only points of interest to the trout fisherman:

It was in Leatherwood, near the residence of "Kelly
Ben" Hamrick, that I caught my first trout, and from
that time down to the present, although in the forty-two
years which have elapsed I have taken many larger ones,
none ever gave me such a thrill. In the summer of 1886,
I was at Webster Springs attending court, and there ran
across Robert T. Herndon, of Charleston, who was a
visitor at the Springs. When court adjourned, Bob and
I decided to go trout fishing, somewhere, and some one
recommended Leatherwood as the ideal stream and
"Kelly Ben" Hamrick's as our stopping place. We rode
horseback the ten miles up to Hamrick's, arriving late
in the afternoon. Being eager for the fray and having
been informed that trout were plentiful in the creek a
little way above the house, I rigged up a hook and line
and grabbed a pole about 9 feet long, leaning against

the house, and attached about 15 feet of line. While
Bob and one of "Kelly Ben's" boys were digging fishing
worms I went to the creek and caught two or three crawfish, the tail of one of which I skinned and placed on
my hook. Selecting a place about a hundred yards
above the house where a small pool ends and the water
rushes swiftly down over a white sand-rock bottom for
about twenty feet, and standing on the left bank where a
grassy meadow binds the creek and breaks off steep
down to the water, I cast my bait just a few feet up into
the pool, above the head of the swift water. Hardly had
the hook touched the water when there was a terrific
rush and splash as a ten-inch brook trout struck at and
missed the bait, which was suddenly whisked away and
carried downstream by the current; then I saw what appeared to be about seven streaks of double-geared chain
lightning playing on the water in the vicinity of my
hook, as it whizzed past me, but which was in fact nothing more nor less than that trout striking at, and missing again and again, the coveted bait, each effort proving futile until at the foot of the swift water, when, with
a hop, skip, and jump and a last vicious lunge, the elusive morsel was captured and the pole almost jerked out
of my hand.

Wow! thought I, as I threw my catch back on the grass,
this trout fishing business is even greater than it was
ever cracked up to be; and I then and there decided that
this was the sport for me; but I will say in all candor
that from that day down to the present, I have never
seen a trout or other fish go through gyrations, contortions, and convulsions approaching those of that, my
first one — nor hit as hard in proportion to its size. It
was the most aggressive, persistent, and uncompromising fish of any kind, stripe, or breed I ever came in contact with.

The next day Bob and I fished up Leatherwood to
the forks, about three miles, and by actual count, our
combined catch was —————— trout, ranging in size

from five to eleven inches, very few being over seven inches. The blank representing the number of trout caught is intentional. If I were to fill that blank with the number actually caught, there would be imputed to me one of two great crimes, either that of being a fish liar or a fish hog; and I would regret being considered the one just as much as the other — if not more so. In other words, if I were to state the actual truth, I am afraid *Wild Life* readers would believe me; and on the other hand, I am afraid they would not believe me; and as I would regret very much to be believed in that particular instance, and would regret almost as much not to be believed—Oh well, you know what I mean, even if I can't express it.

The next day we fished up the left fork until about noon, when there came the most terrific rain and hail storm I ever witnessed, especially the hail part of it. It poured in torrents for about 20 minutes and then changed to hail which peppered us mercilessly, until, after ploughing down the suddenly swollen stream for a couple of hundred yards, we found shelter under a hospitable cliff, where we remained until the hail ceased. In the meantime, the creek had so swollen that we were obliged to scale the mountain side and thread our way through laurel, briers, vines, rocks, and fallen timber for a mile or two down to the forks of the creek, where we struck a path that was traversable.

Talk about cold spells! That day in mid-August was the one on which I suffered more from the cold than any other in my life, and when Bob and I reached the Hamrick home we were both chilled to the marrow. It was mid-afternoon, and no fire in the house and neither of us had a change of clothing: fortunately, we found William Seymour Edwards, who had arrived in our absence, and who supplied each of us with a flannel shirt which he dug out of his saddle pockets, and thus saved our lives for the few minutes it took "Kelly Ben" to have a log fire roaring in the fireplace. That log fire I will always remember as the coziest and most comforting warmth breeder before which I ever stood or sat.

For the next eight or ten years I fished many times in Leatherwood and Bergoo, but never there or elsewhere did I participate in a one day's catch approaching in number that made by Bob Herndon and me our first day in Leatherwood.

By the way, I recall that in the late 80's or early 90's, Leatherwood was stocked with brown trout, by Will Edwards, and by common consent of the neighboring citizens, kept closed for three or four years. The closed season ended about the middle of a certain April, and fishermen from far and near flocked in for the fray. I was invited to join the rush, chancing to be at Webster Springs at the time, but declined, as I never cared for trout fishing until the warm weather, and stated that I would wait till August to get mine. True to my threat, I went to Leatherwood the following August and, while I succeeded in catching a few brook trout, never a brown trout did I see, nor have I ever seen a brown trout in Leatherwood. I have been told that creek was full of them when thrown open for fishing, but in a few weeks was entirely depopulated of that species. What puzzles me is to know what became of the fry and fingerlings. But it is an evident fact that the brown trout, once so prolific, is now extinct in Leatherwood.

Bergoo, which, as already stated, empties into Elk about a mile and one-half above Leatherwood, was once a famous stream for brook trout. I have never fished there since the advent of the Rainbow. It is a much smaller and swifter stream than Leatherwood. In fact, it is almost a succession of short pools and cascades.

Some years ago, having been struck with the peculiarity of the name, Bergoo, I inquired as to its origin and was told the tradition was that in the early history of that section of the country a large party of hunters had camped at the mouth of the creek for several weeks in the height of the game season, and had killed a bear, deer, turkey, pheasant, squirrels, and caught fish in great abundance. They feasted on these articles of diet one after another until the food palled on the crowd, when it occurred to the one who was cook for a certain day that he would vary the menu somewhat by serving it as a composite in the way of a stew. So he proceeded to chop up goodly portions of bear meat, venison, turkey, pheasant, squirrels, fish, etc., for his stew, and by way of adding zest and flavor to the mess, adding, as it simmered in the pot, occasional dashes of applejack. It is said that the whole *posse comitatus* fell to with a relish, and pronounced the meal by far the best they had had on the trip, and with one acclaim they named the place Camp Bergoo, and when the camp disappeared the name clung to the creek. I have looked it up in the dictionary and found "bur-goo" —with the accent on the Bur—and that it jibes exactly with that which tradition says gave us the name Bergoo—with the accent on the "goo."

The present day hunter and fisherman will, of course, be much interested in this dish, so far as concerns the mixed meat content, as it may stand them in good stead when out in the wilds and far from a Greek restaurant, a bunch find themselves with nothing to eat but bear meat, venison, wild turkey, pheasant, squirrel, brook trout, rainbow trout, bass, etc., and they wish to vary the monotony of the bill of fare—but the fluid extract of apple seasoning would not appeal to them at all. Who for a minute nowadays would tolerate such use of such seasoning?

It is pretty hard for me to get away from Leatherwood and Bergoo, but if I were to recount all the haps and mishaps which I have shared or heard of in and around those, to me, hallowed precincts, it would require a book which in volume would lay over Encyclopedia Brittanica as Ossa over a wart, and it would take me just thirteen years to get down Elk as far as Webster Springs—and I never would get to the mouth.

I cannot leave the place, however, without referring to an incident connected with a man who at that time was the oldest resident of that locality. About eighteen years ago, I went from Webster Springs up to Leatherwood, where "Bearskin Bill" Hamrick lived at the time, his father and mother, "Kelly Ben" and "Aunt Naomi," having moved down to Webster Springs years before. Bill and I arranged to leave early the next morning, go up to Whittaker Falls, get Calvin Hamrick, and proceed thence to the Upper River. While we were at breakfast, Sam Dodrill, who lived on the river a short distance below Leatherwood, came with the information that "Uncle Addison" Fisher, who had been ill for several days, was at death's door and could not live through the day, and that the neighbors must get busy and make a coffin for him. "Uncle Addison" lived on the river a short distance above Leatherwood, was about ninety years old, and had lived there practically all his life. Bill had carpenter's tools and some splendid thinly sawed white walnut lumber, suitable for coffin stuff. Of course, our trip was postponed until we, with the aid of "Rattlesnake Bill" Dodrill and Moore Dodrill, the latter being a son of Sam, fell to and by noon had the coffin made and delivered to the Fisher home; whereupon Bill and I proceeded up to Calvin's. Three years later I was passing the Fisher house, and much to my surprise saw "Uncle Ad" standing at the gate by the roadside. "Hello, Uncle Ad," said I, "this is indeed a pleasant surprise. Just three years ago I helped make a coffin for you, and now here you are out kicking up your heels, like a two-year-old."

"Yes," said he, "and I've got that coffin in there under the bed handy, where I can get her when I need her."

VI

THE ELK, THE HAMRICKS AND DODRILLS; KEMP LITTLEPAGE JOINS THE CAMP AT THE END OF THE WORLD

E LK RIVER, at the mouth of Leatherwood, has an elevation of approximately 1800 feet above sea level, showing a fall of 370 feet in the nine miles from Whittaker Falls, or in the twenty-one miles from the junction of Big Springs and Old Lick Forks, an average of 41.5 per mile. The river at Webster Springs at the mouth of Back Fork is approximately 1450 feet, a fall of 350 feet or 35 feet per mile for the intervening ten miles. When you consider the fact that in the 52 miles from Clay Court House to Charleston, with the numerous long, steep shoals between the two points, the fall is but two feet per mile, some conception may be had of the pitch of the water and the ruggedness of the canyon of the upper section.

By the way, it has been my observation that brook trout are rarely if ever found in their native haunts at a lower altitude than 1800 feet. I believe the fish hatchery at White Sulphur is approximately 1900 feet, which is presumably an ideal elevation for the propagation and rearing of brook trout, else the government would not have selected that location. Of course brook trout have been stocked in many streams of this state at a much lower altitude, and seem to prosper fairly well, but the only reason they are found lower down is because they cannot get higher up.

It is well worth the time of any bass fisherman, whether bait or fly, to cover the ten-mile stretch of river from Leatherwood to Webster Springs. I speak from experience of a good many years ago, and when it was very unusual to catch trout in the river between the two points named; but, as stated in April *Wild Life,*

I am told that of late years, rainbow trout have pretty nearly "polluted" the stream for the whole ten miles. "Polluted" is the word used by the fellow who told me about it. I asked him where he got the expression, and he said he heard somebody say that somebody else had "polluted" his whole country with Ford cars. I understood him to mean what the nigger down in Arkansas meant, when the automobile in which he was driving Jim Crawford and me, got stalled in the dry sand with which the road was "polluted." After he had shoveled the car out four or five different times, I said to the colored gentleman, "Some sand," and he replied, "Yes, suh; quite num'ous."

To fish this ground from Leatherwood to Webster Springs with flies, you should take at least three days, and not be afraid to get your feet wet. "Rattlesnake Bill" Dodrill—who was a bait fisherman, but who on this trip used flies, spinners and Dowagiacks—and I have done it in two days, covering the first day the five miles from the Springs up to the Mill Run, where "Rattlesnake Bill" made his home with his sister, Mrs. Isaac Gregory, and proceeded up to "Kelly Ben's" the second day; but that was taking in too much territory. On another occasion we spent five or six days and camped out wherever night overtook us, in spite of numerous pressing invitations of the dwellers along the way to share their hospitality. This is about the finest ten-mile stretch of water for both bait and artificial lures of which I have any knowledge. Many of the pools are so large and deep that it is difficult to whip them with a fly, but afford splendid bait-fishing, while the smaller holes and shallows are ideal for the fly.

"Rattlesnake Bill" was a schoolteacher in the winter time, and a wild man in the summer time, and early in our acquaintance we discovered that we had much in common—that is, during the wild season. Many a day and night we have spent together in and along the banks of the raging Elk. It was not so much to either the number or size of the fish we caught, as to be turned loose without bridle or harness, into the great outdoors. "Rattlesnake Bill" was a chap of varied accomplishments, not the least of which were in the literary line. He published a small volume entitled "Moccasin Tracks," which title was most aptly chosen for the text, dealing as it did with the history of the early settlers of the upper section of what is now the county of Webster. He died a few years ago and in him passed one of the most ardent anglers and all-round wild lifers it was ever my good fortune to meet.

Any lover of the wild and beautiful and beautifully wild, whether a fisherman or not, will find ample compensation in a trip along the river through this gorge, especially if he should get in before the mountain sides are denuded of their timber, which, as formerly indicated, is a matter of a very few years. The fisherman will find great delight, especially at some of the localities which I will endeavor to point out in passing down stream. Not that I would recommend downstream fly-fishing. Quite the contrary; as I am one of those chaps who believe that for either trout or bass the fly should be cast upstream. Many there are who say that it makes no difference; but both experience and reason have confirmed me in my view. A bass or a trout, at ease, naturally stands head upstream, looking for something to float down with the current. Wading and casting upstream, your fly settles on the water in front of the fish, before he sees the angler, and before the wave, ripple or sound of the wading has reached him; and there is nothing to attract attention but the fly itself; whereas these favorable conditions are not present in downstream casting. I do not care to start an argument, but if it should so follow, I guess no harm would result.

At the lower end of the sharp bend in the river, two or three hundreds yards below the mouth of Leatherwood, is a famous fishing hole, called the Metcalf Bank. Many years ago, William Gregory lived in the bottom just below, and an itinerant Methodist preacher by the name of Metcalf frequently came into the neighborhood to preach, and always he held the services at the Gregory home, and enjoyed its hospitality for several days both before and after the "meeting." He was a great fisherman, and this particular pool above Gregory's residence was his favorite haunt; there he would sit hour after hour and day after day, as long as the fish would bite; hence the name "Metcalf"; but why the "Bank" is somewhat obscure, unless because of the steep hillside or bank at the edge of the pool. Probably this bank in his day extended out into what is now the stream, and has been whittled away by the water.

The Sally Hole is a fine pool about a mile below Metcalf Bank. I never knew the origin of the name, but assume that Sally fished there — or probably took her morning dip. However, it is well adapted to either purpose.

Farther down, from the north side, Baltimore Run empties. Though comparatively small, it was once full of brook trout. Here and immediately across the river were two of the "old improvements," the one on the Baltimore Run side, being when I first knew it, the home of Uncle Bob Hamrick — "Bob D" as he was called to distinguish him from the other Bobs; on the opposite side, the old Miller place has been the home of the Millers, time whereof the memory of man runneth not to the contrary.

It was at the ford about one-half mile below Baltimore Run, that "Trigger Ben" Hamrick was drowned. He, with a friend by the name of Cowger, undertook to ride across the river which at the time was rather deep and very swift — according to the vernacular "too deep for fordin'." Cowger was reluctant to venture, especially as his horse was rather small. "Trigger Ben's" horse was much larger and stronger and at his insistence he changed mounts with his friend, who got safely over; but because of his very generosity to his friend, "Trig-

ger Ben" lost his life, the Cowger horse and its rider
being swept away with the mighty current. "Trigger
Ben's" body was found several days later, more than a
mile down the river at Squire Vince Hamrick's canoe
hole.

Among the earliest settlers of this upper section were
the Millers and the Gregorys. Isaac G. Gregory pat-
ented a large boundary of land on the river at and in the
vicinity of Mill Run, above referred to. Here he settled
and reared a large family and his descendants by the
names of Gregory, Dodrill and Hamrick are quite
numerous. One of his daughters married James Dodrill. Their sons, George, William, Isaac, Joseph, Robert, and Judge Charles McC. Dodrill, I knew many
years ago. With the last two mentioned I was very well
acquainted; both of these gentlemen were quite prominent when I first visited Webster Springs in 1885.
Robert — "Uncle Bob," as everybody knew him far and
near, because of what was considered the very high grade
of applejack which he produced in liberal quantities, at
his place on Mill Run; and Judge Charles McC., having
long been prominent in the public affairs of Webster
County, which he served and continued to serve in official capacities such as sheriff, representative in the legislature, member of the county court, and like positions of
honor and distinction.

"Uncle Bob" was quite an old man when I first knew
him, but nevertheless during "court days" and every day
during the season when visitors flocked to Webster
Springs to partake of the far-famed Salt Sulphur water,
"Uncle Bob" rode into town early in the morning, with
bulging saddle pockets. He was very popular with
many of the visitors, albeit they do say that Salt Sulphur
water and spirits fermenti do not associate in peace and
harmony. "Uncle Bob" must have been a producer for
many years before I knew him, because I remember
hearing early in my acquaintance with him a story told
on "Kelly Ben" Hamrick, which carried back quite a

way. Whether the story is true or not, is neither here nor there; it is a good story, and no one must spoil a good story by questioning its authenticity.

When "Kelly Ben" and his wife, Aunt Naomi, then a young couple, lived on the mountain between Elk and Gauley, three or four miles from "Uncle Bob's" place on Mill Run, he told his wife he was going down to the river to get a horseload of apples. He rode down to Uncle Bob's and of course spent the day and partook of all forms of hospitality Bob had to offer. Rather late in the afternoon he filled his two-bushel sack with apples such as Bob had not otherwise utilized, placed the same on his horse and was preparing to mount and wend his way homeward when someone in the house called him back for a farewell farewell. While Ben was so occupied in the house, Squire Vince Hamrick, then a young man full of devilment as a dog is of fleas, went to the creek and carefully selected two bushels of nice creek boulders, apple size, with which he replaced the apples in Ben's sack. The farewells over, Ben came out, mounted his horse and proceeded three or four miles up the mountain to his home, his horse groaning under the weight of a very large man and two bushels of rocks; on reaching home and alighting he called his wife to help him "take the sack of apples" from the horse. She went to one side of the horse and pushed off the bag on the shoulders of Ben, standing on the other side, so successfully that Ben collapsed like an accordion, and his wife had a hard time getting him out from under the avalanche and into the house. Of course, she wanted to know why he brought home rocks instead of apples, when they already had plenty of rocks and no apples. But if "Kelly Ben" ever answered the question the answer was never recorded, so far as I am advised.

Something over a mile below Mill Run is one of the prettiest tumble-down places I ever saw in any river and one of the best bass pools. Carr Falls, it is called, for Pat Carr, a native of the Old Sod who lived near by for

many years. He was a great friend and old chum of
Honorable Patrick F. Duffy, of Webster Springs, who
served two terms from 1885 to 1893, as Auditor of West
Virginia. I use the words "tumble-down" in describing
these falls for lack of a better word. A mammoth castle
constructed of rocks as big as an ordinary house, seems
to have been tumbled down and scattered its component
units helter-skelter from one side to the other and up and
down the river, leaving standing only the foundation,
and that rent and riven. This point has been a regular
Mecca, time out of mind, for visitors at Webster Springs,
who, sometimes singly, sometimes in couples, and often
in large parties, would "take their dinner and spend the
day," in fishing, wading, splashing and enjoying the
wonderful scenery. There are other beautiful places
between Carr Falls and Webster Springs, which have
always been great resorts for visitors. At the Sheep
Rocks, at the mouth of Deep Run, a fine pool at the
mouth of Dyer's Run, and Harris Falls, were great
places for bass in the old days and were much frequented
by visitors.

Harris Falls is named in honor of Quince Harris, who
lived near by, and who for many years had been an active
competitor of his neighbor, "Uncle Bob," a little farther
up the river, but whose activities in that line had practically ceased or greatly subsided before my acquaintance
with him. He had a little mix-up, finally, with our old
friend the "Iron Judge," J. J. Jackson, Federal judge,
who once sat in the seat of Judge McClintic, and who in
a modest way — modest in terms of quantity and not as
descriptive of his manner of dealing — handled the
make or sale of the ardent and inflammatory with the
same celerity and certainty as does the present judge —
in an immodest way — reference still to quantity.

Quince Harris was a remarkable character and had a
most interesting career. How he became a lawbreaker
after the war by reason of his doing that which as a
peaceable and law-abiding citizen he did and might do

before the war, and how he took the bold stand that the
Government had no right to dictate to him what particular use he must or must not make of the fruit and grain
produced by the sweat of his brow, and how he defied
the Government and carried the fight to a finish, till
finally, in seeking to evade the minions of the law, he was
exposed out in the mountains to weather so severe that his
feet were frozen, and it was surrender or die — is an interesting story, as he related it; and his justification of
his own action and motives was quite convincing of the
fact at least that he himself sincerely believed in the
righteousness of his cause. I heard him present his defense to Judge Jackson, and the "Iron Judge" was much
impressed; so much so that glaring fiercely at the prisoner he thundered from the bench: "Sir, that is no defense; you have been guilty of a gross violation of the
Federal Statute; I sentence you to one month in jail, the
term to begin 30 days ago! Marshal! Take the prisoner
to his — boarding house!"

A little farther down, Jacob's Ladder, just above the
old Elbon Mill dam, so called, as I recollect, because of
ladder-like niches in the cliff by which you get down
to the pool, and the Cherry Falls, just below the old
Elbon Mill, at which falls the present state road from
Summersville to Webster Springs bridges the river, are
beautiful spots and good fishing.

Cherry Falls takes its name from T. R. Cherry, a New
Yorker or New Englander, who lived there in the 70's
and early 80's. He rigged up some sort of a water
wheel which was run by the water from the falls and
furnished power for some sort of mill. I do not recall
whether I ever saw this mill. I have been told that Mr.
Cherry drilled for sulphur water at this place, intending
to rival Webster Springs, a mile below, as a health resort.
I presume he failed to find the sulphur water; at least
his project was abandoned and he moved to Buckhannon,
where he resided for several years, but finally returned
to the East whence he came.

A short distance farther down brings us to the "Ad Hamrick Hole," a beautiful pool with magnificent surroundings. Here Adam Hamrick, one of the old settlers, reared a large family, most if not all of whom moved to other sections of the county or country. This brings us to Webster Springs, from which point we will take a fresh start.

———

No Tale of the Elk which I might write, that did not in numerous instances include Kemp Littlepage, would be complete. This tale was not sufficiently progressed downstream to reach that section of the river where Kemp and I have spent together so many delightful days. However, the untoward circumstance of April 24, 1928, has made it seem to me fitting to so far interrupt the orderly course as here to pause and speak of him who was one of the finest sportsmen who ever wet a line in Elk River and one who knew and loved and appreciated the life and flavor of the wonders of the old stream, as few others did.

For a number of years after "The Camp at the End of the World" was established, Kemp shared it with me as though a joint owner; frequently when I was there with my family, Kemp was as a member; and I was often there as a member of his family or invited party of friends.

Kemp Littlepage was one man who in life sounded its allurements to their depth, finding equal pleasure in the discharge of its most arduous duties, as in basking in the sunshine of its diversions; yet strangely and finally, he looked fairly in the face, Death, which he had so often bantered, even as looks the bridegroom upon the blushing bride.

On the highest point of Spring Hill at Charleston, overlooking his beautiful Elk as it finishes its versatile course past the varied scenes with which he was so familiar, and in its flow, serene, impetuous, tranquil, turbulent, placid, tumultuous; so typical of his own career, he sleeps!—in his camp at the End of the World.

VII

FORK LICK; WEBSTER SPRINGS COMES
TO VIEW

FORK LICK took its name from the fact that at the confluence of Back Fork of Elk with the main Elk River, there is a strong salt sulphur spring—strong in volume, taste and odor—which in the day of their abundance was much frequented by the elk, the buffalo, and the deer from far and near coming there to lick the briny fluid that poured forth in such volume. Fork Lick was the early name of the locality and of the magisterial district in which Webster Court House is situated. This spring, or "Lick," is still doing business at the old stand, out on a rocky bar of the main river, but is seldom seen by the visitor, for the reason that a more recently developed outlet for the same vein of water has been found more accessible and conveniently located; and what is now known as the famous Salt Sulphur Spring is about a quarter of a mile up the river from the old Fork Lick, immediately in the present town of Webster Springs, the present name of the county seat of Webster County. Some time about or before 1860, I believe it was, that Col. Addison McLaughlin, of Braxton County, conceived the idea of developing the vein of salt water, which found its vent at this deer lick, for the manufacture of salt; and went so far as to select a plot of ground suitable for a salt furnace, and to there drill a well to tap the salt water stratum. This well—quite a shallow one, only 12 or 15 feet deep, I believe—so drilled by Col. McLaughlin, by means of a spring pole—is the present Salt Sulphur Spring. He "cased" the well with a hollow gum log and allowed it to flow until he was ready to utilize it in his enterprise. My recollection is that the oncoming of the war defeated his project and that the furnace was never constructed. I am stating these facts wholly from memory, for years unrefreshed, and may not be entirely accurate in my chronology. When I first became acquainted with the place it was known as Fork Lick, Webster Court House, or Webster Springs, but the post office name was Addison, so called for Col. Addison McLaughlin. Later it was changed and now bears the name of Webster Springs.

The county of Webster was created by an Act of the General Assembly of Virginia about the year 1860, but, the war following so close upon, was not erected into a full fledged county until about 1865, remaining during all those years of fratricidal strife in a sort of chrysalis state—the cocoon possibly deeming it the part of wisdom to remain in the shell until the war cloud had rolled by. It was a sort of "no man's" land during the entire period of the war, whether from its rugged topography and general inaccessibility or due to the fact that some of its citizens are said to have met in solemn conclave and adopted and caused to be promulgated an edict, ukase or declaration of independence, to the general tenor and effect that the county of Webster, having been so neglected, forgotten and abandoned — treated as a stepchild, so to speak — is and of right should be a free and independent state; and from that time forth "The Independent State of Webster" was hailed as one of the bright galaxy.

I knew a number of the choice spirits who conceived and put in motion this rare bit of state building. George M. Sawyer, of Williams River, was duly proclaimed—or proclaimed himself, I am not sure which—Governor of the Independent State, and wore that title as long as he lived. He was always up to some devilment and never got too old to see the humorous side of everything. He was a natural born actor and mimic, and to hear him relate the incidents connected with his administration of the affairs of state during his incumbency as

Governor was one of the high spots of a visit to Webster Springs.

In August, 1885, I paid my first visit to Fork Lick. I had located at Sutton, Braxton County, a few months before, for the practice of law, and it was customary for the members of the Sutton bar to attend the terms of the circuit courts in the surrounding counties, so with Wm. E. Haymond, who was then prosecuting attorney of Braxton County, I traveled horseback from Sutton by the Wolf Creek route up to Webster Springs, a distance of about 35 miles as the road ran, to attend the August term.

Judge Henry Brannon, of Weston, who presided over the circuit composed of the counties of Lewis, Upshur, Webster, Nicholas and Braxton and held three terms in each county each and every year and received therefor the splendid salary of $1,800,000 annually, was on the bench. John D. Alderson, of Summersville, Nicholas County, was prosecuting attorney, B. C. Conrad, clerk of the circuit court, Ballard P. Conrad, clerk of the county court, Sam Given, sheriff, Tom Daly, deputy sheriff and jailer, and Walter Hollister, county surveyor.

The resident attorneys were C. P. Dorr, Col. Joseph Thompson, James Wooddell, and George A. Revercomb, then a young lawyer from Covington, Virginia, fresh from the University of Virginia Law School, who had just located. Among other visiting lawyers whom I recall as being present at that particular term, were Felix J. Baxter, E. S. Bland, L. M. Wade, and Alex Dulin, of Sutton; W. G. Bennett, W. W. Brannon, and W. B. McGary, of Weston; Capt. A. M. Poundstone, of Buckhannon; Spencer Dayton, of Philippi; L. D. Strader, D. A. (Count) Stofer, J. F. Harding, and Dave Lilly, of Beverly; Maj. Frank B. Smith, John H. H. Duffy, John D. Alderson, Robert A. Kincaid, and E. R. Andrews, of Summersville, and Wesley Mollohan, of Charleston.

The buildings at that time, besides the courthouse and jail, consisted mainly of two or three stores and a half dozen hotels or boarding houses. Jack Miller and Ike Curry were two of the storekeepers, I remember, and then or shortly thereafter, Theodore Horan was also engaged in the mercantile business. Mrs. Wooddell (the mother of J. W. Wooddell, now manager of The Waldo, at Clarksburg, William J. Wooddell, a prominent attorney of Webster Springs, and Bantz Wooddell, present county clerk of Webster County) kept what seemed to be the favorite hostelry, beautifully located in a splendid grove on an eminence overlooking the town. Robert H. Townsend, Levi Skidmore, Walter Stanard, Isaac W. Cool and Mrs. Miller were other hotel or boarding house proprietors. These establishments were usually crowded during the summer season with visitors from the four quarters, but found little doing in their line for about eight months of the twelve. One of the first of the many wisecracks I heard about the place was perpetrated by Tom Daly, who consisted of 250 pounds of avoirdupois, a whole lot of wit and the balance humor. He was a Braxton County product who had migrated to Fork Lick several years before and was always making disparaging remarks concerning the town and county of his adoption and the people thereof—the "natiffs," as he called them. Why some of those six-feet, eight-inch Hamricks, Gregorys, Dodrills, or McAvoys didn't lick him for his tactless comments was not because they were afraid or could not have easily done so, but because of the delightfully amiable manner in which he handed out these left-handed compliments—he got by with that which would have meant a black eye or a busted cranium for anybody else.

Soon after I met Tom he was complaining of the Godforsakenness of that country, and I asked, "How do you fellows manage to put in the year round up here?" "Oh," he replied, "in the summer time we skin one another." "Skinning the visitors," consisted in exacting from them from $3 to $5 per week for room and board—and each with an appetite tuned up to twice normal by frequent libations of salt sulphur water.

How the skinning was conducted during the off season, I never exactly understood, unless he had reference to the continuous performance of the two justice of the peace courts of Fork Lick district—it sure takes a lot of hide to keep such mills grinding.

Among other prominent citizens of the town and county, whom I met at the time, was Maj. Marshall Triplett of Upper Glades, who had been a prominent citizen of that section before the war and had been a member of the General Assembly of Virginia. He was a member of that body when the county of Clay was created, and as a compliment to him the county seat of the new county was named Marshall. Major Triplett was in the Confederate service at the time the State of West Virginia was formed and for that reason the Legislature of the new state changed the name of the county seat of Clay from Marshall to Henry; Uncle Johnny McGuire, who lived at the top of the mountain overlooking Webster Springs on the Summersville road; Peter Cogar, an old residenter formerly in the hotel business; Lewis McElwain, from over on Laurel Creek, where the town of Wainville now flourishes, always with his red hunting shirt, and generally with his flintlock rifle; Hays Rader, from over on Gauley, near the present town of Camden-on-Gauley (he was afterward sheriff of the county); Dr. Benedum, then of Hackers Valley, afterward clerk of the county court; Old Uncle Billy Perkins, long a resident of the town, and Uncle George Miller, who lived about a mile up Back Fork. He was quite a prosperous farmer and was reputed to have brought the first sewing machine into that section of the county. It is said that Uncle George was very proud of his acquisition and would invite the neighbors to come and hear his wife Sally "play a tune on the sewing machine."

Rev. Richard A. Arthur—Uncle Dick, as everybody knew him—lived a mile above town on Main Elk. He had been quite an able preacher in his day and had many important charges throughout the state. He was superannuated when I first knew him, but even then possessed no little fire and vigor.

Uncle Tobe Sizemore from over on Grassy Creek of Holly River, and Uncle Conley Blankenship, both preachers of the Hardshell Baptist persuasion, were also much in evidence, and a joint service conducted by these two eminent divines in the Walnut Grove in front of the court house, was the first "meetin'" I attended in the town. Uncle Tobe preached all Sunday morning and Uncle Conley asserted and labored long and earnestly to prove that "dew and frost is the breath of God."

Bernard Mollohan, a noted land surveyor, Beri Sebastian Delcano Cabot McCourt, who signed his name B. S. D. C. McCourt, and was usually called Beri; his brother, "Andy Shanks" McCourt, Mayor of Puzzle Hole, which will be reached in due course; Charlie Perkins, the owner, operator and proprietor of the water mill several miles down the river, and for that reason could not serve on the grand jury; Charlie McCray, from Hackers Valley; George McElwain, Adam Cogar, Jack McElwain, then and now far famed fiddler; Samp Hamrick, then a young chap who was "sparkin'" one of Uncle Bob Townsend's girls, whom he shortly married; Perry B. Wethered, prominent in business affairs; Neal Hamrick, who later became one of the great political leaders of that section; Allen Armentrout, who some years afterward was elected Squire of Fork Lick district and soon became invested with the proud title of "Chief Injustice" of Webster County; Uncle John Moore, the blacksmith, who with his family were the only Negroes in Webster County; these together with those already mentioned, were among the celebrities with whom I came in close contact on my first visit.

Probably the most versatile and all-round useful citizen of that community was Beverley D. Hutchinson. He was general proxy and all around substitute for anybody, anywhere and any time. In the first place Beverley was a notary public and took all acknowledgments, depositions and administered affidavits; he was a commissioner in chancery of the circuit court, commissioner of accounts of the county court; was deputy clerk of the circuit and county courts, deputy sheriff, deputy jailer, deputy assessor, deputy surveyor, deputy constable; acted as agent in the trial of cases before justices; acted for every justice of the peace in the country in the way of writing up their dockets and making their reports of fines collected; wrote reports for county superintendents of free schools; was frequently foreman of the grand jury, often on the petit jury; wrote all obituary notices and resolutions of respect and condolence; filled out pension papers for old soldiers; if a merchant got sick or was called away from his business, Beverley took charge and carried on for him in his absence; at one time or another he ran every hotel and boarding house in town temporarily during some emergency; he was a carpenter of no mean ability; could paint a barn or a portrait; could make anything in a blacksmith shop; was a good cobbler; as a veternarian he had an extensive accommodation practice; and as a general medical practitioner he was unexcelled by any of the laity. As Tom Daly once said of him: "Beverley Hutchinson does everything for the neighborhood except the preaching and the washing." Beverley was the son-in-law of "Governor" Sawyer, who said to me on one occasion: "There's Beverley Hutchinson who does more work than all the other people in the place—in fact, does his own work and the most of theirs—and he is the hardest up man in town."

It was during the August term, 1885, that the Hon. Patrick F. Duffy had his first home coming after being inducted into office as Auditor of the State of West Virginia, March 4th, preceding. The people of Webster County were very proud of Pat Duffy for his own worth, and doubly proud that in him had been chosen the first resident of their county to hold a state office. Pat was a widower and made his home with his aunt, Mrs. Scaggs, one of the most gentle, loveable and delightful old ladies to be met anywhere, who kept the home fires burning for Pat's return.

I remember of it being in everybody's mouth: "Pat Duffy will be here today or tomorrow!" It was always necessary to give leeway of at least one day in figuring on arrivals at Fork Lick in those days. I had known Pat Duffy all my life, and early the next morning I found him down at the Spring surrounded by scores of his constituency, all eager to greet and welcome him back home. While Pat was holding his reception at the Spring, the courthouse bell rang, and I hastened up the hill in obedience to the summons, leaving right in the middle of one of Pat's inimitable stories.

When Ben Conrad, clerk, had read in open court all the law and chancery orders of the preceding day and the same had been duly signed by Judge Henry Brannon, the clerk was directed to empanel a jury for the trial of a certain case. Very few of those called responded, and the sheriff was directed to call the absentees at the front door of the courthouse. Whereupon Sheriff Sam Given took the list of names to the door and proceeded to call: "Beri Sebastian Delcano Cabot McCourt—Beri Sebastian Delcano Cabot McCourt—Beri Sebastian Delcano McCourt—come into court!"

"Jedge," said someone in the room, "I jist left Beri down at the Spring talking to Pat Duffy."

"Valentine Moats — Valentine Moats — Valentine Moats—come into court!" boomed the voice of the sheriff.

"I seen him down thar, too," said a voice in the courtroom.

"William G. Hamrick"—thrice called the sheriff.

"Billy G. also, Jedge," said the same informant.

"Mr. Clerk," said Judge Brannon, "have the sheriff call Patrick F. Duffy."

A moment later the sheriff was calling at the door— "Patrick F. Duffy—Patrick F. Duffy—Patrick F. Duffy—come into court!"

In due time Pat Duffy with his escort of about 75 people, jurors, witnesses, and stragglers, filed solemnly into the courtroom.

"Mr. Duffy," in stern judicial tones spake Judge Brannon, "the court has found it expedient, for orderly procedure and the dispatch of business, to send for you and request that you occupy the chair here at my right."

Of course, Pat promptly accepted the invitation, and when he was seated the Judge whispered: "Now, Pat, you sit right there until court adjourns, or I will send you to jail for contempt of court."

The old wooden courthouse which served in those days was destroyed by fire about three years later, and for a good many years courts were held upstairs over a store-building, in a narrow, stuffy, ill-ventilated room. There was always an April term of the circuit court of Webster County, and April is the month of "ramps." Does the gentle reader know what that is? Not likely unless you live in or have visited the higher altitudes in the gentle springtime. Once upon a time at a banquet I was asked, "What are ramps?" And the only definition or description I could think of was: "Ramps are— or is— a cross between wild onions and garlic—only crosser." I was puzzled to know something about the pesky things and examined several dictionaries, all to no purpose; you find the words "ramp" and "ramps," but they do not fit the subject. Finally I stumbled on the word and definition "Ramsons—a British species of garlic; broad leaved garlic." While I presume this identifies ramps and ramsons as being about the same thing with the British, I am inclined to stick to my own definition of the American species. If a fellow eats ramps, you can smell his breath the moment he steps inside your magisterial district; and to be cooped up in a close hot room with 116 or 117 ramp eaters, is much worse than death. The only known antidote is to eat a mess yourself—and hate yourself for just three weeks. So you can imagine what an April term of the circuit court meant in those days. It is now a standing rule of the circuit court of Webster County that anyone who appears in the courtroom within thirty days after eating a mess of ramps, is guilty of contempt of court.

Something over thirty years ago a splendid stone structure was erected and now serves as the temple of justice. There was much contention and controversy as to the character of the building to be erected for the new courthouse, whether it should be a small and comparatively inexpensive, or a large, commodious, permanent and more costly structure. The then president of the court was the one most active in favoring the better and more permanent class of construction and it was largely due to his efforts that the handsome stone building was erected. It was the irony of fate that the first case to be tried in the fine new courthouse, was an indictment for felony against the very man most responsible for its building. I had the misfortune to be appointed to prosecute the case in lieu of the prosecuting attorney, who had been counsel for the defendant in the controversy out of which the indictment grew. I not only failed to convict the accused, but came within an ace of being licked by his attorney, who happened to be both an intellectual and physical giant.

Before the erection of the wooden courthouse which was burned in 1888, the courts were held in a temporary structure on the Quince Harris place, a mile or so farther up the river. The story is that as there was no bell available, it had been customary for the sheriff to announce the fact that the court was sitting, by pounding on a hollow log with a knot maul. When Charles McC. Dodrill became sheriff of the county, he decided that the manner of announcing the ascension of His Honor to the woolsack, was rather primitive and that he would employ a more modern contrivance. Securing a large plow point, he suspended the same with a plow line from the rafters at the entrance to the building, and provided an axe with which to strike the plow point. When everything was in readiness for the opening ceremonies, Robert Irvine, of Weston, then judge of that circuit, universally known as "Granny" Irvine, mounted the bench and gave the direction: "Shu-uff, open co'ot!"

With alacrity Sheriff Dodrill responded to the command, and rushing out to the entrance and the suspended plow point, he seized his trusty axe and delivered a mighty blow that made a mighty clang; but alas! "Kelly Ben" Hamrick and some other stalwart mountaineers were standing close by, gazing in wonder at the dangling plow point, and when the axe came in violent contact therewith, the line snapped and the plow point struck "Kelly Ben" full in the mouth, wrecking his frontal dental equipment completely. "Blast," indignantly exclaimed Sheriff Dodrill, "it's jist good for you, gawkin' and gapin' around where machinery is in motion!"

This installment is confined to persons and things seen and heard on my first visit to Webster Springs. In succeeding ones I may be able to present something of interest concerning the place as it grew in importance and favor, as one of the many health and pleasure resorts in West Virginia.

VIII

JOHN E. KENNA DESCENDS THE ELK; REVERCOMB, BYRNE, WILLIAMS, AND THE BRANDY KEG

I WALKED down the street the other day with a friend who said he had been reading my Elk Stories and quoth he:

"I had no idea you had wasted so much of your life fishing and hunting and prowling around over the woods."

My reply was that I considered that part of my life far from wasted, and that as a matter of fact everybody was better off by taking a vacation once or twice a year.

"Vacation—yes, I take a vacation too—but when I take a vacation, I go somewhere where I can see something and enjoy myself."

"So do I."

"Good Lord! What can you see and how can you enjoy yourself back in the woods away from everybody and everything? I spend my vacation down at Atlantic City, Coney Island, New York City, or some place like that. I haven't missed spending a week or two at Atlantic City for twenty summers. Do you ever go there?"

"No, I have the proud distinction of never having been to Atlantic City. I never had business calling me there and would not think of it as a place to seek pleasure."

"But think of the crowds you see—the board walk, the bathing, the wonderful hotels, the fashionable people, the swell people you meet—"

And he wasn't half thro', when I interrupted.

"To illustrate the difference between your point of view and my own, I was in Philadelphia a few years ago on business, with W. W. Brannon, of Weston, and

Ralph Hills Ely, from Buckhannon, West Virginia. Finding we would have a day or so on our hands waiting the arrival of an absent party, they proposed that we run over to Atlantic City, about 75 miles away, and spend the day. I excused myself and they went without me. I spent the day most enjoyably prowling around over Fairmount Park, visiting its most secluded haunts and feasting my eyes upon its wonderful natural beauties, which have been preserved from the spoilsman."

I can only imagine what my friend had in mind as we separated, but if he placed as low an estimate on my tastes and preferences in such matters as I did upon his, to what abysmal depths indeed was I then and there consigned: For what I thought of and concerning him in the premises might be expressed in the words and figures following, to-wit:

Poor Insect!

By the way, I want to say for the benefit of those Upper Elk fellows who have it in for me for tipping off to the world at large the splendid opportunities for trout fishing afforded by their territory, that about the middle of June a gentleman from an adjoining county and remote from Upper Elk, accompanied by his wife and three children, came into my office and introduced himself to me. He stated that he had been reading "The Tale of the Elk" in *Wild Life,* and had decided to take his wife and family for ten days camping on Upper Elk where he could catch some of those wonderful trout, especially the rainbow. That they had accordingly gone to Bergoo and camped there for a week or ten days and had just returned from their trip. "Mr. Byrne," said he, "I would like for you to tell me what kind of flies you use to catch those rainbows."

I told him of the great variety of flies, and of the fact that the angler should be equipped with many different kinds, and often must change from one to another a good many times before finding the one to strike the capricious fancy of the trout at that particular time; I named quite a number of my favorite flies, and asked him what he had found best for rainbow trout.

"Rainbow trout! The mischief! I've never caught a rainbow trout to this good day. I fished up there for ten days, early and late—never fished harder in my life—but never caught a rainbow. I did catch a few speckled trout—but rainbow, no sir—never even got a bite."

He then informed me that he had fished altogether with bait and never had used flies, and that he intended to provide himself with a lot of flies and go back and try it again.

I asked him if anybody else had caught any rainbow trout while he was up there, and he said, "Yes, the Gregory boys caught lots of them; but none of the campers along the river ever caught a single rainbow, so far as I ever heard."

This gentleman, however, need not be cast down because of his inability to catch the rainbow. Only last summer Senator E. H. Morton, of Webster Springs, an old-time speckled trout fisherman, told me he and his family had just been camping at Big Run, a mile below Whittaker Falls, for about a week, and he had worked his head off trying to catch a rainbow, but had caught not one. Fortunately, he said, "Bearskin Bill" Hamrick happened along one morning early and being advised of the situation promptly set forth, and in thirty minutes returned with fourteen fine large rainbow trout and saved the family from going hungry for breakfast.

I have been hearing a great deal about these "Gregory Boys" recently as the fishermen de luxe of Upper Elk. It seems that of late years they wear the horns once worn by my old friends, "Bearskin Bill" Hamrick, Calvin Hamrick, Bern Hamrick and "Rattlesnake Bill." I must run up there one of these days and find out something about these chaps — whether this younger generation has anything on the old.

If people would let me alone, I might write this story

in some connected sort of way and get through with it some time, but with all these interruptions, they are likely to cause it to be strung out forever.

Returning not to our mutton—but to our venison—the only wagonload of venison I ever saw, was at Webster Springs in the month of November, 1885. I was there attending my second term of court and Senator John E. Kenna and Dick Delaney, from Charleston, accompanied by Fleet Porterfield, their true, tried and trusty cook and teamster, drove in via Summersville in a road wagon for their annual hunt. They proceeded on up the river to Whittaker Falls and pitched their camp somewhere in that neighborhood. My recollection is that about ten days later they returned, Kenna and Delaney afoot and Fleet driving — the wagon loaded to the guards with unskinned deer carcasses. There must have been ten or a dozen. I do remember that Mr. Kenna gave a deer to each hotel and boarding house in town, and had five or six left, which they took to Charleston.

In August, 1886 or 1887, Senator Kenna built—and I don't mean had built—a fine johnboat, at Webster Springs, and he and Fleet Porterfield undertook to fish from that point to Charleston. I accompanied them for two or three miles on the trip. I do not mean to say that I rode in the boat with them; for that is not the way that trip is made. If the water is at fishing stage, the shoals and swifts, of which there are many, are so shallow that one man usually wades and guides the boat over the roughs, while the others walk or wade along and do the fishing; and if flush, the current is so swift and the channel so rough and rocky that it would be a perilous undertaking to travel in any sort of craft for the first twenty odd miles from Webster Springs down to the mouth of Laurel Creek, now the town of Centralia. My recollection is that Senator Kenna came to grief on this very trip down at Union Mills, a short distance below Centralia, where his boat was wrecked by coming in contact with a rock, and that he had to call on old

"Squirley" Carpenter who then lived thereabout, to convey him to Charleston in a canoe. Afterward, however, Mr. Kenna built another boat in which he made the continuous trip from Webster Springs to Charleston. So far as I know he is the only man who ever did so.

Mr. Kenna was a great lover of the outdoors, and an all-round "Wild Lifer." While hunting big game, such as deer and bear, was his long suit, he was very fond of fishing for trout and bass. The only time I ever fished in Sugar Creek of Back Fork, Mr. Kenna and I rode up from Webster Springs, making an early start and a late return, and put in a full day in Sugar Creek and at the island near its mouth, in the Back Fork. This was four or five years before his death, which occurred in 1893.

John E. Kenna held a strong hand with the people of Webster County. It was in the old Third Congressional District, which he represented for two or three terms before he was elected to the United States Senate in 1883. He hunted and fished with them during his campaigns and as well in the off year; went to their logrollings and house-raisings, and called them by their first names, and every man, woman and child called him John. The story is told that in his last race for the House of Representatives, Kenna received every vote cast in Webster County, except one, and that was cast by a fellow who had borrowed $10,000 from him and failed to return it.

Webster County is one of the most sparsely settled, and, from the standpoint of population, smallest counties in the State, but if those who lived there forty years ago, when I first knew the place, and all who have been born there since, had stayed at home and behaved themselves, instead of moving out and spreading themselves all over creation, Webster would by this time be by far the most populous county in West Virginia. In those days the average of children per family was from twelve to sixteen, and a fellow with only eight or nine children was looked down on by his neighbors. Currence Gregory's family consisted of himself and his wife, and, if I am not mistaken, sixteen children — all girls but fifteen; and one of his neighbors by the name of Hamrick, had almost exactly the same number, with but one boy in the lot. I wish I could get hold of the photograph of Currence Gregory's family which John Alderson once showed me. It would fit in here just fine.

If anybody should check up on me and challenge the accuracy of these family figures, I hope they will take into consideration the fact that I am speaking merely from memory, and the further fact that it is not out of the way in matters of this kind to add a few, to cover future contingencies.

Once I asked one of the numerous Hamricks — I don't now remember which one — how many children he had, and he replied that he had thirteen, all living. I said "Thirteen! Don't you know that thirteen is an awfully unlucky number?"

"Is that so?" said he.

"That is so," said I.

I saw him about a year later and he said, "Well, Bill, you needn't worry any more about my bad luck. Fourteen."

Not having at hand any of these family pictures of forty years ago, and to show how business keeps up in the good old county of Webster, I robbed John Vicker's photograph album of a picture taken by him eight or ten years ago, down in the Puzzle Hole neighborhood, here shown. This family numbers eleven, and the dog is thrown in for good measure.

John Vickers has fished the roughs of Elk from Webster Springs to Union Mills several times, and has quite a number of very interesting fish yarns to relate. But the trouble about John is — and sad to relate, almost everybody else, excepting the present writer — you cannot depend upon the absolute accuracy of his statements

of, concerning or pertaining to, the fish he caught or
didn't catch.

The old stock of Webster County have always been
pre-eminently a quiet, peaceable, law-abiding people, and
in the olden days and as well the present, when a crime
of any great magnitude was committed — and many
have been committed — it was safe to say that in nineteen out of every twenty cases, the culprit was a "fur-
riner" and not one of the "natiffs," as Tom Daly called
them. Because of its remoteness from the outer world
and its boundless mountain fastnesses, desperadoes and
fugitives from justice from border states, especially
Kentucky and southwestern Virginia, were wont to
seek refuge and isolation in its friendly seclusion. The
most hospitable people in the world, no wayfarer, however humble or forbidding his appearance, ever left the
door of one of the old Webster stock, with his wants un-
provided for. And many was the time that weeks or
months after the event, the news would percolate thro'
to the host, that he had entertained, not an angel un-
awares, but an imp of darkness who was eluding the
gallows or penitentiary for some crime committed scores
or hundreds of miles away.

The first case of any magnitude, with the trial of
which I was concerned in Webster County, was the State
versus Williams, alias Mennifee, upon an indictment
for burglary. This was probably at the April term,
1886. It seems that Uncle Johnny Baughman, who
operated a country store back on the mountains, had sustained one of his periodical robberies, and a day or two
thereafter a suspicious looking character by the name
of Williams or Mennifee was found in the neighborhood, and being a total stranger and wholly unable to
properly account for his antecedents, he was promptly
pounced upon by the minions of the law, charged with
the robbery and confined in the Webster jail to await
the action of the next grand jury. This jail was a one-
story stone structure, consisting of two cells, with a

hallway between, surmounted by a one-story frame structure, which served as the jailer's residence, and from which descended a stairway to the hall below.

A year or so before the incarceration of Williams, one Jacob A. Hosey, a citizen of the lower section of Webster County, had ordered from a Cincinnati liquor house by the name of Sandheger, about $1,000 worth of whiskey, wine, porter, ale and drinks of like nature, which was promptly shipped to the nearest railroad station and there taken over by Hosey and hauled to his home. Some question arose soon about payment for the goods and Sandheger brought a suit in the circuit court of Webster County, and sued out an attachment which was placed in the hands of Sheriff Sam Given, who promptly took possession of the stock of liquors, and conveyed the same to Fork Lick, where it was deposited for safe keeping in one of the two cells of the jail, in the original containers, barrels and kegs. Williams was put in jail about December, 1885, and remained there all that winter. Whether someone told him, or whether he sensed it from the frequent trips made down the stairway and into the neighboring cell, which he could observe through the bars of his cell door, in some way Williams found out that there was something of more than usual interest in the cell across the hall, and being an ingenious devil he proceeded to whittle out a wooden key to the padlock of his door and another key for the other cell, and to make quiet investigation of the mystery. Among the numerous barrels and kegs, he found one of the latter over in a dark corner where it was not likely to be missed, full of liquid of some kind. This he quietly removed to his own cell and found it to contain brandy. Williams' dining table consisted of an inverted empty flour barrel, and this he placed over the brandy keg, thus concealing it. Swiping one of the pint tin cups brought to his cell with his meals, he bent the rim spout shape, hung the cup on the nail in the wall provided for his hat, which, of course, concealed it, when

the hat was in its accustomed place. He was now ready
for business, and, his cell being on the ground floor and
no fence or other obstruction to intercourse with the outside world, except the stone walls and barred windows,
he communicated the fact to some one within who became his confederate, and soon empty bottles coming
in and full bottles going out through the bars was a continuous performance during the hours of darkness.

When the brandy keg was empty, Williams carried it
across the hall and into the other cell, and by means of
a small rubber hose siphoned the liquor from one of the
barrels into the keg which he again conveyed to his own
cell. This he kept going for two or three months. At
first he was careful to tap the barrels most remote from
the cell door, in order that the emptiness thereof might
not be discovered; but alas, business so increased in volume that he threw discretion to the winds and encroached
too far on the front line of containers, and on one sad
day the sheriff and jailer, on a tour of inspection, discovered one particular barrel, which they supposed to
still contain quite an amount of exceptionally fine
"drinking liquor," to be empty as a missionary box.
Their official suspicion being thus aroused, they at once
proceeded to investigate, and to their amazement and
horror discovered that ninety per cent of the liquor was
gone. Why they should have suspected my future client,
Williams, alias Mennifee, I cannot imagine, but sus-
pect they did, and promptly entering his cell they ruthlessly yanked the empty flour barrel from the floor and
so exposed in all its guilty nakedness the brandy keg,
which they found to be then half full of their favorite
brand of Kentucky Rye. The hat was summarily yanked
off the nail and there grinned the battered pint cup and
wiggled the rubber hose. Williams was doomed. Not
that he was guilty of the Baughman robbery wherewith
he was put in jail, because ere the convening of the April
grand jury the perpetrator of that crime was discovered
and confessed, and Williams was completely exoner-

ated. But at the said April term Williams was indicted for feloniously breaking and entering the jail of the county of Webster and stealing, taking and carrying away divers goods, wares and merchandise, to-wit, whiskey, brandy, wine and other liquors, of great value, etc., the property of Jacob A. Hosey.

When Williams was arraigned for trial Judge Brannon asked him if he had counsel. He said he had not, and in answer to the question as to whether he had means to employ counsel, he stated, notwithstanding the winter's business conducted by him, without the payment of any license or rent, that he was utterly destitute of funds. Whereupon Judge Brannon appointed George Revercomb and me to defend him.

John Alderson, who was prosecuting attorney at that time, prosecuted the case with his usual ability and vigor, while Revercomb and I defended with great vigor. Alderson had no trouble in proving by the sheriff and the jailer not only the *corpus delecti*, but all the other *delecti* essential to stick Williams, so far as the facts were concerned; but we, his counsel, raised the "high pint" that as Williams was already in jail he could not under the law be guilty of breaking into jail, and further suggested that so preposterous was the thought that any sane man would voluntarily break into jail, that neither the common law nor the statutes made any provision whatever applicable to such an anomaly. We also raised the question as to the ownership of the liquor as laid in the indictment — as it was questionable under the evidence as to whether it belonged to Hosey, Sandheger, Sam Given or Tom Daly. Judge Brannon knocked us out on our "high pint," and because of some remark made by me in the argument concerning ownership, in which I said the jailer seemed to exercise a peculiar proprietorship over the liquor, Tom Daly threatened to lick me.

Williams was sent to the penitentiary for five years; the Supreme Court of Appeals quashed the attachment under which the liquor was put in jail, Hosey was execution proof; and the liquor was gone. Now, under all the circumstances, I want to propound this question: Who was it that lost the liquor?

IX

WHO'S WHO AND WHY AT WEBSTER SPRINGS

I HAVE TRIED to recall the names of prominent people of my acquaintance who "came to the Lick," as visiting Webster Springs was called in those days, from 1885 to early in the 90's, when the "Big Hotel" was built, but I fear many will be omitted owing partly to a faulty recollection and partly to the fact that it is difficult to distinguish in all cases between those whom I met during the boarding-house era and those who came only after the more pretentious hostlery was erected. In addition to those already named as figuring in the early period, I recall Charles W. Lynch, John Bassel, John J. Davis, Col. Ben Wilson, Charles A. Horner and John R. Boggess, of Clarksburg; Johnson N. Camden, Harry P. Camden, John S. Camden, Judge John J. Jackson, J. W. Vandervort, Dave Leonard, L. N. Tavenner, and Charles T. Caldwell, of Parkersburg; Jonathan M. Bennett, William E. Lively, Andrew Edmiston, Jackson Arnold, Sr., Judge Gideon D. Camden, John Brannon, Louis Bennett, Judge William George Bennett and W. W. Brannon, of Weston; Col. W. W. Arnett, Marshall T. Frame, John H. Holt, William P. Hubbard, John O. Pendleton, Col. Robert White, James B. Taney, T. S. Riley, George W. Atkinson and Alfred Caldwell, of Wheeling; George S. Laidley, W. A. Cracraft, Judge James H. Ferguson, Col. B. W. Byrne, Charles K. Payne, John C. Ruby, B. H. Oxley, George Byrne, Dr. M. H. Dyer, William Seymour Edwards, William Dickinson and C. C. Watts, of Charleston; Judge Homer A. Holt, Alex F. Mathews, Judge A. C. Snyder, Dr. S. H. Austin, John A. Preston and Edgar P. Rucker, of Lewisburg; Maj. Theopholis Gaines and Col. J. W. St. Clair, of Fayetteville; John W. Mason and Judge A. Brooks Fleming, of Fairmont; A. M. Poundstone, George M. Fleming, Coleman C. Higginbotham, William S. O'Brien and Daniel D. T. Farnsworth, of Buckhannon; George W. Curtin, Jacob S. Hyer, E. D. Camden, Charles D. Elliott, John Byrne, Luther J. Berry and Thomas M. Berry of Sutton; Robert G. Linn, Nelson Bennett, Robert F. Kidd, Col. John Hayes and A. L. Holt, of Glenville; John T. McGraw and George M. Whitscarver, of Grafton; Frank Cox of Morgantown; Millard F. Snider and George W. Farr of West Union; Warren Miller of Ripley; Walter Pendleton of Spencer; J. M. Boggs of Big Otter; Richard Shelton of Clay; William Thompson and C. L. Thompson of Huntington; David E. Johnston of Bluefield; J. H. (Fud) McGinnis of Beckley; John E. Roller of Harrisonburg, Va.; William M. McCallister of Warm Springs, Va.; and C. M. (Standard Oil) Pratt of New York City.

When the West Virginia & Pittsburgh Railroad, now the Baltimore & Ohio, was completed to Cowen, transportation to Webster Springs was greatly facilitated, as it is but sixteen miles between the two points, and it was Senator Camden, I believe, who first put on foot the erection of a hotel adequate for the entertainment of the large influx of visitors expected to follow closely upon the improved transportation facilities. Senator Camden was largely instrumental in the building of the West Virginia & Pittsburgh road, and in establishing the town of Camden-on-Gauley at the point then locally known as Lanes Bottom, where a large mill was erected for the manufacture of the timber on the so-called Caperton tract of about 75,000 acres of land. The machinery for this mill was wagoned from Gauley Bridge via Summersville to Lanes Bottom, and installed in the year 1891, more than a year before the railroad was completed to that point; and it seems that about that time Senator Camden had in mind the building of a railroad from Pickens, in Randolph County, to Webster Springs, coming down Sugar Creek to the Back Fork of Elk and thence ten miles down to its mouth; and the Webster Springs Hotel project was part of the general scheme of the Camden development of the Elk and Gauley section.   Later the Pickens-Webster Springs railroad was considered not feasible, because of supposed excessive grades down Sugar Creek, and for that or some other reason the road was never built.

While these things were in the making, I remember of being at Webster Springs on one occasion, and seeing George M. Whitescarver, of Grafton, and a young chap by the name of Charlie Mayo, from Upshur County, come into town on horseback. They fooled around town two or three days wanting to buy Uncle Bob Townsend's property near the Spring, but Uncle Bob wanted more money than they wished to pay, and the next thing I knew, they bought for Senator Camden a big bottom where the hotel was afterward located, and it was not long until the Webster Springs Hotel was under construction.   I was told that all the lumber that went into the section built of this hotel was hauled by wagon from Halo, about four miles below Cowen. My recollection is that the hotel was run under the supervision of Mr. Whitescarver for the first few years of its operation, and was for the greater part of the time, at least, directly under the management of Charles B. Johnson, a nephew of Mr. Whitescarver, I do not know just what connection Charlie Mayo had with the matter, but I believe he was employed by the Camden interests at the time. He is now and for many years has been connected with the Pardee & Curtin Lumber Company in their extensive lumber operations in the Elk and Gauley country.

A few years after the hotel was built, John T. McGraw, who had acquired a large boundary of coal and timber land on the Elk watershed of the upper reaches of Holly River, built a narrow-gauge railroad from Holly Junction up Holly River and over the mountain to Webster Springs, and in connection with his enterprise took over the hotel, adding a new building much larger than the old, and installing up-to-date Turkish bath equipment, where sulphur baths could be had if desired. For many years this hotel was, during the season, taxed to its full capacity by visitors from far and near, and the overflow so increased the demand for other quarters, as to render necessary the building and operation of a number of smaller hotels in the town.

John McGraw died in the year 1920, and his holdings, including the Webster Springs Hotel, went into other hands. In him central West Virginia lost one of its greatest developers and the state one of its foremost and ablest citizens.

I went to Webster Springs at the opening of the trout season this year (1928), mainly for the purpose of showing the Gregory boys how to catch rainbow trout, and found "Bear Skin" Bill Hamrick "rarin' to go." However, the river was so high and discolored that we found it necessary to wait about two days before starting out. The interim I employed very pleasantly meeting old friends and viewing the old and new surroundings. Of those I found there, only seven could I recall as having resided at Fork Lick in 1885, namely, Mrs. M. J. Wooddell, her daughter, Mrs. Conrad, her sons, Bantz and W. L. Wooddell, A. Powhattan Smith, James V. Lough and Steve Woodzell.

Mrs. Wooddell, although 86 years of age, is as hale and active as the ordinary woman of 60, and I spent an hour at her home most agreeably indeed. Jim Lough is 90 and for a man who has spent his life wrestling with a portable sawmill, is holding his own remarkably. Powie Smith is again running the *Webster Echo,* the same business in which I found him 43 years ago, when he and George Revercomb had one white shirt owned jointly—but not as tenants in common. He is back on the job after an absence of many years.

I bumped into Frank Blankenship—and bumping into Frank is like bumping into a feather-bed; he was thin as a racer when I first knew him as a young chap thirty odd years ago; now he is broader than he is long and flabby as he used to be hard—and was reminded of an incident of about 1894. Pat Duffy had returned to Webster Springs after having served eight years as State Auditor, and lived on the Golden Shore farm on the south side of Elk. I prided myself in those days upon my ability to handle a gig, and took occasion to tell Pat Duffy of a large pike I had gigged down near Clay Court House a few weeks before. Frank Blankenship came up and butted into the conversation to say that there was a big blue pike in the long pool right back of the hotel; suggested that we get him that night; to which I readily assented. Jim Wooddell had a boat and we took him in on the deal; and going to Tom Daly's blacksmith shop we found that he had just made a fine three-pronged gig, fitted with a splendid walnut handle, which I promptly borrowed and appropriated to my own use as chief harpooner. As we were leaving the shop Frank spied an old stub of a two-pronged gig, blunt at the points and the beards nearly gone, mounted on an old crooked slunge pole, which he said he would take along to steer the boat. When it got good and dark we rigged up our torch and got aboard, Frank in the stern, Pat Duffy sitting on a plank placed cross-wise on the gunwales near the stern, Jim Wooddell sitting flat on the bottom about the middle, and I in the place of honor in the bow, armed for slaughter, with my new and trusty gig. We began at the lower end of the pool and proceeded slowly upstream in search of the pike; nothing showed up until we reached the V-shaped head of the pool, when Frank yelled, "There!" At that instant I spied an 18-inch sucker and promptly impaled him on my gig, when Frank cried out, "That ain't it!" and at the word lunged forward with his old slunge pole and speared through the middle, a 33-inch blue pike; when Frank brought the fish to the top of the water, Jim Wooddell in wide-eyed astonishment exclaimed, "Well, the durn fool!" and when Frank was floundering around getting the pike into the boat, Pat Duffy fell off his high perch into the river.

I reminded Frank of this incident when I saw him recently, and he asked me to relate the story to a lot of fellows standing around. Frank's face fairly beamed during the whole narrative until the very last, when the length of the pike was mentioned as being 33 inches, and it clouded slightly, and he said, "Yes, boys, that's so—every word of it—but Bill, haven't you got that pike a leetle too short?"

I did not get the full import of his remark until a few minutes later when one of the bystanders told me Frank had been telling the same story for years of and concerning a five-foot pike.

I gazed upon the ruins of the once proud Webster Springs Hotel, which was destroyed by fire two or three years ago. John M. Hoover, attorney for the owners of the property, informs me that the plans are being made for its rebuilding.

I met two of the Gregory boys, Levi and Orlando, and told them "Bearskin Bill" and I were going up to Whittaker Falls as soon as the river got in shape, and they invited me to visit their camp, which is about four miles above Leatherwood.

On July 4, "Bearskin Bill" and I went up to Leatherwood in a taxi, and sent our provisions about three miles up the river, intending to fish up to that point and there camp for the night; but before we had proceeded a hundred yards, Bill became so violently ill from some "store goods" he had recently eaten, that we had to take him to Hanse Hamrick's house and phone to Webster Springs for Dr. Dodrill, who responded very promptly and took Bill back home very promptly.

So I decided to go gunning for those Gregory boys, singlehanded and alone. I borrowed a speeder and pumped it up over the four miles to their camp, meeting Orlando, who informed me that he was on his way to

Webster Springs, but that I would find Levi at the camp. I was somewhat disappointed, as it had been my hope to get Levi and Orlando and Freeman—of whom I had heard but never met—in a bunch and show them how to catch rainbow trout. I found Levi very comfortably quartered in a good-sized tent, superintending the building of a new camp for himself, Paul Rusk and Bill Bolden, of Charleston. We fished from about 5 to 11 p.m. and I did not catch a trout. Of course, I had a perfectly good alibi—two of them in fact, i.e., there was too much water for good fishing, and soon after we began I floundered in the swift water of a shoal and fell on a rock, hurting my hip pretty badly—but alas, and alack, Levi had exactly the same alibis—he fished in the same water and also fell and hurt his hip— and he caught nineteen nice trout, eighteen of them rainbow and one a nice fifteen-inch brook trout.

We tried it again the next day, which was rainy and disagreeable, and Levi caught four and I caught exactly the same number—as the day before. I used to catch an occasional rainbow trout in my trout fishing days years ago, when they first appeared in Upper Elk, but the pesky things do not seem as friendly as formerly— at least with strangers.

But, after all, as I remarked to Levi on taking my departure from his hospitable camp, it was not the durned trout I was after—it was the outing.

X

A GLANCE AT THE LUMBER INDUSTRY AND
A SENATORIAL CARD GAME

IN 1889 the Pardee & Curtin Lumber Company, of which Capt. George W. Curtin was actively in charge, erected at Sutton a large bandmill and a boom, for operating large timber holdings acquired by that concern on Upper Elk and on Holly River. Charles D. Elliott, who afterward held the position of United States Marshal for the Northern District, and Adjutant General of the State, was an active agent of the company in securing such holdings. Thousands of the finest poplar trees that ever grew out of the ground were purchased at the uniform and then princely price of one dollar per, in addition to many thousands of acres of land in fee at $1.50 and $3.50 per acre. These trees stood in the small bottoms and along the mountain sides, near the river, between Webster Springs and Whittaker Falls on main Elk, and on Holly River, likewise conveniently located for putting into the stream. Some of the largest poplar logs I ever saw were cut by Pardee & Curtin between the points mentioned on main Elk, with the intention to float them out on flood stages of the water. Many thousands of these logs from three to six feet in diameter were so floated to Sutton and secured in the boom, but frequently some of the larger ones caught in gorges or behind islands, from which it was so difficult to dislodge them that it was found necessary that they be split in two in order to get them back to the channel of the stream. For several years afterward I saw hundreds of these large logs and half logs along the river, and many of them rotted and became worthless. In those days the best grade of poplar lumber sold for $24.00 per thousand feet.

Probably the largest poplar log ever cut in Webster

County, stood on the mountain side immediately facing
Webster Springs and quite near the old road leading
into Summersville. This tree was cut about 1873, by a
Charleston lumberman by the name of Woodruff, who
thought to float the butt log to his mill in Charleston.
This log was eight feet in diameter and seven feet long,
and in 1879 I saw it at the mouth of Little Sycamore,
where I was fishing that summer. I saw it again the
following summer lodged on the head of Wood Island
about 30 miles above Charleston. Some canoe men or
campers had evidently built their camp fires against
the log in the meantime, as it was about half destroyed
by fire. In 1885, and for several years thereafter, the
stump and greater part of the trunk of this mammoth
poplar tree remained there on the mountain side to be
viewed by all who passed that way.

Apropos of the big trees, big families and big men
of Webster County, I am reminded of the visit paid to
Webster Springs by (Fielding) "Hurry Up" Yost, the
great football coach, on a scouting expedition for football ivory, in the early 90's. I think it was shortly after
he left West Virginia University and went to Michigan.
He had heard of the big men grown on Webster soil
and came out to give them the once-over. I met him on
the occasion of this visit and gave him some pointers as
to where to find likely material. He spent several days
sizing up some of the younger generation among the
Hamricks, Gregorys, Dodrills, Woods, and McAvoys.
He found a large number of youngsters who quite filled
the bill so far as height and avoirdupois were concerned,
but so far as I know took none back to Michigan with
him, for what reason I never knew. The circuit court
was in session while Yost was there, and he witnessed
the trial of a young fellow by the name of McAvoy, I
believe, who was charged with disturbing religious worship at a church at or near Cowen. It seems that McAvoy,
who was about six feet two, edged his way into the church
where a revival was going on and standing room at a

premium, and found he was standing by Tom Jack Woods, who measured six feet eight. After a moment or two McAvoy looked up at Woods and said in a stage whisper, audible throughout the church: "Hey, Tom Jack, throw me down a chaw of terbacker." The titter provoked by this remark so enraged the preacher in charge of the meeting that he caused the indictment of the offender. There were about a dozen witnesses who testified in the case pro and con, all young chaps from 17 to 20 years of age, and whose height averaged about six feet three.

From the great interest and admiration with which Yost seemed to regard these young fellows during the whole progress of the trial, I supposed he had found what he was looking for and that he would carry off the whole bunch, but possibly he knew his business better than I did—although I do believe he made a great mistake in not taking at least half of them.

One day down at the Spring, Melville Davisson Post, then a W. V. U. student, now far-famed writer, introduced me to a long, gangling, gawky young fellow— Professor (A.D.) Hopkins, Chief Entomologist at the University, who had come to Webster County to investigate the ravages of a certain beetle that had attacked the Yew Pine forests in that section. Hopkins had paid a brief visit to the infected territory and showed me some blocks and bark from trees that had been girdled and killed by the insect. Only a few hundred acres had become affected at the time and Hopkins hoped to find something to check the onslaught before the rising sap of the following spring. He later informed me that he had secured in Germany a parasite which he introduced into the blighted area, which made short work of the destroyer and saved hundreds of thousands of acres of Yew Pine forests from destruction. Prof. Hopkins made a world-wide reputation for himself, and I am now informed that he holds one of the most important positions in the Entomological Department at Washington.

Tom Daly once told me that on his first trip to Fork Lick, when he came to spy out the land with a view of taking possession, he walked up the river from the mouth of Laurel Creek, and that as he came through the Puzzle Hole section he traveled a path which led along the mountain side quite a distance from the river. It was early morning, and down near the river he heard a terrible commotion which attracted his attention to a cabin where a man was administering a terrible thrashing to a half grown boy, who was yelling lustily. When the "hickory" was worn out, the man desisted and said to the boy: "Now, dern ye, go up to the 'sarvis' bush and get yer breakfast and go to work!" When John T. McGraw built the narrow-gauge railroad from Holly Junction up Holly River and across the mountain to Webster Springs, this "sarvis" bush boy was successively a pick and shovel man, gang foreman, section foreman and roadmaster. He later drifted out into the world and is now, as I am informed, at the head of an important railroad system in the Northwest.

Charles P. Dorr was the only resident attorney who maintained an office at Webster Springs as early as 1885. He had taken up his abode at that place about 1878, and embarked actively in the practice of law and incidentally in dealing in lands, which were very cheap at the time. He formed a partnership with John D. Alderson, of Summersville, and the firm of Dorr & Alderson, Attorneys-at-Law, was a very formidable outfit for ten years or more. Dorr took quite an active part in politics, both county and state, and was one of the most prominent Democratic leaders of central West Virginia. He it was who was most largely instrumental in bringing about the nomination of Webster County's favorite son, Pat Duffy, for auditor, by the Democratic State Convention in 1884. Dorr represented Webster County in the Legislature of 1887 or thereabouts.

It will be recalled that in the year 1892, in which was held the next congressional election following the passage of the tariff legislation, known as the McKinley Bill, McKinley was defeated for re-election to Congress. It was currently reported at that time that Mark Hanna and other political leaders of the same political persuasion were then grooming Mr. McKinley for the Presidency, for 1896, and that the defeat of that gentleman for re-election was thought to have given quite a setback to his chances for the presidency. The succeeding Congress passed the tariff act which took the name of the Wilson Bill, from William L. Wilson, of the Second West Virginia district, who was chairman of the Ways and Means Committee of the House. No sooner was the Wilson Bill passed than the McKinley supporters, led by Mr. Hanna, set about to encompass the defeat of Mr. Wilson for re-election to Congress, in order to take the sting out of the previous McKinley defeat and to rehabilitate that gentleman pro tanto for the presidency in 1896. Early in the campaign of 1894, I was in the town of Grafton, West Virginia, for an hour or two between trains, and ran across C. P. Dorr with a very distinguished looking stranger in the hotel lobby, and I was formally introduced by Dorr to Mark Hanna. I afterward learned that Mr. Hanna remained at Grafton several days, looking after the interests of Hon. Alston G. Dayton, the Republican candidate for Congress against William L. Wilson. A few days later I was in Webster Springs and was greeted with the news that C. P. Dorr, Tom Daly, and C. C. (Neale) Hamrick, three prominent Democrats of Webster County, had "hung their gate on the other post," as the expression went, and suddenly become full-fledged Republicans.

Happening to encounter Neale Hamrick, I told him of the report that he had left the Democratic Party and joined fortunes with the Republicans. Striking an attitude, both important and impressive, Neale replied: "The Democratic Pah'ty of negation!" Ordinarily Neale sounded his "r's" sharp as the crack of a mountain rifle, so I knew he was quoting the words, pronunciation, manner, and bearing of somebody, but I never learned whom.

Presently, I met Tom Daly and learned from him that the Democratic Party was "the party of the seng-digger, the coon-skin cap, the flintlock and the muzzle-loader," no longer worthy the allegiance of the progressive gentlemen who had so recently renounced it.

It was some time after this that Neale Hamrick burst into sudden political fame. There was a big "do-in's" going on over at Buckhannon, in the adjoining County of Upshur, and Dorr got hold of Neale, dressed him up in a Prince Albert suit, bee-gum hat, "biled" shirt, standing collar, patent leather shoes, and gold-headed cane; got him a haircut and shave, and paraded him down the principal thoroughfare of Buckhannon— "the glass of fashion and the mould of form, the observed of all observers"—introducing him as Colonel Hamrick, prominent political leader of Webster County. Hon. Stephen B. Elkins, who was taking some slight interest in state politics at that time, had driven over from Elkins in the family carriage, accompanied by his wife, and Senator Richard C. Kerens, of Missouri, a close friend and business associate of Mr. Elkins, and, upon being presented to the distinguished looking Colonel Hamrick, invited him into the carriage to drive around over the town and view the ceremonies. Of course, Neale accepted the invitation so graciously extended, and was the guest of the Elkins party for the remainder of the day.

The W. Va. & P. R. R. (now the B. & O.) had been built to Cowen and Camden-on-Gauley, and a hack line from Cowen afforded comparatively convenient means of transportation to Webster Springs, so while in Buckhannon, Dorr and Hamrick urged Mr. Elkins to come to Webster County and look after his political interests, and Elkins promised to make the trip very soon. From Buckhannon, Dorr took Colonel Hamrick to Clarksburg, Parkersburg, Wheeling, and other points, introduced him as a prominent recent convert to the

principles of Republicanism, and it so happened that
on their return home from the trip they encountered
on the train Mr. Elkins and Mr. Kerens, bound also for
Webster Springs, and at Cowen took the same hack for
their destination. At that time Colonel Hamrick and
his family resided in a modest Jenny Lind structure
along the roadside about three miles from Webster
Springs, and as the hack containing the distinguished
personages whirled by Neale's domicile, half a dozen
half-naked urchins swarmed out to see the passing ve-
hicle, whereupon one of them, more precocious than the
others, recognized Neale, despite his disguise, and at
once set up the astonished cry: "Daddy! Daddy! Daddy!" and soon the whole pack was out on the trail
in full cry — "Daddy! Daddy! Daddy!" "Colonel
Hamrick," said Mr. Elkins, "those children seem
to know you and be delighted to see you." "Oh, yes,"
promptly and pompously replied Neale, "all the children along this road know me and are very fond
of me. I usually make it my practice in passing along
to stop and give them candy and small presents, and the
poor things have all learned to call me Daddy."

In the years following, and when the Webster Springs
Hotel was in full flourish, Senator Elkins, Senator
Kerens, Senator Henry G. Davis, and Senator Johnson
N. Camden became frequent guests and indulged in all
the pastimes that were going, from pitching silver dollars to tenpins, bridge whist, and draw poker. It was
fun to see a game of bridge in which Mr. Davis and
his son-in-law Mr. Elkins were opposed. The two had
evidently first met when Elkins was rather a young
man and Davis much older, and while there was apparently a great affection between the two, in Mr.
Davis' eye Elkins had never grown up, but was still
the young chap who had courted and married Davis'
daughter, despite the fact that he had attained full
stature in the eyes of the rest of the world, having held
the portfolio of Secretary of War and being then a

United States Senator; and many was the sound rating given by father-in-law to son-in-law for some slight infraction, real or imaginary, of the rules or proper procedure of the game.

"Senator Elkins, why will you persist in following the card with your hand when you take a trick? Don't you know I can't see what you played?"

And Mr. Elkins' broad face would break into that beaming boyish smile, and he would apologize and promise to be good—and repeat the offense the very next time, and get another scolding.

One night Charles T. Caldwell, of Parkersburg, blew in, and about noon the next day he and Senator Camden met on the porch.

"Why, Charlie, I am glad to see you. When did you get in?"

"I came in last night, Senator."

"Last night? I certainly am sorry I didn't know you were here. We had a big game in my room last night. There was me and Dick Kerens and George Curtin and Steve Elkins, and we had a fine big game. And funny thing, Charlie—funny thing happened—Kerens got all the money and we were all broke but him—and we just kept tab of what we owed on our cuffs. It was a great game—a great game!"

"I certainly am sorry too, Senator; I sure would like to have set in that game. I can play a pair of cuffs as high as anybody in this world."

XI

THE STATE VS. HENON FLEMING; THE LAW GETS STARTED

J. H. Chapman was one of the prominent lumber operators in Webster County in the nineties, having
previously operated a plant near Sutton. He had a camp
within a few miles of Webster Springs and was frequently at the Webster Springs Hotel during the season. Chapman was the most deliberate conversationalist
I ever met. It took him longer to speak a sentence of
a dozen words than it would take three common men.
On the other hand, John T. McGraw was a talker of
the rapid fire variety—three words to the other fellow's one, on an average, was about his normal conversational speed.

I represented McGraw in a case he had against John
E. Roller, in the circuit court of Webster County, which
I expected to submit for hearing at the term then in
session, and was sitting with J. H. Chapman on a settee
on the hotel porch. Chapman was telling me of the great
crop of squirrels in the woods at that particular time,
and right in the midst of the narrative, McGraw came
up behind us and during the lengthy pauses between
the words of Chapman, communicated to me information
concerning the Roller Case.

Chapman's story, with McGraw's communications to
me, which appear in parentheses and italics, proceeded as
follows:

"Coming . . . down . . . from . . . my . . . camp . . . this
. . . morning . . . I . . . saw . . . the . . . most . . . squirrels
. . . I . . . ever . . . saw . . . in . . . my . . . life—(. . *Bill,
about the Roller case* . .)—Along . . . (. . *He wants to take
some more depositions* . . . . . the . . . (. . *and I will take
some more, too* . .) . . . road . . . (*You see Mollohan
right away* . .) . . . I . . . saw . . . (. . *and you and he*

agree on the time . .) . . . anywhere . . . (. . *will both take at Charleston . .) . . .* from . . . (. . *in about a month from this time . .) . . .* six . . . (. . *and be ready to submit next term . .) . . .* to . . . ten . . . on . . . every . . . tree." And McGraw was clear down at the spring before Chapman reached the "tree."

McGraw's interpolations caused no interruption whatever in Chapman's narrative. Both flowed as smoothly and serenely as though in no wise interrelated. Chapman paid no attention to McGraw, nor McGraw to Chapman, each appearing utterly oblivious of the presence of the other. It did take some little concentration on my part to carry both threads, and to be able to reproduce with absolute accuracy.

Many a lawyer has been guilty of "putting up a job" on his adversary in the trial of a case, but I had the rather unique experience of passively permitting my adversary to put up the job on himself, in an important criminal case tried in the Circuit Court of Webster County about thirty-three years ago—the case of State vs. Henon Fleming, indicted for murder. Many West Virginians will recall the atrocious Pound Gap murder in Wise County, Virginia, in which the entire Mullins family was wiped out. It appears that there were two bitterly opposed clans in that region, one headed by "Cap" Hall and the other by Calvin Fleming and his brother Henon. Hall and his partisans immediately set about, justly or unjustly, to hang the Pound Gap murder on the Flemings, and to bring about their apprehension. Calvin and Henon Fleming, whether because of guilt or through fear of the machinations of the Hall gang, sought safety in flight from the state of Virginia and some time later turned up on Birch River, in Webster County, near Boggs Post Office, where a brother-in-law by the name of Thomas had taken up his abode. A reward was offered by the Wise County authorities for the apprehension of the Flemings, and "Cap" Hall, with George Branham and Dock Swindall, two mem-

bers of his faction, became self-constituted sleuths to
follow and ferret out the whereabouts of the Flemings
and return them to Virginia. By some means Hall and
his associates got in touch with John Halstead, of Nicholas County, who had discovered that the Flemings
made their headquarters at the home of his brother-in-
law. Halstead also found that the Flemings paid regular visits on a certain day of each week, to the store of
Billy Boggs where the post office was kept, and received
mail under assumed names. Apprising Hall, Branham,
and Swindall of this fact, Halstead piloted them to a
point near Boggs' store, where the four secreted themselves and awaited the coming of the Flemings. They
did not have long to wait, and as soon as Calvin and
Henon entered the store door, Hall, Branham, and
Swindall followed, six-shooters in hand and ready for
action. Calvin, who was at the time considered the quickest man on trigger in southwestern Virginia, was standing at the counter immediately to the left of the door
reading a letter which Postmaster Boggs had handed
him, and Henon was at Calvin's side, reading the letter over Calvin's shoulder, when Hall, Branham, and
Swindall burst in on them with the shout "Hands up!"
—and the words were hardly spoken before Hall shot
Calvin three times in rapid succession, killing him instantly. Quickly ensued a .44 shooting match between
Henon Fleming on one side and Branham, Swindall,
and Hall on the other, in which fifteen shots were
fired at, and four by, Henon. One bullet fired at Henon struck him full in the mouth, tore away every tooth
on the left side of each jaw, and lodged in his left
shoulder, from which it was afterward extracted. Each
of the four shots fired by Henon took effect, two of
them on Branham, who was fatally wounded and died
in a few hours, one in Swindall's body, and the fourth
passed through Swindall's windpipe, and struck Hall
in the temple, scarcely breaking the skin. Henon was
in the act of firing the fifth shot when a bullet from

the pistol of one of his adversaries struck the rim of the cylinder of his revolver, half the ball entering an empty chamber and locking the cylinder and the other half deflecting, ploughed its way up Henon's forearm to the elbow, leaving a welt as big as a whiplash. Henon made a grab for a smaller pistol in his belt, but before he could use it, fainted from loss of blood—and the battle was over. Calvin Fleming was dead, Branham dying, Henon and Swindall were both desperately wounded, but recovered; Hall was but slightly hurt, and Billy Boggs, the only other person in the store at the time, was scared to death—almost. John Halstead heard, but did not see, the battle.

As soon as they had recovered sufficiently to be removed from Boggs' house, where they were taken after the shooting, Swindall was taken to his home in Virginia, and Henon Fleming to the Nicholas County jail at Summersville, where he slowly regained his strength. The shooting occurred in Webster County, and at the ensuing term of the circuit court thereof, Henon Fleming was indicted for the murder of Branham. Soon after the indictment was found, it became "norated" about that a gang of Henon's Wise County friends were planning to make a raid on the Nicholas County jail and rescue the prisoner. Whether true or false, the report had the effect upon the authorities to cause the Sheriff and several guards to spirit him away one dark night and convey him to the jail at Charleston, for safekeeping, as it was feared that it would be unsafe to risk him for any great length of time in the rather insecure jail at Webster Springs. On the morning of the first day of the term of the circuit court of Webster County, at which he was to be tried, it was announced that Henon Fleming was in the Webster County jail, having been secretly taken from Charleston to Pickens, in Randolph County, by rail, and brought the night before, from that place through the woods to the Webster County jail—to elude any band of rescuers who might be on the lookout—and a strong armed guard was placed about the jail.

Henon was brought into court and asked if he had employed counsel to defend him. He said he had not, but asked Judge W. G. Bennett, then on the bench, to appoint A. J. Horan and me as his counsel; which was accordingly done. Mr. Horan and I consulted with our new client as to his defense, and in a day or two the case came up for trial, which consumed about two days. E. H. Morton, who was prosecuting attorney of Webster County, was one of these savage prosecutors; though quite a young man, he had all the fire and vim and vigor, all the relentlessness, all the vindictiveness, and all the set phrases of invective, of the old, seasoned, time-tried and retested "persecutor."

The night before the trial began, Morton came to me privately and told me that he had reliable information that a band of Henon Fleming's friends from Virginia had left that state a few days before with the avowed purpose of rescuing Henon; that they were desperadoes of the most ferocious type, expert gunmen—every man-jack—and men who would stop at nothing to accomplish their purpose, and appealed to me as his friend to find out from Henon and let him, Morton, know if and when the raid was to be made, and added: "You know if that gang would make a dash into that little crowded courtroom"—court was being held upstairs in a narrow room over a store, as formerly described—"nobody could stop them, and the prosecuting attorney would be the first man they would shoot."

I told Morton I had heard all these reports about a rescue, and had mentioned the matter to Henon, who assured me that there was no truth whatever in the report; that the only person interested in him, whom he expected to come, was his brother-in-law Thomas, from over on Birch River. But Morton would not be reconciled—he knew the gang was on the way and I must find out from Henon all about it and let him know.

Which, of course, I promised to do. Before court convened the next morning Morton asked if I had talked to Henon, and I told him I had done so and that Henon still assured me he was expecting no one but his brother-in-law. When Henon came into court that morning, Thomas, his brother-in-law, was with him and I pointed him out to Morton, who watched him closely all during the trial. At noon and at the evening adjournment I had to repeat my assurances to Morton, that Henon swore to me that no rescue party was expected; but incidentally, I remarked that the brother-in-law, Thomas, had told me that he was going to the country to stay all night.

"That's just what I expected," declared Morton; "he's gone out to bring the gang in tomorrow." Next morning Thomas appeared as usual, and nothing happened to disturb the peace and tranquillity of the proceedings. But Morton was nervous. His cross-examination of opposing witnesses, excepting the accused was notably rigid, searching, and severe, and his tone and inflection carried insinuation and disparagement—as a rule; but not so the cross-examination of Henon. It was polite, though at times rigid—sometimes almost deferential, and never denunciatory. He did lambast Andy Horan and me at times, but his treatment of Henon was most considerate.

When the testimony was in and Morton was about to begin his opening argument, I whispered to Henon: "Tell Thomas that he must get up and walk out of the courtroom as soon as Morton begins his speech." Henon looked at me curiously, but obeyed orders. During the first sentence of Morton's speech, Thomas arose from his chair and walked slowly from the room, the eyes of the speaker following him to the door. The opening argument for the state was mild and unimpassioned. No invective hurled at the head of the prisoner at the bar— no furious onslaughts on the testimony of the witnesses for the defense. Henon was the sole and only witness in his own behalf. When Morton concluded his opening argument and resumed his seat, Thomas was still out of the courtroom. Andy Horan and I each made a few broken remarks to the jury, lambasting the witnesses for the state, lambasting the prosecuting attorney who would have the hardihood and effrontery to prosecute a case on such flimsy evidence; denouncing Hall and Branham and Swindall as murderers of Calvin and intended murderers of Henon, and extolling Henon Fleming as the heroic defender of his brother's life and his own. When we finished our remarks, Thomas was still absent, nor had he returned when Morton began his closing argument. In closing, the prosecuting attorney did make some more or less spirited rejoinders to some of the most outrageous propositions advanced by Andy and myself, but not an unkind word against Henon Fleming, beyond the concluding statement that under the oath he had taken as prosecuting attorney of Webster County, under the law and under the evidence, "it becomes by painful duty to ask this jury to find the defendant guilty." And Thomas had not reappeared.

Henon Fleming was acquitted by the jury. Later he was tried in Virginia for the Pound Gap murder and promptly acquitted of that charge. M. B. (Dock) Taylor was convicted in the circuit court of Wise County of participation in the Pound Gap murder and sentenced to be hanged. (See 17 Southeastern, page 812.) Henon returned to Webster and was for years Chief of Police at Camden-on-Gauley, and had the reputation of a splendid officer. I have not seen him for fifteen or twenty years. He gave me the little gun which he had in his belt during the battle in Boggs' store—a beautiful pearl-handled .32 Smith & Wesson. A few years later he told me the gun belonged to Calvin, whose boy was anxious to possess it; so I gave it back to Henon in order that the boy might have it.

This prosecuting attorney Morton is now one of the leaders of the bar of the state; represented with distinction his senatorial district in the State Senate; served several years as a member of the commission to recodify the State Statutes, and was the Democratic candidate for Congress in the third Congressional district in 1924. He and I often laugh about the job he put up on himself in the Henon Fleming case.

XII

"PUZZLE HOLE" FOR LAWYERS AND
FISHERMEN

IT HAS been a besetting weakness of mine that whenever I land at Webster Springs I've had to tear myself away, and here I find myself in just that predicament. Realizing that I have already loitered too long
when I should have covered a lot more territory on
down the river, with this Tale of the Elk, the time has
come to bid adieu to what has long been to me one of
the most attractive localities in West Virginia and,
therefore, in the whole world.

It seems that I am thoroughly inoculated with the
spirit of my old friend Squire Vince Hamrick, heretofore mentioned in these chronicles. Squire Hamrick, in
common with all the other dwellers in the vicinity of
Webster Springs, always took great pride in the place
and its attractions, notably the restorative, the health-
giving and health-perpetuating properties of the water afforded in such generous quantities by the Salt Sulphur
Springs, which have for so many seasons drawn alike the
ailing and the robust from far and near. About thirty
years ago on one of my visits to Webster Springs, I encountered a friend of mine by the name of Black, from
the city of Buffalo, New York, whom I had known at
Charleston. He and I strolled from the hotel down to
the Spring and there found the aforesaid Squire Vince.
Vince, who was pretty well tanked up on some of Uncle
Bob's best, advanced toward me with the extended hand
of cordial hospitality, as was his wont, and said:

"Hello (hic) Bill; how are you—hic—glad to see you
—hic;—by the way (hic) Bill, who's zis (hic) feller
with you?"

"Beg your pardon," said I—"Squire Hamrick, this
is my friend, Mr. Black,—Squire Hamrick, Mr. Black."

"Powerful (hic) glad to meet you stranger (hic)"—
said Vince with a hearty handshake—"powerful glad
(hic) to meet you. Shay (hic) stranger, where you (hic)
from?"

"I am from Buffalo, sir."

"Buffalo! (hic) which Buffalo?"

"Buffalo, New York, is where I live."

"Buffalo, New York (hic). Hell, stranger—don't
you (hic) hate to live so far away?"

Elk River from the junction of the Back Fork with
the main stream at Webster Springs, down to the mouth
of Holly, about 27 miles below, traverses one of the
most picturesque sections of West Virginia, maintaining to a very great extent the serpentine course and
rugged characteristics of the upper section. But there
is a gradual declension in the height of the mountains
by which it is walled in from an elevation above sea
level of about 3000 feet at Webster Springs to about
1500 feet at the mouth of Holly; the elevation at water
level being about 1450 feet at the mouth of Back Fork
and about 910 feet at the mouth of Holly, a fall of
about twenty feet to the mile.

Between these two points there have always been
wonderful fishing grounds for game fish, such as bass,
blue pike and wall-eyed pike and, as well, catfish and
suckers. The channel-cat of this section will give you
a fight almost equal to a bass of equal size and for the
pan it is surpassed by few indeed of the finny tribe.

Within easy striking distance of Webster Springs
there is a stretch of about three miles of river down to
the Skidmore bottom which, time out of mind, has been
"fished to death," as the expression goes, in season and
out of season, by visitors and "natiffs," but apparently
without exhausting the supply; as I am informed that
fish are as plentiful there today as they were when I
first knew the place over forty years ago; with the qualification, however, that in the past few years the wall-

eyed pike have become so numerous that other species are greatly on the decrease.

For bait-fishing, the Fall Hole, two or three hundred yards below the Forks, the Cat Hole, a mile farther down, the Lower Cat Hole and the Skidmore Hole, were unsurpassed. The two Cat Holes were so called because of the catfish that there abounded in the old days, but I have taken and seen others take many beautiful bass from both places; and the first time I ever saw the old-fashioned phantom minnow in action, a Webster Springs visitor whose name I do not recall, who owned such a lure and did not know how to use it, dragged awkwardly through the Cat Hole and succeeded in snagging and landing a beautiful thirty-inch blue pike, or muskellunge.

Early in my experience in casting a wooden plug or spinner, Wait Talbott, attorney-at-law at Webster Springs, declared that he could take live bait and a pawpaw pole and catch twice as many bass as I could catch with my plugs and spinners. I accepted the challenge, and we went down to the Skidmore bottom for the test. Around that long bend past Painter Lick to Big Run, there is a two-mile stretch of as fine bass water as the world affords, and we put in the greater part of a day very diligently. Our combined catch made quite a large string, I have forgotten the number, but I do remember that Wait has been bragging ever since how he put it all over me with my fancy tackle. But you can't put much dependence in what these lawyers tell you—especially when they get on the subject of fishing.

Speaking of this Big Run reminds me of the many little journeys afoot Judge Jake Fisher—who now presides over the Circuit Court of Webster County—and I have taken in years gone by, from Hardwood Station on the railroad—now B. & O.—over the mountain between Laurel Creek and Elk, down Big Run to its mouth and thence up the river to Webster Springs, a total distance of nine miles. This in preference to con-

tinuing by rail five or six miles to Cowen and riding
the hack sixteen miles to our destination. I believe Jake
has now gotten our time down to about two hours for the
trip, and I accept his figures with the accent on the
"about." I am told that even now in the era of fast trains
and automobiles, that whenever Judge Fisher is in a
hurry to begin court, he gets off the train at Hardwood
and hoofs it over the short cut. Twice in my life I have
made the trip by water from Webster Springs, the first
time as far as Sutton, and the last, down to Centralia at
the mouth of Laurel Creek, where the railroad leaves the
Elk and proceeds up that creek to its head at Cowen
and over to Gauley.

At this point it may not be amiss to make some explanation as to the Laurel Creek's emptying into Elk
River. There are three which bear the name Laurel,
and confusion sometimes results from that fact. The
first is about 36 miles above Charleston, and is called
Big Laurel; the second is seven miles above Clay Court
House and is called Little Laurel, and the third is the
one first mentioned, which empties into Elk about seventeen miles above Sutton, near the Braxton and Webster County line, and called Laurel Creek.

About the year 1892 and before the railroad had been
extended into Webster County, Carl McLaughlin and I
undertook the journey from Webster Springs to Sutton
in a johnboat. Carl lived on Cranberry Ridge, beyond
Camden-on-Gauley and he and I had been together on
several trout fishing and hunting expeditions. A pretty
good fisherman was Carl, but as a hunter of the old
school he was an edition de luxe, fit associate for such
big leaguers as Lewis McElwain, Jess Hammons, and
Elias Sanson.

Neither of us had a very definite idea of what such a
trip would entail. We supposed we would encounter a
few shoals and shallows, but that for the greater part
we would drift idly with the current, fishing when we
cared to do so and traveling when we did not care to fish.

The river was very low and clear and the weather quite warm. At that time I knew but little of the river over which we were to pass except the first mile or two, and, of course, realized that we would have hard sledding to get our boat down that far, but we had been told that when we got down to Skidmore's bottom we would have easy sailing. Well, it took us almost half a day, with the hardest kind of work, to drag that boat over the first three miles, and there we stopped and fished up and down the river until noon the following day, when we moved on down the river, and spent another half of a day in covering three or four miles. With the water at that low stage it was a full grown man's job to get anywhere in a johnboat; but the fishing was fine and we were in no hurry. I think it was about the third day out that we reached Puzzle Hole, where Beri Sebastian Delcano Cabot McCourt and his brother Andy Shanks at that time held forth, both prominent citizens already mentioned in this narrative. The fishing around Puzzle Hole and vicinity was exceptionally good and the river was becoming more easily navigable, so we hung around that locality a whole day and night. I remember of asking one of the McCourts—Beri or Andy Shanks— I don't remember now which, how the place got its name; and he replied, "Oh, some foolishness of Pat Duffy, and them fellers up at town." And that was all the satisfaction I got from that source. Later, at Webster Springs, I pursued the inquiry further, and got two widely divergent versions of the matter. One was to the effect that in the days of the earliest settler who had built his cabin in the sharp bend of the river at this point, a stranger found his way to the cabin, where he spent the night. The next morning he asked to be directed to the cabin of another settler whom we will call X, who lived several miles away, on Grassy Creek of Holly River. His host gave him specific directions and he took his departure immediately after breakfast. Shortly after nightfall the first settler heard a "hullo" out in front of his cabin and going to the door asked what was wanted. "Is this where Mr. X lives?" said a voice, which he recognized as that of the stranger who had been his guest of the night before. "No," was the reply, "but you are back tonight, just where you started from this morning." "Well," said the stranger, "this is the most puzzlenist hole I ever got into or tried to get out of." And if you will familiarize yourself with the geography and topography of this section where Elk River and Grassy Creek for miles run parallel, with only the thin backbone of a mountain between them, both bending, curving, and twisting in such unheard-of convolutions, you will not wonder that the stranger was puzzled.

The other version of the origin of the name was given me by Tom Daly, after he saw the new light politically. He said that the voters at the election precinct down there were all coon hunters and seng-diggers and naturally voted the Democratic ticket; that they always held back the election returns down there until it was known how many votes were needed to elect the Democratic ticket; therefore it was always a puzzle to know how the election had gone, until that precinct was heard from. Hence it became known as Puzzle Hole precinct.

XIII

THE STORY OF THE CHRISTMAS TREE

ABOUT two miles up Laurel Creek from the river, at the mouth of a large run which empties into the main creek from the east side, was located the home of Jerry Carpenter, who was probably the first settler to take up his abode anywhere on the upper waters of the Elk. Here, near the mouth of this run, a large rock or cliff juts out from the hillside at the edge of the creek bottom; under this rock is a space about fifteen by twenty feet and seven or eight feet in height. Jerry Carpenter, with his wife, came across the mountains before the Revolutionary War, and after threading their way through trackless wilderness, finally reached the point in question, and finding this ready-made camp, decided to occupy it temporarily. Within a very few days a son was born to them, and to him was given the name Solomon. The new arrival being in no shape for travel, his parents concluded to prolong their stay at his birthplace, until he should become better able for the journey upward. The winter season was approaching, and Jerry Carpenter sought to make the camp more habitable, by felling and splitting small trees, with which he walled the front of the cavern, leaving in the center a doorway, hung with bearskin portieres — a very comfortable abode, by the way — let me say, having myself on several occasions spent a week or ten days in similar but far inferior quarters. Finding this to be splendid game territory, Jerry Carpenter determined to lengthen his stay indefinitely, and the next year erected an addition to his residence, in the shape of a cabin front. Here he remained for a number of years. What children he had, if any other than Solomon, I have never heard; but this same Solomon Carpenter lived many years at or near the place of his birth, and his progeny were evidently quite

numerous for today his descendants are legion in the
Elk Valley, particularly in the counties of Webster,
Braxton, and Clay.

The large run referred to now bears the name of
Camp Run, so called for this rock camp. When I first
saw the place, some forty years ago, a party of seng-diggers happened to be occupying the camp under the rock;
but at that time there was no vestige of the wooden struc-
tures erected in connection therewith.

Dr. James L. Carpenter, who was, I believe, a son or
grandson of Solomon Carpenter, told me a very interesting story concerning these pioneer Carpenters and their
early home as above described. Dr. Carpenter lived at the
mouth of Missouri Run, which empties into Laurel Creek
eight or nine miles above its mouth, and on the road
leading from Sutton to Webster Springs, and where the
town of Erbacon is located. In addition to being a doctor, he was a farmer and also the owner and operator of
a saw and grist watermill. He lived in a very commodious dwelling, and furnished food and lodging for travelers—"man and beast." I first stopped with him about
1885, at which time he was about 75 or 80 years of age,
and knew him quite well until his death about ten years
later. He was quite an interesting character, and one of
the most fluent and entertaining conversationalists I
ever came in contact with. He was not one of these new-
fangled college doctors, but a homemade doctor. Herbs
and roots were his sole pharmacopoeia.

I stopped at this home overnight one December, a day
or two before Christmas. I mentioned to him the fact
that I had a severe headache, and he immediately went
to his "prescription case" and returned with some dried
leaves in the palm of his hand, which he proceeded to
pulverize with thumb of his right hand. "Here, Bub,
snuff this up your nose," said he. I asked what it was
he was offering me, and he replied, "It is flaters lobelie
or Injun terbacker. Gar-anteed to cure headache, bad
colds, er any mis'ry in the head." Thus assured, I did as

ordered and in an incredibly short time my headache was gone.

It was during this performance that I observed a small and beautifully symmetrical holly bush over in one corner of the large living room. Walking over to inspect it more closely, I found that it had been carefully cut, and the butt whittled down to fit the auger hole bored in a large wooden block which served as its pedestal. The bush bore a beautiful crop of bright red berries and was as fine a specimen as I had ever seen.

"I see you are going to have a Christmas tree," said I.

"Yes, Bub," replied the Doctor — to whom every one was "Bub" or "Sis" — "we allus have a Christmas tree every Christmas. Fact is, it's a fambly failin' with all the Cy-ah-penter generation. They have 'em every Christmas."

"Why so?"

"Well, Bub, you've axed me sumpin' now, an' it's a long story."

And this was the story:

"Sol Cy-ah-penter — Solomon wuz his right name, but everybody called him Sol — he wuz born down here under a rock at the mouth of Camp Run. His paw an' his maw had come here in an airly day from East Ferginny, when there wuz no settlement anywhere around in these parts, an' made their camp down there under that big rock. An' findin' that the huntin' wuz good an' havin' no place in particular they wuz headed fur, they jist decided to stay thar. So they timbered up the openin' fur the winter an' next year put in a corn patch, an' then built 'em a good cabin jinin' up agin the rock. so's to hev more house room, an' thar they lived down to the time of my recollection.

"Well, when Sol wuz a leetle cutter three or four years old, an' when it wuz comin' along towards Christmas, his maw says to his paw one day, sumpin' about hevin' a Christmas tree fur Solly; that over in East Ferginny whar they cum frum, ever'body allus hed a Christmas

tree fur the children ever' Christmas. By that time they
wuz two or three other fellers — among the airly settlers
—hed cum in, one feller down about the mouth uv Laurel
Crick an' another furder down the river at Baers Run
— I disremember their names now — they didn't stay
long in this country — an' they heerd the news about
the Christmas tree an' all gethered up an' holp about
the fixin's. Jist around up Camp Run, a leetle ways,
right in the upper aidge uv the corn patch, wuz the pow-
erfulest big holly tree that ever growed in these woods
— I see the ruins of it many a time when I wuz a boy —
twenty inches over at the stump if it wuz an inch, an' tall
in keepin', an' full uv berries as that boosh thar in the
corner. So the fellers, they gits together, an' fust an'
for'most they goes up on the pint above the camp an'
finds a big pitch-pine log, rich with rosin, an' splits it
up an' packs it down to the crick, an' gethers up a whole
passel uv rosin about the stump an' fetches it down.
Then they hews out two sticks uv the pitch pine about
three inches squah, one about ten an' tother about eight
feet long, an' fixes to pin them together in the shape uv
a cross. Then they takes the extry rosin an' mixes it
with bar grease, an' plasters both sticks with a heavy
coatin' uv this rosin; an' then one feller he climb up the
holly tree with his tommy-hawk an' cut away some of
the little limbs at the top so's to fix a place fur the cross,
an' the other fellers passed him up the long piece which
he wythed in a couple uv places to the stem uv the tree
top, an' then the crosspiece with the wooden pins fer
fastenin' it together, which he done — an' the Christmas tree wuz all fixed an' ready for 'lumination.

"Cum Christmas day they all gethered up again an'
hed a big spread in the middle uv the day. Bub, we
don't hev no sich feeds in these days — venison, bar
meat, turkeys an' fezunts—that's what them fellers et
one day with another, an' on Christmas day they put the
big pot in the leetle one, an' everybody et till they
couldn't eat nary other bite. An' then they want nothin'

else to do but wait till dark an' light Sol's Christmas tree.

"Well, when good dark cum, one uv the fellers gits him a long pole an' ties a pine torch on the end, lights the torch, slips it up thro the branches, an' sets on the fireworks. Well, Bub, you kin take it from me — sich another blazement hain't never been saw in all these woods, fore or sence. The blaze shot straight up an' to the right an' to the left, an' the rosin begin to spew an' sputter an' spit balls of fire down thro the leaves, an' spew an' sputter on the ground. Fer jist a very short space uv time, it done this way, an' all the folks gethered around, off a leetle ways, whar they could git a good view — when sompin' happened! The feller that lashed the upright stick to the top uv the tree fa'led to take into account that hick'ry bark will burn; an' that's what it done — the upper end fust — an' the fiery cross nodded forward a leetle, spread out its arms an' scooted head fo'most over the leaves an' limbs uv the holly tree an' lit flat on the ground, an' the blaze o' sparks that shot up when it fell, wuz a sight, an' it set fire to the weeds an' grass an' leaves in the cornfield — but thar wuzn't nothin' to be burnt, so they jist let it go. They wuzn't no harm done, only the Christmas tree wuz ruint.

"Now, Bub, that is jist half the story, an' you hain't seen the pint yit. Well, that is furder along.

"Sev'ral years later when Sol Cy-ah-penter hed growed up to be a man, still livin' down at Camp Crick, he wuz out in the woods one day when the heered somebody holler like he wuz in a powerful sight uv trouble. He run quick down to whur it wuz, an' thar he seen a big Injun rollin' on the ground an' groanin', an' a big painter makin' off through the bresh, a draggin' a deer. He drawed down on the painter an' plugged him thro the heart, an' then went to the Injun. Sol knowed what hed happened 'thout bein' told — the Injun wuz packin' the deer, an' the painter smellin' the fresh meat, lope on him, bit him thro' the shoulder an' chawed him up somepin' awful, dang nigh killin' him — grabbed the deer an' started off with it.

"Sol tuck the wounded Injun home with him an' doctored him up well as he could, an' when the Injun got a leetle better an' out uv his mis'ry, so's he could talk, he told Sol the other half of the Christmas tree story, jist before he died from blood pizen.

"Your mind uv hearin', don't you, Bub, about the massacree uv the Stroud fambly over on Gauley, an' how the massacree wuz laid on Capt. Bull's gang uv Injuns over at Bulltown in Braxton? Well, they never done it, an' this Injun set that straight, even if the white settlers did 'spicion the Bull Injuns an' wipe 'em out on 'spicion even if they wuzn't guilty. This Injun told Sol that him an' five or six other Injuns hed done the deed over on Gauley, an' that after the raid they crossed over the divide an' down Laurel Crick, an' that a leetle afore dark they jist come across the crick from whar Sol's cabin wuz an' started to fix fer buildin' thar campfire, but diskiverin' the cabin an' the white folks around, they snuck up in the bresh an' laid low ontil good dark, aimin' to rush in on 'em an' massacree the whole fambly, like they done the Stroudses; when it wuz good dark they crope out uv the bresh an' jist as they all got out in the open ready fer their dash in on the cabin — with fresh Stroud blood on their hands an' murder in their hearts — lo an' behold! a cross uv fire appeared in the heavens, lookin' right at 'em, an' in a minute — them standin' thar a-tremblin' an' all ready to run — it div out uv the sky an' over the trees, on the ground, an' tuck right down thro the field after 'em — an' they never stopped runnin' till they hed got back up the crick to about whar Welch Glades now is; 'em — an' they never stopped runnin' till they hed got gyardeen uv the Cy-ah-penter fambly. An' so I told you, Bub, that I would explain to you why the fambly is so strong fer Christmas trees; if it hadn't been fer that one, they wouldn't be a Cy-ah-penter uv the name in all these parts, jist like they ain't no Strouds."

XIV

THE ELK COMES TO BRAXTON

I KNEW full well I was taking my life in my hand in undertaking to weave a Christmas story into these chronicles for December *Wild Life,* and it has turned out even so. It seems that the Stroud massacre occurred in the summer of 1782, about the month of June, and for it to have taken the band of Indians guilty of that atrocity, to travel the eighteen or twenty miles between the mouth of Stroud's Creek on Gauley and the Carpenter Camp full six months, and for the "Stroud blood" to be still fresh on their hands upon arrival, is too much of a reflection upon Indian locomotion and ablutionary traits. I should have known that such anachronism would never escape the historico-critical eye of my old friends Judge J. C. McWhorter, of Buckhannon, or Uncle John D. Sutton, the Historian General of Braxton County. But by way of a mild defense, let me suggest that there is much greater probability that the Indians would wipe out a white settlement in December instead of June. than that the Carpenter family would have their Christmas tree in June instead of December.

However, this is no worse than an actual experience I once heard related by my old friend Dudley Dent, once a prominent citizen of Sutton, now long gathered to his fathers, who was attending a Fourth of July picnic down at the Sugar Grove, three miles below Sutton, when a huge buck dashed through the crowd and down to the river, and fell flat on the ice, and while there struggling and helpless, Dudley ran out and cut its throat with a penknife — just a small, common, ordinary penknife.

From Laurel Creek down to the mouth of Holly River, about four miles as the river meanders, is traversed the section marked by what was one among the earliest settlements along the Elk, in what is now Braxton or Webster counties. There is quite a good stretch of bottom on one or both sides of the river for the whole four miles, and this seems to have recommended the country as being suitable for homes. Benjamin Carpenter, a brother of Jeremiah, and Jesse Carpenter and Amos Carpenter, brothers or near relations of the other two, were the early settlers in this locality. One or more of the Carpenter families lived at the mouth of Mill Creek, a mile below Laurel Creek, one or more at Bakers Run, a mile farther down, and Benjamin and his wife lived in the large bottom at the mouth of Holly. Adam O'Brien, who left his impress upon the Elk Valley from this point down as far at least as Clay Court House, to a greater extent than any other pioneer, lived for a time near the Carpenter settlement. In fact, it is said that by following the "sign" left by Adam O'Brien, leading into the settlement, the Indians found the cabin of Benjamin Carpenter at the mouth of Holly and promptly proceeded to kill and scalp both Ben and his wife.

This same Adam O'Brien, who seems to have been blessed with many more wives than would seem under the present dispensation to receive either moral or legal sanction, will come in for more extended reference as we get along farther down the river.

The story is told that the first wife of the first Carpenter who lived at the mouth of Mill Run, one evening, when her husband was away from home, found it necessary to wade the river after the cows which had strayed across to the other side. Before leaving, she tied her two children to the bed-post to keep them out of devilment and the fire. It took her some time to locate the cows, and on her return to the river, she found that there had been a sudden rise, and that the stream was "past fordin'." With these cows was a little "pennyroyal" bull, a sturdy, stocky little animal, but tame and gentle as a lamb. Panicky with fear for her children in that

"Injun" and "varmint" country, Mrs. Carpenter determined at all hazards to cross that river to the other side, her home and her children. Grabbing the bull by the tail, she forced him into the river, and soon the faithful animal landed her safely on the other shore. A small island at that point in the river long bore the name of Bull-Tail Island. No vestige of this island now remains, excepting a sand and gravel bar.

The county of Braxton was formed in the year 1836, and within probably a decade before that time there was installed at what is known as Union Mills, on the north side of Elk River, almost opposite the mouth of Mill Creek, one of the earliest industrial enterprises that ever flourished in the upper section of the Elk. This was a large watermill equipped for both grinding and sawing, erected by Levi Skidmore, Col. Asa Squires, William McCoy, and Samuel Skidmore. This point was considered the head of flatboat navigation on the Elk. At that time the salt business at Kanawha Salines, the present site of the Malden vicinity, was in its heyday, and the Elk Valley, as far as navigation reached, was the storehouse from which the salt works drew their supplies of panplank, staves, heading, hoop-poles and flatboat "gunnels," and these enterprising founders and finishers of Union Mills were early to grasp the idea that the splendid stand of poplar timber along the Elk from their mill site up for several miles — theirs for the go-getting — was just what was needed to supply the salt makers with plank for their salt pans, gunwales for flatboats to convey the salt to southern markets, and, in addition thereto, to build flatboats at Union Mills, load them with staves or stave bolts, heading or heading bolts, hoop-poles, etc., and dispose of both boats and cargo to the salt works.

This business was carried on quite profitably for a number of years, but finally succumbed to competition from similar concerns farther down the river, where the perils of navigation were decreased not only in proportion to the distance from market but also the lessened ruggedness of the stream, as evidenced by a fall of about seven feet per mile from Union Mills to Sutton compared with about two and a half feet from Sutton to Charleston.

To get back to our trip down the river — Carl McLaughlin and I left the mouth of Laurel Creek in the morning, expecting to fish leisurely down the river and reach Sutton in about two days. The fishing was fine until we reached the mouth of Bakers Run, when there came up a terrific thunderstorm about noon. The rain poured in sheets, and we were compelled to land and seek shelter at the home of my old friend, Jordan Cogar, who lived on the bank of the river a little below the mouth of Bakers Run. I had been there several times before and was well acquainted with his wife, who, by the way, was, before her marriage, Delilah Skidmore, daughter of Levi Skidmore, one of the proprietors of Union Mills — and with their two sons, Ike and John. Carl and I were not slow to accept the cordial invitation to join the family at dinner, which was being put on the table at the moment of our arrival, and, as the rain kept up intermittently all afternoon, to be their guests for the night. At the breakfast table next morning, Uncle Jordan was complaining that the squirrels were literally destroying his corn in a field he had on the hillside some distance up Bakers Run from his house, and, observing that Carl and I each had a gun, he begged us to stay over a day and "shoot the squirrels out of his corn." As the river had risen during the night so as to spoil the fishing, we were glad to change off to a squirrel hunt.

I do not propose to go into the details of this squirrel hunt, although we were quite successful and brought home as many as we could comfortably carry — Carl was a wonderful rifle shot and could hit a squirrel running along a rail fence, three time out of four — nor am I going to extol the virtues of the great pot of delicious

stewed squirrel which Aunt Delilah prepared for our
evening meal. The squirrel hunt is mentioned only because of that which was incidental: In wending our
way up the hillside to and around the cornfield, I observed something I had never noticed before as to the
peculiar formation, conformation and geological structure at and below the mouth of Bakers Run. I had
often observed that there was one large mound-like hill
set off by itself next to the river, but on that day I discovered that instead of only one, there were twins.

These two huge mounds, each about one-half mile
long and a quarter mile wide at the base, and each towering about three hundred and fifty feet above the river,
symmetrically uniform as the two ears on a human head
and much that shape in perspective, roughly representing the figure 8 made by a backhand writer. If you
will take the shell of an ordinary hen egg, cut it lengthwise into halves and place them, oval side up, on an
elongated saucer, side by side, the right half a little in
advance of the left, the rim of the saucer representing
now what are and what once were the surrounding hills,
some vague conception may be gained of this very interesting freak of nature.

The river now runs practically straight for half a mile
to a point a short distance below the mouth of Bakers
Run, almost equidistant from the two mounds, and there
turns sharply to the right, then almost as suddenly to
the left, and continues to the left in a sweeping curve
of almost a mile, more than half surrounding the more
easterly of the two mounds.

It is quite apparent that at some time in the ages past,
the channel of the river ran through the low ground between the two mounds, where the Baltimore & Ohio Railroad now runs. In the slight excavations made in the
construction of the railroad at this point, river boulders
were found in great quantities. It is equally evident
that originally the river bed was around the west side of
the more westerly mound, and that means that in the

years of its onward flow the river even in this narrow, shut-in gorge between two high mountains, has
twice eaten away solid rock stratum, first to make a new
channel half a mile to the east of the old, and again
to make the present channel half a mile farther to the
east; leaving these two grim sentinels to guard against
any westerly encroachment.

The two miles of river from the mouth of Bakers Run
around to the mouth of Holly is prime bass water. The
river has cut into the base of the towering cliffs on the
north side, leaving many deep, dark and shady pools, the
natural habitat of that particular species of the finny
tribe. Kemp Littlepage, who had fished every hole from
Centralia to Charleston, told me that the two miles in
question was the best bass water he had found on Elk
River.

It will pay any *Wild Life* reader who combines a
fondness for bass fishing with the love of the beauties
and oddities of nature to visit the Bakers Run section
and see with his own eyes the things I have tried to
describe.

My recollection is that the river being rather flush,
Carl McLaughlin and I did but little fishing for the
balance of our trip to Sutton, but I have been over the
ground so often and with so many different persons,
that it is difficult to remember the occurrences of each
particular trip.

I should not take leave of Carl McLaughlin without
referring to two certain incidents, not to say adventures,
with which he was connected, one of which at least was
to me quite personal and rather momentous.

One of the many visits I paid to Carl at his home on
Cranberry Ridge was in connection with some surveying
I was having done in a land case involving the location
of the lines of a large house. One evening late in the fall
season of the year, as we were returning home from the
work, and passing the house of one of Carl's neighbors,

who was having a "hog killin'," Carl was presented with a good-sized slab of fresh "hog meat," which we proceeded to carry a distance of about two miles to his home. When we had gotten about halfway on our journey and it was getting pretty dark, we heard a peculiar sound in the road behind us, as of some one striking the ground three or four blows with a piece of rope or the like. Carl stopped instantly and exclaimed, "Painter! Strike a match!" I did as ordered, and Carl, handing me the pork, reached for the small hand axe which he carried in his belt—the only weapon possessed by either. We stood stock still for a few moments and hearing no further sound, had proceeded about a quarter of a mile, when we again heard the sound of the panther lashing the ground with his tail, twenty-five or thirty yards behind us. Again we stopped and struck a match and again all was quiet. This performance was repeated two or three times, the last time being just as we reached the bars at Carl's orchard within less than a hundred yards of the house. We hurried to the house, got a couple of repeating shotguns from Carl's arsenal, cut a piece of pork from the slab, returned and suspended it from one of the bars, and stepped away a few paces, where we styled our guns on the bait, which we could see more or less indistinctly. For half an hour we vainly awaited the advent of the marauder, but finally gave over the quest, recovered the bait and returned to the house.

After it was all over, I said, "Carl, why did you have me make a light, so the panther would know just where to locate us?"

"Locate us, hell," said Carl. "Do you suppose a painter needs anything to help him locate a man in the dark, especially when he's packing a piece of fresh hog meat? And besides, a painter won't go where there is a light."

The other incident, above indexed, occurred in November, 1899. Carl and I had arranged a trout fishing expedition on Cranberry in July or August and went prepared to build a hunting camp to which we would return when the deer season opened in November. We built a pretty good camp about a mile and a half back on the mountain between Cranberry and Dogway, just beyond the Webster County line in Pocahontas County, and about the middle of the following November we reached this camp in a driving snow storm, finding Ben Ritchie, Carl's son-in-law, and John Ritchie, Ben's father, who had gone there a day or two in advance. For two solid days and nights the snow fell in bird-shot pellets, without the slightest letup, and by that time was 18 inches deep on the level, and around under the wind-swept points was drifted to a depth of from five to ten or more feet. Deer hunting was out of the question, but we succeeded in getting plenty of turkeys, by the very unsportsman-like process of shooting them out of the yew pines, where they huddled against the snow storm, and thus kept plenty of camp meat in stock. It was the first snow of the season, the bear were seeking their holes, and one day when Carl and I were out a little distance from the camp, we found a fresh bear track in the snow and determined to follow it in the hope of getting a shot at the bear. We followed the track through an immense laurel thicket that set in within half a mile of our camp and covered an area of about one square mile. The point at which the bear crossed, however, was a narrow neck, scarcely a quarter of a mile across, connecting a much wider expanse on either side. We followed the track several miles over the top of the ridge to our right and thence back to the left, recrossing the same ridge and down to Cranberry River and across to the mouth of Red Run, where we abandoned the chase owing to the lateness of the hour and the distance from camp. On our return toward camp, some turkeys flew out of the trees down near the river to our right and Carl left me and took the direction of the turkeys, calling to me that he would return to camp by a different route from the one we had traveled and cautioning me to cross through the big laurel patch at the narrow neck where we had crossed that morning. It was about five o'clock when we separated and I struck off up the mountain side for the four or five-mile tramp back home. Before I had covered half the distance it began to snow, and the wind to blow a furious gale, and when I reached the edge of the laurel patch and sought to find the bear tracks, and our own, made that morning at the point where we emerged from the laurel, all signs had been obliterated by the fresh snow and wind, although I skirted the edge of the laurel for a hundred yards or more on either side of the point at which I thought we had come out that morning. Finally I decided to take a chance on a certain place as being the right spot to enter, and, after a few minutes travel, was congratulating myself that I had gotten through the laurel and into the timber on the other side, when I was confronted with the startling fact that I had simply reached a little patch of timber growing among the laurel, and that my troubles had only begun. By this time it was nightfall, but it had quit snowing, the air was clear and everything perfectly white about me, so I was able to see fairly well for several rods around. After passing through the little patch of timber I plowed through at least half a mile of unbroken laurel thicket before reaching another patch of timber. Again I thought I was through, but again was doomed to disappointment, as the laurel began again at the far edge of the timber. It had taken me more than an hour to negotiate so much of the thicket, sometimes walking erect, sometimes on my knees or crawling through the dense, tangled laurel, briers and undergrowth, every turf of vegetation with which I came in contact being a soft snowball to slap me in the face and spatter me from head to foot.

Soon after entering the laurel patch, in jumping to the ground from a log which I had walked, I twisted my foot and wrenched my ankle so severely that it brought me to my knees, and it was with much difficulty and much pain that I was able to stand erect, much less walk. Instead of immediately giving an alarm by firing my gun, so that my friends at the camp, a mile away, would come to my rescue, I foolishly thought to brave it out and get through somehow unassisted. So I waited until the pain had somewhat abated and then undertook to manipulate my foot and ankle and get in shape for service. This only renewed the pain, and I had to give it up as hopeless. I could not walk. I had spent probably thirty minutes at this sort of thing, when I called for help by firing my gun three times in rapid succession, and was promptly answered by a shot from camp. By this time I had become thoroughly chilled from my wet clothing and the almost freezing temperature, and when Carl McLaughlin and Ben Ritchie came to me half an hour later, I was just about "all in." It took these two men fully an hour to carry me into camp. What would likely have happened to me but for this timely assistance, may be easily imagined.

Carl McLaughlin died about ten years ago, but with me his memory will always live.

XV

HOLLY RIVER; PALMER LUMBER DAYS; LON KELLY'S FAMOUS FISHING CONTEST

HOLLY RIVER, with its short main stem and many branches, great and small, and with such an immense spread, would remind one looking at it on the map, of a palm leaf fan. The main river is scarcely more than four miles long to the point where it divides into its main branches, the Right Fork and the Left Fork — the two branching off at right angles and each dividing into several large branches almost equal in size to the one to which it is tributary. This almost equal division and repeated sub-divisions, obtain to a greater extent with respect to Holly, than to any other river or large creek in the State — wherever a fork forks, the two forks are "equal forks." The Right Fork, including Grassy Creek, one of its large branches, runs for miles parallel with Elk River with only a backbone mountain, scarcely a mile wide, at its base, between them — to within about one mile of the Back Fork of Elk, at Webster Springs; other branches extending for miles farther to the north and heading close up against Sugar Creek, a westerly tributary of the Back Fork, which empties ten miles up; while the Left Fork with its many branches heads with the waters of the Little Kanawha to the north and Buckhannon River to the east; and it is every bit as far across the fan, sidewise from rim to rim, as it is lengthwise from the end of the handle to the tip. There may be other streams that drain a basin of these peculiar proportions but none has ever come under my observation.

The earliest settlers of the valley of the Holly were the Skidmores, who "took up" and occupied some of the beautiful broad bottoms found along the main watercourses, and after them the Cutlips.

I knew a number of the older and also some of the younger Cutlips, and often pondered over the peculiarity of the name; until once in the argument of the case in the Circuit Court of Braxton County, involving lands in which some of these Cutlips were interested, I heard Honorable Spencer Dayton, of Philippi, who was, years ago, a regular practitioner in that court, and a man of wide general reading and observation — make the statement that Cutlip was but the phonetic spelling of a careless pronunciation of the good old German name Gottlieb.   And I have no doubt he was correct.

At the time of my first visit to the mouth of Holly, "Uncle" Griff Gillespie lived on a large bottom just below, and Johns Salisbury in the smaller bottom just above the mouth.   I remember the fine fishing in both rivers at this point, and also for the first two or three miles up Holly.

Charles Y. Byrne, who was clerk of the Circuit Court of Braxton County from the early 80's to 1895, the time of his death, owned the larger part of the bottom below the mouth of Holly, adjoining the part on which Uncle Griff lived, and he and I went up from Sutton on some business connected with his land, and, incidentally, to do a little fishing.   I presume my fee for the business was paid by the horseback transportation to, and the pointing out of, the fishing ground.

I believe our business was with Uncle Griff, but incidentally I ran across Johns Salisbury and inquired about the fishing there or thereabouts.

"Ah," said Johns, "right around here used to be the best fishin' on Elk River, but 'taint no good any more. Why, sir, a few year back it wan't no trouble to go out an' ketch as many catfish as you'd want — 5 an' 6 an' 10 pounders, an' Griff ketched one that weighed over 30 pound.   Me an' Griff used to keep in meat, that way; but in the last two or three year the black peerch has got in here an' whupped the catfish out — all the big 'uns — an' now all you kin ketch is them peerch, an' you hardly ever git 'em over two or three pound — so we jist quit tryin' to fish.

Dick Byrne and I—everybody knew him and even voted for him as "Dick"—spent three or four hours catching a nice string of those despised two or three pound "peerch"—mostly one pounders, more or less, however—and we were very well satisfied with the locus in quo—so much so was I that my first visit was by no means my last.

Early in the 90's, the Palmer Lumber Company acquired a large boundary of timber land on Holly River, erected a band mill at the mouth, built a railroad from Holly Junction where the West Virginia and Pittsburgh (now B. & O.) crosses Elk to the south side, up to the mill, and extended it, narrow-gauge, up main Holly to the forks and up the Left Fork, about six miles in all to Marpleton, where John M. Marple had a store.

A few years later John T. McGraw took over the Palmer holdings, and extended the narrow-gauge railroad up the Right Fork and Grassy Creek and over to Webster Springs—the West Virginia Midland as it is called. After the death of McGraw this road was taken over by Pardee & Curtin Lumber Company.

The Holly River basin is reputed to have produced a greater yield of yellow poplar timber than any equal area in the state.

From the mouth of Holly down to Wolf Creek, a distance of about ten miles, the Elk mountains have the general characteristics noted from Webster Springs down to Holly—that is, it traverses a narrow, rough and rugged gorge, shut in by high mountains on either side. At the mouth of Wolf the mountains have gradually declined and on the south side, especially, have receded somewhat from the river, and the stream has lost someting of its boisterous pitch, barring Wolf Shoal, which is long and steep, and swift as a mill-tail.

That there is good fishing water between Wolf and

Holly is well attested by the fact that for the past twenty years there have been maintained more fishing camps along there than could be found on any other ten-mile stretch of Elk River. Within the distance of a mile below and a mile above the mouth of Stony Creek, which is about four miles above Sutton, there are no less than half a dozen of these camps—all comfortable for the accommodation of from the ordinary to the extraordinary family during the hot months. Most of these are owned, or were owned, by Sutton people—the Blands, the Haymonds, the Walkers, the Berrys, the Kellys, and others —while farther up, near the mouth of Flatwoods Run, where the railroad reaches the Elk at Gillespie, and also near Palmer Junction, the Parkersburgers, the Fairmonters, the Clarksburgers and the Wheelingites, have from time to time maintained their fishing camps for thirty years or more.

Lon H. Kelly, formerly of Sutton, now (1928) of Charleston, who owned and operated one of the camps just below Stony Creek, a few years ago, conceived the idea of a contest between his two friends, Kemp Littlepage, of Charleston, and Tusca Morris, of Fairmont— both crack bass fishermen.

Each accepted the challenge, and both appeared at the appointed time, armed for the fray. Being host, and not wishing to occupy the precarious position of umpire between the guests, he wisely delegated that office to Joe Kenna, of Charleston, who was also a camp guest. While the other guests, among whom were Judge B. F. Keller, Governor Ephraim F. Morgan, George Rogers, Clark Wiles, and Ed Rider, composed the gallery. Rules were adopted, barring bass under ten inches from consideration; fixing a certain number of points for number of fish caught, total weight, and largest bass, respectively, and providing that the decision of the umpire should be final and conclusive. The contestants left camp at the same hour in the morning, one going upstream

and the other down, and were to return at or before 6
o'clock in the evening.

The gallery, part of whom followed the fortunes of
one and part the other, straggled back to camp before
noon, and about 6 o'clock the contestants appeared each
with a fine string of bass, ranging from three-quarters
of a pound to two and a half or three pounds, and each
handed his string to Umpire Kenna, who was supposed
to count, weigh and render his award accordingly. Joe
carefully removed the bass from Tusca's string and
placed them in a pile on the grass, removed those from
Kemp's string and piled them alongside of the first pile,
and then just as carefully messed them up together,
so it was impossible to tell which from t'other, and
solemnly declared the fight a draw—and each of the
contestants swore the other had bought the umpire.

From the mouth of Wolf Creek up to Stony Creek was
long the favorite haunt of "Squirley Bill" Carpenter,
who, by the way, was a son of Solomon Carpenter, the
chap who was born under the rock, as already recounted.
"Squirley" was an all-round fisherman, a canoe builder
and operator, flatboat builder, and steersman, raftsman
and general water-dog and fisherman; he was the most
inveterate, persistent and uncompromising fisherman
ever known in the valley of Elk. Spring, summer, autumn and winter made up the fishing season for him.
The river frozen over with ice a foot thick didn't daunt
him in the least. He would go up to the deep hole at
Breech Clout, cut a hole in the ice, sit down on the rock
—Breech Clout is the name of a huge rock jutting out
from the north bank of the Elk, about one mile above
Wolf Creek—and catch all kinds of fish, when it was
so cold that any other living man would have frozen to
death. His usual method of fishing when the weather
was warm, was to roll up his trousers above the knees
and wade out as far as he could into the edge of a deep
hole and stand there all day, or until he had as many

fish as he wanted. He was a bait and pawpaw pole fisherman, pure and simple, and despised the new-fangled fishing frumpery of rod, reel, flies or artificial lures, of any kind or character.

Once while fly-fishing I passed "Squirley," with his trousers rolled up, standing out in the river above the mouth of Wolf. Just about that time, he caught a bass and was wading out to put it on his string tied to something on the bank. I said, "How many have you got, Squirley?" In reply he held up a string of some half dozen very nice bass, and asked, "How many hev you ketched?" "Well," I said, "the fact is I haven't caught any yet but I haven't been fishing very long, and it has been most too windy." "No," said Squirley, "an' that hain't all—you won't ketch none with that dern college fishin'." Some time later Squirley and I took a canoe trip or two down the river together, and he learned to have a little more respect for "college fishing"—but for him to use anything himself, other than the old-fashioned pole, line, bait and sinker—no sir, nothing doing.

Squirley died only a few years ago, well up to the century mark; and so passed one of the old-time fishermen of Sutton and vicinity. In making this statement, I am taking it for granted that Tom Cogar, who formerly lived below and near Sutton, has long since been gathered to his fathers. If in error, I will make due apology to Tom the next time we go fishing together.

XVI

THE TOWN OF SUTTON; BIG AND
LITTLE FISHES

M Y ACQUAINTANCE with Sutton, the county seat of Braxton County, dates from the second day of April, 1885, when at the mature age of twenty-two, I located there to practice law. Having been reared principally at Charleston, when I was admitted to the bar in the latter part of 1884, I decided that where a fellow had gone barefoot was a poor place to hang out his shingle as a lawyer, and began to look about for a location elsewhere. Col. J. Bernard Peyton, who seemed to have a life tenure on the office of Clerk of the House of Delegates, offered me the position of first assistant at the session of 1885, which was the last session of the legislature at Wheeling, and the tender was gladly accepted. While at Wheeling I became well acquainted with Hon. B. F. Fisher, who represented Braxton County in the House at that session — the father of Judge Jake Fisher, who now holds down the woolsack in the circuit of which Braxton County is a part — and also ran across William E. Haymond and Jacob S. Hyer, two prominent residents of Sutton, whom I had known for several years, who came down to Wheeling to look in on the legislative doings. These three gentlemen, jointly and severally, had more or less to do with my decision to locate at Sutton. My father, Col. B. W. Byrne, was born and reared in Braxton County and had resided and practiced law at Sutton for a good many years just prior to the War between the States, and had many relatives and friends in Sutton and Braxton County; so it did not take a great while for me to feel very much at home in my new environment.

Sutton at that time was a small shoestring village, closely built up on either side of the Weston and Gauley

Bridge turnpike, a mud road running east and west from Old Woman's Run down Elk River on the north side, about one-third of a mile to where it turned to the left at right angles, to the bridge spanning the Elk, with a few scattering buildings farther down on the north side and over on the south side of the river; the buildings were all of wood construction excepting the new courthouse, which was of brick, and the ancient jail, which was of massive cut stone. It was 44 miles from the nearest railroad, which was a narrow gauge at Weston. A very different place indeed from the very citified and up-to-date metropolis of exactly central West Virginia, equipped as it is with all the modern conveniences and improvements, such as two railroads, two paved highways, paved streets, water works, ice plant, natural gas, electric lights, the buildings modern in every particular, and a population a dozen times greater than it was in April, 1885; greater in number, yes — greater in character and spirit, no — and this goes for the county of Braxton as well as the county seat — no finer class of citizens could then or can now be found in the state of West Virginia or elsewhere, than those I found there in the year 1885. And it is my regret that of those of that day, so very few are left. Of those married and living in Sutton in 1885, W. F. Morrison, J. Taylor Frame, Mrs. Anne Newlon Corley, and Mr. and Mrs. John H. Shuttleworth, are, I believe, the only ones living today. The resident members of the bar at that time were Maj. Pearson B. Adams, Felix J. Baxter, Edwin S. Bland, Archie W. Corley, William E. Haymond, Alex Dulin, and Ledrow M. Wade — of those, Mr. Haymond alone survives (1928).

The visiting attorneys were Jonathan M. Bennett, Judge John Brannon, William E. Lively, William G. Bennett, Louis Bennett, William W. Brannon, and William B. McGary, of Weston; Spencer Dayton of Philippi; John J. Davis and Judge Gideon Draper Camden, of Clarksburg; George Jackson Arnold, of Walkers-

ville; Coleman C. Higginbotham and A. M. Poundstone, of Buckhannon; Marshall T. Frame, of Wheeling; Robert G. Linn and Nelson M. Bennett, of Glenville; John D. Alderson, Maj. F. B. Smith, and Ed R.
Andrews, of Summersville. Not one of these is now
living.

Talk about fishing — and everybody nowadays is
talking about fishing, since the news columns have been
bulging with the piscatorial triumphs of President Coolidge in the North and President-elect Hoover in the
South — why fishing has become one of the most popular indoor sports and topics of pink tea conversation
and has got the stock market and movie stars backed
plumb off the board. Speaking of fishing, let me tell
you one: Late in April, 1885, two or three weeks after
I struck Sutton, I met up with Capt. E. D. Camden on
the street carrying a fishing pole in one hand and a bait
bucket in the other. Before I had a chance to ask any
questions he said, "Get your fishing pole and come over
to Huffman's milldam. The bass are biting like a
house afire after this warm weather." Now, I hadn't
located at Sutton for the sole and only purpose of fishing, and had not, thus early in the season, equipped myself with an angling outfit, but his invitation put the
fever in my blood and I hurried over to Baxter & Campbell's "general store," and hastily supplied myself with
a reed pole and the necessary adjuncts, and got to the
mill dam almost as soon as Camden. In a few minutes
W. F. Morrison and Will Haymond joined us and we
four fished from about 8:30 a.m. until mid-afternoon,
without intermission. Camden's bait bucket was well
filled with live minnows, but they were exhausted long
before noon and we sent a boy with the bucket and a
seine up to Buckeye for a fresh supply, and scratched
around the mill dam and river bank for worms or anything we could find for bait. At the north end of the
dam near the shore, among the leaves and muck and
brush there accumulated, some of us struck a bonanza!

We ran into a large colony of hellgrammites, just emerging from the cocoon, and supplied ourselves with a goodly stock. The bass fairly went wild over this new bait, and when the boy returned with the bucket of minnows, none of us paid them any mind whatever, so more than satisfied were we and the bass with the other bait. We had fished for six or seven hours just below the pour of the dam, covering a space more than fifty feet long, when we stopped and took stock of our catch. The four of us had caught just 225 bass, that we had kept and strung, and they ranged uniformly from ten to fourteen inches — from three-quarters of a pound to a pound and a quarter. There was not a single large bass in the whole bunch. Out of curiosity, I measured and weighed a number of these bass, and then and there first noted that on a general average a thirteen-inch bass will weigh a pound.

The explanation given by Ed Camden, who was a fisherman of long experience, of the plentiful supply of bass at this particular place, was that the warm April days had aroused them from their lethargy of the winter, and that they had started upstream, as is their nature, in search of food, and being unable to get over the dam, had congregated and remained in the deep water immediately below.

Now (1928), there are living witnesses to this episode; William E. Haymond and Wellington Fletcher Morrison, both residents of Sutton—but please allow me to suggest to anyone who may have it in mind to appeal to either of these gentlemen for a verification, that he be kind enough to permit me to see them first. Of course, they are both my seniors by several years and their recollections may not be as good as mine. But what is writ is writ, and it can't be unwrit, I don't care a darn what Fletcher Morrison or Bill Haymond might say about it.

There were some very interesting characters in and

about Sutton in those days and many keenly amusing things were said and done. One of the first and best of those coming under my observation was pulled off by the three old cronies, Maj. P. B. Adams, the Nestor of the bar at that time, Philip Troxell, the wagon maker, and Capt. Jim Salisbury, farmer, general trader, and universal litigant, who lived at Newville, some 12 or 15 miles from Sutton. Maj. Adams' office was on the ground floor of a small two-story frame building fronting Main Street on the corner now occupied by P. J. Berry's mercantile establishment, the upstairs of which was used as the Major's sleeping apartments, access thereto, being had by means of a creaky wooden outside stairway extending from the street and on the west side of the building. Whenever Captain Salisbury came to town, which was always during court time, he made Major Adams' office his headquarters and Philip Troxell would drop in frequently for one thing or another. The Major usually kept on hand a little "drinkin' liquor," as it was termed, and often the trio would repair to the upstairs apartment, where it was kept, for a social chat—and other things. One summer afternoon the three had so foregathered, and had remained in session until the visible supply of the ardent was just about exhausted, when a most vehement discussion arose, audible to any passerby on the street, and in which the Major and Philip had double-teamed against the Captain. The warlike Captain becoming very much irritated, declared that the Major had insulted him in his own house, and casting a glance at the almost empty bottle, announced that he would leave the house never to return —never—never, nev-v-er; and suiting the action to the word, arose and strode majestically out of the room, and clumpety-clump-clump down the rickety stairway. Thereupon Major Adams produced a fresh quart, somewhere concealed, and stepped to the open window at the front of the room where he could see Captain Salisbury as he passed below. Holding the bottle out of sight he said, "Say, Captain, come on back—no use to be a damphool; come on back." "No sir, I'll not come back—I'll never enter your door again. You have grossly insulted me in your own house and I'll never speak to you again, much less enter your house, and that settles it," emphatically spoke the Captain, as he stalked away.

"Ah, what's the use of being a baby," said the Major, "come on back—look here"—and he held up the virgin quart to the full view of the indignant Captain. The Captain turned to look — he saw — he hesitated — he turned completely around — he said: "Well, I'll come back—but I want you to understand it ain't on account of your damned drinking liquor."

One of the first cases I saw and tried in the circuit court of Braxton County, made a lasting impression upon me—not the case itself, for I do not remember either the names of the litigants or what it was all about—but it was a witness in that case. The witness was Uncle Charlie Riffle, who lived over on the waters of the Little Kanawha above Burnsville. He was a fine old chap, about 75 years of age, a man of substance and highly esteemed by every one; but the most excitable and demonstrative old fellow I ever saw. He was a great tobacco chewer—or gummer, rather, as he did not have a tooth in his head. He would wad up a quid of hillside navy about the size of a shell-bark hickory nut, insert it in his mouth and gum it industriously. If you entered into a conversation with him he would listen attentively, and speed up the jaw action while you were talking, but as soon as it was his turn to speak, plop would go the quid out of his mouth into his left hand, and he would speak in rapid fire fashion, gesticulating violently with his right hand, his left, half-closed, palm upward, perfectly motionless, holding the quid as though to prevent spilling—and when he had spoken, plop, would go the quid from his left hand back into his mouth, and the industrious jaw action would be resumed. How often this would be repeated during the conversation, would depend on how many times the other fellow spoke and how many times Uncle Charlie spoke.

Well, in the case in question the attorney who examined Uncle Charlie in chief, knowing his peculiarity, asked him to tell all he knew about the transaction, and Uncle Charlie had to make only one or two transfers of the quid. But the attorney on the opposing side likewise knew Uncle Charlie's peculiarities, and proceeded on cross-examination to fire at him short questions, calling for short answers, and you can imagine the result.

Q. When did that occur? A. (plop) Last June (plop).

Q. What time in June? A. (plop) About the middle (plop).

Q. Where did it occur? A. (plop) At Burnsville (plop).

Q. Where in Burnsville? A. (plop) At Dr. Kidd's office (plop). And so on for fifteen or twenty minutes, and never did he miss fire a single time with left hand, right hand or quid. I wondered what might have happened to Uncle Charlie as a witness if he had chanced to lose that chaw of terbacker.

Ed Camden and I had another fishing bout at Huffman's milldam, which was attended by even more excitement than the bass story above related. This time it was yew pine suckers. In the winter of 1886 there had been a great ice floe from the headwaters of the Elk, which caused quite an ice gorge behind the Huffman milldam. In the early spring this ice had all passed out, and the river had gotten very low and clear. Ed Camden lived on the south side of Elk in the large bottom just below Buckeye, and in coming to town when the water was low, he frequently walked across the milldam rather than go down to the bridge. One morning he came into my office very excitedly and said that the pool above the milldam was full of yew pine suckers, carried down by the ice from the head of the river; that he had just walked across the milldam and had seen in the pool above, which was then frozen over with a thin coat of ice, hundreds of the suckers. We each got a gig and walked across the dam to where Ed kept his trusty canoe, and proceeded to go after the yew pine suckers. It became necessary, of course, to break the ice, which was less than half an inch thick, in order to navigate the canoe, but this was soon done, and the broken ice shoved to one side. The water in the mill pool was quite shallow owing to the sand and leaves and silt that had accumulated just above the dam, and for a time we had great sport gigging the suckers, and could have almost filled the canoe with fish, but for the fact that the water soon became so "riled" from the disturbance caused by our canoe and the scurrying fish, that we could no longer see them, and decided to quit for the day. But, in returning to the bank to land our canoe, Ed caught sight of the fins of a large sucker in the muddy water and made a sudden lunge at it with his gig—so sudden and so violent that the canoe was overturned and we were given a chilly and muddy bath, and our fish dumped out into the river. These we recovered for the most part, but we were almost frozen before we got the fish gathered up, the canoe righted and landed. But the strange thing about the whole performance was, that the next day we went back for more, and found the river cleared up again, and not a yew pine sucker of any kind, size or sort. Hundreds of them must have been frightened the day before to such an extent that they never stopped running until they got back to the head of the river where they came from.

XVII

CAMDEN AND COGAR LOOK AT FISH AND LIFE; McCOURT LOOKS AT A COURT

THE two agencies most pernicious and ruinous to fish life, are stream pollution and the use of explosives; nets and traps run a poor second, and shooting, gigging, and fishing out of season, for anything except trout—are simply outclassed. Two years before I went to Sutton, I saw three fellows who were working on railroad construction, dynamite the mouth of Big Run where it empties into the Ohio about two miles below Williamstown, in Wood County, West Virginia. The river was up considerably and the run was at normal stage, causing backwater for quite a distance, and it being in the spring season, fish in great numbers had congregated just out of the current a short distance up the run. Several sticks of dynamite were exploded, and the result was so appalling that the impression has never left my mind. Probably a dozen suckers large enough for use were recovered, but the surface of the water was white with small fish from an inch to five or six inches long—scores, if not hundreds of them. The sight almost made me sick, and then and there I registered a solemn vow never to be a party to such an unchristian and unsportsman-like method of getting fish. It was this resolution that kept me from getting a great scare and a good ducking the first summer after I located at Sutton—1885. The story runneth thus: Johnson N. Camden, who lived at Parkersburg, was on one of his annual visits to his brother, Edwin D., and a fishing bout was arranged for his benefit, the party consisting of the guest of honor, Will Haymond, Luther J. Berry, Ed Camden, and myself. We all got in Ed Camden's canoe, which was about fifty feet long, and struck out for Beall's Mill, four and one-half miles below Sutton, took the canoe over the dam and did our fishing for the most part in the pool below. I observed in the stern of the canoe a gallon stone jug, and supposing that, of course, it was the ordinary fish bait, asked no questions. Finally, after we had been fishing two or three hours, Ed Camden and Luther Berry took me into the secret that they were going to put, up a job on Will Haymond, who was the Prosecuting Attorney of the county, by making him *particeps criminis* to "blasting" the river with the blasting powder wherewith the jug was filled. I said, "Boys, you'll have to excuse me, as I have conscientious scruples" —and stepped out on the bank, to which the bow was made fast. Ed and Luther fixed the fuse and drove the cork tightly into the neck of the jug and were soon ready for the fireworks, Haymond and Senator Camden meanwhile up about the middle of the canoe, busy with their fishing and oblivious to what was going on forward in the rear. Ed Camden, with a pole, swung the stern of the canoe out in the river, and when directly over the deepest part of the pool, lit the fuse, cast overboard the jug, properly weighted with a good-sized rock, and proceeded to push the stern farther on upstream, a safe distance from the explosion about to take place; he got it up into the swift water just below the dam, where he stopped and held it for a moment with his push pole. By some mischance he moved the pole in such a way that it came in contact with a boulder in the swift water, and the pole was wrenched out of his grasp and floated off down the stream; thus released, the stern of the canoe swung back downstream, retracing the arc of the circle described, and when directly over the bomb just planted, the explosion came. The canoe was half overturned, one gunwale badly split, all the occupants spilled overboard and—not a fish. Whether we had caught all the fish, big and little, or whether blasting powder is not quick enough to do the work of dynamite, I do not know, but the joke on the particular occasion was on the fishermen and not the fish.

Senator Camden was raised at Sutton, and in their boyhood, he and Tom Cogar were companions inseparable. During the warm weather they spent all their time in and on the river, fishing, swimming and ratting around. In his early manhood Johns drifted out into the world, finally located at Parkersburg, where he soon took front rank among the successful business men of the state, and was probably the first millionaire within her borders; oil magnate, railroad builder, owner and operator on a large scale of coal mines; represented his state in the Senate of the United States, and was withal one of the most prominent men of his day. Tom stuck to the old home town and the river. As a man, he lived the same primitive life he and Johns had lived as boys. He fished the year round and could go out and "ketch a mess" any time the notion struck him. Senator Camden never came to Sutton that he did not hunt up his old chum Tom Cogar, and it was quite interesting to hear them recount their youthful exploits. I was out on the old suspension bridge one day with Senator Camden, when Tom Cogar came along, carrying a sack of meal, and the two chatted quite a while over old times. Finally Tom said, "Well, Johns, you left me and went off and got an education, and got rich and made a big business man out of yourself, and I've stayed here and fished and wallered around in the river just like we done when we was boys together; but with all that, I'll bet I've had just as much fun as you have."

"Yes, Tom," said the Senator, with that characteristic quizzical smile, "and a helluva sight more!"

Harvey Bryant was jailer and court bailiff for several years. Harvey usually abstained from overindulgence in the cup that both cheers and inebriates, during all the year, excepting the first day of each term of the Circuit Court, when he seemed to deem it to comport with the dignity of the latter office, that he tank up to a becoming degree of solemnity. On this first day, his manner of calling absent witnesses, jurors, litigants and attorneys was most impressive; after the first day the glamour seemed to wear off, and he didn't care who performed that service; but for that first day, the job was his and his alone. The courtroom was on the second floor of the courthouse and at the front of the hall leading into the courtroom, was a large window commanding a view of the front yard and of the adjacent main street. Harvey would march to this window, and in measured, solemn and stentorian tones call the name of the absentee. Cummins C. McCourt was an absent witness on the first day of one particular term, and Harvey was told to call him, which he proceeded to do. Going to the open window and leaning out so the sound would carry pretty well over the town, he cried in great voice, "Cummins C. McCourt! Cummins C. McCourt!! Cummins McCourt!!!" Some fellow down on the street who was feeling his oats somewhat, after listening attentively to the proclamation, looked up at Harvey, and called out: "Shay, Mister (hic), where in the hell is your court?"

"Damn such a name!" said Harvey, fervently, as he turned and strode indignantly back to the courtroom.

A most interesting trial took place in the Circuit Court of Braxton County a year or two after I went to Sutton. It was the case of State vs. Moss Conrad, for assault with a deadly weapon, to-wit, one rock, stone and dornick.

It seems that there had been a house-raisin' and log-rollin' over on Riffle's Run of the Little Kanawha, and all the countryside was gathered there for the occasion. Very little raisin' or rollin' had been done until trouble started among some of the belligerent ones, and the whole thing broke up in a free-for-all, knockdown and drag-out. When the smoke of battle cleared away it was found that there were no fatalities, but numerous black eyes and bloody noses, and one fellow had a skinned head and a slightly cracked cranium as though from a boulder massage. While it seemed to be a matter of great uncertainty as to when, where, how and at whose hands the wound had been inflicted, owing to the general mix-up of the melee, it finally eventuated that it became the general opinion that Moss Conrad — as the name is writ — Coonrod, "as she is spoke" — was the guilty agent. And I'll tell you why: In the first place, Moss was there on the ground and mixed up in the scrap. In the next place Moss, from the time he was big enough to cuss, through the years of his boyhood and early manhood — he was then 23 or 24 years of age — had been guilty of most of the deviltry that had taken place in the neighborhood. . . . Given cards and spades to both Tom Sawyer and Huckleberry Finn, in any game of devilment known to the calendar, and beaten them out with one hand tied behind him. If a fence "was throwed down and hogs let in the corn," a melon patch or chicken coop raided, a "winder glass broke," a "hoss rode all night," a cow surreptitiously milked, or a hen's nest robbed, "Moss Coonrod done it an' 'taint no use for him to deny it." As the years went on Moss grew in grace and stature along the same line of moral obliquity, so that at the time the story opens he had a reputation not limited to the confines of his own neighborhood, but countrywide and more so, as a seeker and finder of trouble, a disturbing element in the community and a bad egg in general. He had been indicted, convicted and served a jail sentence a number of times for such high crimes and misdemeanors as assault and battery, disturbing religious worship, "whupping the teacher," drunk and disorderly and the like. So when the next grand jury of Braxton County sat in solemn conclave, Moss was promptly indicted for busting the fellow's head open. I do not know just what evidence the grand jury had before it on which to indict Moss, but it wouldn't have taken much, as it would have been difficult indeed to have dug up a panel of sixteen freeholders of Braxton County, of which at least twelve were not hep to Moss's daily walk and conversation, and probably

cause would have been shown to them, simply by showing that somebody got hit with a rock and that Moss
Conrad was anywhere close around.

At the next ensuing term the case came on for trial.
Will Haymond was the prosecuting attorney, and John
D. Alderson, of Summersville, appeared for Moss.
Haymond put a great flock of witnesses on the stand,
about sixteen in number, all eyewitnesses to the row,
each one of whom told all he knew about the fracas, and
some of whom related facts and circumstances to some
degree tending to fix guilt upon Moss; but under the
grilling cross-examination of John Alderson, each of
these was forced to admit that he did not know who
struck the blow; did not see Moss Coonrod strike the
assaultee with a rock or with his fist or anything else;
did not see him with a rock or any weapon; did not see
Moss and the assaultee close together during fracas —
and, boiled down and sifted, it was apparent that each
one of these witnesses simply went upon the theory of
general likelihood.

At this stage of the case there was quite a buzz among
the spectators in the courtroom and some wonderment
expressed that for the first time in his life, Moss would
"come clear." Will Haymond looked worried and
seemed about to "throw up the sponge." John Alderson
looked triumphant and saw victory in his grasp. Then
Haymond, after some hesitation, called Uncle Smithy
Wine to the witness stand. Uncle Smithy had occupied
a ringside seat, first row back of the bar rail, during the
entire progress of the trial. He had paid close attention
to every question and every answer both on direct and on
cross-examination, and with alacrity he responded to the
summons.

Uncle Smithy was a man of about 75 years of age,
short of stature and slender of build, weighed not more
than 80 pounds dressed, smooth face, bald-headed, except for a little fringe of hair back between the two ears,
hatchet faced, prominent nose, keen piercing gray eyes

and florid complexion. He was what might have been termed the leading citizen of Riffle's Run; and was in fact the oracle of that entire community. He had been a squire once upon a time, and in that official capacity had for years settled the controversies of his neighbors for so many years, and dished out even-handed justice to them for so long, that he had so formed the habit that after he ceased to occupy the woolsack, he nevertheless continued to function as arbiter of their differences and adviser in general of his neighborhood. He had acquired the habit or possessed the natural trait of being very direct and unequivocal, positive and emphatic in all his statements, whether of opinion, conviction or fact, and would brook no question or denial of any or either.

He mounted the witness stand, seated himself very deliberately, folded his arms, cocked his head jauntily to one side, glancing first at Haymond and then at Alderson — looking for all the world like a cock-sparrow perched on a limb, looking around for something to pounce upon.

The prosecuting attorney had to ask Uncle Smithy very few questions. The witness knew what it was all about; knew the dismal failure made by the witnesses who had preceded him; knew his own story and knew how to tell it. In a few short minutes he had nailed Moss's hide to the barn door, neat and proper. He had seen the row begin; seen Moss Coonrod, always in the thick of the fight; had seen Moss step aside from the edge of the crowd and pick up a rock — "about the size of a apple—not quite as big as a big apple but a right smart bigger than a little apple"; had seen Moss draw back his arm and then throw the rock with great force; had seen this selfsame rock, so thrown from the hand of Moss Coonrod, hurtle thro' the air, some fourteen feet — maybe a leetle furder and maybe not quite so fur; seen this selfsame rock strike, hit and come in contact with the head of the assaultee — the left side, near the top; seen the blood fly and the man fall, and the rock fall to the ground, and had seen the same man so knocked down by said rock, after the trouble was over, and had seen the blood on the left side of his head and had seen that his head looked like it had been caved in on that side.

"You may take the witness, Mr. Alderson," said Mr. Haymond.

"Mr. Wine," said Mr. Alderson, "will you please tell this jury how it happens that you not only saw and heard all that was seen and heard by all the sixteen who have preceded you in this case but you also saw and heard more than those sixteen all put together, and also things that no other witness saw or heard?"

"Why, yes, Mr. Alderson, I will tell you exactly how it were: I were a leetle late in arriving on the ground and when I got there the crowd had mostly gethered and as I a-proached the aidge of the congregation, I seed frum their manuvering round, that they wuz reclined to git into a general furse among theirselves; and seeing a log heap a leetle ways off — about 12 foot, or maybe 15 — and on a leetle higher ground — ground that laid sorter slaunchways, or some might call it crofting — and I jist climbed up on that thar log heap, whar I could git a exposeraneous view of the whole unseen scenery."

My recollection is that the jury hung.

XVIII

TWO HUNDRED AND THIRTY-FIVE BASS TIE WITH FOOTLOG FOR SUTTON HONORS

I HAVE NOT seen my old friend, Wellington Fletcher Morrison since the March issue of *Wild Life,* wherein I made reference to the catch of 235 bass by four of us of which he was one, but have been informed that Fletcher claims that his memory seems to have failed to record the incident. Of course, I am perfectly willing that Fletcher may have his own way about this thing — being like the young chap once upon a time, who was standing on the street corner jotting down something in a note book; another fellow came along and asked what he was writing in the book:

"Oh, I was just writing down the names of all the fellows I can whup."

"Have you got my name wrote down there?"

"Let me see — Yes — Oh, yes — yours is down here, all right."

"Well, I jist want to tell you — you can't whup me — you couldn't whup one side of me."

"You say I can't whup you?"

"That's exactly what I said, and exactly what I mean."

"All right then — I'll just scratch your name off."

So if Fletcher doesn't care to have his name "wrote" down in connection with that historical episode, we'll just scratch his name off. That will leave all the more fish for Ed Camden, Will Haymond and myself. And since thinking the matter over again carefully — forty-four years is a long time for absolute accuracy in details — I believe Fletcher is right; and that it was Ed and Will and I who caught the fish, and that we got Fletcher to string them; a fellow who simply strung fish would not be so apt to remember as if he had caught them.

Gigging was the great sport among the fishermen in and about Sutton in those days, and many there were who were such experts that in two or three hours' drive one would kill enough red-horse, suckers, carp and an occasional pike, to feed an average family several days. Dr. W. P. Newlon, Luther Pierson, John Humphreys, John Byrne, Houston Humphreys, Ed Camden, and Charlie Newlon were among the finest of the lot. I speak of them particularly because I was out with each of them a good many times. Dr. Newlon was one of the most erratic giggers I ever saw, but withal landed more fish than most anybody. He was quick as double triggers and frequently missed the fish twice and then harpooned him on the third trial.

The best shot I ever saw with a gig — barring a number by myself, which modesty forbids me to relate — was made by John Shuttleworth, the present (1929) Mayor of Sutton. He and I were out in a canoe — I mean a real old-fashioned Elk River canoe — a dugout if you will — fifty or sixty feet long. We were coming up on the south side of Elk Island just below the mouth of Grannys Creek. The river was rather low and we had to keep close to the south bank. Off over toward the island at least forty feet away, John saw a small jack pike, about fifteen inches long, and said to me:

"Watch me hit that little pike in the eye."

"Which eye?"—meaning general disparagement on account of the great distance.

"Right eye," said John.

"Some chance," said I, as the fish was headed down stream with his left side to us.

At that instant the gig left John's hand and the fish suddenly turned about face, just in time to receive one prong of the gig in his right eye. When I complimented John on the rare accuracy of his aim, the scoundrel replied, "Shucks! I can beat that fifty per cent when I'm in practice."

Now I rise to remark right here, that if John Shuttleworth repudiates this story, I propose to eschew the pearl and swine business forevermore. I could just as well ring in on these tales actors who have long since passed from the stage, and thus be wholly without fear of challenge or denial; and when I go to all the trouble of hunting up a few living fellows to bring them into the picture, it is pretty doggoned hard to have their memories shorten up or their consciences tighten up so as to make me out a liar.

I never knew Uncle Archie Armstrong, who in his day was far-famed as a wielder of the gig, and especially for his prowess as a killer of the great blue pike, once so numerous in the Elk. He had been dead for several years when I went to Sutton, but the history of his exploits was still fresh in the minds of many who had known him. Uncle Archie kept a store in Sutton, and lived about a half mile below the town on the lower side of Grannys Creek. Uncle Archie was exceedingly fond of a little "drinking liquor," occasionally, and the drummers who traveled in that section had found that the one sure way to ingratiate themselves into his favor and make and keep him their friend and customer, was to have a "quart" for him on every trip. Under the melting and mellowing influences of such a present, Uncle Archie would lay himself out to contribute to the pleasure of the donor during his sojourn in town, whether it be to buy all his goods, entertain him with a game of poker, or take him "a pikin'," which last named diversion was to rig up his canoe with a wire basket for holding the pine torch and spend a good part of the night on a pike gigging expedition.

On this particular night, so the story goes, Uncle Archie invited a particular friend of his, a member of the commercial tourist fraternity, to go with him after the gay and festive pike. The water was low and clear, he had a splendid light and a good steersman; but luck seemed against them. There was no scarcity of smaller fish, but Uncle Archie was taking no chances in scaring away a pike by gigging the small fry. An hour or more had elapsed and not a single pike had been located, when suddenly, in traversing some very deep water, Uncle Archie spied what in the light, which was becoming a little dim, appeared to be an enormous pike behind a log on the bottom of the river; quick and unerring was the stroke, the barbs of the gig held true and after a few seconds, Uncle Archie brought to the surface a beautiful fifteen pound blue cat. On seeing what it was, Uncle Archie, with a grunt of disapproval and disgust, and with a mighty swing of his gig, cast the catfish out into the river and outer darkness. In astonishment the drummer cried out, "Why, Uncle Archie, what do you mean by throwing away a fine big fish like that?"

"Huh," said Uncle Archie, "I Gawd, when I go a pikin' I go a pikin'."

One dark and blustery night when Uncle Archie and a few of his cronies had foregathered in the back room of his store to partake of some of the liquor which his drummer friends had presented to him, and incidentally to indulge in a little game of "draw" to while away the time between drinks, the party broke up about midnight, and Uncle Archie, with an unviolated "pint" in his pocket, started on his homeward way. The only way by which foot passengers could cross Grannys Creek, which lay between him and his home, was by means of a large footlog, which spanned the creek at an elevation of about ten feet above the water. As Uncle Archie reached the upper end of the footlog he began to realize that in his then condition, the matter of his being able to negotiate the footlog was attended with some uncertainty, and that it would be necessary for him to summon to his aid all the composing and steadifying influences it was possible for him to muster.

"Archie (hic)," said he to himself, "now you listen (hic) to what I shay; if you git (hic) across the footlog (hic) 'thout fallin' in, I'll (hic) give you a drink out this bottle."

Thus reinforced, he started on the perilous journey and had succeeded in getting about halfway across, when his legs begun to wobble, he lost his balance, and came down kersplash! in the middle of the creek in water about two feet deep. When he finally picked himself up, got on his feet and had gouged the mud and water out of his eyes, his first thought was of the bottle and how it had fared in the mix-up. Finding it all there, he carefully removed the cork, and holding the bottle aloft soliloquized as follows:

"Well, Archie (hic), you done the best you (hic) could and durned if I don't give you a little drink, anyway."

John Green, who did the village cobbling, coined a word for me which I believe is entitled to a seat in the dictionary. Not only was John "a surgeon to old shoes," but was mail carrier on one of the routes radiating from Sutton. On several occasions he had taken my shoes for mending under solemn promise to return them at a certain time and left me in a state of hope deferred for periods ranging a day to a week; always putting up the excuse that his mail job required him to get up at four o'clock in the morning three days of the week, and left him little time to shoemake. On the occasion referred to, I gave John the shoes with the strict injunction that I must have them on the following Saturday, or that dire consequences would result; and John swore by every hammer, awl, last and shoe peg in the shop that the shoes would be forthcoming on the appointed day.

I had not been married at that time and had my sleeping quarters in a room adjoining my law shop, and on that fatal Saturday morning at about 4:30 by the clock, I was awakened by a mighty crash at the door as though someone were assaulting it with a battering ram. Supposing as a matter of course that it was either an earthquake or a fire, I sprang out of bed and rushed to the door. There I found John Green with my doctored shoes.

"Bill, here's your shoes. I promised 'em Saturday, and here they are—I'se always mighty 'sponchus' that way."

In trying to go back to sleep, I pondered over this new word, and decided that it was a fair composite of punctual, reliable, responsible and conscientious, and bore a subtle shade of meaning not expressed by either or all; but to myself expressed fervent regret that John Green had seen fit to be so darned "sponchus" at that hour of the morning.

XIX

THE STORY OF TERROR PINNACLE; DR. "NEDMAC" BECOMES A SCIENTIST

I WAS talking the other day with Dr. Roy Bird Cook, Charleston druggist, prominent among the literati of the state, concerning the Camden family, he having married a daughter of the late John S. Camden, of Parkersburg, a brother of Edwin D. Camden and Johnson N. Camden, mentioned in these tales, and another brother, Dr. Thomas Bland Camden, having married Susan Holt, a sister of my mother. In discussing the versatility of Dr. Camden, as a physician, scientist and writer on numerous and varied subjects, themes and topics, I told Dr. Cook that I remembered very distinctly an article appearing in the newspapers of the state, while Dr. Camden was Superintendent of the Hospital for the Insane at Weston, the title of which was "Terror Pinnacle," which made a great impression on me, a twelve-year-old boy at that time.

"I have that 'Terror Pinnacle' story among my papers," Dr. Cook said.

As the Tale of the Elk would not be complete without it, I am, with the consent of Dr. Cook, here and now appropriating the same bodily:

ARTICLE APPEARING IN WESTON DEMOCRAT, DECEMBER 5, 1874

On the 1st day of December we received the following letter:

10 Vesey Street, New York
November 26, 1874

J W. Woffindine, Esq.,
Editor Weston Democrat,
Weston, W. Va.

Dear Sir: — About the 14th of this month a Mr. B. T. Nedmac, of this city, left here for the purpose of exploring "Terror Pinnacle," a high elevation in Webster county, West Virginia, for minerals. Mr. N. is rather eccentric in his habits. We learn that he was accompanied by

Phineas Barton, of Philadelphia. Since their departure nothing has been heard of either of them.

Any information will be gratefully received.

Yours, &c.,

J. F. THOMPSON

Upon receipt of this letter we immediately made inquiry in town and ascertained that no such persons had put up at any of our hotels during the month of November. We wrote back to Mr. Thompson the result of our investigations, and suggested that his friends might have joined one of the hunting parties now in the mountains. Our further investigations, however, were put at an end by the appearance of the following letter in the Wheeling Register of December 3, 1874, which we here reproduce.—Editor Democrat.

Addison, Webster Co., W. Va.
November 15, 1874

Editors Register:

As an unfortunate citizen of the city of New York, I wish to detail to your readers the circumstances of the death of Mr. Phineas Barton, of Philadelphia, which, in some respects, are so unnatural and mysterious, and my position so peculiar, that I wish to lay the facts before the public, and to ask the suspension of public opinion, and to invite science, and scientific persons to come to my rescue, and to examine, for the benefit of science, as well as myself, the mysterious cause of Mr. Barton's death.

I am a resident of Vesey Street, New York, and have been connected in searching for iron and other minerals for some years, and have not only become very fond of it, but financially have been fortunate. Often I have taken long journeys to satisfy myself about peculiar ores, as in this instance. A gentleman well known in New York and in West Virginia, and who has been interested in a contemplated railroad through West Virginia (I believe a Colonel Byrne and Judge Camden are directors) brought with him to New York a peculiar ore found, he said, in Webster county, West Virginia, on a high mountain, and on its very "pinnacle," known on the map of West Virginia as Terror Pinnacle, named, as we afterward learned, from various wonderful and mysterious noises, and unexplained lights, that were often heard and seen on its summit. No one in its locality ever thinks of ascending it. During the late war the Federal soldiers thought these tales were to intimidate them, and that rebels were hid on its top, and attempted to ascend to surprise them one night, when they were driven back awe struck and demoralized — and it is a well known fact, and history will record it, that the "State of Webster" is the only part of the United States that was never conquered. "Terror Pinnacle" is a black barren knoll, and can be seen for miles — and like its antipode, Mount Ararat, it has rarely been ascended by any. After examining the ore I was so struck with its singularity, that I determined to visit the Pinnacle and see for myself. Mr. Barton has often accompanied me on such explorations, and after writing him the facts, he insisted on going with me. On the 6th of November, 1874, we left Philadelphia, and landed in Clarksburg on the 8th, hired horses of McBall, went by way of Weston, and took the near route, as advised by Hon. J. M. Bennett, to Addison, the county seat of Webster county.

From this point we were directed to (as we learned for the first time) the noted place—Terror Pinnacle. Various and wonderful tales were told us, and we were advised not to ascend it.

Superstition has woven many strange and mysterious legends about it. One, that near the 13th of each November great noises and lights could be heard and seen on its summit and some averred that sulphurous odors were perceptible, and that on the memorable night of the 13th of November, 1833, when the never to be forgotten showers of meteors were seen, this mountain blazed like an immense bonfire. So great was the awe created by this mysterious phenomenon that few ever attempt to ascend its height, even in daytime, and never at night, situated, as it is, nearly 15 miles from any habitation. We arrived at Addison on the morning of the 12th, and determined to push forward and spend the night of the 13th on its summit. Although repeatedly warned by the oldest hunters, we thought it but an idle tale. We set out and after a rugged walk, for it is too rough to ride, we discovered the pinnacle about 3 o'clock, living in a solitary grandeur high above all other elevations; and here let me say that Webster county has the highest elevation of any portion of West Virginia, and that Terror Pinnacle is the highest mountain or pinnacle in the county. We arrived at the base of the pinnacle about 4 o'clock, and commenced to ascend. Soon we discovered formations so strange and new to us that we became much interested as we ascended, and examined many pieces of strange looking ore that had evidently rolled down its side, such as I dare say no geologist had ever seen before. Every conceivable size, shape and color, were represented, many round, flattened, grey, red, ash and copper colors, all were found. What struck us most, was that many had a hole through or to one side of the centre, as if they had been hurled into the air whilst in a moulten state, and by centrifugal force had formed the opening. We slowly ascended, and as we got higher, they increased in number. Now and then, we could see huge rocks buried into the side of the mountains, and that nearly all had this peculiar central hole. They seemed to be a mixture of various ores; iron, copper, zinc, antimony and other minerals were recognized. As we neared the top we began to realize the height of the mountain. We found ourselves high above all mountains of note in West Virginia. The Blue Ridge was plainly seen in the dim distance; Droop Mountain was near to us; the Saltpond Mountain, in Monroe county, was also visible, and Mr. Barton thought he could discern Point Lookout Mountain near Chattanooga, in Tennessee. It was a grand sight, and we had forgotten our minerals in contemplation of the beautiful scenery, when suddenly we heard a rushing sound, like the passing of a shell through the air. It lasted but a moment, and all was silent. Soon a similar sound was heard. It was now 5 o'clock, November 13. We had reached the top, and the exercise had sharpened our appetites, and we ate lunch and prepared to spend the night. After our repast I witnessed the most gorgeous sunset I ever beheld — the sky was perfectly clear, the atmosphere transparent, and we could notice its lightness in our feelings and breathing. Our vision was perfect at great distances. The sun seemed larger and more beautiful than ever, and as he neared the far off horizon he almost dropped down and disappeared, and darkness followed quickly.

Later when we were preparing to lie down for the night, we were startled by a brilliant meteoric display; hundreds of "falling stars" were athwart the heavens, and to our horror we soon began to see them strike the earth around us; once or twice we felt a hot stinging sensation, evidently caused by an unburnt but igneous meteor coming in close proximity to our bodies. This alarmed us somewhat, but we were still enchanted at the magnificent and wonderful meteoric display, hardly realizing our danger, when we were made sadly aware of it, by a meteor as large as a man's head falling within a hundred yards of us and exploding like a shell. Soon another fell near — then for the first time it occurred to me that we were in the midst of a meteoric shower, and they were so large that unless we could protect ourselves or get out of their reach our lives would be sacrificed. I communicated my thoughts to Mr. Barton, when he exclaimed: "We are in the meteoric belt that strikes the earth at this time every year, and this height cuts into it"; and I said, "Let us at once leave this terrible mountain." We instantly started, and as we did so we noticed an evident increase in the number and size of the meteors. They seemed all around us, cracking and bursting like so many firecrackers or shells. We gained the brow of the pinnacle and had started down its side, when I saw Mr. Barton fall heavily. I heard a sound as if a shell had burst at our very side. I heard him exclaim, "Oh, my head," and he pitched forward down the mountain. I at once knew that he had been struck, and hurriedly raised him on my back and carried him as fast as I could far down the mountain, until I could see that I was getting below the line of the meteoric storm. Behind and above me I could hear and see the unearthly fireworks. I hastened on until I knew I must be near the base of the pinnacle, when my foot touched a stream of water. I laid Mr. Barton down, and hastily washed his face and forced some brandy into his mouth, when he evinced some signs of returning consciousness, gasped for breath — and was no more. I struck a match and built a fire, and watched over his remains until daylight, when I protected his body as best I could, with logs and brush, after taking all his valuables, watch, &c., and set out for Addison as fast as I could, after the terrible fright, and reached there on the evening of the 14th, and reported as best I could the fearful night on the mountain, and the terrible death of Mr. Barton. I fear my mind wandered and I must have given contradictory statements, for soon I noticed that the crowd became incredulous and after finding Mr. Barton's valuables on my person, placed me under arrest, being convinced of foul play. They asked me to lead them to his body. I at once signified my willingness, and started to do so, but unfortunately I was so excited that I missed my way and after leading them all day, we had to return unsuccessful. Next morning I was informed that a hunter had found the body of a strange man on the opposite side of the mountain from which I, in my excited state, thought it to be. They brought the body in, and upon examination, strange to say, he presented much the appearance of one who had been killed by a pistol shot fired near him, the blackened face, singed hair, and a hole in his temple caused by his falling on a sharp rock, all together, was almost conclusive evidence against me, and makes my case a very hazardous one, unless science and scientific men espouse my cause, and prove beyond a doubt the truth of my statement.

My defense and explanation, which I hope to substantiate and prove beyond doubt, is based upon the well established fact, admitted by all astronomers, that our earth passes through a belt or orbit of meteors once a year, near the 13th of November, and every thirty-three years, owing to the ellipses of the meteoric orbit, our planet comes in contact with a larger portion, hence all astronomers predict with certainty the coming of a meteoric shower at that time. These meteors are doubtless solid substances whirling around in their orbits, traveling with immense velocity, and when they come in contact with our atmosphere the friction is so great that they become incandescent, and most of them are burned up before they reach the surface of the earth, hence we rarely see meteoric rocks falling, but immense ones do fall. There is one in the Smithsonian Institute weighing several hundred pounds, with a characteristic hole through it. Where these meteors have their origin and how set in motion and held in their orbit, is mere speculation. I am led to believe that they are either the fragments of destroyed worlds or they are cast off from the moon by its immense volcanoes, with such force that they pass beyond its attractive power and then become wanderers through space, and by the great law that governs all the heavenly bodies, they fall into an orbit of their own, and are held there by the attraction and repulsion of other bodies. Some say they are the natural fuel for the sun's great furnace.

Terror Pinnacle is doubtless situated on the tract of the meteoric orbit, and being so elevated impinges every year upon it, and receives a quantity of meteors, and owing to the ellipsoid form of the meteoric belt, our earth strikes or cuts into it more deeply every thirty-three years, and hence we have falling stars before spoken of. The vast quantity of meteoric rock and star dust deposited on the Pinnacle and the lack of vegetation show that this theory is correct. No doubt this mountain increases yearly a certain per cent, and every thirty-three years much more, until it is a vast meteoric mountain, and perhaps stands without a parallel with one exception. Mount Ararat is nearly the antipode of Terror Pinnacle, and is on the same degree of latitude, and the only mountain of the same height, and it is singular to say that Ararat has almost the same superstitious legend about it that Terror Pinnacle has. But one or two travelers have ever been known to ascend to its top. Some writers say that "no man within our knowledge has ever reached its summit." Noah, no doubt, ascended, but since his day the climate has certainly undergone a great change; at this day its summit is perpetual snow. The natives around it say that many travelers have tried to ascend, but never returned. Who knows but this mount is not subject to the same disturbances and from the same cause? Who can say but the superstitious awe with which it is held is not based upon the same terrible experience of some hapless mortal like myself.

I am forwarding the facts as set forth in this letter, to many scientific men in the United States, among whom are Prof. Henry, of the Smithsonian Institute, to the National Observatory at Washington, and I am led to believe that, according to my suggestion, they will cause to be created a kind of "bomb proof" building against the 13th of next November, in order to guard against accidents, and to notice the grand display of nature's fire-works.

I will say that the minerals of the "Pinnacle" are well known in this section. I learn that Judge Holt, of Lewisburg; Hon. J. N. Camden, of Parkersburg; Hon. W. E. Arnold, of Weston, have all taken active interest in trying to develop them.

Although confined, as I am, in a close cell, I am happy to say that many have taken an interest in me, among whom is Major Triplett, late representative, and others. The clerk, George M. Sawyers, is especially kind to me. I learn that I will probably be tried by Hon. Henry Brannon, a gentleman of learning and research. The prosecuting attorney, Mr. Joseph A. Alderson, has the reputation of being a high-toned gentleman, and I am led to believe that my sad case will be thoroughly investigated.

Respectfuly yours,

B. T. NEDMAC

The effect of this publication was electric, and spread far beyond the confines of the state. The appeal was not only *ad hominum,* but as well to the scientist and the legal fraternity. Hundreds of dollars contributed in sums of five, ten, and twenty dollars from all over the country, were forwarded to Clerk George M. (Governor) Sawyers and to Maj. Marshall Triplett, to aid in the defense of the accused, and the then Attorney General of Maryland wrote to Judge Henry Brannon, who presided over the Circuit Court of Webster County, that he himself or an assistant would appear for the defendant if apprised of the date set for trial. Scientific research societies of New York, Boston and Philadelphia prepared to send representatives to Terror Pinnacle to investigate the astounding phenomenon, and Capt. Alex F. Mathews, of Lewisburg, Johnson N. Camden and others set about to organize a syndicate to buy up the mountain and surrounding territory, for its wonderful mineral possibilities. Fifteen hundred dollars had been advanced and paid into the fund to be raised for the purpose, by Mathews and Camden, an agent dispatched to Webster County to secure an option, and a meeting called of the members of the syndicate, to be held in Camden's office in Parkersburg to raise a large fund and perfect the organization. A dozen members had assembled, and one of the number read aloud the newspaper article; when he came to the name of the author, B. T. Nedmac, Mr. Camden's brow clouded, and reaching for the paper he said, "Let me see that thing again; B. T. Nedmac— spell it backwards—T. B. Camden—gentlemen, this is one of Tom Camden's damn hoaxes—meeting adjourned."

Most of the contributions to the defense fund were returned to the donors by Governor Sawyers and Major Triplett; but the "Governor," finding that he had about $60.00 remaining in his hands, the donors of which were "unascertainable," in that spirit of deviltry which commonly motivated his action, used this fund for the erection in front of the old courthouse of a duplicate in miniature of the Pinnacle, formed of round, smooth river boulders, carefully placed and cemented together, and about twelve feet high, the apex of which was a limestone slab, cut and placed in the form of an inverted "V," to represent a saw tooth, and through which the "Governor" had laboriously chiseled a round hole. One of the larger boulders bore the inscription "Terror Pinnacle."

I understand this monument did not stand for long, as the vandal visitors at the Springs, urged by the desire for a souvenir of the famous mountain, and need of something to counterbalance a quart or half gallon of "Uncle Bob's Best" in the other side of the saddle pockets, carried the whole bloomin' thing away; all except the limestone saw-tooth shaped, doughnut-holed capstone, which kicked around the courthouse as a door prop, until Pat Duffy, while auditor, brought it to Charleston and deposited it with the Historical and Antiquarian Department, where is should be today.

XX

MEN AND MILLS; "COL." BROWN WORRIES ABOUT "HE-VICKLES AND HI-VICKLES"

A VERY interesting character in those days was my old friend Bill Perkins—William H. was his proper name but few people knew it. Bill was what might be termed a portable sawmill "addict." Of course, nobody ever did anything but lose money on a portable sawmill, but many of them were just like Bill—the more they lost at it the tighter they stuck to it. But I do say that Bill could take a sawmill and a few teams and a bunch of timber and come out with less at the end of the job, than any other man in Braxton County, experience or no experience.

Dick Byrne owned a tract of timber, some ten or fifteen miles from Sutton, and Bill undertook the logging and sawing one winter. Along about April, Dick went over on the job to see how it was coming on. The saw set was near the house of a well-to-do farmer with whom Bill had arranged to board his crew during the job. They started in about December, with the farmer's smoke house well stocked with hams and side meat, his cellar full of dried and canned vegetables and his barn and granary well stocked with "hoss feed." By April that log and mill crew had just about cleaned up on the grub, though not on the job, and when Dick got there he found the main article of diet remaining was pickled beans. Dick told me he liked pickled beans as a rarity but not for steady, and that after a day or two of pickled beans for breakfast, pickled beans for dinner, pickled beans for supper! he returned to Sutton and a more varied bill of fare. A few days later Dick and I were standing on the street, when Bill Perkins came along. Bill had a very peculiar voice—falsetto, high-keyed and shrill; he talked right up in the top of his mouth and put a lot of steam behind it, so he could be heard a block away.

Dick accosted him with,

"Hello, Bill. How's the log job coming?"

"Oh, tolable—tolable."

"How are you coming with the pickled beans?"

"I gawd, wuss, wuss!"

"Worse; what do you mean?"

"I gawd, dried pon'kin!"

Felix J. Baxter had a great fund of stories and anecdotes and always told them well. He and I made many trips together from Sutton to Clay Court House, Summersville and Webster Springs, attending courts at those points, and many a weary hour of what was, in those times, an all-day journey, has he shortened by his inimitable recounting of things seen or heard. I wish my memory were better and that I could recall more than just a few of them. One story he told me with relish, concerning Col. John Brown, one of the prominent citizens of the Birch River section of Nicholas County, long prior to and during the war between the states. In the 50's, Colonel Brown lived at Birch River where the Weston and Gauley Bridge Turnpike crosses. He kept a store and the post office at that point for several years while that road was a mere county road connecting Sutton and Summersville before the State of Virginia took it over and made it a link in its turnpike system. It was in the late 50's that the highway was completed as the Weston and Gauley Bridge Turnpike and opened for through traffic, passing Colonel Brown's place at Birch River. On the day of the opening, travel was naturally very heavy as compared with the conditions formerly prevailing, and of course Colonel Brown, being the only storekeeper for miles, had a "throng" day. Along about sundown, when trade had eased down somewhat, Colonel Brown was sitting on his store porch, when a traveler along the new turnpike rode up and inquired:

"Colonel Brown, have you seen George Fox pass here today?"

"George Fox! Huh! With he-vickles and hi-vickles a passin' here both ways, from mornin' till night, how do you reckon I could keep track of any one particular feller?"

A somewhat embarrassing and altogether "rampising" situation arose on a visit I paid to Sutton about a year ago. Being Irish and a Democrat, I enjoy among my friends and acquaintances the rather unique distinction of never having tasted whiskey. I was standing on the street talking to half a dozen Sutton friends, when "Dock" Skidmore, another old friend, joined the crowd. I asked "Dock" if he remembered a canoe trip I took with him from Charleston up to Sutton about 42 or 43 years before, when he killed a large turtle at the foot of Wild Goose Island, about four miles above Clay Court House. He said he remembered the occurrence, and then I went on to relate to the crowd that I had been down at Charleston and seeing "Dock" there and learning that he was leaving for Sutton in his canoe the next day, arranged to make the return trip with him. It took about four days to make the trip, and I had a fine time gigging in the shoals and shallows, trolling in the eddies and fishing with rod and line wherever we stopped to camp. As to the turtle, I related that at the foot of Wild Goose Island, we came upon the largest soft shell turtle I had ever seen. That "Dock" struck his gig down through the middle of its back and the turtle wrenched the gig handle out of his hand and made its way off into shallow water with the gig handle erect like a mast, and that I had followed and overtaken the runaway, seized the gig handle and stood on the back of the turtle, which carried me around over half an acre of ground before he weakened sufficiently for me to master him. It was in fact an enormous turtle for the Elk River species. "Yes," said Dock, "I remember all about the turtle, and you riding him around in the river. I remember another thing about that trip, Bill. I didn't know you very well at that time and when you started back with us, me and the boys was wondering if you was one of these straight-laced fellers. So we had a gallon jug of whiskey in the canoe and when we was gettin' ready to camp that evening, one of the boys with me said, 'I wonder if we ought to git out our jug before that feller?' And we finally decided to do it; and when we took it out on the bank and pulled out the cork, lo and behold, you took the biggest drink of any of us; and we seen right away that you was an all right feller, all right."

Imagine my feelings at this critical moment. Through all my narrative concerning the trip, the big turtle taking me for a ride, even to the minutest details, Dock Skidmore had stood steadfastly by me and furnished full and complete eyewitness verification. What was I to do—what was I to say—of and concerning his addendum to the story? Gentle reader, I hope you may never be placed in a situation so embarrassing. All eyes were turned upon me—a clear call for me to speak. But I simply sat tight and stood mute. It was Ed Rider who relieved the tension—"Why, Bill, I thought you were the fellow who never tasted whiskey in your life?"

"Now, boys," said Dock, "I may be mistaken about Bill taking that drink of liquor; but something he did on the trip, made us think he was a pretty good feller."

And that made me think Dock Skidmore is a pretty fine chap.

Jesse Crites was one of the notable characters about Sutton back in the 80's. Jesse lived somewhere back on Hickory Wythe, the first mountain south of Sutton over which the Weston and Gauley Bridge Turnpike passes. For the first few years of my acquaintance with him he had pretty hard sleddin'. In the ginseng and "yaller" root season of the year it wasn't so bad, but Jesse was not the sort of chap to take thought of the morrow, and always found it awful tough to get through the winter. He claimed to have done service for his country as a member of the Home-guards, back in the 60's, and had pending for many years an application for a pension. His claim, however, was of such dubious character that its recognition was so long deferred that Jesse was just about on the verge of despair, when some Congressman from his district, more enterprising or more persistent than his predecessors, managed to get it through and Jesse was suddenly flooded with $1,000 back pay and a small monthly stipend. What to do with all this wealth, was the first great problem with which he had ever been confronted, and he solved it partially by the prompt purchase of a horse, saddle and bridle, a new suit of clothes, a new hat and a pair of "fine shoes." Dyer Duffield was a prosperous farmer who lived on the Turnpike, two and a half miles south of Sutton, and for years Jesse had trudged by his place afoot, on his way to market his ginseng and "yaller" root. On the day, however, that Jesse acquired his new outfit, Dyer, standing at his front gate, observed the approach of a well clad and well mounted horseman, whom he soon discerned, to his great surprise, to be none other than our friend Jesse. "Ah, good morning, you," burst forth Jesse, "when I was poor an' needy an' hard up, all you rich fellers gave me the high-shoulder, an' it wuz ole Jesse Crites! But now, sense I've got my money, it's— 'Ah, good morning, Mr. Crites.'"

During the time I lived at Sutton, 1885 to 1897, "Uncle Ben" Huffman operated the watermill at the south end of the milldam previously described. Uncle Ben was one of the most indefatigable workers that ever lived anywhere. He was out early and stayed out late and never stopped for wind or weather. But six days he labored and did all his work, but the seventh—well, Uncle Ben was a devout and consistent Baptist and his daily walk and conversation typified the sincerity of his professions. This milldam was a source of constant concern and uneasiness to Uncle Ben. Though constructed of heavy timbers, well fastened together, weighted down and buttressed by many tons of rock on which were placed alternating courses of poles and rock to catch and hold the sediment, but notwithstanding, almost every tide or considerable freshet would cause such damage as to impair its security at one point or another, and between times Uncle Ben, with some one or more of his sons, Granville, Jake, or Daniel, and a pair of mules, spent most of the time hauling rock and poles and brush, to mend or fortify the dam. While in Sutton a short time ago, Jake Huffman told me of an incident in this connection: He said that on one occasion a freshet had washed out a small section of the dam over near the mill, and that as soon as the water had subsided sufficiently, his father, with all the boys and the mule team set about to repair the mischief. Several days were required for the work and Saturday night came and found it incomplete by only a few hours work. It rained hard Saturday night and bright and early Uncle Ben was out to see about the chance of a rise in the river. He found that the river was beginning to rise pretty fast, and expressed the assurance that unless the breach were healed at once not only the work just done and almost completed would be swept away, but the entire structure greatly imperiled. In all the years he had kept up that dam, he had never struck a lick on Sunday, and it went awfully against the grain for him to do it now, even in the face of an altercative so disastrous, even though the Bible said what it did about ditches and oxen. But the river kept rising and the danger becoming more imminent with each speeding second, Uncle Ben grabbed a cant hook, started down the bank and called the boys to follow. In two hours time the last log was placed and the last drift bolt driven. The job was done and the dam was saved. At this moment Jake was chopping off the end of a projecting timber, in order to more improve the looks than the security of the job, and had it about half done, and was in the act of making another lick, when his father said, "Well, the ox is out of the ditch! Jake, drop that axe." Jake said he was so used to obeying his father literally and on the jump, that he dropped the axe in the river.

Well, this leads up to the fact that the old Huffman milldam is a thing of the past. The mill has been gone for years, and the superstructure of the dam has entirely disappeared. The foundations, however, which must have been set deep and broad, are still there and visible in low water, and there are likely to remain until "Gabe" toots his last toot.

Since this dam was destroyed many years ago, there has formed gradually an island along the north shore, extending from a point two or three hundred feet above the dam site, down the river to a point almost opposite the mouth of Skidmore Run — near a quarter of a mile in length. While the dam was intact, there was no semblance of an island anywhere along, but the disappearance of the dam has so changed the course of the river currents, as to make this deposit, which has rapidly grown up with willows, water-birch and sycamore trees, the roots of which grip and hold the successive accretions. Luther Pierson, an old residenter, tells me that Old Man River is simply replacing that which he took away; that before the dam was built, the shore of the mainland extended out even farther than the island now reaches, and that in the 60's when the Federal troops occupied Sutton they used that space as a parade ground. and that it was all cut away by the change of currents caused by the milldam erected in the late 60's.

Evidently this newly made ground will eventually attach itself to the mainland and will be sufficient to afford a parade ground against the time of the next war between the states.

XXI

SAW LOGS, YELLOW POPLAR, AND
SHOOTING MATCHES

A FEW DAYS after the issue of June (1929) *Wild Life,* Lon. H. Kelly, an old Suttonite, now a prominent Charleston lawyer, told me I had gotten shipped up wrong in my narrative about Uncle Archie Armstrong, the footlog and the pike. He said Uncle Archie never lived at Sutton at all, but lived at Birch River, and that the footlog was over Birch River instead of Grannys Creek, and that he went "piking" in Birch River instead of Elk. The next day I ran into Okey Johnson, born and raised on Birch River, who slapped me on the back and told me that he was tickled pink to read the stories about Uncle Archie Armstrong; that he had been raised on those yarns, and seeing them in print made him feel like he had met an old friend. I told him that Lon Kelly had jumped on me for locating the scenes on Elk instead of Birch, where they actually belonged

"Huh!" said Okey, "I don't see what that's got to do with it."

This simply goes to show the difference between these pesky lawyers — always trying to get somebody in a hole — and a good honest hardware man.

Many were the shooting matches we used to have at Sutton, with the mountain rifle, percussion or flintlock. The rifle range was over in the Ed Camden bottom; the usual distance 40 or 60 yards with a rest or two-thirds that distance offhand. A beef, a sheep, but most frequently turkeys, would be the prize. If a beef, the first prize was the heavy hind quarter; second, light hind quarter; third, heavy fore quarter; fourth, light fore quarter, and fifth, the "hide an' taller." It happened on rare occasions that one marksman so outclassed the field that he took all five prizes, and "drove the beef on foot."

One of these matches that made a lasting impression on me, was participated in by about a dozen of us, among whom I remember Dr. W. P. Newlon, Jacob S. Hyer, W. E. Haymond, Edwin D. Camden, James A. Johnson (who had but one arm), Charlie Newlon, Will Hyer, and last, but by no means least, Henry Evans. Henry was raised on a farm near Sutton and drifted into town in his early manhood, working as a teamster, hauling coal and at other jobs. Before many years he had so established himself in the confidence of his fellow townsmen, that he was triumphantly elected to fill the important office of Town Sergeant, and he made a good one. Henry was meticulously correct, exact and orderly in every way, shape and form. One thing in which Henry took particular pride was his name — Henry Clay — which, however, he abbreviated when he became Town Sergeant, and his official signature was H. C. Evans.

At the shooting match in question Henry appeared with his trusty rifle and paid his entrance fee. There was a long list of shooters, and someone on the ground was designated official announcer and it was his business to call out the names of the participants in their proper batting order.

Henry examined the list to find out whom he followed, and didn't need anybody to tell him when his turn came. At the crack of the gun of the fellow who preceded him on the list, Henry promptly stepped forward and took his place on the firing line. Taking his stance, left foot a little forward, slowly and with great deliberation he brought the rifle to his face, sighted carefully along the barrel, drew a fine bead on the target and was almost ready to touch the trigger, when the tardy announcer called out, "Henry P. Evans!"

Henry paused; and lowering the gun and bringing the left foot back even with the right, turned head and shoulders half around in the direction of the announcer and solemnly and in a tone bristling with earnestness, exclaimed, "H. C.!" Then pivoting on his hips, he turned and again faced the target, raised the rifle to his face, again sighted along the barrel and drew a fine bead on the target. In that tense moment between "gittin' a bead" and touching the trigger all eyes were glued on Henry; he applied the slight pressure, the hammer fell and — the cap snapped! And some dirty dog back in the gallery sung out, "Henry, it wouldn't mattered a damn what name you shot under for that shoot!"

The good old town of Sutton had a "close call" in the month of June, 1896. About 9 o'clock of the day in question, "Jink" Waybright, who was then deputy sheriff and jailer, remarked to me that we were going to have big water. I expressed some surprise, and suggested that we had not had rain for several days; he replied that it made no difference about rain — that he had seen Mort Thayer pass up street carrying a rope and ring dogs, and that this was a sure sign of a big river. Sure enough within an hour the river began to rise rapidly, and by noon was out of its banks, indicating that there had probably been a cloudburst up about the headwaters.

In 1889 Pardee & Curtin Lumber Company acquired a vast area of timber on Upper Elk and Holly, and in that year erected a large band mill at Sutton, immediately below the mouth of Grannys Creek. In Elk River, at that point, there is a large island, which extends from a short distance above the mouth of the creek, down the river two or three hundred yards. At the lower end of, and along this island, Pardee & Curtin Lumber Company erected a boom, for the purpose of securing the timber which was floated out from above.

In the fall season of 1895 and the winter and spring of 1896, millions of feet of poplar logs, ranging from two to six feet in diameter, had been deposited in and along the stream of the Upper Elk and Holly, to be borne out by the usual spring and summer freshets. Shortly before noon on that June day, these huge poplar logs began to arrive, and within less than two hours the boom was full, and the river clogged with timber and driftwood, almost as far up as the suspension bridge in the town. To form an idea of the immense quantity of timber this would involve, be it known that logs, thus floated into a boom on the swift current of a high tide, will pack solidly to the bottom of the river, those last to arrive diving underneath the logs already lodged and forcing the upper stratum high above the crest of the tide. By the middle of the afternoon the jam was complete from one side of the river to the other, the water still rising, and the outlet below almost entirely cut off. In less than twenty minutes, the river raised almost six feet, and by this time saw logs and driftwood were bumping the sills of the bridge and the water covering some portions of the main street of the town. Up to about that time, hundreds of people had congregated on the bridge to witness the scene, but with the first bump of a saw log against the bridge, the crowd scattered and from that time on the bridge was deserted. Consternation spread throughout the town, and all the merchants, and those living between the river and the hill, made speedy preparations to move their belongings to the higher elevations. If the river continued to rise for another thirty minutes as it had risen in the last, the main part of the town was doomed. Every one prayed that the boom would break and break quickly; but the boom held tight and showed no signs of letting go. Gen. George W. Curtin, who lived at Sutton at the time and was in charge of the Pardee & Curtin Company operations, was just at the point of relieving the situation by dynamiting the boom, when the structure suddenly let go of its own accord, with an awful crash and roar, and the pent-up poplar logs moved forward like an avalanche. So great was the force and velocity of the release, that huge logs were thrown up into the road in the sharp bend just below the boom, fully ten or fifteen feet above the crest of the water at that point. In an incredibly short time the channel was opened on the south side of the island where the break occurred, and the flood subsided much more quickly than it had come upon us.

Thousands of huge logs were left deposited in the Skidmore bottom, now South Sutton, on the street leading from the main street to the railroad station at the mouth of Grannys Creek, and the railroad tracks at the station were piled high with logs and debris. Fortunately, I was able to get some pretty good photographs at the time of and immediately after the flood, and they will convey a fairly good general idea of its extent and effect, to those familiar with the surroundings.

Several million feet of the logs that escaped by the breaking of this boom were recovered by Pardee & Curtin Lumber Company, and conveyed out into the Kanawha River and down to Sattes, twelve miles below Charleston, opposite the town of St. Albans, where they were sawed into lumber by Burns Bros., who operated a band mill at that place.

It is doubtful if any other boom ever held as large a number of large high-grade yellow poplar saw logs as was contained in this Elk Island boom at the time of its breaking. Those logs were culled from the virgin forests of the world's greatest yellow poplar region — the upper reaches of the Elk and the Holly River. In fact, it was the virtue of this timber from the standpoint of the lumberman that constituted their chief menace to the town. Smaller and less buoyant timber could never have accumulated in such a short time and in such volume as to have caused the flood in question and so threaten the destruction of a town.

XXII

A DRUGGIST, A DISTILLER OF MOUNTAIN DEW, AND A QUART

IN THESE DAYS when bootlegging is so prevalent, it would arouse but little interest to point out any particular person as being engaged in that profession. But in the late 80's, Sutton and Braxton County had the unique distinction of possessing an official bootlegger, in the person of Jake Ferguson, who conducted his business in and about the courthouse. Jake owned a rickety wagon and a span of aged, decrepit and underfed horses with which he made a bluff of making a living, but his real source of revenue was derived from illicit commerce in "drinkin' liquor." Braxton County was a bone dry county, so far as concerned its legal status, but there was the usual complement of thirsty citizens, and Weston, forty-four miles away, was the nearest irrigating station, and a mud road of that length and great depth, the only means of ingress and egress. Jake, under the guise of hauling store goods for his own consumption, would bring an occasional wagon load of liquor from Weston, and dispense it in pint and quart doses among his customers. His *modus operandi* was as follows: The Sutton Drug Store, as was the custom, carried a small stock of liquor, for strictly medicinal purposes, but it was about as hard to get spirits fermenti, with or without a prescription, from that drug store, as to get money out of a bank without security or with a jimmy. Jake usually wore a heavy knit woolen wammus, tied in front at the waist and bulging all around, whether loaded or empty. On leaving home in the morning he would slip a few bottles in his wammus and appear on Main Street in the vicinity of the courthouse. Jake didn't fool with the town folks, but would await the coming of a customer from the outlying districts, with whom he had previously done business. On his arrival in town the customer would spy Jake hanging around the temple of justice, and the following dialogue and scene would be enacted:

"Jake—you got any liquor?"

"No, sir—don't handle it in no way, shape or form."

"Know where I can get some?"

"Not unless you git it at the drug store."

"No use me tryin' to get it at the store—they always turn me down."

"Well, that's because you hain't got the pass-word. No trouble if you got the pass-word."

"Can you git it for me?"

"Why, sure, I kin git it."

"How much a quart?"

"Why, they ax a dollar and a half a quart."

"All right, here's the money."

Armed with the long green, Jake saunters across the street, probably walks up and down past the drug store a time or two, and finally, casually enters.

"All right, Jake—what will you have today?" says the druggist.

"Oh, nothin'—jist lookin' around."

A few minutes later Jake saunters out and across the street to the waiting customer, takes him back in the hall of the courthouse where they will not be observed, pulls a quart of whiskey out of his wammus and makes due delivery thereof.

If this customer was called before the grand jury, his examination was something like this:

"Did you within the past year buy any whiskey or other intoxicating drink from Jake Ferguson?"

"I did not."

"Buy any from the Sutton Drug Store?"

"I did not."

For at least two years Jake plied his trade successfully and without detection, owing to the well known fact that the liquor purchaser will go to every extreme of equivocation to protect the illicit seller—or at least it was so in those days. Jake was finally rounded up, however, his subterfuge exposed and he was duly chastised for bootlegging.

Speaking of Jake Ferguson, reminds me of his son George, with whom I had an interesting experience. On one of my numerous trips between Sutton and Clay Court House, I left the latter place for Sutton one morning, horseback and alone.

The road at that time left the river at the mouth of Buffalo, just opposite the upper end of Clay Court House, and traversed about 19 miles of the wildest, most desolate, sparsely settled and loneliest sections anywhere to be found, to the mouth of Strange Creek, where it again comes to Elk River. I hadn't seen a soul from the time I left Clay until I stopped for dinner with my old friend George Goad, at Strange Creek. Leaving Strange Creek, the Sutton road follows the river for a short mile, and there leaves it and crosses over to Birch River which stream it follows for two or three miles, and thence through the Twistville country and comes again to the Elk at Sutton, a total distance of 16 miles. I left Strange Creek after dinner and had proceeded three or four miles on my journey, still without companionship, when I spied in the distance, a horseman traveling in my direction. Spurring my horse to increased speed, in my eagerness to find a fellow traveler, I soon overtook the horseman, whom I found to be none other than George Ferguson, Star Route mail carrier between Sutton and Strange Creek.

George was a lad of about 15, tall, slender, angular, awkward and ungainly, about as unprepossessing a youth in his appearance as you will encounter in many days of traveling; besides, to say he possessed sixty-six and two-thirds per cent of the average intellectual equipment, commonly called "his marbles"—would have been putting it a little strong—and he was tongue-tied and spoke with a magnified lisp. While I at once realized that my newly acquired companion was not much of a find from a conversational standpoint, it was any port in a storm with me, and I straightway set in to make talk.

"Hello, George—how are you?"

"Hello, Mither Byrne—how are you?"

"Don't you find this road pretty lonesome, George?"

"Oh I don't know—I don't mind it."

"How often do you travel it?"

"Three tripth a week—down an' back."

"Three trips a week?"

"Yeth, thir."

"Well, I guess you get pretty good pay—they would have to pay me pretty well to make three trips a week over this road."

"Yeth thir, I git purty good pay—twenty-five cents a trip."

"Twenty-five cents a trip—well that is pretty good pay."

"Yeth thir, twenty-five cents a trip; a dollar a week; ten dollars a month; forty dollars a quarter; one hundred dollars a year!"

I was then a young limb of the law, and like most young limbs of the law prided myself on my ability as a cross-examiner; and here was a witness who had laid himself open to utter demolition by even the most obvious and simple processes of arithmetic. But before proceeding to destroy him, I would close every gap and avenue of escape by repeating to him his exact figures and having his tactic reaffirmation of his astounding proposition.

"Now let's see, George—let me get that again. Three trips a week and you get twenty-five cents a trip."

"Yeth thir."

"Now you say that is one dollar a week; ten dollars a

month; forty dollars a quarter; one hundred dollars a year! George, how do you make that?"

"Carryin' the mail!" promptly and triumphantly replied George.

George and I rode along together for the balance of the journey in perfect silence; neither spoke; George didn't seem to have anything further to say, and I am darned sure I didn't.

Nearly forty years ago I sent this "Carrin' the Mail" story to the *West Virginia Bar,* then as now the official organ of the State Bar Association, and it was printed at that time. Of course I have told the story a great many times since, but never knew of it being in print except the one time. Several months ago I was listening in on a radio program of WLW, of Cincinnati, and heard some chap put this story through the air. I was not able to get all he said, but got enough to recognize it as "Carrin' the Mail," with some slight variations.

XXIII

PRICE, CORNWELL, CONLEY, LIVELY, CLEVELAND, AND OTHER FISHERMEN

I HAVE just read with great interest and pleasure the article written by Hon. Andrew Price of Marlinton, and published in the *American Bar Association Journal* for July (1929), on the assigned subject, *Is the Fishing Lawyer an Outcast?* I emphasize the fact that this subject was assigned to Andy, for I know that if he had been asked to cover the general subject and choose for himself the title to his article, it would have been cast in very different words; it would have been in form of substance as follows, to-wit: Can any Lawyer amount to a continental, who does not Love to Fish; or if he has never had the opportunity to fish, would not love to have the opportunity, and love to fish if he knew how.

I certainly would like to see Andy, instead of taking the defensive as he was forced to do by the way the subject was phrased for him, turn himself loose on the proposition as I have stated it above—take the offensive, and forcibly demonstrate, as he most assuredly would, that the man who does not love to fish or would not love to fish if he knew how and had the opportunity—is fit for treason, stratagems and spoils and is the outcast of his profession. You handled the subject in a masterly way, Andy, for the chance you had; but don't you ever let them hornswaggle you again by forcing on you a theme, the title of which carries such an imputation, and compels you to defend rather than attack.

I'll bet a jitney that the fellow who prescribed that dose for Andy never wet a line in his life; never paddled a canoe or rowed a johnboat; never saw a bass pool or a trout stream; never listened to the delightful music of the boisterous shoal, or contemplated the smooth, rhythmic glide and the swirl of the eddying pool; never traversed three consecutive miles of any portion of God's footstool except in a conveyance; never saw a flower outside of a hothouse, nor heard a bird sing except in a cage and never even saw the glorious sunlight except through a smoke screen.

Are all angels devils—is a question I might propound to that chap, and let him chew on that and make due delivery.

As a matter of fact it is true that whereas under the old regime, horseracing and foxchasing was the sport of kings, now, under the new and improved order of things, fishing has always been the sport of Presidents— aye, and of chief justices, governors, statesmen, divines, lawyers, philosophers and men of large affairs. Read the biography of any American who has left his mark on anything worth while, for the last 150 years, and in nine cases out of ten you will find it recorded—"His favorite recreation was fishing."

Take George Washington and start back with the story of the cherry tree as it was originally told. Be it remembered that when that cherry tree was chopped down with that little hatchet, it was nothing but a small bush or sapling, which a small boy would cut down with one fell swoop of a small hatchet; true it has, in all these years that have since elapsed, grown to the proportions of a huge tree, and that little hatchet has likewise grown to the size of a meat cleaver—a growth quite common, as is well known, to fish or anything in any wise appertaining thereto. Well, when George chopped that cherry tree and his father found out about it and asked George who had done it, George's reply was, "I cannot tell a lie, father; I cut it for a fishing pole." The old gentleman, who by the way was something of a fisherman himself, simply said, "That's all right, young feller; but paw-paw makes a lot better fishing pole than cherry." And so endeth the first lesson.

From that first time forth, in his youth and early manhood and during his whole career as a land surveyor, military man, land proprietor, president of the United States, and father of his country, George spent a great deal of his spare time and all his vacations, with a fishing pole in his hand. It is historical that he and Lord Fairfax, when they went to spy out and locate the country covering the upper reaches of the North and South Branches of the Potomac, granted to Lord Fairfax by the British Crown, and long known as the Fairfax Estate, caught skads of bass in the main branches and slews of trout in the side streams and headwaters, just like John J. Cornwell did when he was Governor of West Virginia, and Governor Conley and Judge Frank Lively will do next year and for years to come.

The next great fisherman in the White House, of which history speaks, was Thomas Jefferson. He was called in off of a fishing trip to write the Declaration of Independence. While President, he slipped off and went fishing every chance he had, when Congress was not in session, which was only for a few months of the year.

I do not happen to have at hand exact data as to the piscatorial habits and accomplishments of all the presidents, but I do know that every one of them tried his hand at it more or less—and some of them a great deal more.

Take "Andy" Jackson for instance—he got his nickname "Old Hickory" from the fact that he always used a hickory hoop-pole for a fishing rod. He generally fished for the big ones, and wanted something staunch and strong to land them with.

It is said of Abraham Lincoln that when he was a young man he would maul rails all day and fish half the night, and that after he began the practice of law. many is the time he would have the court adjourned for a day or two so he and the Judge could go fishing. He was considered one of the crack fishermen of his day, and as a fish storyteller he was far and away ahead of all competitors — always dealing with his own personal experiences. And that's how he got the name of "Honest Abe." True, he could not spend much time fishing while he was president, owing to the war, which kept everything, both land and water, "riled" up; but even at that he used to slip down to the Potomac back of the White House and set a few bank hooks.

Grover Cleveland was probably the most confirmed and inveterate fisherman of the lot. Every chance he got during each of his two terms, he would go fishing or duck shooting, and usually he combined the two. It will be recalled that some of the metropolitan newspapers, who knew as little about it as the little fellow who got up the question for Andy Price, used to jump on Grover roughshod every time he went fishing, charging him with wasting his own and his country's valuable time, with such trifling, neglecting the public business, etc., etc., but Grover just kept on fishing and said nothing and it wasn't long before all such critics laid off of him, and most of them got ashamed of themselves and apologized — and went fishing "their own selves."

But the piscator de luxe of the whole galaxy was President Roosevelt. He caught everything catchable by hook and line, from the sardine to the man-eating shark, besides having gigged and speared salmon, pike, muskellunge, red-horse and suckers galore and harpooned whale and walrus without number. But the crowning act of his career as a fisherman, was when just off the California coast, he tangled with an Octopus — "son of the terrible Cuttlefish, the quivering, shivering Octopus!" After a seven-hour battle with the sixteen-foot monster, during which it reached out one of its eight arms and yanked overboard and to his destruction the only other man in the boat, Teddy finally succeeded, singlehanded, and alone, in subduing, taming and beaching his horrible catch.

And to speak of statesmen and men of large affairs, as we go along, don't you remember back in the stormy days of 1896, when Mark Hanna, as national chairman, was making the fight of his life to elect McKinley, and certain statesmen of his party were standing aloof and playing the role of Achilles, Mark startled the country by reading their names out in meetin' and telling them that they must fish or cut bait! Instantly, every one of those fellows got busy, and from that time forward they had the most industrious little fishing party this country ever beheld.

What makes all this fit into the Tale of the Elk is the fact that when in the spring of 1928, it got "norated" around that President Coolidge wanted to go fishing — trout fishing — and the West Virginia Game and Fish Commission and the Wild Life League got busy and joined in an invitation that he come to the head of Elk River, where both speckled and rainbow trout abound — and where they are to be had for the mere catching — if you know how. After a time a most courteous reply came from the Washington spokesman, to the effect that upon investigation it had been learned that the Upper Elk trout would rise to a fly only, but the President had located a place out West where they were trained for worms, and for that reason he chose to run out there rather than come to the Elk. Of course we are sorry, for we surely would have given the President a touch of high life up about Whittaker Falls and the Big Spring Fork.

It seems that in these days fishing is as "ketchin' " as the measles and everybody is "all broke out" with it, especially Presidents, cabinet members, ambassadors extraordinary, and ministers plenipotentiary. Since Mr. Coolidge took that fishing spree out West, there has been more fishing tackle sold than in any previous like period in our history. President Hoover didn't wait to get his seat warm until he had spied out, staked off and taken over choice fishing territory over in Madison County, Virginia, on the Rapidan River. I have fished in the Rapidan years ago, around Madison Court House and Criglersville. There were a few speckled trout in those days, but never did it compare with Upper Elk, Upper Gauley, Cranberry, Williams River, North Fork of Cherry, Big Clear Creek or Mann's Creek. But doubtless it is quite different now, as the government hatcheries would most likely and properly stock that region with choice trout of every sort, so tame that they would eat out of your hand.

It is said that the other day when President Hoover was entertaining Premier Ramsey McDonald at his Rapidan camp, the President asked the Premier if he cared for trout fishing.

"Oh, ver-r-ry fond of trout fishing," was the reply.

It was accordingly arranged that the two chieftains of the two greatest countries on the globe, should together hie themselves off to a choice and secluded fishing hole, not far from the camp where they could discuss in private the weighty matters concerning wars and rumors of wars, peace and rumors of peace, disarmament, naval ratios and the other things which had brought the Premier over to this side. A large rock jutted from the bank out into the deep pool. On one end of this rock the President caused the Premier to be seated, and seated himself on the other end, and the bout was on.

Five minutes passed in perfect silence and without action — finally —

"Ahem," said the President, and proceeded with some very general observation concerning disarmament.

"Very true," said the Premier.

Another five minutes of silence and inaction, followed by another "Ahem" and a very general observation concerning naval parties, from the Premier, which in turn evoked from the President the response, "I think so."

And so the conference proceeded and so the fishing went on for an hour.

It was the Premier's time to speak and he spoke —

"Mr. President, don't you think it is a long time between bites?"

"I certainly do," replied the President.

Simultaneously the two rods were raised, and it was discovered that each fellow had forgotten to bait his hook. Which goes to show that the fellow who goes fishing does not always fish for fish.

XXIV

DOCTOR NEWLON, THE TOWN, AND ITS ACHES AND ILLS

DR. WILLIAM P. NEWLON, who spent his life in devoted service to his fellow men, particularly in Sutton and its environs, was a man well worth knowing. He practiced medicine and surgery for the love of it and the question of a *quid pro quo* for the service performed never entered his head. But for the fact that he was a man of fine business judgment, and was able to make a good turn now and then in buying and selling lands, he would have starved to death, as nobody ever thought of paying anything for his professional services. As a young man he graduated from one of the foremost medical colleges and kept step with the progress of the science by occasional courses of post graduate work. A man of fine intellect, an omniverous reader of worth-while books, his stock of general information was never permitted to dwindle. He was as thoroughly human as any man I ever met. A hunter and a fisherman, especially with the gig, in the use of which weapon he had few superiors; he loved sports and games of all sorts and sizes; chess and checkers were indoor sports in which he excelled, and at the good old national game he was by no means a novice.

At any time of the day or night and in any brand of weather, Dr. Newlon would promptly respond to every call, from high or low without distinction or difference, if within the length of his cable tow — and frequently stretched the cable, five, ten, fifteen, twenty miles through the mud and snow and ice and rain and sleet, never stopping to think whether the fellow had paid or would pay him for his last visit or for this one. "Old Jack" would carry him to the home of the afflicted, as quickly as he could pace the distance.

"Old Jack" himself was almost as much of an institution about Sutton as was the courthouse. He was a rather under medium sized bay, flea-bitten on the rump, giving him somewhat the semblance of a strawberry roan. He was a pacer by nature and by training — not a long swing pacer — but a short, stubby and rather choppy pacer, as though "stoved" in the shoulders; but to have suggested that he was in fact "stoved," would have meant a mix-up with his owner then and there, and would have been a slander on the horse, because during the fifteen or more years that I knew him there was no change for better or worse in his gait. "Old Jack's" footfalls on the streets of Sutton and adjacent roads, were as readily recognized by the people therealong, as his own cowbell is by the farmer or the music of his own hound to the fox hunter; and many a husband or wife in the wee small or even larger hours of the morning, would nudge the sleeping mate and say, "Wonder who is sick? I hear Old Jack and Doc."

Dr. Newlon was essentially and distinctly a "common sense" doctor. He has told me frequently that the main causes of many serious ills that the flesh is heir to, were eating too much, rot-gut liquor and dosing with medicine; and he always added that psychology and the mental state of the patient were most potent both as a preventive and a cure. That a fellow of natural courage would get well while one lacking in that element would die. That it is essential to buoy the mind in order to get the best results from the body.

"Let's see your tongue! Quit eating; and take one of these pills every six hours," was one of his favorite diagnoses and prescriptions — handing the patient a dozen formidable looking pills.

"Can't I eat nothin', Doctor?"

"Oh, some bread and milk or a little broth. Come back when you have taken all the pills."

"Bread pills, sugar-coated, was what I gave that fellow," said the doctor when the patient had gone. He'll

be back here in three days feeling like a fighting cock,
and will be in good shape until he overloads his stomach
again or gets on another toot. Then he will come back,
and it will be the same thing over."

If any M.D. in any of the neighboring counties ever
came in serious need of medical attention Dr. Newlon
was usually called and always responded if possible.
He was known far and wide as "the doctor's doctor"—
the very highest station to which the medicine man may
aspire. Senator Johnson N. Camden was his double first
cousin, and whenever anything got out of kilter with
him, he would send for Dr. Newlon to come to Washington or Parkersburg, as the case might be. If, however, when the summons came, Dr. Newlon had on hand
a local patient who needed his immediate and constant
attention, whether a prosperous farmer or merchant or a
common laborer or a washwoman, the Senator would
wait.

To illustrate the princely income this particular physician derived from his profession: I moved from Sutton to Charleston early in 1897; Dr. Newlon had been
my family physician ever since I had a family, and during the last five years of my stay, had rendered quite a
bit of professional service. Two of my three children
were born under his ministration, the oldest having been
born at Lewisburg, and my calls upon his professional
services during that five years were quite numerous, involving all manner of ills and ailments, and in some instances protracted illness of several weeks.

Just before leaving Sutton, I told Dr. Newlon that I
had not paid him anything for four or five years, and
that I would like to have his bill. He replied that he
didn't have time just then to fool with matters of trivial
importance, but that he would look the matter up and
mail his bill to me at Charleston. Two or three weeks or
months later, I received the bill by mail: To professional services to date $26.50.

For several years, Dr. Newlon had his offices in the old Sutton Drug Store building, consisting of two rooms on the second floor, access to which was gained via a wooden stairway between and common to, the drug store building and a frame building, the second story of which was occupied by the *Braxton Central,* J. H. Dunn, Editor and Proprietor. Occasionally a number of us would gather in his back office in the evening and while away a few hours in the festive pursuit of fortune via the National Indoor Sport. On one particular night four or five of us were thus engaged, the blinds closely drawn and the keyhole plugged, so that no ray of light emitted from the kerosene lamp would be visible to the other world, when about 11 p.m. steps were heard ascending the wooden stairway. Instantly Dr. Newlon turned down the light almost to the point of extinction, whispering, "Sh-h, that's Fletcher Morrison after me to go out to see John G. Morrison's wife," Fletcher being a very straight-laced gentleman, who frowned on all frivolity or dissipation.

We all sat in perfect silence; soon there was a knock on the door, and, sure enough, Fletcher's voice demanded:

"Dr. Newlon, are you in? You are needed out at John G's at once."

Perfect silence within; and soon we heard Fletcher go down the stairway and out on the street. In the meantime the doctor had explained to us that the lady in question who lived out in Flat Woods, ten miles away; was quite sick, and that he was expecting the call; and that as soon as Fletcher gave him the chance, he would go down and give him an opportunity to deliver the message. Soon as Fletcher's steps died away on the street, Dr. Newlon got up and started to open the door, but just as he was on the point, he again heard footsteps on the stairway, which he supposed to be Fletcher's, returning to the quest.

"Durn the fellow, why doesn't he give me a chance to get out," said the doctor as he resumed his seat at the table.

But this time it was George H. Morrison who knocked at the door and delivered the same message as that just conveyed by Fletcher. Receiving no response, George H. soon went away, and again the doctor went to the door, intending to reach the street and hunt up the messengers. At that moment, however, we heard the voices of Fletcher and George H. at the foot of the steps, relating how each had vainly tried to find Dr. Newlon and concluding with the suggestion, "We'll just wait here till he comes," and we could hear them wait.

There was only one avenue of escape for the doctor, thus beleaguered, and that was to climb out the back window onto the roof of a one-story wareroom extension then under construction from the drug store back to the rock cliff, and drop from there to the ground, which might be done either on the up-river side or the down-river side. Dr. Newlon figured that it would not do to come out to the street on the upper side, as that would place him near and in plain view, on that moonlight night, of his pursuers.

Some of us recalled that between the third and fourth buildings below the drug store, there was an open space of about three feet, and it was suggested that the doctor drop off the lower side, walk down in the rear of those three buildings and step from the open space out on the street, which would bring him a considerable distance from the besiegers. This plan was adopted, and quietly and cautiously the doctor climbed out the window onto the roof and we heard him land safely on the ground, and each breathed a sigh of relief.

He threaded his way between the rear of the buildings and the rock cliff, a space none too wide for comfort and none too free of tin cans, goods boxes, and trash, for safe and silent travel, and emerged into the open space between the buildings. Even more carefully, cautiously and noiselessly he proceeded toward the exit at the street, and there found that someone had placed an empty goods box in the aperture at the edge of the sidewalk, which just about filled the space to the height and length of about thirty inches. Silently and cautiously he mounted the box on his knees, and was proceeding on all fours to reach the outer edge of safety, when the towering form of Fletcher Morrison looked before him in the moonlight.

"Well, Dr. Newlon! I am surprised to see you here!"

"Well, you're not a damned bit more surprised to see me here than I am to see you there," replied Dr. Newlon.

It was the irony of fate that a man who had done so much to minister to and ameliorate the sufferings of others, should himself be victim to a fell stroke that left him for years almost helpless, and wholly beyond the aid of human agencies, and finally took him hence. He died a few years ago at the home of his younger daughter, Mrs. H. Roy Waugh, in Buckhannon, Upshur County.

If Ivan MacLaren could have had the advantage of an intimate acquaintance with Dr. William P. Newlon, he might even have enriched that superb classic, "A Doctor of the Old School."

XXV

DOCTOR HUMPHREYS LOOKS AT ARTILLERY, CREEK AND FISH

O NE OF THE most persistent fishermen with whom I ever came in contact was Prof. Milton W. Humphreys, who along in the late 80's, when I knew him best, was at the very zenith of his fame as a premier among the world's intellectuals, if not in fact the leading luminary. I believe Professor Humphreys was born in Greenbrier County, but in his early boyhood his father, who was a physician, moved to Sutton, where Milton and his brothers, James W., John C., J. Handley, Dan'l, and Houston, and his sister, afterwards Mrs. White, were reared. His widowed mother and all his brothers, except Dan'l, lived at Sutton when I located there in 1885, and in that and each succeeding summer for several years until her death, Milton visited his mother for three or four weeks.

Before I met Professor Humphreys, I heard stories of his youthful precocity, when as a mere child in Greenbrier County, he had embellished the limestone rocks around about his home with "figgers," working out arithmetical problems in multiplication, addition and subtraction, worthy the genius of the average sophomore, and how he had persisted in his figuring and studious practices generally, until he had figured himself through school and college, always at the head of his class in every department. Just what opportunities were afforded him of which he took advantage, or whether, without waiting for the opportunity to hunt him up, he went out and hunted up opportunity, I do not know, but most likely it was the latter, judging the man as I knew him.

I often noted the striking similarity in physiognomy and family traits, between Milton and his brothers Jim,

John, Handley, and Houston — the same shapely head, broad, full and massive forehead, and especially the shape, set and keenness of the eyes — with the oriental slant and almost almond shape, it was very deeply set and when in repose, mild and defensive — but stirred up in the slightest, it showed the glint and spark of the repressed fire that lay behind; and that selfsame fire that had in Milton, burst forth in flame and illuminated the world, was there in Jim, John, Handley, and Houston, latent indeed, but nevertheless always present. Jim was a small storekeeper and sometime postmaster, John a carpenter and joiner, Handley the village watchmaker and jeweler, and Houston, like John, a carpenter and joiner; and in their little world and respective lines, each stood pre-eminent, as did Milton in his. I dare say the controlling factor in shaping the career and destiny of these five brothers, was the fact that he fared forth and sought and made his opportunity, while the others were content to wait for opportunity to come and find and make them, and it never came.

Professor Humphreys first came into prominence in higher educational circles in the chair of mathematics and later that of Greek, in some of the great universities of the country; and while occupying one of these, probably at the University of Virginia, he was called upon to take charge of the University of Texas. In a few years he put that now great institution on the map, and later took charge of Vanderbilt, then struggling for recognition amongst the foremost universities, and soon gave it the coveted standing. He then returned to what he told me he always considered "home" — the University of Virginia, where he remained until his death, which occurred only a few years ago.

During all these years of service, in addition to the work immediately in hand, Professor Humphreys was acquiring a vast, broad and comprehensive knowledge in every field of erudition, piling Ossa on Pelion, so to speak, until he came to be considered one of the few, if not the very most highly educated man in the whole world. Higher mathematics in all its branches and off-shoots, ancient and modern languages, chemistry, geology, botany, biology, art, music, medicine, surgery, philosophy, theology, law, literature—he knew all that anybody else had ever known and written, and a lot in addition which he had found out for himself. He probably was the author of more textbooks upon the high branches of learning than any other American, albeit as a general thing someone else stepped in and took the credit and the emoluments; the real author being indifferent to all other considerations except the consciousness of his work well done.

The story is told that while professor emeritus at the University of Virginia, it was the custom for the faculty to meet each Saturday night at the home of the President, to discuss and exchange views upon such subjects as might be introduced by any member, and that almost invariably Professor Humphreys would take the play away from the whole bunch, exhaust the subject, whatever it might be, and leave nothing to be said by anybody else. After this thing had been going on for several months, two of the professors put their heads together to find some subject with which Humphreys was not familiar and thus head him off and give some of the others a chance. They finally hit upon Chinese music, as the theme on which he could not possibly be posted. At the next Saturday night meeting, one of these conspirators took time by the forelock and launched Chinese music as the theme for discussion, he and his pal having in the meantime boned upon the subject by reading and studying carefully all the encyclopedias within reach. The proponent held forth briefly but learnedly on the subject and then turned it over to his pal, who spoke both learnedly and at length, reciting about all he had read in the encyclopedia. When the recitation was ended, Professor Humphreys said, "Well, gentlemen, when I wrote that article for the encyclopedia from which you are quoting, I gave the generally accepted version of the subject and endeavored to set forth practically everything that was then known to the outer world; but that was written more than twenty years ago, since which time a new edition of that encyclopedia has been published, in which you will find I have revised and made very material additions, alterations, and corrections"; and proceeded to set everybody straight on Chinese music.

Milton Humphreys knew everything; had most unusual powers of concentration and possessed a mind which was incapable of allowing to escape any impression made upon it. He reveled in philological research; dead and buried languages were a diversion and a pastime; he toyed with the tongue of the Chaldees, ancient Greek and Hebrew, Sanscrit and Pure Irish, Aztec and Choctaw, as the modern kid with a "Yoyo." Whenever the scientific societies in their excavations of cities of antiquity dug up a hieroglyphic, cuneiform inscription or other linguistic puzzle that stumped the wise men of the east, west, north or south, they always called on Milton Humphreys to help them out. Why, if he had lived in the days of Belshazzar and had been invited to the feast and commanded to interpret the handwriting on the wall, he could have told them what it was all about without ever looking on the book.

On his visits to Sutton, Professor Humphreys spent most of the daylight hours fishing. He was a bait fisherman and preferred hellgrammites to any other lure. Many an hour was spent by Lon Kelly, Jake Fisher and other small boys in the neighborhood, at the Huffman Mill dam or up at Buckeye Shoals, catching hellgrammites for Professor Humphreys. He fished sometimes at the milldam which was a splendid place for bass, but he didn't like it there very well, because usually there were

too many people around, especially boys. Like all other
good fisherman, he disliked fishing where "fishing was
crowded." He wanted to fish either alone, or with but
one companion, which fact alone was sufficient to mark
him a wise man. I fished alongside him at the milldam
late one afternoon; there were several men and boys
about, and he said to me, "There are too many people
around here; let us go up to Beech Clout tomorrow
morning." I agreed, and the next morning he and I
set out for Beech Clout, which is a large rock formerly
described in these annals, three or four miles above
Sutton, on the north bank of the Elk at the edge of a
large pool. Once afterward during the same visit and
several times in the next few years, he and I fished together at this same place. In that way I came to know
him from contact which in its character is most intimate.
A few days on the river or in the woods with a man, and
you know about him all you are capable of finding out.
Do not understand from what I have said about his dis-
liking a disturbance around him while fishing, that he
wanted to keep always silent. On the contrary he was a
great talker, and the most interesting and instructive I
ever listened to. True, he would sit for fifteen minutes
or an hour, without a word, and then in response to some
remark of mine or of his own accord, he would launch
forth and hold the floor for fifteen minutes or an hour.
He never "made talk" or discussed the commonplace,
but on any other subject, whether it be ancient history
or a toadstool; Shakespeare or Bret Harte; a hellgrammite or the components of the Pleiades; pre-historic man
or the latest discovery in coal tar derivatives; "shoes or
ships or ceiling wax, or cabbages or kings," he would
tell you all there was to be told; pedantry, euphuism,
stilted phrase, subtle simile or the manner didactic, were
wholly absent from his discourse, and the loftiest thought
was clothed in language the most simple, clear and con-
cise. If I had been able to retain, digest, and assimilate

one-tenth part of the things Milton Humphreys told me, I would deem myself to have a first-class liberal education. While he was telling me a hundred things I had never heard of, I added to his vast stock of knowledge by but a single item, which, inconsiderable though it may seem to many, was by him much appreciated and put to use. I taught him how to bait a hook with a combination of hellgrammite and crawfish, so adjusted that neither could hurt the other, although each kept up attempted murder without intermission, thus keeping the bait in constant motion and not only being a greater attraction to the fish, but also rendering the hook less liable to get snagged. Sometimes we caught bass and plenty of them, again we caught none, or none to speak of, but it was all in the day's work with him, and "fortune's buffets and rewards, he took with equal thanks." As with all true fishermen he loved fishing for its own sake and not for the catch or the meat, and he would apply himself just as faithfully though the prospect be poor or even hopeless—holding with Cyrano de Bergerac in a very different line of sport—it is much finer to fish when it is no use. And when not playing or landing a fish, he had all the more time for uninterrupted meditation or discourse.

On one occasion I said to him, "Professor Humphreys,"—every one spoke of him and to him as "Professor," just why, I often wondered, because the double "Ls" and double "Ds" that had, and should have been conferred on him, gave him a better right to promotion to and recognition by the honorary title of "Doctor" than any other man I ever heard of—"I have been told that you were the only gunner in either army, Confederate or Federal, or any other army, who was able to figure trajectory with such precision as to shoot a cannon ball over a mountain and down a chimney, miles away, into a room occupied by enemy officers with their maps, and thus set fire to and destroy the maps."

He did not immediately reply, and I thought for a moment he might for some reason be offended, but glancing at him, I was assured from the expression on his face that such was not the case. After ten minutes gazing intently off into space, he said:

"That was a pot shot"—the only time I ever had heard him use a slang expression—"I was a gunner in Bryan's Battery with Stonewall Jackson, in his campaign in the South Branch Valley. Our battery was planted in one valley and the enemy was over across a wooded ridge in another, about two miles away.

"We had maps of that whole section, the enemy's location as well as our own. These maps showed a large farmhouse which we knew, or took for granted, the enemy officers had appropriated for their quarters. I calculated as closely as I could from the data at hand, and aimed the shot to strike the house. A few days later, the enemy vacated that section, and, with some of my comrades, I visited the house and found that the cannon ball had gone down the large chimney in the center, and had evidently scattered the wood fire on the hearth, and set fire to some articles in the room. I saw some of the objects that had been partially burned. It was rumored that the maps were burned, but I do not know for a certainty."

That this shot of "Gunner" Humphreys, the initial scientific application of indirect cannon fire, was heard around the world, is attested by the fact that in every great conflict since that time, and notably in the World War, the science has been applied and perfected, and the Humphreys shot duplicated again and again—in everything but its accuracy and precision. These more modern marksmen may be able to shoot the chimney down, but none of them has ever yet succeeded in shooting a cannon ball down the chimney.

I last saw Professor Humphreys in 1915. My son George was then a student at the University of Virginia, and I stopped off between trains at Charlottesville, to be with him a few hours. While we were at the railroad station waiting for a night train to take me on my journey, I noticed a familiar form on the platform and asked George if that were not Professor Humphreys— whom I had not seen for more than twenty years. Being assured that I was not mistaken, I walked up, and interrupting a profound lecture on astronomy which he was delivering to the baggage man, who was standing there with his loaded truck, made myself known to my one-time fishing companion. He greeted me cordially, and as my train was just pulling in, our conversation, though cut short, was very much to the point. It consisted of just three questions and three answers. The questions, which were his, were: "How is fishing on Elk?" "Have you been to Beech Clout recently?" "Do you still use the hellgrammite-crawfish combination?"

XXVI

AROUND THE RIVER'S BEND TO CLAY; JAKE FISHER'S TYPEWRITER GIGS A FROG

I FIND it necessary to get away from Sutton if the Tale of the Elk is ever completed. But on the eve of departure I must relate an incident of which I was recently reminded, of and concerning Bill Dillion, who eked out a precarious sort of existence at Sutton, and his brother Monk, who lived on a farm on Poplar Ridge, about four miles out in the country, in the edge of a large scope of wild territory where the citizens for miles around were wont to range their swine on the mast which there abounded; and it was darkly hinted, that the meat found in Monk's smokehouse was not always from his own hogs. Bill would do odd jobs around town, such as being handyman about a livery stable, spading gardens, cleaning out wells, and other things which an unattached old codger of 75 might do. Somehow or other he seemed to be able to "make buckle and tongue meet" for the warmer eight or nine months of the year, but when winter set in, he would pay a visit to his brother Monk, who was always pretty well provided with "hog and hominy," and invariably such visits would be protracted until the buds opened up in the spring, when he would come back to town and take up the usual grind. It was rather understood that when Bill stayed with Monk, the latter, who was the younger, lorded it over his elder brother, to an extent well calculated to be sufficiently offensive to cause him to leave, but Bill couldn't be insulted away from his meal ticket in any such manner. When Bill returned to town and Monk would come in, as he did occasionally, Bill would make it a point to hunt him up and start a conversation which would afford the opportunity for him to get back at Monk for

indignities suffered while a guest at his home and fire-
side the preceding winter. On one occasion Bill spied
his brother Monk standing on the street talking to a
bunch of fellows, and approaching the crowd he heard
Monk conclude a sentence with the words—"You knew
I couldn't do that as a honorable man."

"Honorable hell!" interrupted Bill, "you talk like you
wuzn't the feller whut stole Norm Squires' old fat sow."

"Well, ef I did," said Monk, "you holp eat it."

In the early summer of 1894, a party of us consisting
of Jake Fisher, Ed Rider, Charlie Bland, Charlie
Ervin, and myself, planned a fishing trip to Clay Court
House and return, and arranged with young Squack
Carpenter to furnish the transportation by means of a
canoe belonging to "Old Squirley," his father. Each of
us had a different motive for taking that trip, in addition to the common urge of fishing. Jake Fisher, Ed
Rider and Charlie Bland had finished the law course
at Washington & Lee the year before and returned to
Sutton and hung out their respective shingles. One of
the first cases to engage Jake's attention, was known as
State vs. Fisher, in which the defendant was charged
in a warrant issued by a justice, with unlawfully and
feloniously casting and throwing at, in and against a
moving railroad train and passenger coach, a dangerous
and deadly missile, to-wit, one rock. This was in the
fall season of 1893, the first year of my incumbency as
prosecuting attorney of Braxton County, and the railroad brakeman who swore out the warrant came and apprised me of the fact that the same was in the hands of a
constable who was hot on the trail of the culprit; that
the case was likely to be heard very soon and for me to
hold myself in readiness to uphold and vindicate the
majesty of the law at the trial.

Upon inquiry as to the details of the offense, the
brakeman informed me that Jake was on his train out
near Flatwoods coming into Sutton, and that when the

conductor came for his ticket, Jake claimed to have
lost it and that the conductor, believing Jake was stall-
ing and meant to beat the railroad out of a ride, stopped
the train and ordered Jake to get off; that upon his
refusal to obey the order, he, the brakeman, a six-foot,
two-hundred pounder, had been delegated to eject him,
which was accordingly done, with great difficulty and
after a struggle which landed both Jake and the brakeman flat on the ground outside, locked in each other's
embrace; that the brakeman finally succeeded in extricating himself, and while he was in the act of getting back in the coach Jake threw a rock at him, which
he barely succeeded in dodging, in consequence of which,
the missile sped on and struck an iron upright on the
platform, shattered, and a portion thereof as large as
a filbert flew into the coach through the open door, and
hit "Aunt Lizey" Newlon on the foot.

I was not much impressed with the seriousness of the
charge and treated the matter rather lightly. But not
so with Jake. He had meant murder, and believed he
had really committed a high grade felony—or at least
pretended like he did—I have always had my doubts
about that, for there has always lingered the sneaking
suspicion that Jake wanted to take a trip West and incidentally take in the World's Fair at Chicago. At any
rate Jake went to his father, told him of the awful
crime he had committed and inveigled him into giving
him $100.00 to make his get-away. That night he hoofed
it over the mountain and down Cedar Creek. Later he
made his way to Parkersburg, where he took the train
for the Far West. After spending several months and all
his money in such wild and woolly western sections as
Chicago, Kansas City, and St. Louis, Jake made up his
mind he would return home, live down the awful disgrace, and be elected Judge of his circuit—which he
did, thanks to another contribution from his father—
that is, he did return home. He did not become Judge

until many years later; and as for living down that disgrace,—why bring that up?

Well, Jake had not been back very long from his
western trip and, believing that the process of healing
reputation is sometimes accelerated by occasional ab-
sences, he got Will Haymond to give him a job of ab-
stracting down at Clay Court House, and furnish him
an old typewriter with which to do the work. This typewriter was an early edition of the old Caligraph, the
first writing machine ever brought to Sutton. It was as
bulky as any two modern typewriters and weighed something less than a ton.

Jake's main reason for going on that fishing trip
was to get himself and that typewriter down to Clay.

Edgar Rider also had other reasons for wanting to
get away from home. It was right in mid-season of his
courting days and there had been a little flare-up, such
as is apt to occur pending such proceedings—this one
being of sufficient consequence to cause Ed to resign
as President of the Epworth League. For the life of
me I never could understand what the Epworth League
had to do with Ed and his girl; but it is fact and not
theory that concerns us. At any rate things were in such
a state, that Ed wanted to get away for awhile. And by
way of parenthesis, let me say his judgment was fully
vindicated, as the wedding followed within a few months
after his return.

Charlie Bland had some idea of spying out a new location to practice his profession and thought he would
give Clay Court House the once over. Charlie Ervin,
about 18 years old, went because he just liked to "wal-
ler around in the river" as he expressed it. Squack Carpenter, who was about the age of Charlie Ervin, was
induced by certain promises of remuneration for the use
of his dad's canoe and for his own services as chief
navigator. For my part, the trip was greatly to my liking, as I wanted to attend the then approaching term of

the Circuit Court of Clay County, as was my custom, and was thus afforded a fine opportunity to get down and back and do a lot of fishing enroute.

The day selected for our departure happened to fall on "show day"—that is, the very day on which a large one-ring circus was to hold forth in Sutton; consequently, we arranged to have everything ready to make our get-away immediately after the afternoon performance was over, as there was not a member of the party who would have thought of foregoing such a prime attraction; and the hour of leaving made but little difference, as we were equipped with one of these street faker gasoline lamps, attached to the bow of the canoe, and ten gallons of gasoline in two five-gallon cans, and it was our purpose to do most of our traveling at night and gig by the light of the gasoline lamp. I had a gasoline stove at my home, and bought gasoline by the barrel, which by the way, cost in those days nine cents a gallon, or $4.50 per barrel, family being away for the summer, I appropriated what gasoline was left in the barrel at the time.

The instant the show was over, I made a break to get through the crowd, but hadn't gone thirty feet until someone in the crowd yelled, "Hey there, Bill, I have been robbed—I had $3.75 in my pocket, and it's gone. You are prosecuting attorney and I want you to get my money." Another fellow had been shortchanged somewhere on the lot, and two or three others had been buncoed by some of the old threadbare devices. I had to stop and listen to all these complaints before I got away from the show grounds, and by the time I reached my office in the courthouse, where I had left my gig, fishing rods and other articles which could not safely have been left out in the open, there were seventeen men waiting for me, to register complaints similar to those already heard, and another half hour was consumed before I could tear myself away from this bunch. Finally

I grabbed the gig and rod and a large basket containing other articles, and rushed off down the street in the direction of the canoe. I bumped into Jake Fisher staggering along—under the weight of the huge typewriter. He informed me that he and the other boys had waited for me, down at the canoe for about an hour, and that he had suddenly remembered that he had forgotten his precious typewriter, and had hustled back up to town to get it, and that he would have been "plumb ruint," if he had gone off without it. When we reached Bridge Street, we saw a knot of people gathered around my old friend, Dr. Job McMorrow, who was holding forth eloquently and lustily concerning an outrage over at the circus. On spying me, he crossed the street and grabbed me by the arm: "Here, Bill, you are our prosecuting attorney, although I didn't vote for you, as I am a Republican—but lots of Republicans did—and I want to tell you I've been robbed of $20.00 and you've got to get it back for me."

"Dr. Job" as everybody called him—and not half of whom even knew he had "McMorrow" hitched on to his name, was a splendid type of that sturdy citizenship which populated Birch District, which embraces the lower end of Braxton County. He had practiced medicine among those people for 50 years and was universally respected and beloved. Gruff and rugged in his manner, speech and action, his heart was tender as a woman's and every instinct that of the highest order.

The story as reeled off to me by Dr. Job, was about as follows:

"A fellow come to me over at the show grounds and asked me if my name was Dr. Job McMorrow, and I told him it was; and he said he had heard of me as the most prominent physician in Birch District and a leading farmer and citizen in the community, just the kind of a man his company wanted to represent them in selling their farm gates—they always wanted the very best

—Big Chicago concern with $10,000,000 capital and factories in seven states. He showed me a picture of the gate—best lookin' gate you ever saw. Was to consign 100 of these gates to me at Frametown and send a man later on to sell them for me, and I wouldn't have anything to do only the use of my name and would get one-third of the profits, and two gates worth $15.00 apiece —just for the use of my name. And all I had to do was to put up $20.00 in escrow to guarantee my good faith, and he would give me the receipt of a $10,000,000 corporation and an agent's contract; and I gave him the $20.00 and told him to give me the receipt and the agent's contract, and he said he would have to get the papers out of his grip and stepped around the corner of the tent, and I stood there waiting for him to come back, and—he never did come back; I ain't seen or heard of him since; and he's got my $20.00 and you are the feller to get it back for me."

I asked him a number of questions as to the name of the guilty party; whether he was some local chap or one who seemed connected with the show; but Dr. Job could give me no information on any of these points; and I finally told him it looked as though his case was hopeless and that I did not know anything to do under the circumstances.

Then Dr. Job blew up: "Do you mean to tell me, sir, that a man can be robbed that way in broad daylight and nothing can be done for him?"

At this junction a lad of about 12 years, son of Phil Corley, spoke up from the crowd: "Say, grand-pap, the only thing I know is to have a gyardeen appinted fer you."

"Well, bub, I guess you are right," replied Dr. Job; and the incident was closed. Jake and I struck out to join our party as fast as the typewriter would permit him to travel, and we shoved off about 6:30.

We took advantage of the hour and a half travel-light yet remaining, to get as far down the river and beyond the zone of the Sutton giggers as possible, before dark, and then lighted up our gasoline torch and set in to gig. The river was low and crystal clear and I suppose we got plenty of fish, although I do not remember particularly; but do recall that along the steep mud bank just above Frametown on the north side of the river, we ran into bullfrogs galore — whether it was a state convention or a spring festival, we were unable to determine, but for half a mile along that bank there was the greatest frog congregation we had ever beheld, and the truculent challenge of their combined and co-ordinated jug-a-rums was well calculated to strike terror to the heart of the uninitiated. However, nothing daunted, we charged upon the whole kit and bilin', speared them right and left until we had filled a gunnysack with our victims, and without casualty to any of our party, beyond the fact that when I gigged at one fine large juicy specimen, perched high upon the bank, Jake Fisher was in the canoe immediately behind me, hovered over his typewriter to prevent it getting stepped on or frog bit. It was a long reach for my gig handle, and my aim was so bad that I just "scammed" the frog sufficiently to cut the skin on his underside. Instantly that frog gave a mighty leap, almost parallel with my gig handle, and exactly in the direction of Jake as he huddled over his typewriter. As good-or-otherwise-luck would have it, Jake sensed that something unusual had happened or was about to, and raised his head to see what was going on, just in time to receive the slightly wounded and badly bleeding bullfrog full force on the chin and the shirt-front. The air was somewhat chilly and Jake had his coat buttoned and of course the frog went down between coat and shirt and there hung until Jake got up and shook him loose. On dropping on the bottom of the canoe, the bullfrog took another leap, which landed him among the running gear on the underside of the fatal typewriter. For the next few seconds one would have thought he was in the office of the West Virginia Code Commission, with a whole battery of typewriters in constant action. Every kick that bullfrog made, seemed to set off the whole machinery and keep it going until every letter on that Caligraph double keyboard had responded with a click that could be heard across the river. Even the bullfrog serenade suddenly ceased, probably because the choristers thought it was some sort of a musical instrument that they were supposed to tune in on. Jake finally succeeded in extricating the frog from the machinery, and it seems that no particular damage was done, further than that after he got to Clay Court House, he had to spend about a week removing the frog blood and frog hair from the mechanism, before the typewriter would typewrite.

That was the bloodiest bullfrog I ever heard of. Jake swore there was at least a half pint of blood in and about the works of the typewriter, and we all decided there was at least an equal amount on Jake's face and hands, coat and shirt.

Somewhere down below Frametown a couple of miles, we made our camp for the balance of the night, not going to the trouble of putting up our tent. We had not stopped for supper, as we were supplied with sandwiches to eat on the way, so we made up a roaring campfire; made some good, strong coffee and ate a substantial lunch before stretching out on the ground near the fire for a few hours rest.

And it was the next morning that Charlie Bland found himself in bed with a black snake.

XXVII

TROUBLES CONTINUE; THE GROVES MILL
PIKE; OR "WAS IT A RED-HORSE?"

THE WHOLE BUNCH of us slept soundly, sprawled on the naked ground around our campfire, until long after daylight when we were awakened by a blood curdling yell from Charlie Bland, and saw a huge black snake gliding away from the smouldering campfire. "Look at the gol durned thing," said Charlie, "and it was right here in bed with me," and he pointed to the snake which was making for cover as fast as its legs — they do say that a black snake has very diminutive legs — could carry it. After some one had followed and dispatched the awful intruder, Charlie proceeded to explain what the row was all about. "I woke up and saw it was broad daylight and the fire was pretty near out, and I thought I'd get up and put some wood on and let you fellows sleep, and put my right hand out to help me up, and grabbed right a-hold of that gol durned snake — and I don't know whether I am snake-bit or not. I never thought of a snake being there, or I never would have put my hand on it." After a thorough inspection, Charlie finally satisfied himself that he had got off with a whole skin and was apparently greatly relieved.

Such a frog-leg feast as we had for breakfast that morning, I have never seen before or since — all but Squack, who declared, "If I had my druthers, I'd druther eat Charlie Bland's black snake than eat one of them danged things that tries to hop out uv the skillet when you're fryin' 'em and will still kick after you git 'em down in ye." So Squack didn't have anything better than fish for his breakfast.

I don't remember about the fishing that day until we got down to Fish Pot, about half a mile below Strange

Creek, and so called because of the great abundance of fish there to be found at all times, — as it was in those days. It is a rather short pool, not very deep, and along the southerly side of which were many good-sized rocks. Just why it was such a favored haunt for fish of all kinds, I have often wondered, but nevertheless I have seen more fish in Fish Pot than in any pool of equal size on Elk River — or any other river, for that matter. We killed a few pretty good ones in Fish Pot, and doubtless would have gotten more, but for the fact that Charlie Ervin took it into his head to change his location from the stern of the canoe to a point up nearer the bow, and in the act of so doing was just on the point of steppin' on Jake's precious typewriter. Jake's howl of alarm and caution so startled and unbalanced Charlie Ervin, that the typewriter was saved, but poor Charlie went out of the canoe and kersplash! into the river. The disturbance he raised going in and the commotion we made fishing him out, put a crimp in all further fishing in Fish Pot for that day.

There was an incident in connection with our crossing the county line out of Braxton and into Clay, which I had forgotten and of which Ed Rider reminded me a short time ago. The county line crosses the river at the mouth of Duck Creek, at and immediately above which is a rather deep pool. As we were passing through the lower end of this pool, I picked up the gig and was standing in the bow of the canoe in readiness for such fish as might be in the shallow water at the head of the shoal, just below, when I suddenly caught sight of an enormous red-horse in the deep water off to my right; I started to gig at him, when he turned suddenly and ran under the canoe diagonally toward the stern; turning to my left, I saw him come out from under the canoe fully twenty feet behind me, still in the deep water. I threw the gig, and as good luck would have it, struck the fish mid-ships, and after some difficulty owing to the depth of the water, succeeded in landing him. This was, under all the circumstances, the best stroke I ever made with a gig, and the largest red-horse I ever killed. The feat elicited much praise from my companions, and especially from Squack Carpenter, who declared, "I tell you that feller William Burns is a slick gigger all right." I mention this remark not so much in the spirit of self laudation as for reference later on.

Now as to the size of that red-horse, being always reticent to gauge the length or weight of my catch, I will give you Ed Rider's version of it as he stated it to me recently, so that if anybody's reputation for truth and veracity is to suffer, it won't be mine:

"Well, sir, I never will forget that red-horse you killed at the mouth of Duck. That was far and away the biggest red-horse I ever saw. You remember that we stopped down at the mouth of Snake, half a mile or so below Duck, to cook our dinner, and we decided to eat that big red-horse, and while we were cooking our dinner, all the Duffields in that whole country, about sixteen of them, came in on us, and we invited them to help eat our red-horse; which they did, and their crowd and our crowd were not able to eat it all, and — don't you remember? — we gave them a lot of it that was left, to take home with them." Of course, I remember — who wouldn't?

Well, there were six of us, — of that I am sure; and if there were sixteen of the Duffields, that makes twenty-two able-bodied and valiant trenchermen that feasted on that one red-horse; so you can judge for yourself how big it was, even without taking any account of what they may have taken home with them.

Ed Rider has a splendid recollection, and I got him to help me out on another matter in connection with crossing the county line. I said, "Ed, what was the incident about Charlie Ervin and Squack Carpenter, who were minors at the time, and the liquor?"

"Why, don't you remember? Some of us had a little liquor along — just for medicine and in case of snake-bite, and we wouldn't give Charlie Ervin or Squack any, or a chance to get any, so long as we were in your bailiwick as prosecuting attorney; so as soon as we crossed the county line into Clay one of the minors suggested that we stop immediately and get dinner. So the first likely place we came to — a nice sand and gravel bar at the mouth of a creek—we landed. Somebody asked the name of the place and you said it was the mouth of Snake, and then one of the fellows said, 'Hell's bells! Snake for breakfast and snake for dinner — where's the snake-bite antidote?' And then somebody put the bottle and the tin cup out on the bank in the edge of the weeds, and commanded the two minors to let it severely alone, which they immediately proceeded not to do; and while they were in the act of disobeying orders they saw at a distance our visitors approaching, and retired up in the brush; and in a few minutes Squack emerged from the undergrowth and said with a grin, 'I was jist hidin' them anecdotes so them fellers comin' wouldn't see them'."

We continued our journey without incident worthy of note until we reached Groves Mill, which at that time and for long years afterwards, stood on the north bank of Elk River at the foot of Groves Shoal, at the end of the long millrace. This mill was supported by massive uprights of hewn oak timber, fifteen or twenty feet high, at each end of the building and on either side of the mill-race which extended under the center of a construction sufficient to withstand the assaults of flood tides and their incidents. This, by the way, was probably the last mill of its kind between Sutton and Charleston to succumb to the ravages of time and disuse.

As we approached the mill, Squack remarked, "You fellers ort to git William Burns to tell you about how Old Squirley met his defeat four or five years ago, over thar at Groves Mill."

Of course, I had to tell the story then, and, to avoid anything like repetition, may as well put it in right here:

About five years before that time Maj. W. D. Rollyson, of Salt Lick Bridge, Hon. J. W. (Wes) Morrison, of Flatwoods, and myself, contracted with Squirley Carpenter to take us in his canoe, from Sutton to Charleston; and Squirley took his son, Young Squack, then a lad of about fourteen, with him on the trip. I took along a gig and used it occasionally when a good opportunity afforded. Just below O'Briens Creek Shoal, about a mile above Groves Mill, I had killed a blue pike, about three feet long. Just before we reached the mouth of Groves Creek, there came up a quick thunderstorm, and as we entered the long shoal, it began to rain so hard that we decided to take shelter under the Groves Mill. Landing our canoe at the foot of the shoal quite near the mill, we were soon under cover. Presently Major Rollyson made some remark about the nice pike I had just killed and stated that it was about the largest one he had ever seen. At this old Squirley perked up immediately: "Fellers," said he, "that jist reminds me — an' it's a funny thing — jist about ten year ago, I was takin' some fellers from Sutton to Charleston in my canoe, jist like I'm takin' you fellers now, an' as we got down along out thar, a big storm come up an' we landed an' come in under hur fer shelter, an' while we wuz all standin' hur on the side uv the millrace, pine blank like we air now — I wuz lookin' down in the water thar — the sluice gate wuz up an' the water about four feet deep an' powerful swift — I looks down in thar an' sees the biggest pike I ever seed in my life — an' I've seed big 'uns in my time — an' this 'un — why Bill Byrne's pike wouldn't a made a good bait fer it — an' I run out right quick to the canoe an' got my gig an' when I got back the pike wuz still thar, headed downstream jist like it wuz — too long to turn 'round in thar

an' git back out — an' standin' right thar on this
identical spot, I slammed my ole gig into him, an' sich
a shine as he cut, an' it wuz me an' him fer it — but I
had hit him down thew the backbone, right in the jint uv
his neck, an' the beards wuz good an' held all right, an'
finally, the other fellers helpin', we landed him right
thar whar I am standin' — the monster pike I ever seen,
an' he wuz jist exactly 69 inches long, that pike wuz —
by actual measure — an' I'll swear it on a stacks of
Bibles that high."

This all delivered in a more or less excited tone, getting more excited all the time, and accompanied with a
great variety of contortions and gesticulations, illustrating his every action in spearing and landing the huge
fish; and when, at the final windup, Squirley raised his
right arm high above his head, to indicate the height of
the stack of Bibles on which he was willing to swear, he
became overbalanced, or his foot slipped, or something,
and overboard he went, kersplash, into the mill tail. Maj.
Rollyson, Wes Morrison and I immediately sprang to
his relief, and after great difficulty succeeded in yanking Squirley out on dry land and thus rescuing him
from a watery grave, Squirley puffing like a porpoise
and gulping down all the bad words which he did not
have the breath to utter.

During all the course of Squirley's narrative and as
well while we three were putting forth strenuous efforts
to fish his papa out of the water, Squack stood by, leaning against one of the upright supports, as uncon-
cernedly as though he were watching a dog fight between
two dogs, neither of which belonged to him. Midst all the
commotion and excitement, his face was as expression-
less as that of a wooden Indian — he moved not a hand
or even a muscle; but when we had landed Squirley
safely, high and dry, Squack looked up and remarked,
in level tones, "Pap, ef that thar pike hed ben jist one
inch longer, damned ef you wouldn't a drownded!"

And now, for the sequel to this story of Squirley's pike: I told and retold that story as an actual experience of my own, for many years, — quite often enough to have caused me to honestly believe in its absolute truth, even tho it were sheer fiction, — when one day I picked up a Charleston newspaper and saw staring me full in the face, this identical story, told, however, in much more readable style, as a personal experience of my distinguished friend and fellow townsman, Ex-Gov. Wm. A. MacCorkle. Upon the impulse of the moment I addressed a short communication to the same newspaper, complaining that Gov. MacCorkle who was possessed of such a vast wealth of anecdotes, reminiscences and personal experiences, should see fit to thus ruthlessly appropriate my ewe lamb.

Shortly after these publications, I happened to be in Sutton, and some of the boys who had noted the controversy between Gov. MacCorkle and myself, concerning the proprietorship of the story, called my attention to old Squirley Carpenter on the opposite side of the street, and suggested that they call him over and let him sit as final arbitrator and court en banc between us. Thinking I could not lose anything by having the case tried in the absence of my adversary, I readily assented, and Squirley was called over and joined the crowd. I admit that before the main question was propounded, I "approached the court with honeyed words of approximation," by reminding him of the fine times we had had in the long ago, on fishing trips, long and short. The old chap was very responsive, and played up beautifully to every allusion or suggestion, so I was ready and eager to have the fatal question put. Lon Kelly was in the crowd, and when I was through, he said to the old fellow:

"Squirley, there is an important question we want you to settle: Will Byrne here, says he was with you when you were telling about the big pike and fell on the mill race down at Groves, and Gov. MacCorkle says he was with you and Will Byrne wasn't there at all. Now you tell us the truth about it?"

"Well, fellers," said Squirley, "I've took that same trip with Bill Byrne thar, an' I've took it with Gov. MacCorkle — an' its them fur it!"

And this was all the verdict anybody ever got out of Squirley until the day of his death which occurred two or three years later. Some there are, I believe, who are even man enough to attribute Squirley's reticence, not to a dislike to decide between the two claimants to the distinction, but in fact to save the face of both Gov. MacCorkle and myself.

From Groves Mill around the "End of the World" bend, to the foot of Lower Seventy-four island, we traversed three miles of what was at that time, before the advent of the railroad, the best stretch of fishing water, especially for bass, anywhere to be found. It is a succession of short shoals and eddies, swifts and "plouts," many large rocks and other haunts and feeding and hiding places such as seem to appeal particularly to bass. But alas and alack, what was then a bass paradise, became also the paradise of the dynamiter during the construction of the railroad therealong, and has continued to be his happy hunting ground even unto this good day; so that there is now a pitifully small percentage of bass or other fish, in comparison with the number that once inhabited those waters. The small plouts in which fish congregated, and the large rocks there about, greatly increased the destroying power and deadly effect of each shot of the explosive, and the harvest of fish of "skillet" size is, of course, always negligible in comparison with the small fry and the eggs destroyed. What a great pity it is that our penitentiary is so crowded with bootleggers, that there seems to be no room for dynamiters!

We did not stop to do any fishing except with the gig,

on the down trip, as we were in somewhat of a hurry, but left other sorts of fishing for the return trip, on which we were to spend about a week.

At the head of Standing Rock, about eleven miles above Clay Court House, we stopped and cooked supper, loaded up our gigging lamp with "gasoline oil," as Squack always called it, and at dark, "shoved off" with the full intention of killing enough fish that night to supply the town of Clay for a week — ourselves included. Well, we got a good many fish, it is true, but there were some we didn't get, as you will later be told.

One of the main essentials for such night gigging is to have a good steersman. He must know his river in minute detail. He is required to know every shoal and shallow, and when the water is low, every channel and chute, and, in going downstream, must know or be able to locate quickly by the action of the current, every sizeable rock on or in close proximity to the "chute," otherwise there is always danger of coming in contact with a rock and upsetting if not bursting your canoe. A steersman who knows all this and can let you down over a long shoal as smoothly as tho you were floating in eddy water, is worth his weight in fish for every night he is out with you — provided always, that you are able to handle the gig as well as he handles the canoe. Now Squack, tho but a youngster, was no slouch as a steersman. Of course, he could not be compared with Jim Rogers — "James Alias," as he was called for short, — Josh Woods, Rile Holcomb, or Billy Nichols; — but neither could anyone else be compared with either of them except it be another one of the quartette. By the way, Josh is still living, at Clay, the sole survivor of the four premier night steersmen of the age — they all used to live at or near that town. But Squack had "follered the river" with old Squirley ever since he was big enough to lift a push pole and would have ranked only a few notches below the best.

Well, that night he let us down easily and smoothly over some pretty long and difficult shoals — Standing Rock, Little Laurel, Big Spread and Wild Goose, without a jar or a scratch; but it was when we got to White Oak Top, a little, measly old shoal half a mile below Wild Gooose, and three miles above Clay, that the balloon went up. This is a very short shoal, but with a considerable pitch right at the head. Now about a year before our trip the Government of the United States of America having decided to make Elk River, in fact, what in about the year 1803 it was declared to be, a navigable stream, expended divers sums of the coin of the realm in picking the rocks — not all the rocks — out of a few of the shoals and therewith erecting wing walls to concentrate and deepen the water in the channels, in order to accommodate craft of greater tonnage than formerly. Well, White Oak Top was one of the shoals so treated and Squack didn't know, or had forgotten about it. Of course, it was mostly my fault, because I was up in the bow, just back of the light, and it was my business to look out for breakers. But I was dog tired, the light was burning low, so I sat down, intending to land and "mend the light" as soon as we got through that little shoal. Well, just a little below the entrance to the channel down in the very swift water, had been left, or placed, a good-sized rock to the left of and about eight feet from the wing wall, and standing five or six inches out of the water. Squack saw this rock just before we struck, and gave the canoe a mighty heave to the right, hoping to avoid the rock. But the heave was so mighty and the current so swift and our speed so great, that the bow of the canoe, grazing the rock, shot across the channel and became wedged between two rocks of the wing wall, while the stern settled against the rock against the channel; the craft tilted to the left, almost dipping water on that side. The impact was so great that the occupants were almost thrown out of the canoe, some of our goods and chattels went overboard, our light went out and we were in total darkness. The canoe, thus wedged slaunchwise across the channel, formed a partial dam for the fast rushing water, some of which was forced hissing, splashing and roaring over the wing wall. Jake Fisher and Ed Rider were near me in the bow, and my first thought was of Jake's typewriter. I yelled loud enough to be heard above the torrent, "Jake, where's your typewriter?" "Safe, thank the Lord! Shall I swim out with it?" And then I heard Ed Rider praying: "Oh Lord, Thou knowest that it wasn't anything I had against Thee that caused me to resign as President of the Epworth League — but it was other people butting into my business; Oh Lord, Thou knowest that it wasn't our fault that Charlie Ervin and Squack drunk the liquor we put on the bank where they could — I mean where they found it; Oh Lord, Thou knowest that Jake Fisher didn't mean any harm or commit any real crime when he rocked the train; Oh Lord, Thou knowest that Bill Byrne don't mean nothing by telling such big—" At that juncture the canoe gave a lurch and in order to catch himself Ed shot one foot out in the water on the lower side of the canoe, — and concluded his prayer with — "Hell! this water ain't a foot deep." Thereupon Jake stepped out in the water and waded over to the wing wall, where he sat hugging his typewriter, until the rest of us righted the canoe and again set it afloat.

Filling our lamp with some more of Squack's "gasoline oil," we went our way without further mishap — except what happened to me. Down at Butlers Bend about two miles above Clay, as we got to the head of that little shoal, a blue pike, about 36 inches long, sauntered leisurely up to me like he was going to shake hands with me. I made a quick stab at him with my gig, but succeeded only in speeding him on up the river; whereupon Squack remarked, "I wisht I'd a bin up thar with this push pole: I'd a broke his back"; — and I don't

know to this day whether he referred to me or the pike.
We got some nice carp and a red-horse and a sucker or two
down in the Eagle plains, and with all had a fine lot of
fish, even if I did make the muff at Eagle plains —
and no sun in my eyes, either.   But just as we were at
our journey's end and rounding into our landing in the
rear of John Pettigrew's hotel, came the opportunity to
wind up the campaign in a blaze of glory; atone for the
Eagle Bend bonehead and re-establish myself in the esti-
mation of my comrades as worthy to wield the lance;
for there, close to the edge of the river, in water not over
ten inches deep, and not ten feet away and fast asleep,
was a blue pike a few inches longer than the one I had
so recently missed.   This time I took deliberate aim and
directed the gig for the center of the body of the sleeping fish.   I overshot the mark by an inch, and the pike
tore out of there and away, the worst scared fish in Elk
River.   And Squack again came to the front with the
remark, "And that's the same William Burns what
gigged the red-horse at the mouth of Duck."   Of course,
I had some alibi at the time — but alibis don't count for
a thing on an occasion like that.

XXVIII

CLAY COURT HOUSE; "FISH, BENCH AND BAR"

A T 5:30 the next — or rather the same — morning, — we had gotten to bed about 2:30, all huddled in one room — we were awakened by a thunderous pounding and thumping on our door, and Jake Fisher called out, mad as a hornet, "Who's there?" A voice answered, "It's me," — thump, thump, on the door.

"Who's me?"

"John Pettigrew," thump, thump.

"What do you want?"

"I want you fellers to git up"—thump, thump.

"Oh," said Jake, "I thought you wanted that door."

"No," replied John, "I don't want the door, I want you fellers to git up and clean your fish for breakfast — that is, if you want any of them fish for breakfast, — we ain't got no time to fool with 'em."

"To Helligoland with the fish!" declared some one in our crowd — "we want to sleep," and our landlord retreated, — and yes, we had no fish for breakfast today, that morning.

After breakfast Jake took his typewriter down to the county clerk's office—the small two-room log structure then standing down on the street near the courthouse, and installed it on a table. It was the first typewriter ever seen at Clay Court House, and a crowd at once gathered to view the strange looking machine. George Griffin, attorney at law, from over on the West Fork, and a member of the Clay County Bar, was standing by, and someone asked, "George, what is that thing."

George looked quite wise and owlish for a moment, and with great deliberation and in tones judicial, replied:

"Well, I am not exactly certain whether it is a new patent cornsheller or a knitting machine."

Hon. Virgil S. Armstrong, of Ripley, Jackson County, was judge of the circuit which included Clay County at that time, and the local bar was composed of Mortimer W. Frame and Ed R. Andrews, all residenters, Henry C. Lockney of Calhoun and Clay, William P. Gould, who edited the weekly newspaper and "practized a leetle law" on the side, James M. Frame, son of Mort, and Patrick M. Summers, recent converts, and Henry B. Davenport, who had just landed and hung out his shingle.

The visiting attorneys who at that time attended the courts with more or less frequency, were Capt. Absalom Knotts, of Calhoun, John E. Hays, R. G. Linn, J. Scott Withers and R. F. Kidd of Gilmer, Felix J. Baxter, L. M. Wade and Alex Dulin of Braxton, B. W. Byrne, James F. Brown, Malcolm Jackson, E. B. Dyer, Murray Briggs and J. W. Kennedy of Kanawha, John D. Alderson and Maj. Frank B. Smith of Nicholas, J. W. C. (Chap) Armstrong and Geo. F. Cunningham of Roane, A. B. Wells, Dave Brown and Alf. W. Beall from Roane or Jackson, and John Mac. Butcher and George Griffin from Clay County's outlying precincts.

Mort Frame was the Nestor of the Clay County Bar. All that Mort lacked in profundity of knowledge of the law he more than made up in forensic effort, and, as an advocate before a jury, was one of whom an adversary, however able and astute, had needs beware. With an average education, coupled with his natural zeal and application, Mort Frame would have been a splendid lawyer; but as he has often told me, he was in the Confederate Army for the full four years, covering that period of his life from 16 to 20 years of age, when most other boys were getting an education, and that after the war he was suffering so terribly from a bullet shattered leg, received in one of its last battles, that he was wholly incapacited for three or four years. Mort had acquired the habit of being prosecuting attorney of Clay

County late in the 70's, and with the exception of two or three quadrennial periods, when some Republican took it away from him temporarily, he held that office until the time of his death.

Ed Andrews was one of the greatest natural orators I ever met; eloquent and fluent—a wonderful vocabulary, perfect diction and superb bearing. He could prepare any sort of a court paper, whether a bill in equity, a declaration, a decree or other order with greater facility and rapidity than any other lawyer of my acquaintance. If he had only been blessed with Mort Frame's knack of unremitting zeal and constant application, he would have been a wonderful lawyer. But Ed didn't love work —between terms of court he marked time so far as the law was concerned, and depended on courthouse inspiration alone. But Ed did like to fish, and he was as hard to match with a gig as he was before a jury—and I've tried both many times.

I mention these two celebrities in particular because they are likely to figure more or less conspicuously in these tales.

After the second day after our arrival at Clay, the boys who were not tied up in court decided to go back up the river about six miles to the head of Spread, pitch our tent and start in for regular fishing. We had a good-sized tent which would "sleep" nine or ten people by a little crowding and all "flopping" at the same time, and were equipped with a "cookin' and eatin'" fly of corresponding proportions. So, leaving Jake and myself, who had some court business—Ed Rider, Charlie Bland, Charlie Ervin and Squack took the canoe and all equipment and departed, and Jake and I were to join them when court was over, and bring Ed Andrews, fisherman in general and master gigger in particular, along with us.

After two or three days of court and with but two cases remaining on the court docket to be tried, we

started into the one next to the last, Andrews on one
side and I on the other. During a lull in the proceedings,
I mentioned to Judge Armstrong that as soon as we
finished that case, Ed Andrews and I were going up
to our camp at the head of Spread, and the Judge expressed a keen desire to go along with us; on reflection,
however, he stated that there would be no chance for
him to go because of an engagement elsewhere, unless
we could go the very next day, and that such would be
impossible, because Mort Frame was in the case following the one being tried, and was insisting on a trial;
and that our case and Mort's would consume the whole
of the following day. Chap Armstrong heard our conversation and expressed himself also as anxious to go
with us. Chap was on the opposing side in the case Mort
was so bent on trying, and had already moved for a continuance which the court had refused to grant. Ed Andrews was called into the conference and it was then and
there that a deep, dark-dyed and diabolical plot was
laid against Mort Frame, whereby the Judge and Chap
might be able to go fishing on the morrow, instead of
of wasting the precious hours in a stuffy courtroom. Im-
primis, first and foremost, the court would hold a night
session that night, if necessary to finish the case then
on trial, and Chap, Ed and myself would have a chance
until court opened the next morning, to work on Mort
Frame. We had all heard Mort in his most strenuous,
earnest and emphatic resistance to Chap's motion for a
continuance, and were fully aware that it would be use-
less to employ honest methods to accomplish our purpose; but that we must resort to trickery, connivery, chi-
canery and skulduggery; this we proceeded to do in
the manner following: Mort Frame lived in the extreme
lower end of the town, about a quarter of a mile below
the courthouse, and bright and early the next morning,
I strolled down past Mort's residence and lay in wait
for him to come out of the house on his way to court.

Presently he appeared, walking quite briskly, and I timed my pace so as to meet him face to face at his gate. Looking at him intently for a moment I said, "Mort, what in the world is the matter with you?"

"Me—Oh nothing—I feel all right."

"Well, you don't look it—why man, you are pale as a ghost."

"Well, the fact is I didn't sleep good last night—my old Confederate leg, you know—was hurtin' me again."

"You look like a sick man to me, Mort."

By this time we had walked about 50 yards up the road, and happened to meet Ed Andrews, who greeted us: "Good morning, gentlemen — why Mort Frame! What on earth is the matter with you?"

"Oh, I don't know—just didn't sleep good last night—I guess."

"You look like a ghost to me—you ought to be taking care of yourself, old man," said Ed as he passed on. I took Mort's arm and we proceeded only a short distance when we happened to meet Alf Beall who chipped in with—

"What's the matter, Mort—sick? Where are you taking him, Bill? To the doctor?"

"No," said Mort, "not much sick—guess I must have eaten something last night that didn't agree with me—didn't sleep much and couldn't eat much breakfast."

We next encountered Henry Davenport, who had just located at Clay, who expressed great concern and alarm at Mort's emaciated condition, his pallor and his apparent general debilitation — felt his pulse and pronounced him on the verge of total collapse; whereupon along came Alex Dulin, who stopped to comment upon Mort's woebegone appearance and to express concern and sympathy. By this time Mort remembered that he had been working very hard in court all week and had lost a great deal of sleep, and that his Confederate leg had bothered him a good deal.

I still held on to Mort's arm and by the time we met Jake Fisher, Mort's gait was rather wobbly. Jake was very solicitous about Mort's welfare and asked many questions and offered many suggestions, among which was that he go immediately for Dr. Carr. Mort was getting sicker and sicker all the time, but demurred to Jake's suggestion about calling in a physician—explaining that he hadn't felt well when court began, and that he had worked unusually hard during the term, had been up late every night and not able to sleep when he got to bed, and nothing he had eaten seemed to agree with him, and his Confederate leg pained him all the time, and that he was just about all in, but would be all right when court was over and he could rest up a few days. "Well," said Jake, "if you take my advice you'll go right home and go to bed where you belong."

I next steered Mort into Judge Armstrong, who likewise was greatly shocked to see him looking so awfully bad, and expressed great solicitude for his well-being, and then, casually, "By the way, haven't you a case you wanted to try today?"

"Well, yes, Judge, I did want to try that case, but the way I'm feeling, I thought if it was all right with you and we could get hold of Chap Armstrong, maybe we could arrange to let it be continued till next term." Just at that moment, by some strange chance, Chap emerged from Hans Reed's store, and under the circumstances agreed to a general continuance. Somebody's horse and buggy happened to be standing close by, and into that buggy we tenderly loaded Mort, and instructed the driver to straightway deliver him to his home and put him to bed; which was accordingly done; Judge Armstrong promptly adjourned court, and in thirty minutes our fishing crowd, in Ed Andrews' canoe, was on its way to the head of Spread.

True to his promise, Mort was up and about in a few days, fully recovered; and I am glad to say that when

I next saw him, about two months later, Mort was in finer fettle than he had been for years, and told me he believed I had saved his life by putting him to bed.

On our way up to camp, Ed Andrews killed a pike in that little shoal at Butler's Bend, where I had missed one on our way down. When we exhibited it to Squack and told him where it was killed, that gentleman swore that he was able to positively identify it as the same one "William Burns missed—cause you see it hain't got a mark on it only where Andrews hit it—and neither did William's."

We had taken our time going up, passing over some splendid gigging ground, and it was almost noon when we arrived at the camp. The boys were rather expecting us, and Squack greeted us with the information that they had had a big pot of "mark tortle" soup. It seems some of them had killed an enormous soft-shell turtle, too big and tough to use except for soup purposes; they had out a trotline, and had been fishing diligently with pole and line for several days, some one had killed a lot of squirrels and gigged fish and bullfrogs, until they had the makin' of a pretty good dinner, everything considered, and we certainly "et hearty."

There was but one thing to mar the enjoyment of that dinner, and that was the utter ruination of Squack's prize and only story. On the evening we left Sutton, as we were proceeding down the river, some of the boys were telling stories, and finally Squack chipped in with one that made quite a hit, which we had Squack repeat on several occasions after the first telling which he always did, gladly and verbatim et literatim.

While we were absorbing our "mark tortle" soup, someone suggested that Squack tell his story for Judge Armstrong, and Squack snapped into it without any urging whatever:

"There wuz a feller that got married an' his woman died an' then he married another woman—an' there was a ole colored feller had lived with him when his fust woman wuz livin'—an' a feller come along an' says to the old colored feller, that he heered his boss had got him another woman, an' he told him he had, an' then the feller axed the old colored feller had his boss tuck her ary bridal tower yit, an' the old colored feller said he didn't know, but that when his tother woman wuz a livin' he allus tuck a paddle to her."

Generous applause, led by Squack himself, greeted the recital, Judge Armstrong joining in, but with a rather puzzled expression on his face.

"Young man," said the Judge, "I have heard that story before, but not exactly that way; in fact I don't believe you just get the point of the story—when the old darkey told the man that his master had married a second wife, the man asked, "Did he take a bridal tour?" and the darky, misunderstanding the question, answered that when his old missus was alive, he took a paddle to her. You see young man, it is a play on the words "tour" and "to her."

Poor Squack! While he understood but vaguely, it was well enough to realize that there was something radically wrong with his story, and no amount of persuasion or cajolery could induce him ever again to repeat it; and only one who had heard his recital can appreciate our loss for the balance of the trip.

The only allusion I ever heard Squack make concerning the unfortunate incident, was a week later when we were homeward bound and all of us with two or three visitors were gathered around the campfire spinning yarns, Squack was sitting rather apart from the rest of the crowd, listening intently to every story told, and quite restless during each intermission, but uttering never a word. Something was gnawing Squack's vitals, and I knew what it was. He opened his mouth to speak, and I thought glory be! here comes that story for the benefit of our visitors; but what Squack said was: "Them judges think they know so damn much!"

The afternoon of Judge Armstrong's visit to our camp was a red letter day in his fishing life. Unaccustomed to fishing, except for the smaller varieties to be found in the rather small streams of Jackson County, he was anxious to catch a real Elk River bass—man's size—or a blue pike. I got a nice bucket of creek chubs —horny-heads—and took him over to those cliffs opposite the mouth of Little Laurel and in thirty minutes he had landed a beautiful 22-inch bass that would have weighed something over four pounds. Then happened something the like of which I never saw before or since; there was in our bait bucket a fine seven or eight-inch horny-head, and I put it carefully on the Judge's hook—a large size bass hook—and told him to go forth and catch a pike. In a few minutes something took his hook and moved off down the river. I was sure it was a pike, and as the Judge did not have much line, I paddled the canoe, gently following downstream, and cautioned the Judge to give him line and plenty of time to swallow the bait. Suddenly the line stopped, and the Judge, supposing the time was up, gave a mighty jerk; out of the water and high in the air snapped the line bait, and the horny-head, still on the hook, landed splash in the water within a foot of the canoe—when almost instantly the "tiger of the water" again seized it with a ferocity and an impetus that made the water boil, and struck out for midstream. Luckily, the line did not foul and again we followed with line and canoe until the pike stopped, and then gave him plenty of time to turn in his mouth and swallow the horny-head; which being done, he moved off slowly, and the Judge struck him. A thirty-two inch blue pike, as this one proved to be, puts up no mean scrap especially for a fellow who is not accustomed to such warfare, but the Judge handled him beautifully, finally wore him down, and we towed him out on the bar at the mouth of Little Laurel.

That night Ed and I, with Squack as steersman, took the Judge and Chap out gigging, covering the stretch of about three miles up to and through Turkey Run plains, always good night-ground in those days. I suppose we killed a lot of fish, as we usually did, but the outstanding recollection of that entire day was the spectacular assault that pike made on the horny-head, and how tickled the Judge was over his thrilling experience.

XXIX

ED ANDREWS, CHARLIE BLAND; FLOODS, FLIES; SAVAGETOWN AND ELK RIVER IRON; A STRANGE MAN ON STRANGE CREEK

OUR CAMP was one of the choice locations, for fishing of any and all kinds, to be found on Elk River. Splendid water for gigging up and down the river for three or four miles; the river was full of bass and pike; and we set in to make a regular "killin'." But I think it was the second day after Ed Andrews, Jake Fisher and I joined the party, that it began to rain, and kept at it, with but slight intermissions, day and night, for two or three days, and soon there was a log tide of eight or ten feet in the river, which, of course, put a quietus to all fishing and likewise prevented us from getting back up the river until the flood subsided and the swift current abated. But the worst feature of the whole business was that when the first rain came, it found everybody away from camp, and all our belongings scattered about helter-skelter, so that by the time the first to arrive got back to camp, we found everything soaked and sopping; bedclothes, grub and wearing apparel — everything wet as water could make them; and to add to our discomfiture, the intermittent rains and showers following the first, gave us no show to dry out anything except such articles as we could shelter under the fly and expose to the heat of the campfire five or six feet away. The upshot of it was that we laid around camp three or four days until the rain quit and the river fell sufficiently to permit up-river navigation, when we struck camp and started for Sutton — losing Jake Fisher and Ed Andrews who returned to Clay in Ed's canoe.

About the only fun we had after it began to rain grew out of a mix-up caused by the fact that Ed Andrews introduced Charlie Bland to some of our neighbors as being Ed Rider, and some amusing incidents resulting; but we will have to postpone that story to another time, as we must be getting up the river before it rains some more.

We could not make much speed on our return trip owing to the stiff current, so it was later in the afternoon of the first day out that we neared the mouth of Groves Creek, about twelve and a half miles above Spread. Marshall Colebank had lived for several years at the old William Waggy place a short distance up Groves Creek from its mouth, and his wife was a splendid cook, as I could well attest from numerous occasions on which I had enjoyed the fine hospitality of their home; so I told the boys that as we were approaching a place where we could get some real grub, we would dispose of all the water-soaked and mildewed stuff we had on hand — and overboard went all our bread and flour and meal and everything else except what bacon we had left. As we came up over the long shoal I spied Marshall Colebank and one of his small boys standing on the bank at the mouth of the creek, and with all the impudent assurance of an old acquaintance called to him, "Marshall, run up to the house and tell the boss that five hungry friends of hers are about to pay her a visit — she'll know what to do."

"Well, gentlemen," said Marshall, "I know she'd be glad to see you, if you will go over the mountain on Frame's Run where we've moved to — but we don't live here any more." And that was that, — all our grub thrown away and nothing in sight. Finally Marshall suggested that we go up and occupy the house which he had vacated and that some of us go with him over the mountain two miles away and he would let us have enough grub to keep the wolf from the door for a short spell at least. So Charlie Bland and Charlie Ervin volunteered as the forage squad and went along with Marshall and his boy, returning long after dark with about a half bushel of fine biscuits, half a dozen nice fat pullets, a small razor-back ham — for which the Colebank table was always famous — and other odds and ends to suit the occasion.

In the meantime Ed Rider had gone across the river to Groves Mill and gotten a bucketful of corn meal. Squack and I had a good wood fire burning in the fireplace by the time Ed returned with the meal, and I concluded we would have ash cakes to supplement what the boys might bring back from Colebank's. I mixed up a goodly batch of meal, with water and a little salt, dug a couple of fair-sized holes in the glowing red embers and ashes on the hearth, filled them with the corn dough, raked the ashes and embers over the top, and sat down and awaited the outcome, keeping the hot ashes and embers well replenished all the while. When the Colebank provisions arrived and supper was ready, I dug out my ash cakes and placed them on the festal board. The outward appearance of these cakes was anything but inviting — charred black as they were, — but remembering that an uncouth exterior is oft presented by the rarest virtue, nothing daunted, I took the butcher knife and chopped one of the cakes into five as nearly as possible equal pieces — showing no favoritism. Squack, deciding he would take corn bread in his'n, and reaching for a hunk of the ash cake, stuck one corner in his mouth; we heard a crunch—a snap! Squack slowly rose from his "hunkers," with a pained expression on his face, walked to the door with the piece of ash cake in his hand and came back in a few moments minus the ash cake and one front tooth. The remaining four of us ate Colebank biscuits — preferring them to corn bread, anyway.

The other four pieces of the particular ash cake got lost somewhere in the shuffle; but the other cake remained an unviolated unit and one of the boys took it home with him as a memento of the trip. I saw it two or three years later, used to prop open a cellar door.

We got as far as Strange Creek the next morning, when it began to rain, and we left our canoe and hustled off to George Goad's store for shelter.

And now something about Strange Creek, or Savage-town, as it was generally called in those days:

About the early or middle seventies, two very enter-prising gentlemen from Jackson, Ohio, Jesse S. Savage and W. A. (Al) Savage, brothers, had prospected the country at and near the mouth of Strange Creek, and found numerous and rather extensive deposits of a very superior quality of iron ore on and along the adjacent hillsides, points and ridges, and a more or less capricious stratum of limestone in the same vicinity. Talk of a railroad to be immediately constructed from Charles-ton up the valley of the Elk, was rife at the time, and the Savage brothers decided to take time by the forelock, and build, equip and have in operation against the ad-vent of the railroad, a charcoal blast furnace to convert the iron ore into pig. This was accordingly done, and along with the furnace they built up quite a thriving village along the river front about the mouth of the creek and in the creek bottom nearby. This village was christened Savagetown, in honor of its founders and finishers. Quite an active business was carried on for awhile until the project was fully set on foot and put in operation; but the railroad having failed to materialize, it became necessary to devise some other method of transportation for their product, and the barge and flat-boat were built at a boat yard on the river bank above the mouth of the creek. One barge, heavily laden with pig iron, set out on a flush stage for Charleston, manned by the most experienced log-raft and flatboat steersman and bowmen to be found on Elk River; but the craft was so heavily laden that in going around the "End of the World" bend, the boatmen were powerless to hold it off the south bank, and it was so ground and battered by the rocks therealong, that it wrecked and sank a short distance below. Later, the cargo was transferred to flatboats, moderately loaded, and floated out to its destination; and thereafter the heavily loaded and unmanageable barge was discarded and only lighter draught flatboats were employed. Many a flatboat loaded with Savagetown pig iron went down Elk River to Charleston, Ironton, Ashland, and Portsmouth. But the disposition of these flatboats soon became a problem. There being no possible way of getting the boat back to Savagetown, each cargo of iron meant the building of a new flatboat, and as a matter of course the boat must be sold where the cargo was marketed, else a dead loss. For a time there was a ready market for such craft, largely to Kanawha salt makers; but just about that time the Michigan salt makers dead-rented the greater part of the Kanawha salt works, closed them down and eventually put them out of business, thus killing the market for flatboats, formerly in such great demand for transporting Kanawha salt to the lower Ohio and Mississippi. The handicaps became so numerous and insuperable that about 1879 the plant was closed down and abandoned, and in 1885, when I first became acquainted with the place, the once pretentious Savagetown was but a memory, and but a grinning skeleton of stonework, stood to mock and to mark the place of the once proud edifice known as the Savagetown Blast Furnace.

George Goad came to Savagetown in its early days, and in the year 1885, he was the "Last of the Mohicans" —he and his family being the sole and only residents of the town. George had become quite a prominent citizen of Braxton County; was an extensive farmer and stock-raiser, timber dealer, merchant and general business man; then and later, quite active in politics, serving his county one or more terms in the House of Delegates and one term as Sheriff. He was well known and knew everybody throughout the county and was universally regarded as one of the shrewdest traders and dealers anywhere to be found. He had accumulated a goodly portion of worldly goods, and was as able to take care of what belonged to him as the next one.

Wet and dripping, we had rushed into his store, bitterly complaining that our homeward journey should be interrupted by the rain, and were greeted most cordially by the proprietor, with whom we were all well acquainted.

Only a few minutes later a horseman rode up, alighted, hitched his horse at the hitch-rail in front of the store, and hurried into the room. This newcomer proved to be Dave Evans, of Frametown, who came to see George Goad on a very special mission it seemed at the start, as Dave beckoned George off into a secluded corner, and sought to have private converse with him; but George seeming to feel that we were his guests and entitled to all the attendant amenities, brought Dave and his proposition out in the open, where we could all be included in the conversation, with the statement— "So you say, Dave, the idea is to start a new bank at Sutton."

"Yes," said Dave, "that's the idea, exactly."

"Do you really think, Dave, that there is enough business for two banks at Sutton—doesn't the Sutton Bank seem to be able to take care of the business all right?"

"Well, you see there's lots of fellers around over the county complaining that they can't get no accommodations; that the way "Jake" Hyer is running the Sutton Bank, it's just him and a few friends of his that gits the benefit, and anybody on the outside has a hard time to borrow any money."

"Well, Dave, I've got a little stock in the Sutton Bank —not much—and I've been at some of the meetings, and I know everybody interested in the bank thinks Jake Hyer is a mighty good and safe banker, and he's running it just like we want him to run it—safe and sound."

"Well, but the trouble is, they ain't got enough capital. The idea is to organize a new bank with a big capital stock and run it on a more up-to-date plan and be in shape to accommodate more people—do a big business all over the country."

"Who are the fellers you're counting on to run this new bank, Dave?"

"Why, there's a lot of them—there's So and So, and So and So"—naming on his fingers seven or eight well known citizens of the county, well distributed to cover every important section—everyone named being a man well known to George and also well known to us to be congenitally and habitually of the borrowing type, and not so careful of their financial obligations.

"Now let's see," said George, "you say there's So and So and So and So"—carefully renaming on his fingers, each of those named by Dave—"they are the fellers that's to run her?"

"They are the ones," said Dave.

"Well, say, Dave—don't you reckon she'll suck herself."

Dave didn't stay long after the rain quit—nor did we, for that matter; but we did not depart until each of us had told George how we had enjoyed our short stay with him, and how genuinely glad we were that we had been driven by the rain to seek refuge in his store at that particular time—and every fellow meant it. That story, each of us felt, had not cost us half its worth.

No one is ever allowed to write anything of or concerning Strange Creek without answering the inevitable and natural question—"How did that creek get its name?" I have heard numerous versions, but the one which seems to be most authentic is this:

About the year 1795, a party of surveyors, engaged in locating some large land grants made by the State of

Virginia along Elk River, found on the high river bank at the mouth of the creek in question, the bleached, but well preserved skeleton of a man at the root of a huge beech tree, and nearby, a small pile of rocks and some remnants of charred wood, indicating that there had once been a campfire; and the smooth bark of the beech bore, quite legibly but somewhat crudely carved by means of what was doubtless a large hunting knife, the inscription:

> Strange my name,
> And strange the ground,
> And strange that I
> Cannot be found."

I saw a man who said he saw the original inscription on the bark of that beech.

Whether the eponymist—I saw that word forty years ago, when reading a review of "Robert Elsmere," and have ever since been honing for a good chance to use it—of that creek was a man by the name of Strange, or whether the meaning of the inscription was that his was a name that would be strange to the finder of the remains and the epitaph, has always seemed to be more or less a question of dispute; but I have been inclined to the view that there was a man by the name of Strange, and in a spirit of humor that later developments made gruesome, intended a play upon his own name in his reference to the ground and to his hopefully hopeless condition.

I knew John Strange who lived in another section of Braxton County. His forebears came from Virginia to Braxton County about 1840, but he was not aware that any of his connection had ever so disappeared.

As we proceeded up the river from Strange Creek to the mouth of Birch, the sun came out with great brilliancy and in the trees along the river's edge a lot of squirrels got on a rampage among the wet branches, making of themselves an easy mark to shoot from the canoe. Some of the boys bagged four or five nice plump ones, and those squirrels and one of the nice fat pullets we got from Colebank, made us a mighty fine dinner that day. This cooked in the canoe as we traveled along, by the following recipe: Cut up squirrels and chicken as you would to fry; one-half pound fat bacon cut up in small chunks; and place in a ten-quart tin bucket, with a little water; pour carefully into one pint tin cup some one-third of a pint of gasoline; set tin cup flat on bottom of canoe; strike one match and apply same to the gasoline, and when ignition gets under full headway, take the bucket by its bail and hold same over and within two or three inches of the top of the tin cup. To replenish your gasoline, which must be done several times, let the tin cup burn perfectly dry, and let it cool before touching with hand. When thoroughly cooled, cool it some more by dipping in the river, and let it dry thoroughly, then carefully give it another dose of gasoline; repeat until meat is thoroughly done; take the large biscuits gotten from Colebank, split each one through the middle as nearly as possible, drop tenderly in the bucket; remove bucket from tin cup; let simmer a few minutes by the watch, if you have a watch, if not, by the sun, season to taste; eat. But don't touch that tin cup until the gasoline is gone.

Well, that's the way we did it—and five hungry men never sat down to a finer meal. I would not, however, recommend this for a steady diet—that is the gasoline feature—as I have been told that what we did was both foolish and dangerous; and the fact that we got by with it, does not detract in the slightest from its folly. And they do say that gasoline of 1894 was not nearly so "quick on trigger" as the product of the present day. So don't try it unless you have double indemnity accident policy written in large figures.

We got back to Sutton without further casualty or outstanding incident; and in checking up, voted that we had not done so bad for a fishing trip, all things considered; having lost only one man—and he not a very big one—not nearly as big then as he is now—one second-hand Caligraph typewriter, and one front tooth.

XXX

A LOOK AT LAND TITLES AND STREAM NAMES; SAM FOX, THE MERCHANT, SELLS OUT

FOR a great many years following the earlier settlement of the Valley of the Elk, there was a stretch of almost exactly fifty miles extending from the mouth of Birch River, which is 76 miles above Charleston, down to the mouth of Queen Shoal Creek, 26 miles above that city, which, owing to its inaccessibility to the outer world, was very sparsely settled, and was commonly called "The Wilderness." From Charleston up, the river hills rise gradually, but do not attain any very great elevation, until the mouth of Queen Shoal Creek is reached, and there are many good-sized streams on either side which drain comparatively low hilly sections, which were taken up by actual settlers very early in the nineteenth century; so from Sutton down to the mouth of Birch River, a distance of about twenty miles, the hills are comparatively low and the back-lying lands inviting for agricultural purposes, and settlers along the river and upon adjacent back lands became quite numerous. But this fifty miles of intervening "Wilderness," for a great number of years, with the exception of a very few cabins along the river, was almost entirely unpopulated as late as the year 1850. Gradually, the settlement increased from Queen Shoal up, and from Birch River down, so that the fifty miles of "Wilderness," so called, had been reduced by the year 1870 or thereabouts, to the nineteen miles from Clay Court House up to the mouth of Groves Creek. Another reason for the dearth of early settlement of this section, was the fact that the entire south side of Elk River, from the mouth of Birch River to the mouth of Queen Shoal Creek, was covered by two surveys made in the year 1795, for William Wilson, one of 93,000 acres, later granted by the Commonwealth of Virginia to the said Wilson, and the other 12,300 acres granted to Benjamin Martin, Assignee of Wilson.

At that time the County of Kanawha extended almost as far up Elk as the present Frametown, several miles above Birch River, and the two Wilson surveys were embraced wholly within that county.

I have often had occasion to examine these two old surveys; and believing they may contain something of interest to persons acquainted with the Valley of the Elk, I secured photoprints of each of the original plats of these surveys as they appear in Surveyors Book No. 1, in the office of the Clerk of the County Court of Kanawha County, and they are here shown.

Both these surveys were made by Andrew Johnson, assistant of Reuben Slaughter, Surveyor of Kanawha County, the 93,000-acre survey reported as being made on the fifth day of May, 1795, and the 12,300 acres on the following day, May 6.

It will be interesting to note the names of the streams as indicated on the plats, not one of which, excepting Birch River, is the name by which any stream mentioned is known today.

The report of survey accompanying the 93,000 acres calls for beginning at two beech trees at the mouth and upper side of Birch River and running thence down Elk River with its meanders and binding thereon, 8546 poles to short bend in the river 92 poles below the mouth of Sycamore Creek, "crossing the creek that's named in the plan, at the following distances each of their mouths from the two beeches at the mouth of Birch River"—to Turkey Creek 644 poles; thence to Falls Creek 1684 poles; thence to Camp Creek 590 poles; thence to Raccoon Creek 2166 poles; thence to Island Creek 2454 poles; thence to Sycamore Creek 916 poles; and thence 92 poles to the corner. Any one familiar with Elk

River, upon inspecting the plat, will recognize the bends
in the river as a fair representation of its meanders, and
will further realize the fact that with the exception
of Birch River, not one of the side streams as laid down
on the plat bears the same name at the present day as
that given it on the plat; Turkey Creek on the map is the
present Strange Creek; Falls Creek is now known as
Groves Creek. Note the marks extending zigzag from
one side of the river to the other as shown on the plat at
this point. And this verifies the tradition that formerly
two strata or ledges of sandstone each about 18 inches
thick and about ten feet apart horizontally, presented
their broken edges and extended across the river at this
point, forming distinct falls. Later, in order to facilitate
the passage of canoes and light water craft, a chute was
made by cutting or blasting out the ledges so as to give
the water a uniform pitch, from the head to the foot of
the long, steep shoal which begins at the mouth of the
present Groves Creek. This is, next to Queen Shoal, probably the longest and steepest shoal on Elk River, having a fall of more than six feet.

The next creek, shown on the plat as Camp Creek, now
bears the somewhat less euphonious name of Jumping
Gut. Here will be noted on the plat, immediately above
the mouth of this creek, the small triangle diagram
which was commonly employed by old surveyors to
mark the place at which they camped while making
the survey. And the circumstances would seem to indicate that Assistant Surveyor Andrew Johnson gave
this the name of Camp Creek in commemoration of the
fact that he and his surveying crew had camped on its
banks; and to me this all bears a peculiar significance
in the fact that on the identical spot, represented by that
triangle, now stands the Camp at the End of the World,
my fishing camp.

The surveyor has largely magnified the importance
of this creek on the map; as it would appear by com-

parison, to be almost equal in size to Falls or Groves Creek, while, as a mater of fact, Groves Creek is about ten miles long, and Jumping Gut is little if any more than two. He was doubtless deceived by its appearance at the mouth, which would indicate a much larger stream than it really is, owing to the fact that its pitch is so great that what little water falls within its basin comes out to the river so quickly and with such a rush and fury as to tear up and carry off everything in its way to cut a wide swathe, so to speak—especially at the mouth. I suppose that is the reason the name was changed from sober Camp Creek to riotous Jumping Gut.

Raccoon Creek on the plat is easily recognized as Standing Rock Creek, about two miles below Otter. Island Creek is the present Big Buffalo, opposite the upper end of the town of Clay, and immediately at the mouth of which the important railroad station, Dundon, is located. Note the three islands in the river, one immediately at the mouth of the creek, one above and one below. Within my own recollection the two uppermost islands were there in all their integrity, and the third and lower one, was represented by a great bar. There are three sand and gravel bars there now, but nothing which might be properly called an island. As late as 30 years ago this upper island consisted of about half an acre of ground as high as the adjacent river bottom lands, fringed with trees as large as two feet in diameter, and for many years Solomon Reed and afterward, Dr. Claudius Carr, used the land thereof for a garden. The middle island, though covered with large trees, did not rise so high above the water and was never put to any use.

Sycamore Creek on the plat is the present Big Leatherwood, three miles below Clay.

Just why Assistant Surveyor Andrew Johnson should have so proceeded, may be something of a mystery, but according to his official report, having surveyed the

93,000 acres on the fifth day of May, on the following day, the sixth, instead of continuing on down the river from the corner 92 poles below Sycamore or Big Leatherwood, it appears that he went down the river 6608 poles to the mouth of a small creek, and there began and ran back up the river to the same place he had quit the day before; for the report says, May 6, 1795, began at 2 beeches on the bank of Elk River, on South East side, at mouth and upper side of a small creek, corner to John Barclays survey of 50,000 acres. This small creek is easily identified as Queen Shoal Creek, which is the line on that side of the river, between Kanawha and Clay counties. The report proceeds: "Thence up Elk River with meanders and binding thereon, 6608 poles to a short bend in the river 92 poles below Sycamore Creek, corner to survey of William Wilson of 93,000 acres, crossing the creeks that's named in the plan at following distances each of their mouths from the 2 beeches."

To Johns Creek, 510 poles; this is the present Porters Creek; thence to Otter Creek 3556 poles—now Little Sycamore; thence to Leatherwood Creek 584 poles— now Big Sycamore. Here is another triangle camp sign, showing that the party camped on the high bank just above the creek; thence to Mountain Creek 770 poles— now Middle Creek—"and 240 poles above that said corner."

The fact that the names of these creeks have been changed since these two surveys were made in 1795, and especially that Leatherwood and Sycamore have swapped names; that Mountain Creek is now called Middle Creek, Otter Creek is now known as Little Sycamore, and Johns Creek is the present Porters Creek, was judicially determined in the year 1896, by the Supreme Court of Appeals of West Virginia, in the ejectment case of Bishop John J. Kain vs. Samuel E. Young, 41 W. Va. 618, in which Judge Henry Brannon, the learned jurist who wrote the opinion, takes occasion to declare:

"Time has made in the century, such changes in perishable things, that though he (the Surveyor) named in the old surveys from Birch River to Sandy, in what was forty years ago known as the "Wilderness," have changed the names from those given them in the surveys. * * * But, although the names of the streams have gone, the streams themselves 'go on forever,' * * * The name 'Leatherwood Creek' is not the same as the name 'Sycamore' called for in the grant, but is clearly the stream intended."

Anyone good in arithmetic will discover a discrepancy of almost 1000 poles between the distance stated in the report from the mouth of the Small Creek—Queen Shoal—up to the corner of the 93,000-acre survey, the distance called for between the intervening creeks "that's named on the plan"; and it is clear to one familiar with the ground that this discrepancy may be accounted for in the distance called for between Leatherwood or Big Sycamore and Mountain or Middle Creek, as it is nearer 1770 poles or five and one-half miles than 770 poles, or two and four-tenths miles, between these two points. But what was a mere matter of a thousand poles in those days when land was so plentiful that nobody would pay two cents an acre for it and keep up the taxes, which, plus the cost of surveying, was all it cost in the year of grace 1795.

According to tradition the survey made by the surveyors, Johnson, along the Elk River for these two Wilson surveys, was made by the use of two canoes, a compass and a small line about the size of a trotline, and three hundred feet in length; the surveyor and a helper in one canoe would plant his Jacob-staff at the edge of the river and send two men in the other canoe down the river with one end of the 300-foot line; at the end of the distance they would plant a sight-rod in shallow water or on the edge of the bank according to the conditions, on which rod the surveyor would take his sight with the compass; the surveyor and his helper would then drop their canoe downstream winding up the line, until their canoe had passed the other one, which was held stationary with the aid of the sight-rod planted as aforesaid, and then unwind the line and proceed downstream until another 300-foot point was reached, there again plant the sight-rod—and so on down the river from the mouth of Birch River to the mouth of Queen Shoal Creek. The question of the accuracy of this sort of measurement naturally arises; and the answer is, first that this line was kept thoroughly wet all the time, and those who handled it were careful to give it the same tension each time as measurement was taken; second, it was not accurate; and third, there was no particular reason why it should be accurate, as the creeks were there to speak for themselves, and such natural monuments will control both distance and magnetic course. And but for the fact that these plats show with fair accuracy the very peculiar meandering of the river, there would be no reason to suppose that a compass was used at all, or anything in fact except something with which to measure distances.

The next puzzling question would seem to be how the surveyor was able to run all the lines of the 93,000-acre survey, not only involving about 28 miles of river front, but lines reaching back many miles and taking in a large territory of the Gauley drainage, on the fifth day of May, and on the sixth to run the 22 miles of river frontage of the 12,300-acre survey and as well the numerous back lines, and the answer to this puzzle is that the reports were made on those dates and that the surveying itself was the work of weeks. But what I cannot understand is that they camped only twice in running out the river lines from Birch River to Queen Shoal Creek, however it may have been surveyed.

When I first became acquainted with the territory at and near the mouth of Birch, Benton Mollohan owned and operated a water mill just below and on the opposite side of Elk from the mouth of Birch River, and Sam Fox had a store nearby.

Sam Fox was one of the most prominent and influential citizens of Braxton County at that time and was held in the highest esteem by all who knew him. He was a member of the County Court at the time I was Prosecuting Attorney of the county and I was in a position to know and appreciate his high character as an official and as a citizen. He was an "Old Virginian" by birth, but came to Braxton County when quite a young man. In manner he was suave and affable — serene as a May morning ordinarily; but when, on rare occasions, under great stress and provocation, he did lose his temper, he went straight up and never got back on his feet until the flurry had blown over, after which his gentle manner would assume its sway and it would be months before another outbreak.

A typical Sam Fox story is that not long after he had established the store at the mouth of Birch and had built up quite an extensive trade in the general neighborhood, his being the only establishment of the kind within a radius of several miles — weather and river conditions, such as to prevent him from operating a canoe between his place of business and Charleston, his only means and source of supply, prevailed for such a great length of time, that his stock on hand had become depleted almost to the vanishing point, and his patrons were clamoring for "store goods" which he had not. So, as soon as he could safely venture forth, he and two other sturdy canoemen, set forth for Charleston in his canoe of about 3,000 pounds burden. After about six days the canoe, loaded to the guards, hove in sight and was hailed with delight by the expectant multitude assembled on the bank at the then almost vacant store. Sam and his two men, weary from their six days' arduous toil, proceeded promptly to unload the canoe and carry the boxes up the bank and into the store. No sooner was the first load deposited than at the demand of some customer he had to open the boxes or packages, and in a jiffy all the contents were gobbled up by the waiting customers; the next load and the next met the same fate, and then Sam began to get mad, and not only began to get, but got — and rising upon his hind legs and waving both arms wildly about him he commanded — "Git out of here, git out of this store, every goldarned one of you git out, I say, and git out quick! Do you suppose I'm going to spend a whole week pushing this load of goods from Charleston, and then sell 'em all out in one day? Not by a darn sight!!" And he put everybody out, locked the store, put the key in his pocket and went home. And there he stayed until the next morning.

John Vickers, one of Charleston's far-famed fishermen, has, for several years, maintained a fishing camp at the mouth of Birch, and that is the main reason for the scarcity of fish in that vicinity and for several miles above and below. While he does no off-color fishing either by prohibited methods or out of season, the bass and other game fish just naturally flock to his fly or other lure, and he gets his bag limit every day — he just can't help it. John invited me to his camp two or three years ago when the season was well under way. He explained that he had caught everything in the main river, but that he had not done any fishing in Birch, and suggested that we try that stream. John had one little fourteen-foot canoe, in which we started off; he was the host in the stern with the paddle and I was the guest, in the bow with the fly rod. We had proceeded about a mile, when I insisted that we swap ends and that I paddle while he fished. We tried it; but, as John weighed 230 pounds and my weight at that time was just one hundred pounds less, the bow of the light canoe ploughed so deep in the water and elevated the stern to such an extent that it was impossible either to propel or to steer the craft, and we were compelled to change ends again, and I was compelled ,to do all the fishing for another mile up to where we landed, and from which point we waded and both fished for another mile or such a matter.

On our return to the canoe, John, in a tone of high command, said, "Now, Bill, you get back in the stern and grab that paddle." I meekly obeyed. Whereupon John hunted around on the bank and soon came lugging a huge rock of about a hundred weight, which he carefully placed in the canoe in front of the bow seat. I said, "John, what in the world are you doing?"

"Never mind, Bill; just keep your mouth shut and your eyes open, and you'll learn something." And with this remark he pushed the canoe for deep water and stepped in close behind the rock. The canoe responded immediately with a nose dive, turned over and sent John, the hundred-pound rock, and myself, lumbering into the river.

All John said at this time was, "Oh, you just looked like you needed a bath." But later, when we were back in the canoe, John paddling homeward and I in the bow with the rod, he volunteered the remark apropos of whatever it was apropos of:

"Well, sir, it's strange how the best minds will get flabbergasted and act exactly backwards sometimes."

XXXI

BIRCH RIVER DAYS, COL. ALBERT LEWIS, A HIGH SILK HAT; JUDGE JOHN BRANNON

IN THE Chronicles of the Elk, Birch River is of sufficient importance to entitle it to more than a mere passing notice. It is Elk River's largest tributary, being almost 50 miles in length from its mouth to its head branches, which extend to within less than a mile of Cowen in Webster County, which is exactly on the divide between Laurel Creek of Elk River and The Big Ditch, a small tributary of Gauley, the lower two-thirds of its length being in Braxton and the upper one-third in Webster County, and the old Weston and Gauley Bridge Turnpike, now State Highway No. 4, crosses it at Birch River P. O., now so called — formerly the Ford of Birch — about halfway between head and mouth. From this crossing downward, Birch River drains a comparatively good farming section, which becomes exceptionally good for the last six or eight miles of its course, the hills low-lying and many of them comparatively flat on top. But for the upper half of the Birch drainage the hills have gradually grown to mountains with the exception of the narrow river bottoms, the land is steep and rugged, and offers little inducement from the standpoint of agriculture. And it was this very characteristic that, in the days of big game in central West Virginia, made the upper reaches of Birch River the favored section for the hunter and the trapper. The earliest settlers of that locality were hunters who went for the deer and bear and wild turkey which there abounded, built a camp here and there, and being so pleased with the prospect, these camps were succeeded by log cabins to which these hunters moved their families, cleared out a few acres for a garden, corn, 'tater and sorghum patch, and took up their permanent abode. A marvelous change has been wrought since I was first in that locality, forty-five years ago on a hunting expedition, when we had to follow a pack-saddle trail to get up the river from the ford, and found only a few log cabins, along the way,—and what I found last summer, when Holmes Morton of Charleston, and Frank Fisher of Sutton, and I drove over the identical route in Holmes Morton's big Graham-Paige, from this same ford, now supplanted by a handsome concrete bridge, up the river and out at its head and on to Cowen; not a paved road, it is true, but a rather decent dirt road, navigable for an automobile—if skillfully managed—as was the one in question. The log cabins which had followed the hunting shacks had in turn given place to comfortable and commodious frame dwellings; good looking farms along the bottoms, and grass land along the hillsides had succeeded the cleared "patches"; store buildings had sprung up along the way, and a general air of thrift, prosperity and contentment was manifest throughout.

While driving along on that trip I was reminded of a story, told me many years ago, by my father, B. W. Byrne, of an experience he had in that locality, many years before.

Be it known that the hospitality of all dwellers within the drainage of the Elk, is proverbial; long years ago I heard it said that — up to that time — there had never been an instance when the wayfaring man had gone to the door of any abode on the watershed of the Elk and applied for food or lodging, and been turned away. Tho the pickin' might be slim and the shakedown rough, the welcome was always cordial. And that is a part of the story:

Col. Albert A. Lewis and my father, who both lived at Sutton at the time, were interested in some lands on Birch River in the 50's and decided to pay a visit to the premises. They set forth on horseback, rode over to the Ford of Birch and thence up the river to their possessions. A little before nightfall they came to a log cabin and applied for food and lodging. The man of the house gave them a most cordial welcome and told them he would be delighted to entertain them, and that while he could feed them all right, he was very much cramped for sleeping quarters and for beds, as his cabin afforded but one room; but suggested that if they would be satisfied to sleep on a pallet up in the loft, the difficulty might be solved. As it was any port in a storm with them, the offer was gladly accepted. They partook of a first-rate supper, and in due season their host conducted them, by means of a ladder and the light of a tallow dip, up into the loft overhead, where a very comfortable "shakedown" of bearskins and homespun woolen blankets was spread on the floor. Just before going to bed, Col. Lewis suggested that he would like to have a cup of water to take to his room, as he usually awakened about the middle of the night and always craved a drink of water. This was provided and placed on the floor near to Col. Lewis' side of the pallet and he and my father undressed and retired by the dim light held by their host.

My father said he had been asleep but a short time, when he was awakened by his bed fellow:

"Col. Byrne, are you asleep?"

"I was asleep — yes; what's wrong?"

"Why bedbugs! This bed is alive with them."

"They are not bothering me," said my father, who was asleep again in a few seconds.

Again, about midnight: "Col. Byrne, is it possible you can sleep through all this? These bedbugs are literally eating me up! Why, man, they are all over everything!"

My father merely grunted and promptly went back to sleep.

My father said he awakened about daylight and found Col. Lewis in a terrible stew:

"My God, Col. Byrne, I haven't closed my eyes tonight. The bedbugs have actually eaten me alive; they are all over these blankets and all over the floor, and I have been catching them all night and putting them in this cup of water so they can't escape, and you have slept through it all! Just come over here to the light and let me show you."

With that he picked up the cup of water from the floor and my father followed him over to the light, only to behold about half a pint of flaxseed, which Col. Lewis had spent the night carefully and laboriously gathering up from the floor, where by some mischance they had been spilled.

Col. Lewis figured very prominently in connection with the formation of Braxton County and was chosen the first Justice of the Peace when the county was erected in 1836. I first met him in 1885, at which time he lived at Weston where he was for many years engaged in the mercantile business. He was then a dashing bachelor of 75 by his own count, but most people insisted that he had broken at least five years off his notch stick. Notwithstanding his persistent celibacy, he was a great beau and society man generally, and attended all dances and social functions along with the crowd of boys and girls who were a matter of some fifty or sixty years his junior. He always dressed in the most scrupulously correct fashion; was most dignified, suave and even courtly in his manner, punctiliously proper in every appointment — generous, considerate and thoroughly unselfish. As a term of endearment he was known as and called "Prince Albert," or "The Prince," by all his large circle of acquaintances, which embraced a large portion of the northerly half of the state. He was a staunch Democrat, and never missed a Democratic convention held for his county, district, or state. He took a lively interest in every election, was liberal in his contributions to the party war-chest, and made a few stump speeches in every campaign.

In the early spring of 1886, some of the Democratic newspapers in the First Congressional District proposed the name of Col. Albert A. Lewis for the Democratic nomination for Congress. I happened to be in Weston soon after these publications and mentioned the matter to "The Prince."

"Yes, sir," he replied, "I see they are booming me again this year. They wanted me to run in 1884, and of course I would have been glad to accept the nomination; but Marsh Frame wanted to run, and I told him to go ahead — that I could wait. Now if they want me again this year, of course, sir, I shall obey my party's call."

A few months later, Judge John Brannon of Weston went to his townsman, "The Prince," and told him he was somewhat in the notion of aspiring for the nomination for Congress.

"All right, Judge; go right ahead, sir; I can wait."

In 1888 there was another early spring boom for Lewis, who again stood aside, that time for John O. Pendleton; and again for John A. Howard; and so on each recurring two years until the dear old fellow was gathered to his fathers at an age upward of 90 — always willing to run, but always more willing to stand aside at the request of some friend. "Go right ahead — don't bother about me; I can wait." I have said that "Prince Albert" was a bachelor, which may account for the fact that the type is now extinct.

Getting back to Birch River: For several generations the Johnsons, the Piersons, the Mollohans, the Givens, and the Deans, the forebears of some of Charleston's most active and progressive business men, have lived in the lower section of the Birch drainage, notably in the Twistville or Diadda Run section, the Herold community and the section near the mouth of the river. One of the main roads from Sutton to Strange Creek traverses this Twistville and Diadda Run section, and on that road lived my good old friend of long ago, Burton Pierson. His residence was on the hillside over-looking the Birch River, half a mile or more away, his farm and grazing land extending along both sides of the river. Uncle Burton was a great fisherman and his special delight was gigging, at which art or accomplishment he was quite proficient. He always kept a good canoe down at the river, which served the double purpose of transportation across the river and for gigging when the water was right. Birch was always a good stream, not only for bass, but red-horse and suckers as well, the two last-named species belonging to the same fish family and being as closely related probably as first or second cousins, — though to the uninitiated, the red-horse is generally regarded as simply the big brother of the sucker. This is a great mistake, however, as the bones, if not the blood, will tell; the sucker being a very bony fish, as a rule, and the red-horse rather free from troublesome bones.

Burton, knowing of my fondness for the sport, often invited me to come down and go gigging with him in Birch River, always promising that we would find plenty of red-horse and that it would be no trouble to kill as many as we wanted. Finally I accepted his invitation and stopped overnight with him on a return trip from Clay Court House to Sutton. He had all preparations made, with plenty of torchwood, two gigs and a steersman; but from some cause we had very poor luck that night, and with the exception of a few suckers, we got nothing at all — not a fish of any considerable size and never saw a single red-horse.

About a year later I was riding past his house about 11 o'clock one morning, expecting to reach Strange Creek by dinner time. Burton was out in his front yard and as soon as he recognized me, rushed out in the road very excitedly and started to pull me off my horse.

"Bill, git off and come in and stay fer dinner; I've got something you shorely will like."

I remonstrated and tried to beg off, as I had a long journey ahead of me and couldn't afford to lose time. But he would not be denied — assured me dinner would be ready in a very short time, and as he was yanking me off my horse, remarked, "They're in thar fryin' the red-horse right now."

"Red-horse!" said I. "So you finally got some of those red-horse you were bragging to me about, did you?"

"I'll tell the universal universe I've got red-horse!"

"How did you get them?"

"Well, sir, I'll tell you — and I had the master time I ever had in my life — and I'll swear it on a stack of Holy Bibles as high as my head! Well, sir, I was going across Birch this morning to salt my cattle, and, thinks I, maybe I'd better take my gig along — not expectin' to fish — but thinkin' I might just straggle on something — you know I never leave my gig at the river — fear somebody snoopin' around might steal it —tain't safe to leave a good gig like that one of mine laying around, — and, sir, just as I shoved the canoe off, there at my landing at the foot of the shoal, I seed more goldurned red-horse than ever I seed in any one place — the bottom of the river was black with them as far as I could see, and, sir, — and I'll swear it on a stack of Holy Bibles as high as my head — the least one of them red-horse was the biggest goldurned red-horse I ever seed in my life; and when I shoved off, and by the time I had grabbed my gig and got the canoe turned, them red-horse had lit out down through the plout, and me after them — an' I overtook 'em down the plout nigh the head of the next shoal — and they turned and back up the river they come — and as they passed me, I slung my old gig into a big one — and then I turned and follered them, and overtook them again nearly up to the foot. of the shoal where they first started from, and they turned again, and here they come — and as they passed me I got another big one, and then I turned and after them again; and, sir, I'll tell you the truth, the whole truth and nothing but the truth — me and them had it up and down licketysplit fer who laid the chunk fer at least a half-hour — through the plout — up and down and up and down and back — me pushin' 'em strong and slingin' the gig in a big 'un ever time they passed — until, swear it on a stack of Holy Bibles, — I didn't have a dry stitch on me, and every goldurned one of them red-horse was in a perfect lather of sweat!!!"

XXXII

POLITICS, A CAMPAIGN SPEECH, McCUNE, CADLE, AND A "HOG WITH A SWALLOW FORK IN LEFT EAR"

M Y FIRST acquaintance with the "End of the World" section dates from the year 1880. In the election of that year my father was the Democratic candidate for the State Senate from the District composed of the counties of Kanawha, Clay, Nicholas, and Webster, and Alf W. Burnett of Charleston was the coalition candidate of the Republicans and Greenbackers, opposing him. As that was before the Australian ballot system had been adopted by West Virginia, providing for an official ballot, it was up to the candidate or party managers to provide the ballots for each of the election precincts and see that they were on hands for use on election day. It seems that the Democratic ballots for all the precincts in Clay County had been printed in Charleston and duly forwarded to the proper places; but something less than a week before election day it was reported that the ballots for two precincts, Flat Fork, in Buffalo District and O'Briens Creek in Otter District, had been entrusted to a faithless messenger and had gone astray — had probably fallen into the hands of the enemy. A new lot of ballots was prepared immediately, and I was commissioned by my father to deliver the one package to Morg Bragg at Flat Fork, and the other to John Duffield at the Groves Mill, both of whom were well known to me. In those days the state elections were held in the month of October, and it was nearly nightfall of that October evening, that, mounted on one of Ed Ervin's best saddle horses, I fared forth on my mission. I got as far as Stephen Stoffel's, just below Jarrett's Ford, that night, and resumed my journey quite early the next morning, reaching Clay Court House in mid-afternoon. At Clay Court House I found a number of friends among whom were Uncle Jack Stephenson and Mortimer W. Frame, and knowing them to be Democrats, tried and true, confided to them my errand, having been warned not to "make a blowin' horn" of my business, lest a second mischance overtake the ballots. Mort Frame, who was the Democratic candidate for prosecuting attorney of Clay County at that election, told me that he had a J. P. case to try at Groves Mill the next day, and that he was just getting ready to start and go part of the way that evening, and would be glad to deliver both packages. I thanked him for his kind offer, but told him that my instructions were to deliver one package into the hands of Morg Bragg and the other to John Duffield and that I was going to do it if it took the hide off. So Mort kindly volunteered to go with me, out of his way, to Morg Bragg's that night, and over to Duffields the next morning.

We got to Morg Bragg's residence just as Mrs. Bragg was preparing to clear away the supper dishes, and she informed us that her husband had just gone up to the schoolhouse to attend a political meeting. She gave us a good supper, which she hurried up so we could attend the meeting, and it was just a little after dark when we reached the schoolhouse, less than half a mile away. As we approached, we found the meeting was under way and that some one was making a speech. The room was dimly lighted by a kerosene lamp on the speaker's table and two or three lanterns suspended from pegs driven in the wall. The only persons we were able to recognize in this light were Strother B. Grose, the speaker, and Morg Bragg, who was seated at the table as chairman of the meeting. Mort Frame and I found a bench at the extreme rear and just to the right of the door at which we entered, and took our seats where we could dimly observe, without being even dimly observed.

For some moments after our arrival, the speaker dealt in generalities and platitudes, but presently launched forth on that which seemed to be uppermost in his mind; he said that one of the very most important offices to be filled at the approaching election was that of State Senator from that district; that he should be a man who had the interests of the common people at heart; a man who would not in that high office be the tool and puppet of corporate power or organized greed; a man who would stand foursquare to every wind that blew and serve his whole constituency with fortitude and fidelity. He had in fact so fully outlined the very characteristics which I had always understood my father to possess, that I was not only abashed, but literally astounded, when he capped this fine shaft with the declaration: "And such a man, my fellow citizens, is my distinguished friend, the Honorable Alf W. Burnett, of the County of Kanawha." But even more astounding to my ears was what followed. "And, my fellow citizens, who is his opponent? Old Ben Byrne, a man you all know to your sorrow. He was the man who, as Attorney for Allen T. Caperton and William H. Edwards who claimed to own the Wilson 93,000-acre survey, robbed you of your lands, your homes, and your firesides!"

Ye gods, and small tadpoles! Imagine how I felt. A boy not quite 18 years old, sitting there in the dark among strangers, and hearing his own father, for whom he had always had the very highest respect and whom he believed to be held in like esteem by everybody, thus spoken of! I tried to climb out over Mort Frame who sat between me and the aisle, fully intent on committing murder; but Mort kept me back and said, "Wait till he gets through and I'll reply to him."

But when Strother finished and sat down, I forced my way past Mort and rushed up the aisle to Morg Bragg, who had risen at the table, and, extending my hand excitedly, said, "Mr. Bragg, I am a son of Col. Ben Byrne and would like to say a word."

"All right, young man, go right ahead; we'd all be glad to hear you."

Turning and pointing my finger at Strother, who had seated himself on a bench across the aisle about six feet way, I made this, my first campaign speech, which for brevity, fervor and effectiveness, has never been approached by any subsequent effort of mine:

"The man who says that my father, Col. Ben Byrne, ever robbed, wronged, defrauded or mistreated any man, woman or child in this county or any other county, is a liar, a scoundrel and a coward!"

Strother Grose was a man of about 6 feet 2, and weighed about 225 pounds. My weight was about 100 pounds less; and when he jumped up and started toward me, I just took it for granted that he would grab me by the scruff of the neck and the seat of the pants and pitch me out of the open window. But Morg Bragg who had never resumed his seat, promptly stepped in between us and laying his hand on Strother's shoulder spoke as follows:

"Hold on thar, Strother, what this boy said about you ain't a bit worse'n what you said about his pap. But the difference is we all know Col. Byrne better'n you do. He settled up all these titles in here where we was either squatters or holding by shaky titles, and give us all a fair deal — better'n we deserved, most of us — an' we know that what the boy said, was every word true; and you didn't have no business sayin' what you did."

Now Morg Bragg, though not so heavy as Strother, was about equal height and was a gentleman who had the well earned reputation of being a scrapper, whenever the occasion demanded it, of all which the aforesaid Strother being well aware, the incident closed then and there; and a few moments later, while Mort Frame was making his speech, Strother exuded from the schoolhouse.

In after years when I became well acquainted with

the people of that neighborhood, I came to know a goodly number who attended that memorable Flat Fork
schoolhouse meeting and heard my maiden effort.
There were John Butler, Spider Collison, Marsh Rose,
Hiram Young, Mack Triplett and Thomas Riley Dean
—who have often since referred to the fact that Morg
Bragg kept me from getting a good licking at that
time and place.

I turned over the ballots to Bragg, and the next morning Mort Frame and I went over the mountain to Groves
Mill, where I delivered the other package to John Duffield, and my labor and responsibilities there ended.

The lawsuit which Mort Frame was to try, was that
of Pete McCune, plaintiff, vs. Martha Cadle, defendant, being an action in detinue for the recovery of one
hog, before William A. Riffle, Justice of the Peace for
Otter District. It seems that the plaintiff McCune who
lived over in the edge of Clay County, next to the Calhoun line, claimed that a year or so previously he had
turned a lot of his hogs out on the mast, all in his own
proper mark—which was a swallow fork in the left ear
and an under-bit in the right—and that one of these
hogs had strayed from the others and "come up missin' "
when the general roll was called; that six or eight
months later, in passing the home of Martha Cadle, on
the waters of O'Briens Creek, he had seen what he
recognized as his long lost hog, in the hog lot, and among
the swine of the said Martha; that he was able to identify it by its "general countenance," and peculiar "red-
sandy color and black spots," notwithstanding the fact
that the ear marks had been changed, by cropping the
left ear so as to cut away the swallow fork, and cutting
a second under-bit in the right, to convert the same into
the proprietary mark of the defendant Martha, which
was a crop off the left ear and two under-bits in the
right. The case went to trial about ten o'clock in the
morning, with Mort Frame as the attorney representing

the defendant, and against him was pitted Tom Chapman, representing the plaintiff. While Tom was not a lawyer in the sense of having been licensed to "plead" in courts of record, he was just about as keen a J. P. practitioner as you could scare up anywhere in central West Virginia—and that's taking in a lot of territory. Each side was well supplied with witnesses, there being six or eight for the plaintiff and about an equal number for the defendant, and a jury of six was duly empaneled, tried and sworn according to law to try the issue joined. The plaintiff and his witnesses positively identified the hog as belonging to the plaintiff, having been "personally acquainted with it," since early pighood, and having last inspected it at Martha Cadle's on their way to the trial. They emphasized its peculiar red-sandy color and black spots, and that it was the only hog of that peculiar coloring found among the hogs of the defendant, and all stressed the fact that the crop off the left ear "must have cut off the swaller fork," and the ease with which two under-bits might be made to appear where only one originally existed. Tom Chapman handled his witnesses with great skill and adroitness, and every man Jack responded nobly; and Mort's most rigid, skillful and searching cross-examination didn't make a dent anywhere.

Having already conceived the idea that I would be a lawyer some day, I became greatly interested in the trial, and followed every step and hung on the words of each witness with great care. Naturally, my sympathies were with Mort who was my friend, and his client who was a woman, but I could not close my eyes and mind to the fact that Tom Chapman had made a dangerously strong case.

But Mort had a Roland for every Oliver of Tom's. He proved by witness after witness, close neighbors of Martha Cadle, that they had known the hog in question ever since it was littered; referred to the difference of its coloring from the rest of the litter, noted and commented upon it at the time as being a throwback and of no uncommon occurrence; traced its whereabouts from its earliest history down to the present hour; identified the crop off the left ear and two under-bits in the right, as having for years been the true and lawful and generally recognized mark, or that they had marked that particular hog in that particular mark when it was a suckling.

This evidence made me feel much better, but I didn't like Tom Chapman's constant and continual reference in cross-examining the defendant's witnesses to the fact that a crop off the ear would cut off a "swaller-fork" if one had been there; he made every one of them admit this, over and over again.

And then came the argument. Tom opened the case, and rehashed the evidence pro and con with great skill and ability and soon developed as the "high pint" in his case the presumption that the crop off the left ear had cut off some previous marking—that previous marking was a "swaller-fork." And then Tom played his trump card: "And now, gentlemen of the jury, I want to read you the law of this case. Here I have one of the greatest law books ever written, recognized as authority in every civilized country on the globe—Williams on Personal Property; and let me read you what it says: 'In the ear-marking for identification of cattle, hogs and swine, which are permitted to run at large on the range or for the mast, the fact that any considerable portion of the ear has been entirely cut away, shall establish the conclusive presumption that a previous marking has been cut away and destroyed."

Mort was on his feet, instanter: "Let me see that authority you are reading from, Tom Chapman!"

"No, sir," said Tom. "This is my own personal property, and you have no business with it; and he slapped the book together and put it under his arm.

Mort appealed to the court to compel opposing counsel to permit inspection of his authority, but the court decided that he was powerless in the matter and that if Tom didn't want Mort to see his book he knew of no law to compel him.

When Tom finished and sat down, Mort followed with a brief discussion of the evidence—too brief as I thought, for I expected him to elaborate some of his stronger points, and was rather disappointed when he said, "And now in conclusion, gentlemen of the jury— Mr. Chapman has read to you from an authority called Williams on Personal Property—now I have some authority here myself, that I want to read. I was expecting Mr. Chapman to quote this very authority to you, and I came prepared." He stooped and from his saddle pockets on the floor, took a bound volume and proceeded: "I have here, gentlemen of the jury, the Acts of the Legislature of West Virginia for the year 1879—the Supreme lawmaking body of this great state of ours, and turning to Chapter 44 on page 169, I read as follows: 'Be it enacted by the Legislature of the state of West Virginia: That the law book known as Williams on Personal Property shall no longer be held, treated or considered as binding authority in any of the courts of the state or by justices of the peace. All acts and parts of acts coming within the purview of this act and inconsistent therewith, are hereby repealed.' "

"Hold on there, Mort—let me see that book," said Tom in great agitation.

"No, sir," said Mort, "this is my own personal property and you have no business with it," and he slapped the book together and put it under his arm.

What might have been the result of the case on its merits will never be known, but when Mort repealed Tom's law, Tom never rallied, and when the case went to the jury, they found for the defendant without leaving the box.

About the time the lawsuit ended, Leslie Frame and Sherman Hyer, in a canoe, with their passenger, Andrew Brockerhoff, stopped and came up the bank. Brockerhoff was at that time interested with Don Cameron and others in the Wilson survey, and I was quite well acquainted with him. It was his custom to visit the lands about once a year and he usually went to Clay Court House to pay the taxes. He told me he was having an awful trip—that the river was so low that they had to wade and let the canoe through the shoals, for fear of bursting it. I saw their gigs and asked about the fish. They said they had killed all they cared for. Then a bright idea struck me; I proposed to Brockerhoff that he ride my horse to Clay Court House, and that I would take his place in the canoe. He was surely too glad to swap, and it was so ordered. I believe he and Mort stayed at John Duffield's that night and went to Clay the next day, as it was late in the afternoon when they arrived; but Leslie and Sherman were fixed for camping out, and we started down the river. The river was indeed very low—both Leslie and Sherman said it was lower than they had ever seen it. Poor fellows, they are both dead, but if they had lived until the present writing they would see it fully four or five inches lower than it was at that time or at any other time in the memory of the living. At that time and a few other times since, I have seen it so low that at many of the shoals one could wade across and the water would be scarcely over the ordinary shoe tops, but never until the present summer have I seen it so low that you can cross in forty different places, by stepping from rock to rock, and never get your feet wet.

I am told that the river is so low at Sutton, where they are temporarily operating a ferry while the bridge is being built, that they have to haul water for the ferry boat. You can take this for what it is worth, but Fred Clemens told me, and he lives there. But it is a fact that the present appearance of Elk River, its serpentine course, with the rocks exposed everywhere from side to middle, and but a thin stream trickling between, reminds one of the skeleton of a huge snake bleaching and glistening in the sunlight.

About halfway between the foot of the End of the World shoal and the head of Jumping Gut shoal, I caught sight of an enormous pike some twenty feet away, moving rapidly downstream. I was pretty handy with a gig at that time, and struck the pike midships but well up toward the back. The gig handle went in the air, thrown with great force from the powerful fish, and the badly wounded pike kept on downstream to deep water at what is known as Pike Rock. We followed and searched for him quite a long time at Pike Rock and on the opposite side of the river among the rocks and sunken tree trunks. But all to no avail. While searching for the crippled pike, some of us recognized Old Sol Nelson, on a rock bar down at the mouth of Jumping Gut, working at something, we could not tell what. We decided to go down and see what Old Sol had, and come back later and renew the search.

Sol was skinning a big buck which was hanging against a tree at the edge of the bar, and which, as he expressed it, the dogs had run over him right there at the mouth of the creek a couple of hours before. He told us casually, that it was nothing uncommon for him to kill half a dozen deer or more every year. It was then that I learned that he lived there at the mouth of Jumping Gut. He pressed upon us a good-sized piece of venison and we concluded to camp there for the night.

We told Sol about the pike I had crippled up in the eddy and he said he had seen that pike many times and that he was five feet long if he was an inch.

I was all eagerness to go back and resume our search, and Sol, seeing my anxiety, said, "Now, Bub, you fellers git your supper and when it gets good and dark we'll fix up a good light and go and git him. I've got a lot of pitch pine and a good basket up at the house."

I went up to his cabin with him to help with the pine and basket and found that both his wife and his daughter were sick in bed, which he stated was the reason he had not invited us to be his guests.

After supper and while we were waiting for good dark, Sol brought down his fiddle and played for us his full repertory of fiddle "chunes" for which he was famous throughout the Elk Valley from Clay Court House to Sutton where he was known as "Old Sol Nelson, the Fiddler of the Wilderness." He played Flat-Foot-in-the-Ashes, Horneo, Sugar in the Gourd, Sourwood Mountains, Wild Goose, Cumberland Gap, and Forked Deer (Fauquier being the baptismal name of that tune, corrupted by years of mispronunciation and misapprehension), to my uneducated ear all sounding very much alike, but doubtless markedly different to the musician.

We spent fully two hours hunting my crippled pike, but, although we never saw hair nor hide of him, Leslie Frame found a four-foot pike fast asleep at the head of Jumping Gut shoal, which he struck and we all succeeded in landing after a terrific battle down through the shoal. While a four-foot pike and a score or more of red-horse, carp and other splendid fish which we killed in the search, should have been considered a pretty fair haul, I was far from satisfied. I wanted my five-foot pike and would be satisfied with nothing else.

We resumed the hunt the next morning but with no better success and it was with great reluctance that I abandoned the field and we proceeded on down the river.

About a year later Sherman Hyer told me that Old Sol had gigged my pike and that he was just 61 inches long. He was able to identify him by a big white spot about the middle, a little too high on the back for the gig to have penetrated the hollow of the body and thus inflict a fatal wound.

From this short visit to Sol Nelson, I was so attracted to his place on the river as a location for fishing and hunting that I said to him that I certainly would like to own it. Whereupon the old fellow said that when he was through with it he would be glad for me to have it. And this I then and there made up my mind to do, if within the length of my cable-tow. I think it was that five-foot pike inspired me most with desire to own the place—and by the way, his mate is there today hanging around that same old Pike Rock.

The land on which Old Sol Nelson lived, consisted of 50 acres at the mouth of Jumping Gut, taking in both sides of the creek and extending for about half a mile along the river. After Sol's death the premises passed into other hands and in 1892 I purchased it from Wm. R. Reed, the then owner, for myself and associates, John B. Dunlap, and William E. Haymond of Sutton, whose interests I later acquired. About the year 1907, I sold the timber to James Reed and Levi J. Reed, who owned the timber on the 1400-acre tract surrounding the Nelson tract, and gave them permission to use the bottom land for the mill site and lumber yard and dwelling houses for their men. They finished their work on Jumping Gut drainage about the first of the year 1911, and left two or three pretty good Jenny Lind houses on the land. On March 31, 1911, my fellow townsman and boyhood chum, Walter L. Ashby, and I went up to look the situation over, with a view to converting one of these houses into a fishing camp. We selected the house which had been built for John Parsons, the head sawyer on the job, and arranged for building a ten-foot porch surrounding the house, which made it quite comfortable for camping purposes. We found Anise Nichols in the house at the lower end of the bottom, and arranged for him to act as caretaker, and he and his family lived there for a number of years.

I decided from the first to use the "End of the World" in giving the camp a name, and as somebody told me that the two Greek words "Cos" meaning world and "Omega" meaning the end, would fill the bill, it was first christened Camp Cosmega. This name did not seem to "set well," and when, about the second summer, a bunch of boys and girls were applying cold creams, lotions and powder to sunburnt backs and arms, and one young lady suggested that the name be change to Camp Cosmetic, that brought about a re-christening under the name of Camp Ashburne — by the way, a very pretty play on the names of the two proprietors. This name, too, was short-lived, for when I applied for fire insurance, and told the agent the name, he said, "My God, man. You could never get fire insurance on a fishing camp with a name like that." So after all, we reverted to our first intention and gave it the full name, in plain United States lingo — "The Camp at the End of the World," — rather a mouthful, it is true, but a mouthful is what you want in and at a fishing camp.

XXXIII

DEVIL'S BACKBONE GETS A NAME; DOGS, GIGS, AND FISH

ON THE occasion of my first visit to the "End of the World," as related in the August (1930) number of *Wild Life,* as Leslie Frame, Sherman Hyer and I proceeded down the river from Groves Creek in our canoe, as we swept around the point of the sharp bend at the "End of the World" Shoal, I was struck with the tall perpendicular cliffs rising on our left, and afterward, while we were sitting around our campfire waiting for it to get dark so we could use our pine torch to good advantage in searching for my wounded pike, I remarked to Uncle Solomon Nelson about those beetling cliffs and their peculiarly picturesque appearance.

"Yes," said he, "them cliffs is called the Devil's Back Bone — just a narrow clift of rocks raised up thar between the river an' Jumpin' Gut — an' up at the shoal, ef you would cut a hole through, a hundred yards long, you'd come to the creek over a mile above its mouth. An' under them clifts you see from the river side, purty high up next the top, you'll find purty good campin' quarters, back under thar."

"Did anybody ever live there?" I asked.

"Well now, Bud, you've axed me sumthin', an' I low to tell you — but I ain't goin' to name no names: In an airly day in this country there wuz a young feller strayed in hur a huntin', an' he didn't have nothin' but his rifle, his fryin' pan an' butcher knife — an' his fiddle, an' a couple uv blankets an' some salt an' a few things he could pack on his back. It wuz summer time when he come, an' again cold weather he had killed three or four bear an' a lot uv deer an' coons, an' he tuck up winter quarters under that clift, usin' them skins to side up a room under thar an' fer a bed to sleep on. The next

spring he packed up a part uv his fur, an' after bundlin'
up the balance that he wuzn't able to pack, an' swingin'
it from a limb sose the varmints couldn't git to it, he
started off a straight shoot to the Ohio River, to sell his
fur an' git him a supply of ammunition an' some salt an'
things — takin' his rifle an' fiddle along. He had to
cross the Ohio River into the State of Ohio to sell his
fur, an' the feller he sold to had a big store an' lived on
a big farm. He was a purty old feller, uppards uv 50
years old, an' lived in a fine big house, an' wuz a purty
high flyer. Had fine hosses an' kerridges an' lots uv
everything. The young feller hadn't done so powerful
well sellin' his fur, an' 'lowed he might hire out to the
feller to work a spell on his farm to git him enough
money fer what he wanted. So the feller hires him an'
puts him to work on the farm an' jimmin' around the
place. This feller's wife wuz a young woman not over
twenty-five year old, an' purty as a peach. Shortly after
the young feller went to work, one even' he got down
his ole fiddle an' played a chune or two in the room
where he stayed, an' the feller an' his wife put at him to
bring his fiddle down to the parlor whar they was company an' give 'em some music. So they soon got to
dancin' and frolickin' around, an' havin' a master time
— an' the young feller he jist spread hisself an' made
that ole fiddle fairly talk. An' after that, it was a dance
about ever other night, an' when it wuzn't a dance the
young feller wuz down on the front porch evenin's, a
playin' the fiddle an' the feller's wife settin' thar sew-
in' her silk things an' 'broiderin' an' tattin' an' sich
fancy doin's. It went on this way fer about a month—
the young feller workin' on the farm ever day an' fid-
dlin' ever night—an' her settin' on the porch listenin'
when they wuzn't dancin'. An' when the young feller
had a month's wages in his pocket, why, one mornin',
shore nuff, him an' the feller's wife turned up missin'.
This Ohio feller he hunted fer 'em high an' low—up

the river—down the river—across the river—but they couldn't find hair ner hide ner track ner sign uv 'em, nowhar. Well, sir—how they ever found the place, the Lord only knows—but nigh onto two months later the Ohio feller an' two other fellers with him, snuck up the steep hillside thar to them clifts an' found the young feller thar in under the rock fryin' fish fer dinner, an' the Ohio feller's wife settin' thar on a rock with a bearskin throwed over it, silk 'broiderin' a buckskin waist-coat fer the young feller. They all had thur guns, but they jist passed the time of day an' stood thar a leetle spell, an' then the Ohio feller said they must be goin', an' the young feller told them not to be in a hurry—to stay an' git their dinner; but they thanked him an' said they'd be gettin' on—an' so the Ohio feller an' his wife an' the tother fellers they all left. An' that's the last the young feller ever seen or heered uv any uv 'em."

We had pitched our camp at a spot long used for the purpose by rivermen passing back and forth. Two very large elm trees growing on the edge of the low bank adjoining the great rock bar just above the mouth of the creek, stood about ten feet apart, the space between smooth, level ground well adapted for a camp site, the huge spreading branches of the two trees overlapping this space, and their dense foliage forming a canopy overhead which afforded complete shelter from an ordinary shower. By the way, these elms are standing today, the lower portions of their trunks gnarled and knotted by frequent batterings and bruises from icefloes, floating logs and debris, coming in violent contact therewith during the stages of high water and the interlaced roots of the elms exposed for a depth of three or four feet below the former level.

While Old Sol was relating the story of the "young feller," and the Ohio lady, I discovered in the low forks of one of the elms, the skeleton of a huge boar's head, and, later, taking it down from its perch, I asked him where it came from. Taking the skeleton in his hands, the old gentleman related the following history of the Wild Boar of Jumpin' Gut:

"I've done a lotta huntin' in my time an' killed lotsa deer an' bear an' several painters, but the terriblest varmint I ever had any dealin's with wuz that boar. He was a full grown hog—must a been four or five year old—when he strayed in hur from summers, five or six year ago, an' tuck up hur on the watershed uv Jumpin' Gut, whur they wuz allus lotsa mast, sich as chestnut, walnut, hickory, beech an' oak. Right up the crick thar about three hundred yards, jist above whar that fust leetle right-hand fork puts in, thar sets in the master laurel patch anybody ever seen—an' it runs way up the hillside on both sides uv the crick an' runs up the crick above the falls, about a mile above hur—the laurel is so thick a rabbit can't hardly git through, an' the only way to git up the crick is to foller the crick-bed mostly an' in lots of places the laurel laps across the crick, an' when the crick gits up a leetle, you can't git through at all. Fer the most part that boar spent his time ravagin' an' depredatin' around—sometimes he would break in my cornfield on the hill—no stake an' ridered fence couldn't stop him—he would go right through same as they wuzn't no fence thar—he didn't bother me none down hur on account uv my dogs—but he'd kill half the pigs I had out on the mast when they wuz leetle, an' sometimes half-grown shoats — kill 'em an' eat 'em — an' once he killed an' et a calf fer me.

"I tried many times to run him down an' kill him. I would take my dogs—five or six uv 'em an' jump him out in the woods an' try to shoot him—but allus he would wind me, go right through the whole bunch of dogs an' break fer that laurel patch—outrun the dogs— why they never wuz the dog born that could keep in sight of that boar in a foot race. That boar wuz built special fer runnin'. He wuz about as tall as a good size

calf—awful slim an' peaked in his hind parts, but he
had the powerfullest big shoulders you ever seen on a'
animal, an' the awfullest snout—well you can see fer
yourself whut a snout an' tushes he had. I guess I've
shot at that boar at least a dozen times—an' I never
teched hair ner hide uv him, fer as I know—never did
git a shot at him only when he wuz a tearin' through the
woods an' bresh. Fust time the dogs run him into the
laurel, they tried to foller him in, an' one of them come
up on him in thar, an' what that boar done to that dog
in thar wuz a plumb sight—he give him a couple uv
rakes with them tushes, an' jist financially tore him all
to pieces, an' he wuz dead afore I could crawl into the
laurel whur he wuz. An' that wuz the last time airy dog
ever follered that boar into the laurel.

"Well, one day me an' the dogs—three uv 'em, went up
the crick a couple of miles lookin' fer turkeys—the creek
wuz low an' we follered the path in the creek-bed goin'
up; but fore we started back they came a hard rain, an'
Jumpin' Gut riz sose we had to come back by the path
that tops out on top uv the Devil's Back Bone, up thar
overlookin' the river. I wuz ahead of the dogs when we
topped the Back Bone—ole Sound an' ole Trailer an'
ole Drum wuz with me, jist behind—when, jist as I got
nearly to that big flat rock layin' up on top, woof! come
that boar around the end of that rock, quarterin' toward
me—but afore he got fairly started, ole Drum nailed
him by the flank, an' hur come ole Sound an' ole
Trailer, an' jist as the boar turnt on ole Drum an' rip-
ped open his shoulder with a swipe of his tushes, ole
Sound clevised him by the year on one side an' ole
Trailer by the tother year, an' the old boar give back
up the hill, an' I thought to see the terriblest fight I
ever seed—I couldn't shoot fer fear uv hittin' the dogs—
when lo an' behold! they got back right up to the
aige uv the clift, an' over they goes, an' down one hundred feet fore hittin' the ground — an' fightin' ever'

step uv the way—an' slid off into the river, whar all
the life that wuz left by the fightin' an' the fallin' wuz
drownded out uv 'em.

"I gethered up ole Drum an' packed him out the
Back Bone an' down to the house—he wuz butchered
up sumpin' awful, but I finally brung him 'round. So
I gits in my cun-noo—me an' Amos—you know my son
Amos—an' we went up to see 'bout the dogs an' the
boar. Well, sir, the way that boar an' them dogs wuz
smashed up wuz a plumb sight. I got a grapevine an'
hitched it 'round the boar an' drug him behind the
cun-noo an' towed him down hur, an' we used some uv
him fer dog meat an' biled his carcass down fer soap
grease—an' that's how I come to have the head. But
losin' them two dogs was sumpin I certainly did hate. I
wouldn't a tuck the best hoss in Clay County fer airy
one uv 'em. Why sure, you're welcome to the boar's
head ef you want it. I hain't got no use fer it. Mebbe
when you git this place an' fix up yer camp—which you
say you 'low to do, sometime—you kin bring the ole
boar's head along an' put it up, to remind you uv ole
Sol Nelson."

And now, all that is of the earthly remains of the
wild boar of Jumpin' Gut, greets you, like unto a grinning gargoyle, from its niche at the Camp at the End
of the World; the present whereabouts of its other component elements, would seem to depend—according to
the testimony of old Sol Nelson—upon whether or not
there is a hell for hogs.

About 1894 or '5 Henry Waggy, of Sutton, who owned
the 2000-acre tract of land at the mouth of Groves
Creek—and Kester Gorrell, also of Sutton, erected a
circular sawmill at the mouth of Groves, and sawed
a portion of the timber from the Waggy land. They
built a boarding house on the river bank about a hundred and fifty yards above the mouth of the creek, and
my old friend Marshall Colebank, with his family,

moved in and took charge. The Waggy and Gorrell
business was carried on for several years, and I availed
myself of every opportunity to pay them a visit and
do a little fishing. In those days the river was usually
clear except during freshets, and, as heretofore stated,
the stretch of river for the three miles from Groves
Creek around the End of the World bend to Lower
Seventy-Four Island, was at that time the best fishing
ground for hook and line, gig and spear, anywhere to
be found. Kes Gorrell was quite a fisherman, especially
fond of gigging, and several nights he and I have put
in traversing the territory down and back, as above
described. As illustrating how tricky is that End of
the World bend, especially in the night time: Kes and
I started out one night and gigged down to about Lower
Seventy-Four, and there turned and started on the return trip. We had just gotten up to the head of the End
of the World Shoal when our torchwood gave out; and
as it was very dark and more than a mile to go, we
landed our canoe on the north side of the river, lighted
our lantern and took up the bank to walk back home. We
had landed exactly in the sharpest point of the bend,
and that long strip of bottom land was all grown up in
brush and weeds and briers. There was a dim path
about midway of the bottom, leading up and down the
river, and we soon found this path and struck off in
the direction of Groves Creek, as we supposed—and
which supposition was indeed true, so far as direction
was concerned, as it was due north whichever end of
the path we took—but after having traveled half a mile
we heard the roar of a shoal to our left, and for the
first time realized that we had been traveling downstream instead of up, and that we were down at Jumping Gut Shoal instead of being up at Paddy. As we
retraced our steps and trudged homeward, I made all
manner of fun of Kes, "an old woodsman, getting lost
on the bank of Elk River," until he reminded me that

he wasn't much older than I and didn't pretend to be half as "knowin'."

But I did get it on Kes Gorrell, after that, good and proper. I went down to Groves one day with Henry Waggy, and we arrived just about supper time; Kes Gorrell immediately took us out in the kitchen and showed us a fine big pile of fish, part of which Mrs. Colebank was frying for supper. There were several nice bass and a dozen or more catfish—mud-cat and channel-cat—sixteen pounds of cleaned fish, Kes said, that he had caught that day partly on hook and line and partly on a trotline. For supper that evening and breakfast next morning, we cleaned up that sixteen pounds, and I started out early next morning to replenish the larder. I fished up around O'Briens Creek, and Grassy Place and Frames Run, and on my rounds stopped at Elve Sirk's store at the mouth of O'Briens. There I ran across Wash Tanner, an old friend of mine. He wanted to know where I was going, and I told him I was going down to Waggy & Gorrell's place. He said, "Bill, here's a nickel, I wish you'd give to Kes Gorrell. Kes was passin' here yestiddy, an' I jist got thew cleanin' a passel uv fish I'd ketched on my trotline, an' he put at me to buy 'em, an' I tole him he could have 'em fer ten cents a pound, an' he sez he'll take the lot, an' I fetched 'em up here an' we weighed 'em on Elve's scales, an' they weighed jist 16 pounds, an' Kes he hands me a $2 bill, an' the fish jist come to $1.60 an' all the change I could rake an' scrape was 35 cents, an' I tole Kes I'd give him tother nickel next time I seen him."

I was most delighted to accept the commission, and hastened down to Groves to deliver the nickel. Finding Kes and Henry Waggy together at the mill, I walked up with the money in my hand and said, "Kes, Wash Tanner asked me to give you this nickel."

"Did that lyin' old scoundrel tell you I bought those fish from him?" said Kes, as he stuck the nickel in his pocket; but his question remains unanswered to this day.

On one occasion when I was at Groves, I was sitting on the porch at Colebank's one evening just a little before dusk, when Jake McNemar came up from the mouth of the creek, and told me he had just seen a big wild turkey gobbler fly into a hemlock on the lower side of the creek and that he was roosting on a limb down near the ground, and asked me if I had a gun. I rushed in the house and grabbed a shotgun and put out down to the hemlock in question. From the top of the creek bank on the upper side, I had plain view of the gobbler roosting on a low limb not over 100 feet away. My first impulse was to blaze away at the turkey, but on a moment's reflection it occurred to me that the setup was by all odds too good, and, knowing Jake McNemar as I did and that he was a chap who was not above "putting up a job" on an innocent and unsuspecting fellowman, and recalling the fact that Frank Young or some of the other Youngs who lived up on Groves Creek, had a lot of tame turkeys, and the light being so dim that about all I could see was the bulk of the bird, not distinctly enough to tell whether it was wild or tame— I lowered my gun and walked back up to the house.

Jake said, "What's the matter—scare him away?"

"No, Jacob, he's right there where you left him. You thought you'd have a good joke on me—have me shoot somebody's tame turkey.—But you can't fool your uncle Dudley."

"Gimme that gun," said Jake.

In about three minutes we heard the gun go bang! and presently Jake hove in sight with a fine, large and juicy wild turkey gobbler; and the joke was on me for fair.

On the occasion of one of my visits to Groves while Waggy & Gorrell were operating this mill, I ran across my old friend Coonrod Eagle. Coonrod then lived on

Snake Creek, up near the Braxton line, but was raised at Butler's Bend, or Eagle Bend, as it was latterly called, on Elk River, about two miles above Clay Court House, and I had known him for many years.

Now Coonrod Eagle was and has always been no common ordinary chap; he had a wider spread of accomplishments than almost any man of my acquaintance, and his versatility was a matter of common knowledge and general report. He was a blacksmith, carpenter, wheelwright, millwright, farmer, miller, boatman, canoeman, shoemaker, tanner, veterinarian, cabinetmaker, machinist, gunsmith, dentist, teamster, ox-driver, whipsawyer, stone mason, timber cutter, raftsman, cross-tie hewer, watchmaker and clock fixer—in fact he could make a stagger at anything any other fellow could do, and much that nobody else ever tried to do.

Coonrod, like many gentlemen of great diversity of accomplishment, was very thin skinned and sensitive to criticism—censure or unfavorable comment of or concerning his handiwork, or of any error or mistake however small on his part, was gall and wormwood to his soul, while ridicule directed toward him for a bone-head he might pull, made him to wear the shirt of Nessus.

Coonrod "spicioned" Kes Gorrell and me for having in mind to go gigging that night, and "put at us" to go along. Being a splendid gigger, and "give up" to be the best gigmaker on Elk River—two most important qualities inadvertently omitted from the foregoing list— we were glad to have him. While Kes was busy at the mill, Coonrod and I busied ourselves making the necessary preparations, such as fixing for the light, hunting up the gigs, etc. We found two good gigs, both of the "Coonrod make," but the handle of one of them being broken or defective, Coonrod said we would go down to the mill and find a good piece of seasoned poplar, out of which he would make a new handle. We found the very piece we were looking for—an edging off of an inch and a quarter board—square and sound, except a few inches of "feather" at one end which Coonrod said he would fix in a jiffy, by taking it to the cut-off table in the mill. This cut-off table was on the second story of the mill building and the cutting was done by a large circular saw, which the operator, by means of a hand lever, pulled toward him while in motion, through a slot in the floor and likewise a slot in the table. Coonrod placed the stick carefully on the cut-off table and asked me to hold the end farthest from the saw, while he, holding the other end at the proper place with his left hand, grasped the lever with his right, and drew the saw toward him. Now, whether it was the haste and excitement of the moment, or whether it was because he had not built or operated a sawmill or cut-off machine like that for a long time, that was responsible for it, I do not know, but Coonrod certainly did "slip a cog," when he placed his left foot over the slot in the floor where that saw traveled. I heard a queer buz-z-z down at the floor—Coonrod jerked back his left foot, released the lever, and, as though to conceal his mishap, turned his back on me and stepped quickly around the end of the cut-off table, the blood spurting from his shoe.

I did not at first fully sense what had happened, and asked, "What's the matter, Coonrod?"

"Oh, nothing—nothing! I tell you."

By that time I was around the table and could see what was wrong. I said, "Why man, you've sawed your foot off!"

"No—jist my toe—it don't make a bit of difference."

"Let's see, Coonrod—which toe is it?"

"Oh, it's just the same old big toe that the cow broke and the old sow bit off."

I saw Coonrod a few months ago and asked him about that big toe, and Coonrod, always quick at repartee, came right back at me—"Still gone."

XXXIV

A DEAL IN BOATS AND LAW

IT WAS the year 1910 I believe, that I had my trouble with Uncle Jackie Townsend. Uncle Jackie was a fisherman of note, generally well known on Elk River, but whom I had never met until on the occasion of the incident I am about to relate. He sometimes lived on a houseboat and sometimes shantied along the river, and during the fishing season usually put in all his spare moments indulging his fondness for the piscatorial art. He was accustomed to do odd jobs about a sawmill wherever he could find one in operation along the river where the fishing was good, and where the duties of his employment would not too much interfere with fishing. When the Reeds had completed their sawing on my tract of land at the End of the World, they moved their mill up to the mouth of Paddy, just one mile above, and John Parsons, who had been their head sawyer down at my place, moved his family up to the mouth of Paddy, and continued to run the mill. Among the other numerous employees about the mill was this Mr. Jackie Townsend who did such odd jobs as cutting slabs for firing the boiler and other things of like kind that might be useful.

In the summer of that year, I had occasion to visit Sutton, and there ran across John Parsons. John was very fond of gigging, and learning that I was coming to Charleston on the same train on which he was going down to Paddy, he suggested that I stop off with him and go gigging that night. I was glad to accept the invitation, and we arrived at our destination rather early in the morning. It so happened that I had in my grip a "Sunday" rod, which is the name by which fishermen designate the rod made up of short joints, so that it may be carried in a grip without attracting the attention of the public.

When we arrived at Paddy we found the mill shut down on account of some mishap to the machinery, and while I was fixing up my rod preparatory to doing a little fly-fishing during the day, Uncle Jackie Townsend sauntered up and seemed very much interested in the operation. Someone introduced me to him about that time, and while I was rigging up my leader and flies, Jackie wanted to know what the thunder I expected to do with "them things." When I answered his question the best I could, he spoke very slightingly of the whole contraption and made the public announcement that with hook, line and bait he could catch ten times as many fish in a day as I could catch with my outfit; and then and there challenged me for a trial of the issue, saying that he had a good boat down at the river and plenty of bait, such as live minnows, hellgrammites and crawfish, and was ready to start at the moment.

We pulled out down the river, Jackie paddling the boat, while I took advantage of his inaction from the mouth of Paddy down through the first eddy, the foot of which was our first stopping place, to catch a couple of fair-sized bass, but, much to Jackie's disgust, to allow a fine two and one-half or three pounder to get away from me. When we stopped for bait-fishing, I took off my fly and used the same bait which Jackie was using. During the day we covered a stretch of about two miles down the river, stopping at four or five good bait-fishing places, and in moving from location to location, I replaced my flies and in that way caught half a dozen or more bass while Jackie was doing the paddling.

When we quit fishing and started back home, we counted our fish on our respective strings, and found that I had 17 bass and that Jackie had 16 fish, of which 15 were bass and one jack pike, which was a little larger than any bass which either of us had caught. When the count had been made, checked and double-checked, I saw that Jackie was worried, and I knew it was because of the "razzing" he expected to get when we got back up to Paddy, from the boys who had heard him boast that he could catch ten to my one. Finally he said, "Well, we might say we both caught exactly 17, for this jack pike of mine orta count for two." I said, "All right, Jackie, let it go at that."

When we got up to Paddy, the boys were merciless in their taunts of Jackie, and soon had him as mad as a hornet; and I could see that I also had become an object of his wrath. Well, that is the first chapter of the incident.

John Parsons and I, with a good steersman, that night at dark started from the mouth of Paddy down the river on our gigging expedition. We had just turned into the long pool below Paddy when we saw a bank hook set against the steep muddy bank, back of John Parsons' house, at the upper end of the deep water. Some of us lifted up the line as we passed and found the hook to be baited with a doughball, which up to that time had not been disturbed, and Parsons remarked that it was Jackie Townsend's bank hook. We proceeded down the river as far as Lower 74 Island and returned about two o'clock in the morning, having killed twenty-five or thirty nice red-horse, suckers and carp. As we approached Jackie Townsend's bank hook on the return trip, I noticed from the movement of the pole that it had caught a fish; and raising up the line I took off an 18-inch catfish and dropped it in the boat. The doughball had been forced up the line above the hook, and was there intact. So when I took the fish off the hook, I carefully rebaited it with the doughball, which I pressed back into compact shape and form.

When we landed, John Parsons said he and the steersman would take care of the fish, and that he would fix up some of them, and the nicest of the bass that I had caught during the day, for me to take home with me, and suggested that, as I wanted to go down on the early train the next morning, I had better go up to the boarding house and go to bed right away, so that I could get a little sleep. The next morning about six o'clock I was awakened by hearing someone yell, "Hello, Jackie, where did you get him?" and I heard Jackie reply, "I ketched him on a bank hook right down here back of John Parsonses." Looking out of the window I saw my friend Jackie, lugging a fine catfish, which on being weighed and measured was found to be an eight pounder and thirty inches long. As soon as I could get my clothes on I went out into the yard and interviewed Jackie a little more definitely, and learned from him that he had caught this fine fish on the very hook from which I had taken the small catfish, and on the very doughball that I had replaced. But I did not mention to Jackie the fact of having taken the small catfish off his line. Soon after breakfast, John Parsons appeared with a basket containing the fish I was to take home, and he accompanied me up to the railroad station at Groves, three-quarters of a mile away. Going down on the train, when I was exhibiting my fish to some fellows, I found among them Jackie Townsend's small catfish.

Now after I left, that scoundrel John Parsons, who was as full of devilment as an egg is of meat, told Jackie that I had taken the catfish off his hook, and furthermore that I had taken it home with me.

About a month later I ran across Jackie at Clay Court House, and as it happened, John Parsons was with him. John said, "Bill, Jackie Townsend here has brought a very serious charge against you; he says you stole his catfish." I laughed and looked around at Jackie expecting to see at least a smile on his face; but not so. Jackie showed no sign of being pleased. He said, "Mr. Byrne, I wouldn't have thought you would have took my fish without axing me for it." I said, "Jackie, it seems to me that I conferred a great favor on you by

taking that 18-inch catfish off your hook, and fixing
back the doughball for you to catch the thirty-inch catfish—the eight pounder that you took off of the very
same line and the very same bait; I think instead of
getting cross with me, accusing me of doing you dirt,
that you ought to feel very thankful for what I did,
helping you trade an eighteen-inch—pound and a half
catfish—for a thirty-inch—eight pounder." "Well,"
said Jackie, "you may beat me with your lawyer talk
and argyfying, but as I look at it, it was nothing but
a damn defraud, and that is all anybody can make out
of it."

It is a nice thing to collect lawyer's fees, and especially nice juicy ones; but the one, the collection of
which afforded me more real, genuine satisfaction and
pleasure, was a $10.00 fee, which I got under the fol-
lowing circumstances:

In the year 1911, just after Walter Ashby and I arranged to institute what is now the Camp at the End of
the World, I chanced to be at Strange Creek, waiting at
the station for the afternoon train to Charleston, when
I saw Cam Fox and Phil Corley down at the river, just
landing from a boat. I sauntered down to find what
they were doing, and was informed that they had gigged
down from Frametown that day, and were going on
down to Otter, and they invited me to go along, saying
that I could take the early morning train at Otter the
next day. I was not hard to persuade and the arrangement was so made. Before we had gotten very far on
our trip, Phil Corley, who owned the boat, which was
a very nice one, twenty feet long, built especially for a
gigging craft, offered to sell it to me for $10.00, and
that he would throw into the bargain, a good walnut-
handled gig, which, as he said, was worth any man's
$2.00.

Realizing that a boat like this and a good gig would
come in quite handy for Ashby and myself at the camp,

I closed the deal and paid over the $10.00. About two
o'clock in the morning, after gigging about all night
up to that time, and having killed quite a lot of fair-
sized fish, we landed at Otter, and went up to the hotel
or boarding house kept by an old friend of ours, whom
I will call Dave. We got him out of bed and turned
over our fish to him, telling him he could have all of
them except six or eight, which we selected to take home
with us. We told Dave that Corley and Fox wanted to
take the early north bound train the next morning, and
that I wanted to go to Charleston on the early south
bound train.

At breakfast the next morning we, as well as all of
the other boarders and guests, had all and more fish than
we could possibly eat. When we came to settle our bill,
Dave charged the three of us a little more than the customary price. I had brought my gig up to Dave's the
night before, and as I was leaving that morning, told
Dave I would like for him to look after my boat down
at the river and also take care of my gig, until they
were called for by Will Reed, whom I would get to take
them for me up to the End of the World in a day or
two. Dave said he would be glad to look after them for
me until Reed came for them, and before leaving Otter
I wrote a note to Reed, asking him to take the boat and
gig up to my camp. A few days later I saw Reed, who
told me that he had gone to get the boat and gig and
that Dave turned the boat over to him, but would not
let him have the gig, as he "charged Bill Byrne the
price of the gig for taking care of the boat."

About seven years later, which I believe was the term
for which Jacob served for Rachel—and having seen
Dave many, many times during the interim, I was sitting in my office in Charleston one day, when Dave
stepped in and handed me a paper, saying: "Bill, I have
got an option here that I want you to examine for me;
I am buying a lot over on the West Side, and am to pay

a fellow $650.00 for it; just want you to look at the
option and see if it is all right." He handed me the option, which was on an ordinary blank form, and I read
it over carefully, which took something like ten minutes.
When I got through I said, "Dave, I believe this is
all right, it seems to be regular," and handed him back
the option. Thereupon Dave said, "Well, Bill, you
charge me anything?"

Now, I knew Dave well, and had known him for a
great many years, and knew him to be close as the
bark on a tree and also to be one of those fellows who
always counts on getting his legal matters attended to
for nothing, and was so in the habit of getting by that
way, that what I was about to say to him would be the
greatest shock of his life. I said, "Dave you owe me
$10.00."

"What-a-a-t!"

"$10.00."

"My God, Bill, you are not going to charge me
$10.00 for that little work."

"Yes, Dave, $10.00."

Now to the ordinary client, a fee for that service
would have been considered very moderate, and would
have been paid without question or hesitation. But I
was banking on the fact that Dave was no ordinary
client, and his reaction certainly did verify my estimate.

Slowly he reached into his pocket for his wallet, and
slowly he brought it forth; slowly he unwound the
string with which it was bound; slowly he opened the
wallet and took therefrom a $5.00 bill—the beads of
perspiration meanwhile studding his forehead. He extended the $5.00 toward my outstretched hand, reluctant-
ly letting go of it, looked at me most appealingly and
as though to say in the anguish of his soul, "Great God,
isn't that enough"—but I kept my open hand containing the $5.00 extended, and simply looked him in the

eye. Finding me obdurate to his appealing glance, he went down into the wallet again and brought out a dollar bill which he laid on the five, again directing toward me his glance of entreaty; but meeting no sympathetic response, he went back again and again until the five and the four ones were piled up on my hand. Then he looked at me again, but seeing no sign of compassion in my glance, he dug up a fifty cent piece and laid it on the pile, then a twenty-five cent piece, then a dime and another dime, and finally with a sigh that almost shivered his frame, he capped the sheaf with the last nickel. Then it was he said, "My God, Bill, I wouldn't have thought you would have treated me that way."

I said, "Dave, do you remember about that boat and gig?" His answer was a hasty retreat.

I felt so good over the collection of that fee that I took the ten over and gave it to the Salvation Army.

I guess it is true after all, that a fellow will take more to heart anything that happens to his dog, his boat, his hunting outfit or fishing equipment, than any other calamity which may befall.

XXXV

"THE LARGEST SMALLMOUTH BLACK BASS I EVER SAW"

THE largest smallmouth bass I ever saw taken in Elk River was a seven pounder which was caught by a Negro boy in the summer of 1875, at the old dam in Elk River, just above the mouth of Elk Two Mile, a short distance above the present corporation limits of the city of Charleston. He was fishing with a stubby hickory pole and a short, stout line, and when he felt the fish on his hook, he gave a mighty heave and threw his catch over his head and out in the brush on the steep bank behind him. Two or three of us white boys, who were fishing nearby, ran up the bank and helped him keep his fish from flopping back in the river. A number of us, 12- or 13-year-old boys and several men, who were present, formed an escort for the colored boy and his fish, and proudly marched down to town and to the butcher shop operated by E. Cragg and Jim Smoot, on Summers Street, where the bass was duly weighed, measured and hung up for exhibition, at the front door of the shop. The weight was almost exactly seven pounds to the very ounce and the length about 26 or 27 inches. Fish liars were not as plentiful in those days as at present, and my recollection is that there was none who saw the one in question, who claimed to have seen a larger smallmouth black bass. Even Joe Jones, then a young man of about 20, looked with admiration upon this fish, and stood mute.

The next largest was a five-pound bass which I caught immediately at the foot of the End of the World Shoal about 35 years ago. Either the year following or the second year after my memorable trip from Sutton to Clay Court House, with Jake Fisher, Charlie Bland, Ed Rider,

Charlie Ervin and Squack Carpenter—when Jake had such a terrible time with his typewriter—Capt. Edwin D. Camden of Sutton, commonly called Ed, and I, undertook the same trip in a canoe belonging to him. As we approached the End of the World Shoal on the downward trip, I told Ed that there was a big pike always to be found in the pool below that shoal and suggested we try to devise some plan to get him. Observing a rack-heap that formed about the upper end of a large tree that had lodged on the rock bar at the foot of the shoal, which seemed a likely place to catch a goggle-eye, we landed just above the rack-heap, and I proceeded to try for a goggle-eye with which we might troll down through the pool for the pike. I had in the canoe a light 8-foot trout fly-rod, equipped with a reel, a light line and a number 10 trout fly, which we had used from time to time to catch chubs and minnows for bait-fishing, by placing a worm on the hook of the trout fly. I took up this rod, placed a piece of fishing worm on the hook and cast the bait to strike the water just over the rack-heap from where I was standing. I am not sure that bait ever struck the water, for immediately the rod was jerked almost out of my hand, the reel began to sing and the line sped away downstream. Fortunately I had about 50 yards of line, comparatively new, though of only ten or twelve-pound test, and finally succeeded in checking in his mad career this Mr. Fish — I did not even know his baptismal name — whereupon, out of the water he came, and then I saw that it was a huge bass. Realizing that the place where I was standing, with the rack-heap between me and the fish, put me in no proper position for a winning fight, and also seeing that the bass was headed for some large rocks in the river and had almost reached his objective when I checked him and he broke water, I walked up the bar a few steps and waded the shoal to the other side of the river, where I would have a clearer field for action, meanwhile playing him as gently as possible, to keep him from making another dive for those rocks. While I was making the crossing that bass weaved and seesawed from one side of the river to the other, but took little if any more line than he had when I checked him. But it seemed that when he knew that I was all set and ready for the battle to begin, he began it in earnest. Up to that time I had held him with the spring of the rod, but suddenly he made a nose dive for a big rock in the middle of the river, and I was compelled to give him line for fear he would get a straight pull and break the slender thread that held him, but again I was lucky enough to check him just before he reached the rock and again he broke water almost at the rock. Of course, when he came out and splashed back into the water I stole back a lot of line from him. Then he began to seesaw, back and forth from one side to the other, but I was taking line on him all the while, slowly but surely. Finally I had him coming my way, and when he was about 30 feet away and still coming, I wondered how I was going to land him on that rocky bar — not having sense or presence of mind enough to move ten steps farther down where there was a smooth sand bar — and happened to think of a little .22 single shot pistol we had in the canoe — the barrel about a foot long, with a shoulder piece attachment, by means of which it was convertible into a squirrel rifle. So I called to Ed, who had watched the battle from the canoe on the other side of the river, and asked him to bring over the pistol so he could shoot the bass when I reeled him up in the shallow water. Whether or not the line between the bass and me operated as a conductor of speech or thought, I do not know, but at the mention of the word "pistol" that tired bass turned tail, kicked up its heels and took a straight shot for that big rock, and I had it all to do over again; and tired as that bass may have been, he was not at his worst any more tired than was I — nor half as much excited. But I finally whipped him out again, reeled him up into shallow water at Ed Camden's feet, and that gentleman shot him through the head. As the bass turned over from the effect of the shot, I tightened on the line, and the hook came out of his mouth. The shock of the shot may have had something to do with it, but an examination showed that the hold of the tiny hook had gradually lessened and must have been well nigh worn away when the shot was fired.

The bass measured just 24 inches from fork to tip, and according to the scales we found that afternoon at Friend's store just below the mouth of Big Otter, weighed a fraction of an ounce over 5 pounds.

I suppose lots of other people have caught bass quite as large or larger on tackle correspondingly weak or weaker, but I defy any man to say that he got a greater thrill while the proceedings were going on, or was worse used up when the battle was over, than your humble servant on that occasion.

About a year later I caught a 4-1/2 pound bass at Clay C. H. near the bridge; and in August, 1927, I caught a 22-inch bass that weighed 4-1/4 pounds. These three are the only bass I ever caught weighing over 4 pounds.

In 1913 Kemp Littlepage and I went up to the Camp at the End of the World, to fish on the Fourth of July. That was several years before Kemp had developed into the fisherman of renown which he afterwards became — and long before he broke the world's record down in Florida by hooking and landing an 80-pound Tarpon with a 5-1/2 ounce bass rod, and a correspondingly light line. Up to that summer Kemp had never done any fly-fishing, but had been content to devote himself entirely to the use of bait.

At that time Dick Carmichael and his associates were carrying on an extensive lumber operation at Groves Creek, and we invited him to join us in our Fourth of July fishing bout. Dick also was a bait fisherman exclusively; and after supplying ourselves with a liberal allowance of nice creek chubs, we "set in" early and fished late. At the end of a long and arduous day, we wound up at the camp a little before dusk, with just four bass — nice little fellows, they were, averaging between 8 and 9 inches, but just the size which the ordinary fisherman usually "throws back." Having had but a light breakfast and no lunch, we immediately set about to clean our fish and have dinner. Whether because we had such great confidence in our own skill and ability to provide enough fish to supply an abundance of "camp meat," and had failed to bring along ample foodstuff to afford a second line of defense, or whatever may have been the reason, when the meal was fully prepared, the three of us sat down to the table on which were spread those four pitiful little bass, baker's bread, and black coffee. Each fellow took unto himself a fish from the platter and proceeded to feast thereon. We all finished at the same moment, and I grabbed the platter and offered the remaining fish to Dick Carmichael, our guest. "No," said Dick, "I have had plenty, I don't care for any more."

"Here, Kemp, you eat it then," said I, shoving the platter over to him.

"Me? No-o; I'm full, plumb up to the neck. You'll have to eat it if Dick doesn't want it."

"No indeed," said I, "I couldn't swallow another bite to save my life."

And while this Alfonse and Gaston business was seesawing back and forth three ways, the door opened and in strode Annis Nichols, carrying a huge black pot; "Here, fellers, is a pot of snap beans fer you. My wife and the kids went down to Ivydale to a celebration and to stay all night; and she left this pot of beans and some other grub for me to warm up for my supper, but there was ten times more beans than I could eat, so I just 'lowed you fellers might like to have 'em."

In ten minutes that entire pot of beans and as well the chunk of fat bacon half the size of a paving block, with which they were cooked, had disappeared, and Kemp, Dick and I were thus saved from starvation. All of which simply goes to show how self-sacrificing and self-effacing is the ordinary fisherman — and what big liars they are — at times.

Dick Carmichael, by the way, strayed from the Elk, upon the completion of his lumber job, and I did not see him for years, but three or four years ago, as I was passing along the Elk River Road about seven miles above Clay, I saw on the river bank at the mouth of Whetstone a very attractive looking fishing camp, sporting the sign "Camp Sunshine. Dick Carmichael"; and I knew that Dick had yielded to the urge, ever present during his absence, to return to lick the salt of the old Elk; and when I read the sign "Camp Sunshine" I did not need to look further to know whose camp it was.

It was in September, 1914, that I caught that wonderful blue pike — muskellunge seems to be the proper name — in the first pool above and around the bend from the End of the World Shoal. Kemp Littlepage and I had spent a few days at my camp and were returning home on the afternoon train on Sunday. Annis Nichols and his son, Algy, then a boy about 15 years old, were taking us and our baggage up to Groves Creek Station in a johnboat, and when we got to the foot of the End of the World Shoal, I picked up my plug casting rod and a Dowgiac plug and stepped out on the north bank, remarking that while they were getting the boat through the shoal, I would walk up the shore, and catch a pike. I made a rather long cast over near the rib of rocks extending upstream from the rocky point which juts out into the river about middle way the pool, when the pike struck. By that time the boys in the boat were just rounding the point about 100 yards below me, and seeing that I was playing a large fish of some kind, they sped up to lend a hand in the landing. After about 8 minutes play, during which time he broke water beautifully 3 or 4 times, I brought him up into the shallow water 8 or 10 feet out from the edge of a perfectly smooth and gently sloping sand bar, the most ideal spot imaginable for landing a fish of any dimensions, notwithstanding which, however, Kemp grabbed a gig out of the boat, Algy gathered both hands full of rocks and Annis waded out into the water and started to take hold of the line. What I yelled at Annis, was so sudden, vociferous and convincing as to cause him to desist instanter, wade back to shore and let the line alone, and also to deter the others from interfering with gig or rocks in the business, while I gently hauled the pike out on the bar, high and dry. But a few years later, when Rev. Ernest Thompson of the First Presbyterian Church at Charleston was a visitor at my camp, and he and Annis were out fishing near the place, Annis told him of the incident and gave as his version or recollection of the words spoken, the following:

"Don't touch that line, you blank fool! Don't you know that the best way in the world to lose a big fish like that is for some blankety blank idiot to grab the line?" And I must say, if those were my words, they contained much wisdom.

We took our pike on up to Groves Station, which at that time was at the store kept by Charlie Ebert, just above the mouth of Groves Creek. There we weighed him and found the weight to be exactly 12 pounds. On the porch at the front end of the store building, was a bench made of heavy oak boards to seat waiting customers, and after weighing the pike we laid him down flat on this bench and cut deep notches in the board, to mark his length; then with a yardstick we measured and found the length to be thirty-six and one-half inches — three feet and one-half inch — from fork to tip; and you must keep in mind that one-half inch, for around that one-half inch revolves the main point in this story. That board, and the notches representing the length of the pike, remained intact on Charlie Ebert's store porch for several years; but one summer, when my

son-in-law, Dan Mohler and I went up to the store, I
noticed that the old board was gone, having been replaced by a new one. I said, "Charlie, what became of
the board that had the length of my pike notched on it?"

"Oh," he said, "it was getting rotten and I had to
throw it away and put in a new one."

"Yes, and there you have gone and destroyed all the
evidence of the length of my pike."

"No, sir — I'm your evidence on that — and the
weight too — and I'll remember them both as long as I
live. It was three and a half — yes, three feet and a
half — forty-two inches long, and weighed twenty-four
pounds. You needn't be afraid of me ever forgetting
about that pike."

A few years later, and after Charlie had moved his
store down to the present Groves Station, my other son-
in-law, Bob Mesmer, and I, called on him. I had told
Bob about that pike and that I was going to introduce
him to the man who weighed and measured it, and let
him speak as to its size. The introduction over, I said,
"Charlie, I've been telling Mr. Mesmer about that
pike—"

"Oh, you mean that big one you caught and I weighed
it and measured it and cut its length on the bench up
at the old store. Well, sir, that was some fish—the biggest pike I ever seen and I've seen lots of big ones. You
know things like that will git fixed in a feller's mind,
and he never fergits. I always will remember the length
and weight of that pike—he was four and a half—yes
sir, fifty-four inches long, and weighed forty-eight
pounds, and I'll never fergit that as long as I live—the
length or the weight ary one."

In undertaking to reproduce these two statements of
Charlie Ebert, I have, at the risk of making his language
appear most unnatural and wholly unrecognizable to
his friends, deleted all the cuss-words, with which he
invariably embellished his speech. Charlie was one of the
few men of my acquaintance who would even divide his

words into extra syllables in order that he might inter-
lard more expletives.

Now Charlie Ebert did not mean anything criminal
by these statements about that pike, any more than he
did by his inordinate employment of cuss words. He
was simply a bully good fellow; he and I had been
friends for many years, in which time I had done him
some good turns, and he was willing to help me along
by word or deed. And to analyze the matter a little
further, here was that fatal "one-half," that figured in
the equation. Thirty-six inches being just three feet, I
can well understand why Charlie might naturally and
honestly get it fixed in his mind that the one-half applied to feet instead of inches, and that the actual weighing having passed out of his memory, he sought to supply it with figures that would comport with the length,
albeit his spur of the moment conception of proportions
was rather faulty; but when we come to the second stagger which Charlie made at the proposition, a satisfactory
analysis, consistent with probability, is more difficult.
To confuse thirty-six and one-half inches with three
and one-half feet, is not unreasonable, and to raise the
weight in proportion, would of course be natural, although the proportion of twenty-four from twelve
pounds, because of an increase of five and one-half
inches in length, would be considerably out of line, yet
even that might be accepted as within gunshot of
veracity; but the broad jump from thirty-six and one-
half inches and twelve pounds, to fifty-four inches
and forty-eight pounds, or even from forty-two inches
and twenty-four pounds, is to me something more of a
—well, I will leave you to work that out for yourself.
But I will always maintain that Charlie Ebert meant
nothing criminal—knowing full well though he did,
that to lie about the size of a fish is a crime, and a most
heinous one.

Charlie moved away from Groves several years ago,

and I have not seen him since, so it seems that with the notched board and Charlie Ebert both gone, my "best evidence" is no longer at hand.

I am making this public for the first time, not so much to adorn a tale as to point a moral—which is that a fish dead and out of water will oftentimes grow much more rapidly than the same fish if left alive and swimming around; and in so doing am taking the risk of this falling under the eyes of Dan Mohler and Bob Mesmer, and so disabusing their minds of false and lasting impressions—with the making of which, however, you will bear me out, I had nothing to do.

XXXVI

STEPHENSON AND ANDREWS HIRE STUTTERING BILLY "NICKLES"; HENRY DAVENPORT, THE LAW, AND THE PIKE

ONE very interesting character of Clay C. H. and its environs, was William Nichols, commonly called Billy Nickles. Billy lived on the mountain in Spread Bend, about three and a half miles above Clay C. H., on a small farm to which he gave some slight attention, but put in most of his time doing odd jobs for his neighbors, near or remote, leaving the greater part of his own farm work for his "weemin folks." He had the happy faculty of getting in debt to almost every one roundabout, and the unhappy faculty of putting off payment so long as humanly possible, and then "working it out" by slow and easy stages. Billy was a strapping, great big fellow — six feet two in his moccasins — (he wore the last pair of moccasins I ever saw in commission) — and was proportioned accordingly. He was straight as an arrow from his heels to the base of the neck, but his neck, which was quite long, protruded forward from his shoulders almost at right angles to his body, with his head twisted very perceptibly to the left side, which gave him a rather peculiar appearance, and he had a very pronounced squint, which detracted nothing from his distinguishing marks generally. Billy was an expert canoeman, and many is the time Ed Andrews and I have had him steer for us while we gigged all night from Clay C. H. up or down the river six or seven miles and return. He could hold a canoe as steady, in letting it down easily over a shoal, as any man in Clay or Braxton counties—and that is speaking a mouthful.

Billy had a manner of conversation that was peculiarly and exclusively his own. His voice had the alternating coarse and fine break as of a boy with the "goslins," and he had the trick of repeating the last word of every sentence and considerable fraction of any considerable sentence—the repetition being immediately preceded by a slight forward movement of the head, and a semi-guttural sound something between a clearing of the throat and a hacking cough of one syllable; "k-huh," with a distinct rising inflection, beginning with subbass and ending in high tenor, would describe that sound, not accurately, but as nearly as may be; and the word repeated was always peculiarly emphasized and in a high cracked baritone; his manner of speech slow and deliberate, his words chosen with great precision and uttered with a puckered compression of the lips, almost as though prepaiing to whistle. If you asked Billy to do something for you he wouldn't answer you directly, yes or no, to save your life; but after much qualification and a palaver, he always argued himself around to acceding to your request whatever it might be.   He was quite punctilious in giving every man his title "Mister," no odds how familiarly other people might address or speak of him.

One evening when Ed Andrews and I were preparing for an all-night gigging bout, we saw Billy Nichols in the street, and Ed said to him:

"Billy, can you go fishing with us tonight?"

"Well, Mr. Andrews—k-huh—Andrews, I had 'lowed to go to Blue Knob—k-huh—Blue Knob, tonight, to see a feller—k-huh—feller; but I guess tomorry will do—k-huh—will do; and I ain't got nobody—k-huh— Nobody, to send word by to my woman—k-huh—woman —that I won't be home—k-huh—home — but I guess —k-huh—guess, I can go fishin' with you fellers—k-huh•fellers—nevertheless—k-huh—the less."

A. J. Stephenson, who died several years ago, the father of D. H. Stephenson, present (1931) Sheriff of Kanawha County, was a most prominent citizen of Clay C. H., for at least half a century, and well known to every one living in the valley of the Elk. "Uncle Jack," as he was affectionately called by old and young, was clerk of the County Court of Clay County for more than a generation, and for a good part of that time was clerk of the Circuit Court as well. During that period the two clerks' offices were housed in the small two-room hewed log building which stood on the upper corner of the present courthouse lot, immediately on the main street. The residents of Clay C. H. were wont to rely for their coal on a bank which had been opened on Camp Creek, two miles below town and on the same side of the river. Billy Nichols was pretty handy with a coal pick and was frequently called upon by town people to dig their winter's coal for them, which they would haul from the bank by wagon or sled.

Uncle Jack Stephenson's deal with Billy Nichols for his winter supply of coal, is worth relating, albeit the reader who never saw and conversed with Billy will not get all its tone and flavor.

Billy was indebted to Uncle Jack — as was almost everybody else in those days — and Uncle Jack conceived the idea of getting his coal dug as part payment on the account. One day when Billy dropped into the clerk's office, as was usual every time he came to town, Uncle Jack asked him to go down to Camp Creek and dig his winter's coal.

"Well, Mister Stephenson—k-huh—Stephenson; you know I hain't shucked my corn—k-huh—corn an' the old woman is poorly—k-huh—poorly, an' my biggest gal's got the janders—k-huh—janders, an' I promised Mister Mack Triplett—k-huh—Triplett, to help him do a job uv loggin', over on Buffler—k-huh—Buffler; but I guess—k-huh—guess, I kin git my shuckin' done later—k-huh—later, an' Mister Triplett kin git somebody—k-huh—somebody—to help do the loggin'—k-huh—loggin'; so I guess—k-huh—guess, I kin dig your coal next week—k-huh—week."

Billy did not show up the next week, nor the next;

but eventually he came to town, and Uncle Jack wanted
to know why he had failed him.

"Well, you see Mister Stephenson—k-huh—Stephenson, when I promised you about the coal—k-huh—coal,
I thot I had a pick—k-huh—pick, but somebody had
stole it—k-huh—stole it—an' of course—k-huh—course
—a feller can't dig coal without a pick—k-huh—pick."

The upshot was that Uncle Jack agreed to furnish
the pick, and Billy again agreed to dig the coal. On the
appointed day Billy showed up, true to promise, Uncle
Jack purchased a brand-new pick, with which on one
shoulder and his grub sack on the other—or likely
pick and grub sack on the same shoulder—Billy strode
through town on his way to Camp Creek.

Three or four days later Uncle Jack happened to
be looking out of the window and saw Billy Nichols,
away over on the far side of the road, going past the
clerk's office and in the direction of his home at a gait
much more rapid than usual. Wondering why this was
thus, Uncle Jack opened the door and called to Billy,
who slowly turned and wended his way across the road
and into the office.

"Well, Billy, did you get my coal dug?"

"Well, you see, Mister Stephenson—k-huh—Stephenson, as I was goin' through town that mornin'—k-huh
—mornin', to dig your coal—k-huh—coal—Mister Mort
Frame—k-huh—Frame—you see he's prosecutin' attorney—k-huh—'torney; an' I been owin' him ten dollars on a fine—k-huh—fine—an' he axed me where
wuz I goin'—k-huh—goin'—an' I told him down to
Camp Creek—k-huh—Creek—to dig coal fer Mister
Stephenson—k-huh—Stephenson; an' he threatened to
jail me—k-huh—jail me, ef I didn't dig him that coal—
k-huh—coal, an' pay off that fine—k-huh—fine; so I
had to do the diggin'—k-huh—diggin', fer Mister
Frame—k-huh—Frame."

"Well, where's my pick?" said Uncle Jack, hot as
pepper.

"Well, you see, Mister Stephenson—k-huh—Stephenson, I owed Mister Frame ten dollars on the fine—k-huh—fine, an' my coal diggin' only come to eight dollars—k-huh—dollars, an' I jist give him the pick—k-huh—pick, an' he agreed to call it square—k-huh—square."

While Billy Nichols died a good many years ago, he will never completely have passed away, so long as Dr. Ben Sears, once a resident of Clay, but now a practicing physician somewhere in Calhoun County, is alive and able to impersonate him, as I have heard him do on many occasions. If Dr. Ben could be prevailed upon to quit pill rolling and go on the vaudeville circuit with his impersonations of Billy Nichols, he could travel in his own private car between points and buy the hotel during the stops.

Take him by and large and as a class, you will find it entirely safe to rely absolutely on any and everything a fisherman tells you. It seems that it is peculiarly inferential of that pursuit or sport to imbue the devotee with the very essence of truth and veracity, and to exercise every element of guile, duplicity or falsehood. There are, of course, notable exceptions to this, as well as to all other general rules; and I have encountered rare instances of a fisherman—even of fair standing and repute, who has sought to put something over on a guileless and unsuspecting brother.

In the month of November, 1914, Henry B. Davenport, who at that time lived at Clay, but who was a frequent visitor at Charleston, came into my office, and with an air of triumph handed me the photograph of which the accompanying picture is a reproduction, and said:

"Now you old pike fisherman, let me show you a real pike that I caught."

I took the photograph and examined and commented admiringly upon the beautiful fish.

"Where did you catch him, Henry?"

"I caught him off the bridge at Clay."

"Forty-two inches long; 24 pounds," I read. "He certainly is a beauty. I see Porter Hyer was along with you."

"Yes, Porter was with me when I caught him."

After the first rather casual examination of the picture, I sat down and began to make a more thorough inspection of the layout. The setup did not appear to me as altogether natural, and I began a mental analysis of the details. Here were shown in the picture a light casting rod, the plug showing as a light wooden contraption; and there was a bait bucket; a fellow would hardly cast from the bridge for pike, and especially with such a frail outfit; if he did snag such a pike as that and on that outfit, how in the world did he ever land him? And, if he caught the pike on that plug, why the bait bucket? The expression on the face of Porter Hyer, whom I knew very well, attracted my attention —that bland, innocent childlike expression, which Porter is wont to assume when he is on the eve of springing some diabolical prank on an unsuspecting victim—that to me, was a "stop, look and listen" sign; I then transferred my gaze to Henry Davenport in the picture, and noted that sinister expression about his eyes and mouth, so foreign to his usual appearance; and then, looking at Henry in the flesh, as he sat there in front of me, intently watching my every movement, I detected the identical expression delineated in the picture.

I knew that there was some hokum about the layout, but of course did not know wherein it lay; but venturing to guess, I bent over the picture intently a moment and then remarked—"That little black spot up there near the head—it looks like it might be a bullet hole—."

"Let me see that!" said Henry, as he reached over and grabbed the photograph out of my hand—"well, I'll be durned!"

Well, that's all there was to it; Henry broke down

and confessed that he and Porter Hyer had gone out on the bridge with a high-power rifle, shooting a steel-jacket ball, and murdered the poor defenseless pike; and that they had conceived the idea of the photograph with the fishing paraphernalia, in order to create the impression in the public mind that the pike had been taken in the more approved manner.

But it certainly was a fine pike, and a fellow could not be greatly blamed for getting one like it any way he might and then telling any sort of a yarn which seemed to best fit the occasion.

XXXVII

BILLY "NICKLES" CALLS ON J. G. BRADLEY; JUDGES OF THE LAW AND OF FISH

I CHANCED to run across Henry Davenport on the street a few days after the story of the pike came out in the last issue of *Wild Life,* and he indicated that I had not done him full justice in recounting that story. I stated how sorry I was that such should have been the case, as it was always the chief aim and purpose of The Tales of The Elk to do equal and exact justice to all men with whom it dealt, and assured him that if he would point out wherein he had been wronged, I would be only too glad to make the amends honorable.

"Well," said Henry, "you make it appear in that story that my fishing tackle had nothing to do with catching that pike. The fact is, I was down under and a little below the bridge, casting for pike, and while engaged in the act, Porter Hyer came out on the bridge with a high-power rifle, and seeing this pike in the clear water, cut down on and shot him through the body. The pike immediately came to the top of the water opposite where I was standing on the bank, and about 60 feet out in the river—and I made a quick cast with my wooden plug just over and beyond him, and reeling the line in snagged the pike in the gills and landed him. So as a matter of fact, I did catch that pike with that tackle."

I am glad indeed to have this correction made, in order that all the participants in the transaction may have their exact dues.

In that conversation the other day Davenport reminded me of another Billy Nichols story, which I had forgotten:

Mr. J. G. Bradley who has for many years been the executive head of the Elk River Coal & Lumber Company, which owns the greater part of what was originally the Wilson 93,000-acre survey, already described in these Chronicles as embracing practically all the territory of Clay County on the south side of Elk from a point three miles below Clay C. H., up to the Braxton County line, has resided for several years near Dundon, on and near the mouth of Big Buffalo Creek, which empties into Elk opposite the upper end of the town of Clay. In the past two decades Bradley has developed two of the largest coal operations in the state, at Widen, on Buffalo, about 25 miles from its mouth. He has served two or more terms as President of the National Coal Operators Association and was for a long time, and probably now is, President of the West Virginia Coal Operators Association.

From all surface indications, Bradley is the very personification and double-distilled quintessence of sober-sided seriousness and gravity, but deeply underlying, is a sub-stratum of humor and keen appreciation of the facetious turns of thought and action—those subtle intellectual convolutions, which tend so greatly to relieve the deadly monotony and corrosive effects of the humdrum daily grind.

As a matter of course Mr. Bradley became well acquainted with Billy Nichols, and it was one of his delights to push the button which would set Billy in motion, when the two came in casual contact. Billy was an ardent Democrat, and Bradley was wont, in a quiet and apparently casual way, to provoke him to a political discussion, in order that he might enjoy the reaction.

About the time Woodrow Wilson was elected president in 1912, Mr. Bradley had completed a large band-mill at Swandale, which is a few miles up Buffalo from its mouth—for use in manufacturing the timber on the lands of his company.

For some reason this mill was not put in operation until about two years after its completion. During the campaign of 1914, Billy Nichols happened to run across Mr. Bradley and this conversation ensued:

"Mr. Bradley—k-huh—Bradley—whenever you git ready—k-huh—ready, to start your mill at Swandale—k-huh—Swandale—I would like to git me a job—k-huh—job."

"Why Billy, I am very sorry, but I have decided not to put the mill in operation as long as Woodrow Wilson is President."

"Well, Mr. Bradley—k-huh—Bradley—it 'pears to me like you was calculating—k-huh—calculating—to let her rot down—k-huh—down."

About twenty years ago, when Judge Samuel C. Burdette was Judge of the Circuit Court of the Circuit which comprised the counties of Kanawha and Clay, I was engaged in the trial of a case in the latter county, which occupied about a week. My old friend, the late John T. Harris, Clerk of the State Senate at the time—by the way, one of the most excellent court reporters I ever knew, and who was in Charleston closing up the work of a legislative session—at the request of Judge Burdette, went to Clay to report the case in question. Judge Burdette, John Harris and I stopped at what was then the Hotel Stephenson, and in the long evenings when we had nothing else to do, the three of us, with such others as might from time to time join the circle around the old Burnside stove, whiled away the time, swapping stories—for the greater part of the piscatorial variety. Judge Sam was no slouch of a fisherman, as many of the old-timers on the Elk, the Gauley, the Greenbrier and Coal River can well attest; John Harris had had large experience in that line, and each of these gentlemen was chock-full of incidents of personal experience in that behalf, and able to recount them in manner and form both instructive and entertaining. Each story told by one of the three would remind one of the others of a similar happening; and after two or three evenings, we began to run short of true and actual occurrences, and as each fellow began gradually to inch on the truth and take occasional flights into the realms of fancy, and the others in turn would take the same liberty and aim to go him at least one better; along toward the last, it became rather common for the veracity of the last narrator to be challenged by the other two, by such delicate methods as the arching of eyebrows, a mean, questioning smile, an insulting, long-drawn whistle and, if possible, such an inoffensive remark as— "Witnesses all dead—I presume?"

After the term had adjourned, the Judge, Harris and I, took the same train for Charleston, and while walking from the hotel over to the railroad station, Judge Burdette bethought him of a story he had overlooked in his repertory. He said he was bass-fishing up on the Greenbrier, with live minnows, and in rowing up through a long pool, he observed a fellow standing on a large rock in the middle of the river, with a fishing pole in his hand and looking quite disconsolate. In replying to the usual inquiry, "Catching anything?" the fellow replied, "Out of bait." Judge Sam had but two minnows in his bucket, but like a true sport, he split them 50-50 with the chap, wished him good luck and proceeded to the head of the pool. Half an hour later he returned, to find the same chap, standing on the same rock. As he passed, some distance away, he asked, "What luck?" and the fellow reached down and held up a red-horse about twenty inches long. Never having heard of catching a red-horse on a live minnow, in some wonderment the Judge asked if it could be possible that he had caught that red-horse on the minnow. The answer was in the negative, but that the red-horse had come to the top of the water at the edge of the rock, and that the fellow had prodded him with the butt of the fishing pole, so stunning the fish that he caught it with his hands.

"Witness living, Judge?" said John Harris.

"Hold on, John," said I, "I will not permit you to question that story in the slightest; it reminds me of an actual occurrence in which I was chief actor."

I then proceeded to relate this story:

When I was a boy of sixteen, my father and Hon. Henry S. Walker, owned a large tract of timber land on the Adonijah (Donager) Fork of Big Sycamore Creek which empties into Elk ten miles below Clay. They determined to have the oak timber made into staves, which were to be "splashed" out of Big Sycamore into the river by means of a splash dam at the mouth of Donager, and thence at Charleston; the "splash" being so timed that the staves should reach the river when it was at a sufficiently high tide to carry the staves on its crest. Always after a splash, it was necessary to have a follow-up crew, to go along and gather up the straggling staves which had lodged along the creek banks, throw them into the current and follow them down to the mouth of the creek. As the tide in the river had always subsided before these stragglers reached the mouth of the creek, it was found necessary to place a boom consisting of two "gunnels," across the mouth of the creek to keep the staves from going into the river at a low stage and drifting idly down behind a small island or bar at the head of the shoal, a short distance below the mouth of the creek, and on the same side of the river. The water in the creek for some distance above this boom at its mouth, was fairly deep, and when these staves had all been driven into the boom, the practice was to detach the upper end of the boom, swing it out in the river as far as the two "gunnel" lengths would reach—some 150 feet, anchor it there, push the staves out along these "gunnels" and let them float down into the shoal, ready for the next freshet.

"Tige" Johnson, an old Wetzel County stave man, was put in charge of the enterprise, and he and his family were quartered at the camp at the mouth of Donager. He had three boys, Bill and Ves and Johnny, the first two mentioned being grown young men. I spent two summer vacations and two Christmas holidays at Johnson's camp while this stave job was going on, fishing and hunting.

I happened to be present on one occasion when the crew was at the mouth of the creek, conducting these staves out of the boom along the "gunnels" and out into the current. A stout stick or long cane, forked at the end, by means of which a goodly sized batch of staves was pushed by a person walking on the "gunnel," was the process used; and on this occasion, seeking to be helpful in the work, I had taken a hand and a stick. Returning on one trip from the outer end of the "gunnel" toward the shore and at a point where the water was very deep, I saw a large red-horse come to the top of the water within three feet of me, and quickly reversing the ends of my stick, I prodded him viciously alongside of the head with the butt end. He turned belly upward, and like a flash I was on him, and luckily caught his gills with the fingers of my right hand, my thumb in his puckered mouth. You may imagine the tussle we had. The fish but slightly stunned, quickly came to life and set about to battle for it—and some battle it was! He was in his element and I was out of mine. Half the time we were on top of the water and the other half at the bottom of the river. I had to hold on with one hand and try to swim with the other, which was no easy matter, with the fish twisting, darting and cavorting in an effort to extricate himself. After a struggle lasting a few hours—or minutes, or seconds— I do not know which—it has been so long ago—I finally got back to the "gunnel" and landed the red-horse; and I dare say, like Uncle Burton Pierson's flock of red-horse in Birch River—both this red-horse and I were in a "perfect lather of sweat." Gentlemen, when that red-horse was dressed it weighed six pounds—one of the largest I ever saw.

"Witnesses all dead, I presume?" said the Judge.

I replied that there were doubtless some witnesses still living, but that I would not take the trouble to locate them, and would resent the dirty insinuation. At that very instant I looked down the platform and saw a man standing 30 feet away, whom I thought I recognized. I beckoned to him and he came up to where we stood. I said, "Are you Ves Johnson?" "Yes, sir; but you've got the advantage of me—why if it ain't Billy Byrne. I haven't seen you for 15 or 20 years."

I introduced Ves Johnson to the Judge and Harris, and simply said, "Gentlemen, take the witness."

"Mr. Johnson," said the Judge with more than usual judicial gravity, "do you happen to remember anything about Will Byrne, when he was a boy, killing a large red-horse?"

"Red-horse? Let me see. I mind about him doing a lot of fishing down about Big Sycamore when we was on a stave job. He spent two or three summers—Oh, yes, I mind all about it now—some kind of a big fish—guess it was a red-horse."

"Do you remember how he killed that fish, Mr. Johnson?"

"Well now, I don't remember just exactly how it was; but 'pears to me he hit it with a rock or something—No, I guess it must have been a stave maybe he hit it with— we was working with some staves there at the mouth of Big Sycamore. 'Pears to me he was on a gunnel and hit that fish with something, and stunned it and then jumped in on top of it. What I mind most about it was, that him and the fish had it up and down there in the deep water fer quite a spell, sometimes his head was out and sometimes under, and us fellows out on the bank was just getting ready to go out to him, when he finally landed his fish."

Now this was what I call corroboration, and I am sure that the pride with which I swelled up, was pardonable.

Then the Judge said, in deeper and more judicial tones: "Mr. Johnson, how big was that red-horse?"

"Well, sir, that was a powerful big red-horse—powerful big. It was the biggest red-horse I ever seen. That red-horse must have weighed — let me see — (gazing skyward)—gentlemen, that red-horse must have weighed nigh on to twenty pound!!!"

"Will," said the Judge, "I understood you to say six pounds."

"Judge," I replied, looking at my witness standing there like a stone wall, and determined not to desert one who had stood by me so nobly, "you misunderstood me; I said sixteen;—and you, gentle reader, would have done the same thing, under similar circumstances.

XXXVIII

THE PIKE THAT BROKE UP COURT; GEORGE E. PRICE DOUBTS JURY AND FISH

IN THE year 1912, Dr. B. C. Eakle, of Clay Court House, and myself, as attorneys for George Goad, brought a suit in the Circuit Court of Clay County to recover the possession of certain land lying on Elk River at the mouth of Waters Defeat Creek, against Walker and Reed and others. While the action was unlawful detainer, the trial involved practically all the elements of ejectment, and every question pertaining to color of title, location, boundary, possession and tenancy, was raised and hotly contested. Senator George E. Price, of Charleston, represented the defendants. Everybody, and especially every lawyer, knows Senator Price and knows him to be a most dangerous adversary at the bar. His fighting qualities are unexcelled even by the "Fuzzy-Wuzzy in his home in the Soudan," and no lawyer ever engaged with him in a legal battle and came out with a hide wholly whole.

The first trial lasted about four days and resulted in a hung jury. The second, which was held six months later, consumed a day or two longer and again a hung jury. A third trial, covering more than a week, ended with practically an instructed verdict for Senator Price's clients.

Mr. Eakle and I took the case to the Supreme Court of Appeals and obtained a reversal of the judgment and the award of a new trial. 73 W. Va. 431. The case was docketed for the fourth jury trial at the September term, 1914, of Clay Circuit Court, and under an arrangement with Judge Samuel C. Burdette, who occupied the bench, our case was set specially for a certain day in the term, when presumably the other business of the court would be out of the way. Both sides made full preparation for the coming trial, and everybody was equally anxious to write the final chapter to the long drawn-out litigation. The witnesses, about 20 per side, were all summoned, and everything was supposed to be ready for the day set for trial. On the morning of the appointed day, Senator Price and I boarded the Coal and Coke train at Charleston and together traveled to Clay Court House. We occupied the same seat in the coach, and I was holding a round canvas case in my hand.

Senator Price, referring to the canvas case, said:

"What's that—a map?"

"No; a fishing rod."

"What are you going to do with it?"

"Catch a pike."

"Where?"

"Clay Court House."

"Didn't know there were any fish up there."

"Not in the Court House, but in Elk River, at, near, or in the vicinity of that certain city, town or village commonly known, called and designated Clay Court House."

"How big a pike do you expect to catch in Elk River, at, near, or in the vicinity of that certain city, town or village commonly known, called and designated Clay Court House?"

"Oh, ten or twelve pounds. I caught a twelve pounder about ten days ago, on this same rod."

"In Elk River?"

"Yes."

"At Clay Court House?"

"No; up at my Camp at the End of the World."

"Don't believe there are any such fish in Elk River."

"All right, I'll show you."

Reaching our destination we proceeded to the court-room and found Judge Burdette, with a jury, trying the case last on the docket before ours. As we walked into the room, the Judge saw us, and asked if we would be ready with the case of Goad vs. Walker and Reed, at the conclusion of the case on trial, stating that his reason for making the inquiry was that if there was no probability of a trial he would like to know in advance of the actual calling of the case, so the court, jury and witnesses might arrange to get away as early as possible. I answered that the plaintiff was ready if his witnesses were present, and Senator Price made a similar statement for the defendants. The witnesses were called, and all but two or three for the plaintiff and about the same for the defendants, responded. The plaintiff announced ready for trial, and Senator Price stated he felt sure the defendants would be ready against the time the case would be called, but that he would rather not definitely so state at the time. The court then stated that he must have a definite answer at one o'clock, on the reconvening of the court after the noon recess.

Finding I would be free for that time — about 11:00 a.m. until 1:00 p.m., I decided to put in the time making good my promise to Senator Price regarding the pike. On the train that morning I had seen L. C. McKim, who showed me a brand-new pike spoon—a very attractive lure, it seemed to me; and on going to the hotel to get my fishing tackle, I found McKim, and proposed that we go fishing and try out his new spoon. He was more than willing, and, borrowing a boat from Bank Cashier McLane, we were soon afloat and headed downstream from the bridge. I had suggested that it was fine pike water from about the bridge down to O'Briens Ford, a distance of less than half a mile, and it was agreed that McKim would row and I would fish going down, and that we would reverse the order coming back. I attached McKim's spoon to my line and rod, and trolling the deep water near the north

bank about halfway between the bridge and the north
I got a strike, and after a nice little scrap landed a ten-
pound pike. We got nothing on the return trip, so we
proceeded with the boat up as far as the rear of the
hotel lot. As I came out to the main street with the
pike, I met the whole court outfit, Judge, jurors, lawyers, witnesses and everybody else, in front of the hotel,
court having just recessed for noon—and, in the very
forefront of the array, Senator Price. On seeing the
fish which I was proudly sporting, that gentleman
made some explosive ejaculation—"Well, I be—," I
did not clearly catch the fourth word of the sentence
but as he never cusses, I am inclined to think it was
"blest." Everybody had to see and feel and heft the
pike, and crowd into an adjoining store to see it weighed.
I then took it, still alive and kicking, and put it in the
hotel bath tub, where the whole posse comitatus went
to view and review it.

Promptly at 1:00 p.m. court reassembled, and the
plaintiff in Goad vs. Walker and Reed, again announced ready for trial. Thereupon Senator Price, for
the defendants, arose and soberly stated that some of the
witnesses for the defendants were still absent, and that
as there was no assurance that such witnesses would be
present, the defendants would be compelled to ask for a
continuance, as he did not believe they "could safely go
to trial under the circumstances."

We strenuously opposed the continuance, emphasizing
the fact that all parties had made extensive preparations
to try the case; that it had been thoroughly understood
that it would be tried at that term, and that special arrangements had been made by the court to give it clear
right-of-way; that about forty witnesses had been summoned, all but four or five of whom were present, probably a larger per cent than could ever be had again, and
we presented other strong reasons why the trial should
proceed.

Senator Price again made an earnest appeal for a continuance on the ground of the absent witnesses. We pressed him for the names of the absent ones, and he named two. We turned to the printed record in the Supreme Court and called attention to the fact that these witnesses had testified on the former trial and their testimony appeared in full in that record and could be read on the present trial. Senator Price insisted, however, that the reading of testimony always lessened its effect as compared with having the witnesses present before the jury, and appealed to the court more earnestly even than before, to continue the case.

Greatly to our surprise, the court continued the case, discharged the jury, and adjourned court for the term.

Returning home on the afternoon train, I said to Senator Price:

"Why the sudden change; I thought you were anxious to try the case."

"I was; but was not going to try it before a jury that was so much interested in that pike."

Before the coming of the next term the case was settled by compromise.

I had another experience, which, however, I am always reticent to speak of, and never even now, after the lapse of so many years, refer to it, except to my most intimate friends: About twenty years ago an old chap by the name of John Hall, lived on a tract of land in which I was interested, on Elk River at Middle Creek about four miles below Clay C. H. He was a great fisherman, and the most monumental fish liar I ever met. I used to visit him for two or three days at a time and join in both pastimes. One day he and I were out in his boat bass fishing; the fish had quit biting and as we were floating down toward home through a long pool, John pointed out, on the far side of the river, a large, old, dead tree which had uprooted on the bank and fallen into the water, "Do you see that big log over thar in the edge of the river—or did I tell you about ketchin' that catfish outen that log last year?"

"No; you did not; let's have it."

"Well, I was fishin' over nigh thar last summer, an' I noticed a big hole in that log, about three foot under the water, an' I knowed that catfish made their nestes in such places, an' I had heerd—but never paid no attention, thinkin' it were jist a durn fish lie—that if you wuz to poke a stick in thar an' a catfish wuz on the nest, the catfish 'ud grab the stick in its teeth to get it outen thar an' hold on long enough to land him in the boat. So thinks I, I'll jist try it wonct to show they ain't no truth in the danged lie—about ketchin' the fish ef they wuz one in thar. So I paddled over to the log, an' they wuzn't nobody with me, so I ties the boat to that limb you see stickin' up out of the water—right nigh the hole—you could see the hole if you wuz over thar. So I picked me up a stick layin' in the boat—about five foot long—by gosh, thar's the same durn stick layin' thar in the boat yit—an' I oozed the end of the stick e-e-zy like, in the hole an' right off peerintly, I felt sumpin' grab the stick, an' could feel his teeth grittin' on it; I let him get a good holt an' then I oozed the stick out e-e-zy like, an' brung him up to the top of the water an' into the boat, an' the danged thing held on till he hit the bottom of the boat—a twenty-inch cat, by gum!"

"O ye gods, ye gods! Must I endure all this? John Hall," said I, "if a thunderbolt should come out of yon clear sky and strike you dead for that infamous, outrageous, unreasonable, insulting and gratuitous lie you have just uttered, I would simply sit here and smile. But for the fact that you own the only decent boat in this neighborhood, and are such a good hand to get bait, I would never speak to you again, and would feel myself everlastingly disgraced even to be caught in your society."

"Ha, ha, I knowed it. Them's the very words I said to the feller that told me he ketched a catfish that a-way.

I wouldn't a believed it ef he had swore it on a stack uv Holy Bibles high as my head. I don't blame you nary bit — never woulda believed it myself ef I hadn't did it myself."

"Now, you unmitigated old liar," said I, "paddle over to that log you are talking about, I just want to see if you are even lying about the hole in it; and I'll bet my hat you are."

"Well, I ain't needin' a hat particular, or I'd take that bet."

We went over to the log, and there in the trunk about three feet under water and near the projecting limb, was a hole about the size of a dinner plate.

"I don't know whuther they is a catfish at home or not," said John Hall, "but you mout take thet stick an' ooze it e-e-zy like, in the hole an' see."

"All right, you old scoundrel," said I, "I am going to do it, just to show you up. If there should happen to be a fish when I punch in there with the stick, he'll break his neck getting out."

"Don't punch; ooze it in e-e-zy."

So I proceeded to "ooze it in e-e-zy," and before the stick had "oozed" very far, much to my surprise, I felt something take hold, and John Hall cried exultantly— "Let him get a good grip an' then ooze him out e-e-zy."

Which I did—and in much less time than it has taken me to describe the business, a 22-inch mud cat was flopping on the bottom of the boat.

"John Hall," said I, "ordinarily I would offer you a most humble, abject and contrite apology, but I have decided simply to let what I have said about you in this connection, stand firm and binding, as applicable to other horrible lies you have told in this fishing business. But I hope you will so far forgive me as to pledge me your word—the sacred word and honor of a fisherman, that you will never by word, sign or token make reference or allusion to what has just transpired, unless and until I release you from your promise. In years to come I hope to establish such an irreproachable and unimpeachable character and reputation for truth and veracity, that I may afford to tell and have told the true story of this incident; but until then forget it and let it be as though it had never been."

John Hall carried the secret to his grave, some ten years ago, and it has been only within the past year or so that I have felt that the moment had at last arrived that I might safe-venture to relate the story.

I here adopt the sentiments of the fellow—doubtless a fisherman—who said—

"I do not fear to follow out the truth, albeit along the precipice's edge."

XXXIX

A VISIT TO UPPER ELK; BATS AND SNAKES

IT IS surprising how very few trout fishermen are aware that fly-fishing by moonlight is the best way to take trout. Next best to moonlight is the first streak of dawn, and next to that, early twilight. But this story has nought to do with twilight nor the dawn, but with moonshine.

About fifteen years go, I was on one of my annual visits to the trout waters up toward the head of Elk and Gauley rivers, from twenty to thirty miles above Webster Springs, with "Bearskin Bill" Hamrick, referred to in the early stages of this Tale—who, by the way, was one of the best fishermen and all-round good scouts it was ever my good fortune to meet. Year after year, usually in August, I would journey to his place, and we would set out for a trip during the light of the moon, each equipped with fishing rod and "pack-poke," the latter containing little else than a frying pan, bread, fat bacon, coffee, sugar, salt and such necessaries—as our only impedimenta. On this occasion we went first to Gauley at the mouth of Straight Creek, and thence up the river to its head and over the mountain to the junction of the Big Spring and Old Field Forks of Elk. For about two and one-half miles below the forks the water pursues the even tenor of its way, and then suddenly changes that tenor, sinks and comes to light again after traversing a distance of six miles underground, at Cowger's Mill, as heretofore described.

We fished in the daytime with varying success, our catch ranging in size from under six to nine inches; then, waiting for the moon to rise, we would go over the same ground, catching usually more in number and always larger ones, than in daylight.

One evening we built our campfire and had supper at a point about halfway between the forks of the river and the "Boiling Hole," so called because there the greater part of the water sinks, causing air bubbles to rise to the surface, as when water boils. When the moon rose, "Bearskin Bill" started off upstream and I downstream. After fishing several hours, I found myself, about 3 o'clock in the morning, at what is called the "Twin Pools"—two small pools about thirty feet square, separated by a large flat rock jutting from the bank on one side. I stepped out on this rock and, facing upstream, stripped a few yards of line preparatory to making a cast in the upper pool, but was careful to observe the menacing, overhanging branches of the hemlock tree, standing just below the rock. I made two casts without a strike and in making the third, I felt my line come in contact with some object behind me. Thinking I had snagged the line on a bough of the hemlock, I turned in that direction to see about disengaging it; at that instant, much to my surprise, I felt a sharp tug from about the surface of the water in the upper pool; I gave a jerk, thinking that when I snagged the line I had jerked hard enough to disengage it, and that the spring of the rod had carried the fly to the upper pool into the waiting mouth of a hungry trout; then I felt a tug to the left, and then I thought—no, then I quit thinking! Then came a tug to my right, a tug straight up in the air and on all sides and in every direction. Excitedly and with nervous fingers, I began mechanically to reel in my line which, meanwhile, was making all manner of fantastic gyrations.

Imagine a fellow at 3 o'clock in the morning, out on a rock in the middle of the river, in the wildest section of God's great outdoors, five miles from the nearest habitation or human being—except his fishing partner, then two miles away—after a strenuous day and night, yes, several days and nights, of the most arduous, incessant and nerve-depleting toil—tired, weary, fagged, and both physically and mentally all in—with a flying fish cavorting and galumphing in the very immediate ambient.

I recall that my mind wholly ceased to function during the seconds it took me to reel in that line, except to suggest and cause me to repeat inaudibly, over and over again: "Is dis hu'h me or not me, or has de debbil got me?" Well, to shorten the longest short story I ever lived through, it was a BAT! He had evidently mistaken one of my flies for the genuine, just at the trout is supposed to do—made a grab at it and hooked himself in his leather-like wing, from which, when I finally landed him on the rock, I had trouble to disengage it.

A year later my son and I were in that section together. We had fished below and at Cowger's Mill, and walked up over the six miles of "Dry Bed" as it is called, arriving at the upper river a little after nightfall. We noticed a good place for a campfire along our path, and stopped for the night. After starting the fire, we went through a brush thicket down to the river to clean, for our late supper, some of the trout we had caught during the day.

I had told my son about my experience with the bat, and while at the water's edge, cleaning the fish, I recognized the place and observed that we were directly across the river from the flat rock above described.

I said: "George, that rock you see across the river is the very one on which I stood when I caught the bat; and you see those branches—that is the hemlock—"

"Wow," yelled George, "What's that? Something fell on my hand!"

I turned my flashlight in his direction and there, struggling among the rocks, were two baby bats that had evidently dropped out of a nest in an overhanging hemlock, and fallen on George's hand.

This story is intended to be read by the elect only—

and by the elect is meant those who are equipped with sufficient knowledge and experience of and concerning the subject matter treated of, to be able to recognize and appreciate the truth when they see it in print.

Bats are more or less suggestive of snakes, and thinking of snakes reminds me to relate in this connection an experience of mine at a rattlesnake den, not far out of the Elk watershed.

Doubtless many *Wild Life* readers would consider it a wildly and hazardous undertaking, to invade a den of rattlesnakes and take alive the "whole kit and bilin'." Well, the main excitement connected with the enterprise, according to my experience, was the long and arduous climb up the mountain side, finding the exact den and finding the quarry after the den had been located; and the hazard was negligible as compared with the robbing of a bee tree.

In the summer of 1896 or 1897, I had occasion to be at Camden-on-Gauley, in Webster County, and decided to visit my old friend Carl McLaughlin, who lived about three and one-half miles distant therefrom on Cranberry Ridge, and with whom I had been on many hunting and fishing expeditions, to make arrangements for a fall hunt. On going to his house I was informed that he, with a party, was trout fishing over on Cranberry River, and camped near the mouth of Fox Tree, which flows into Cranberry about 10 miles above its mouth. Though not equipped for fishing at the time, I proceeded to his camp, and found Carl, with John Foulke and Emmett Thorne and Carl's two boys, Elden and Roy. When I reached their camp, the party was about ready to sally forth in search of a rattlesnake den, reputed to be located in a cliff on the point of the mountain between main Cranberry and Fox Tree, and "just to be sociable," I went along. The way to our objective lay up the rough and rocky way around and among large rocks that had broken away from the upper cliffs and were dispersed along the mountain side. After a climb of a thousand or more feet we came to the lower base of the cliff presenting a perpendicular face of about fifty feet, which we supposed to contain the den; but upon careful inspection were unable to find any indications whatever that this cliff, so far as concerned that part of its face which we could see from the ground, had ever been the habitat of snakes. However, as the upper portion was not visible from our viewpoint, we decided that there was a chance that the den might be in the top section of the rocks. To reach the top we were compelled to traverse the mountain side up and along the Fox Tree slope for more than half a mile, until we found a place where there was sufficient slant to the rocks to admit of our ascent. From this point we took a photograph in direction down the ridge, showing the cliffs in the middle foreground. Having reached the top of the point ridge we walked down the point and came out on top of the cliff first described. We neared the edge of the precipice and were looking for some cleft in the rocks which might house our reptiles, when we heard a gentle b-z-z-z, and Roy McLaughlin, eight years old and barefoot, called out, "Here they are!" and pointed to the underside of a semi-flat rock on the top and fifty feet back from the edge of the cliff. By stooping down, we could see an opening under one side of the rock, and there, all entwined as in one huge plait or braid, we discovered nine, as they were afterwards counted, rattlesnakes, of varied hues and sizes, gazing at our party of intruders, as calmly and unflushed as though they were as many pigs in a pen—the occasional b-z-z-z being almost inaudible and unaccompanied by any manifestation or gesture of fear, anger or flight. Our first thought was to get a snapshot as the snakes were huddled together under the rock, when first discovered, but the idea was discarded for the reason that the apperture was not large enough to afford sufficient

light to show under the rock. We then decided to raise
one side of the rock sufficiently to let in the light so
the snakes would show in the picture. This rock was
about four by five feet by ten inches, and by means of
a log for a lever and a stone for the fulcrum, we pried
it upon one side. While this was going on the snakes appeared a little restless and once or twice seemed about
to dissolve the union and glide out in different directions, but being armed with long sticks provided for the
purpose, when a snake would start to break ranks, we
were able by a gentle snip on the nose to cause him to
change his mind and resume his proper place.

After the rock was turned up and the snakes nicely
huddled, we took a snapshot of the layout; but there
was not sufficient light to show the snakes.

The process of taking the snakes alive was simple,
very easy and attended with no more danger than the
catching of a butterfly. The sticks we had prepared
were about six feet long and on the small end of each had
been tied a cord with a slip noose. When everything was
in readiness, the ones herding the snakes let them out, one
by one—holding the others back for their turn. There
was but one avenue of escape and that was through the
waiting noose, which was promptly snapped the instant
the head of the snake had entered. The stick with the
snake dangling from the noose, was placed upright
against a tree, until the job was done.

One of the large snakes on being placed upon the
flat top of the cliff and the pressure of the noose upon
its throat somewhat relieved, disgorged nine baby rattlers
as shown in the picture. Thus the mother rattlesnake
nourishes and protects her young until they are from ten
to twelve inches in length.

We had provided a good strong meal sack into which
all the snakes were deposited, one at a time—the sack
securely tied and fastened to the middle of a long pole,
so that two men could easily and safely carry the load,

and in this manner the "Cranberry livestock" was delivered to the camp. We had some thought of preserving our catch alive, and for that reason took them down to the camp; but afterward abandoned the idea, and killed all of them, skinning the larger ones and intending to tan and preserve the skins; but unfortunately they were all spoiled in the process of tanning.

The largest rattler measured almost four and one-half feet and was the biggest one I ever saw. We dissected its head and took the fangs; which I kept for several years and finally lost or misplaced them.

In this connection I make the observation that it is quite rare to find a rattlesnake on a trout stream. They may be plentiful back on the ridges and mountain tops but not so along the stream. During an experience of more than forty years trout fishing I have encountered only one rattlesnake along the immediate watercourse, and that was a rather small one which I killed on Mann's Creek in Fayette County about ten years ago.

XL

THE STATE VS. HAVENS; THOMPSON
BECOMES A WITNESS

IN THE years of my acquaintance and association
with Ed Andrews, while he was located at Summersville, in Nicholas County, as well as afterward
when he moved to Clay Court House, we were on opposing sides in the trial of quite a number of jury cases.
In only one case that I remember, were we on the
same side. That was the case, notable in its day in
Nicholas County, of The State vs. Margaret Havens,
upon an indictment for murder, tried in the year 1895.
I was located at Sutton at the time and was a regular
attendant at the Circuit Courts of Nicholas County,
then presided over by Judge William G. (George)
Bennett, of Weston. Ed Andrews then lived at Clay
Court House, and likewise attended the terms of court
in Nicholas. John D. Alderson and Andrew J. Horan,
of Summersville, Ed Andrews and I were employed on
behalf of the accused. Theodore B. Horan, Prosecuting
Attorney of the County, and George H. Morrison, of
Sutton, represented the State in the prosecution.

Margaret Havens, a spinster of about 45, the defendant, was charged with having, in cold blood, murdered
Harriett Frazier, a young woman of about 20 years of
age, by deliberately shooting her brains out with a gun.

The case, as made out by the evidence of the State on
the trial, was substantially as follows:

Bob Thompson, a widower, with four children, one a
daughter of about 18, by the name of Abbie, a son of
about 15 or 16, named Stonewall, and two boys of about
five and seven respectively, lived about four miles from
Summersville, on a small tributary of Muddlety, and
Margaret Havens, who was a sister of Thompson's de-

ceased wife, had made her home with them for several years during the life of her sister, and upon whose decease, had continued to so make her home. The house occupied by the Thompsons, was a one-story, Jenny Lind structure, consisting of three rooms, the main or front room being about 16 feet square, and two rooms, each about 8 x 10, in a lean-to built on the rear—a door opening into each of these smaller rooms, from the larger one. Since the death of his wife, Bob and his older son had slept together in a large bed in the left-hand corner of the main room, and the two younger boys, in a trundle bed that was kept under the larger bed, when not in use; and Margaret Havens and Abbie Thompson slept in the small room on the left, the one on the right being used as a kitchen.

Abbie Thompson and Harriett Frazier were chums, and visited one another frequently; and on several occasions, when Bob Thompson was to be away from home overnight, Harriett would come over and spend the night with Abbie. On these occasions they would amuse themselves until bedtime with various diversions, in which Margaret Havens and Stonewall Thompson usually joined, one favorite pastime being that of having their fortunes told by Margaret, who was quite proficient in the magic art, which she practiced not only at home, but on occasional gatherings in the neighborhood. In telling fortunes, Margaret would sometimes use a deck of cards and sometimes "coffee-grounds."

On the fatal night Margaret had used both methods, and had told the fortunes of Harriett and Abbie and Stonewall, by both systems. In telling those of Abbie and Stonewall, there had been nothing of a strange or startling character, but in looking into Harriett's future through the medium of the coffee-grounds, the seeress saw "a dark man" who would be connected in some intimate way with Harriett's fate, and of whom Harriett should beware, as she "saw blood in the cup"; and in the cards she found this same "dark man," and also saw other dire forebodings which spelled disaster unless Harriett heeded the admonition to "beware of the dark man."

On retiring for the night, Harriett and Abbie occupied the large bed in the main room, Abbie sleeping behind or next to the wall, and Harriett in front; Margaret Havens slept alone in the small back room, usually occupied by Abbie and herself, and the boys slept "three in a bed," in the trundle bed, which, when pulled out from under the larger bed, extended across the door opening, into the room where Margaret slept, the head being six or eight inches from the wall and doorcasing.

Lodged upon two pegs in the large room and immediately over the door into Margaret's room, when they all retired, was a double-barrelled shotgun, belonging to Bob Thompson.

Sometime after midnight, the household was awakened by the report of a gun in the house, and immediately the shotgun, which had been over the door, fell on the trundle bed, striking Stonewall with such force as to leave a lump on his head; whereupon he and Abbie and Margaret Havens, lighted a lamp and found Harriett Frazier, lying there in bed with the top of her head shot off—the blood and brains oozing out on the pillow. Neighbors were summoned immediately, and several there were who quickly responded and viewed the gruesome spectacle.

At the ensuing term of the Circuit Court, Margaret Havens was duly indicted for the murder of Harriett Frazier.

The theory of the state as developed at the trial, which began on April 10, and was concluded April 18, 1895, was that Margaret Havens was desperately in love with her brother-in-law, Bob Thompson, and likewise insanely jealous of Harriett Frazier, who was quite a pretty and attractive young woman, who Margaret feared was trying to "cut her out," and whose frequent visits to the Thompson home were calculated to ingratiate her with the Thompson family and pave the way to the desired end. That there was great significance to be attached to the fortune of Harriett as told by Margaret only a few hours before the tragedy, especially when coupled with the fact that on previous occasions and at various homes in the neighborhood she had told Harriett's fortune, and in each instance the dark man of whom Harriett should beware, and "blood in the cup" and similar forebodings of disaster, had always been prominent features, whereas long life and happiness had been found in both cards and coffee-grounds for all others whose future she read.

With the motive of jealousy thus established and the proper emphasis being laid upon the psychological connection between bloody predictions and bloody intentions, on which certain law books lay great stress, and which books, in those days, by the way, the attorney was permitted to read to the jury in argument—the state claimed and undertook to support the contention by the attending circumstances, that Margaret Havens availed herself of the opportunity afforded to put her rival out of the way, by lying quietly in her bed in the back room, until all the inmates of the house were sound asleep; then slipping noiselessly to the open door, reaching up and taking the gun from over the door—which, it was shown, she could easily do—and then, knowing as she did, that Harriett was sleeping on the front side of the bed—placing the gun near the head of her sleeping victim—and pulling the trigger.

Stonewall Thompson was an important witness for the state; as by him it was shown where the various persons slept and the general surroundings; and also that he had placed the shotgun over the door and that it was loaded in one barrel, and that Margaret had seen him place it there and that she knew it was loaded; that on the afternoon Abbie had gone for Harriett to bring her to spend the night, and before they returned, he and Margaret had seen a hawk circling around overhead, and that he had taken the gun off the pegs over the door, loaded one barrel and had gone out in the yard and was about to shoot at the hawk, when it suddenly darted out of range, and that he took the gun back without firing it, and replaced it on the pegs over the door.

Stonewall Thompson told a straightforward story, without bias, fear or favor. Ed Andrews, in cross-examining Stonewall, had him take in his hands the shotgun from which the fatal shot had been fired and which the state produced at the trial, and show the jury just how he had handled the gun when and after loading it, preparatory to shooting the hawk.

The boy, then holding the gun in his hands, said, "After loading one barrel and putting the cap on the tube, I walked a few steps further out in the yard, where I could get a better view of the hawk, and then cocked the gun so (illustrating); I put the gun up to my shoulder and was about to shoot, when the hawk darted around some trees, and got out of range, and then flew clear away and out of sight. And then, I let down the hammer of the gun, so (illustrating) and then took the gun and put it back on the pegs over the door, just where I had gotten it."

"Stonewall," said Andrews, "when you uncocked the gun on that occasion, did you let the hammer clear down on the cap?"

"Yes, I suppose I"—and then glancing at the gun and seeing that in his illustration on the witness stand, he had unconsciously left it half-cocked—he continued rather confusedly—"that is, that's what I aimed to do— and I thought I had it down on the cap."

"Stonewall, a moment ago, you aimed to let the hammer down on the cap, and thought you had done so; did you not?"

"Yes, sir—because I didn't know the hammer would stop on the half-cock—I had never handled that gun. My father had only had it a few days, when this thing happened."

"Where did your father get this shotgun?"

"He traded Mr. So-and-so his rifle for it."

"How long had your father owned that rifle?"

"Two or three years."

"How long was that rifle?"

"Oh, I don't know, but it was one of those long-barrelled mountain rifles."

"Where did he keep the rifle?"

"When he got it, he put those pegs over the door and kept the rifle up there."

"The same pegs on which you kept the shotgun?"

"Yes sir."

"Stonewall, are you right-handed or left-handed?"

"Right-handed."

"In placing the gun back on the pegs, did you hold the butt with your right hand?"

"Yes, sir."

* * *

"What awakened you the night Harriett was killed?"

"I heard the crack of the gun and at the same time felt something heavy hit me on the head—seemed like it was both at the same time."

"When you were awakened what did you do?"

"The first thing I did was to jump up and light the lamp to see what hit me in the head. By the time I was up I heard Abbie and Aunt Margaret talking and wanting to know what's the matter, and by the time I got the lamp lit they were both out in the room, and just as I turned around with the lamp and saw the shotgun lying on the trundle bed where it had fallen on me, we all saw Harriett laying there in the bed with her brains and blood out on the pillow."

"Then what did you do?"

"They told me to run down to the road right quick and holler over and tell our nearest neighbor, that Harriett had been killed and tell him to come right quick."

"Did you call this neighbor?"

"Yes, sir, I hollered over and he answered me right away, and got over in just a few minutes."

"Was it raining when you went out?"

"It had been, but was just letting up."

The state put on the stand the man called by Stonewall, who was the first neighbor to reach the scene of the tragedy, leaving his folks to spread the word among other neighbors. He lived two or three hundred yards away, and came as quickly as possible.

He stated what he saw on reaching the Thompson home: "Harriett lying on the bed with her brains blown out and the shotgun lying on the trundle bed, Margaret and Abbie wringing their hands and moaning, the children crying, and Stonewall the only one who was not excited to death."

On cross-examination the witness was asked how many times Stonewall called him before he answered. He said, "Only once, I am sure; because we had just had a hard rain and windstorm, and it woke me up, and I got up and shut the door to keep the wind from blowing the rain into the room; and it was about to quit raining and I got up to open the door, and stepped out on the porch to see whether the rain was actually over; and while I was standing there looking, I heard Stonewall holler about Harriett being killed; and I jumped back in the room and pulled on my boots and breeches and run right over—telling my folks to tell the neighbors."

He was asked if the face of Harriett Frazier showed any powder burns, and answered that neither that night nor the next day after the body had been dressed, did he see any powder marks.

Other witnesses, who had reached the scene that night in response to the neighborhood alarm, testified as to the conditions there found, much the same as related by the neighbor first on the ground. Some of them remembered the rain and windstorm; others did not. None had observed powder burns about the face.

Neighborhood sentiment was quite pronounced against Margaret Havens, and a number of neighbor women and young girls testified that Margaret Havens thought a "mighty heap" of Bob Thompson, and that she would always "get red" when Bob's name was mentioned and that she "always seemed to like to be teased about him"; that Margaret had frequently expressed her dislike for Harriett Frazier, referring to her as "that snippy thing"; and they stressed the fact that in telling fortunes, Margaret would always find in the cards and in the cup, impending evil in connection with Harriett and "a dark man"; and that Bob Thompson was of dark complexion. And one very willing female witness got it to the jury in spite of court and counsel, and before she could be stopped, that, "Having heard Margaret tell Harriett's fortune several times the same way, "with blood in it," and knowing how she hated Harriett, I knew Margaret was the one that shot her, soon as I heard she had been shot"; nor could the court's severe rebuke to the witness and his admonition to the jury to disregard the statement so volunteered, wholly eradicate its effect.

On Saturday afternoon the state concluded its evidence, and on Monday morning the defense would have its innings. On that Saturday night we held a counsel of war in Alderson & Horan's office to formulate our defense.

XLI

ANDREWS AND BYRNE SOLVE A
MOUNTAIN MURDER

OUR client, Margaret Havens, had stoutly protest-
ed her innocence from first to last. The story told
by her to her counsel was that when she went back in
the little room to retire that night, the two little boys
were already asleep in the trundle bed, and that Abbie
Thompson and Harriett Frazier had sent Stonewall
Thompson out in the yard while they were preparing
for bed; that about the time she got in her bed she
heard the girls get in bed and heard them call Stonewall. Heard him come in and get in the trundle bed,
after putting out the lamp. Then she heard the girls
talking up to the time she went to sleep, and knew from
the sound of their voices that Harriett was sleeping in
front and Abbie behind. That in going into her room
she had walked around the trundle bed and edged
through a space of about eight inches between the head
of the trundle bed and the wall in order to enter the
door of her room. That she was a sound sleeper and that
several hours after she had gone to sleep, she was awakened by the report of the gun, and heard Stonewall make
some loud exclamation; that it was very dark when
she awoke and that she immediately jumped out of bed
and groped her way into the front room, meanwhile
calling to know what was the matter. That when she
got around the trundle bed, Stonewall was in the act
of striking a match to light the lamp; and that when
the lamp was lighted Abbie was out in the room, near
the lamp. That Stonewall had said something about
having been hit in the head, and that looking toward
the trundle bed they first saw the shotgun lying partly
across the two little boys who were yet in the trundle
bed and who had not awakened; and that then her glance

fell upon Harriett Frazier, lying on the larger bed, her head and face smeared with blood; and that Harriett was dead when they got around to where she lay. That it was hardly possible that any person could have entered the house from the outside, committed the deed and escaped from the house; and that the only way she could account for what had happened was, that the gun had fallen from the pegs over the door and in some manner had been discharged and shot Harriett Frazier. She had seen Stonewall take the gun down from the pegs; had seen him load one barrel and try to get a shot at a hawk; and failing in which, had seen him replace the gun, loaded at it then was. She knew nothing of the windstorm, but knew it had been raining and was raining slightly when Stonewall went to give the alarm.

She said she had told the fortunes of Harriett, Abbie, and Stonewall on the fatal night, both by the coffee-grounds and the cards, and that she had found "blood in the cup" and a dark man of whom she should beware, in telling Harriett's fortune; and did not remember any evil in the fortunes of Abbie or Stonewall. That she had no thought whatever of Bob Thompson in connection with the "dark man" although Bob's complexion was rather dark. That she had told Harriett's fortune several times before, but had forgotten entirely whether she had or had not found "blood in the cup" or a dark man, on any of those occasions, or whether she had found Harriett's different in any marked degree, from the fortune of others. That it was all just a lot of fun and foolishness and that she had no cause to remember such things, except what occurred on the fatal night, and her ability in that behalf was due to the fact that a day or two later, Abbie had mentioned the matter, and that her attention having been called to it when it was fresh, she had remembered it ever since. That she was very fond of Harriett; that they had always been great friends and she was always glad to have her come to the house. And Margaret's statement, and as well her manner in making it, was such as to impress one with her sincerity.

Bob Thompson, her brother-in-law, stood by Margaret loyally; assured us that the jealousy proposition was pure fabrication and utterly groundless; and we believed him. But the seeds had been sown very adroitly, and fruit was something to be feared. The tide of public opinion had set in strongly against our client; this we fully realized, and also unwholesomeness of the atmosphere thus created; and there was no mistaking the fact that the case was most desperate.

It is obvious to the reader that there were seven points developed in the cross-examination of the state witnesses, that might prove important factors; first, the fact brought out wholly by accident—as none of us had been permitted to see the shotgun in question, until it was brought into court and placed in the hands of Stonewall Thompson in the witness chair—that in letting down the hammer it would stop at the half-cock; second, that when Stonewall placed the gun back on the pegs over the door, it probably—or possibly—stood at half-cock; third, that the shotgun, short in comparison with a mountain rifle, had been placed on the pegs which had been provided to accommodate the longer gun; fourth, that the gun, when placed back on the pegs, pointed to the left of the person placing it; fifth, that there had been a rain and windstorm about the time the gun was discharged; sixth, that the building in question was of Jenny Lind construction and not very substantial; and seventh, the face of the victim showed no powder burns.

But any idea, plan or scheme as to how to connect, correlate, synchronize or fit into the mosaic of a defense, these circumstances on which the case was believed to hinge, is probably about as nebulous in the mind of the reader as it was with defendant's counsel, when we met for our conference.

When Ed Andrews joined us that night he brought with him a double-barreled shotgun which he had borrowed, and which he had been assured was an exact mate to the one from which the fatal shot had been fired. He also brought a small file and a box of percussion caps. Having already experimented with the trigger and hammer, and found that this gun could not be pulled off at the half-cock; he proceeded to remove the lock and file the notch slightly, so that it could be pulled off by the trigger. Then putting a cap on the tube, he pulled the trigger and demonstrated the fact two or three times, that the hammer would explode the cap from the half-cock.

It was then decided that our only salvation was to reconstruct the whole scene and layout in order to see whether we could find any way by which that cap might have been exploded when the gun was in a position to have pointed directly at the head of Harriett Frazier as she lay in the bed. Thereupon it was arranged with Bob Thompson, who was present at the conference, that some of us would meet him the next morning at the house in which the tragedy had occurred—the same being vacant at this time, as Bob had moved away shortly after the sad occurrence.

Taking the borrowed gun along with us, we visited the premises Sunday morning as arranged, and, after certain preliminaries, we did a little experimenting, the result of which was so satisfactory, that on Monday morning when court convened, we moved the court for a "view of the premises,"—i.e., that the jury, accompanied by the Judge and Sheriff, visit the *locus in quo,* and see for themselves what was there to be seen. The court granted the motion; whereupon we asked that the time for the view be fixed for an hour in the afternoon, as we had some testimony we wished to offer before the view was had; and it was so ordered.

This being settled, we instructed Bob to go to his home and get the identical bedstead and trundle bed, and take the same over to the old house and set them up in the room and equip them with bedclothes and bedding.

We put Margaret Havens on the witness stand, and she testified substantially as above indicated. We also recalled Stonewall and Abbie and showed by them that they had moved to another house and that the house in which the accident occurred was now vacant; that the bed and trundle bed in question were both at their new home; and that they would be able to place these articles of furniture exactly as they were disposed on the fatal night; and Stonewall stated that he could place the gun on the pegs over the door as he had left it.

The view was held early in the afternoon. The court and jury entered the room where the large bed and the trundle bed had been set up, and we had the court direct Abbie and Stonewall to place them in their proper positions; the larger bed in the left-hand corner of the room and the trundle bed rolled back under, as it was kept when not in use. The shotgun which had caused the tragedy had been brought on the scene by the sheriff, and, after being carefully examined and found to be empty, was turned over to Stonewall; a percussion cap was handed him, and he was directed to place the cap on the tube of the proper barrel and let the hammer down on the cap; then to cock the gun, and from the full cock, let the hammer down to the half-cock. This being done, under the direction of the court, he placed the gun on the pegs, which there remained over the door—as he had done on the former occasion. In placing the gun on the pegs he naturally turned the weapon upside down, so that the hammers pointed downward, and the muzzle pointed to the left, the side on which the bed stood. As so placed by him, the muzzle of the gun extended about three inches over the peg on the left, and the butt extended four or five inches over the peg on the right, thus bringing a part of the butt of the gun to within five or six inches of the overhead board ceiling. When the gun had been properly placed, the trundle bed was pulled out by Stonewall and Abbie, and when it had cleared the larger bed, it was found to extend across and barely beyond the open space for the door leading into the small back room, and to leave a space of six or eight inches between its head and the wall, or doorfacing. Three pillows were placed at the head of the trundle bed, to represent the three boys who had slept therein on the night in question, the pillow on the right, or outer side, to represent Stonewall Thompson. Two young men were placed in the larger bed to represent the exact positions of Harriett Frazier and Abbie Thompson, as they slept that night.

When all was in readiness, by permission of the court, granted, however, with some reluctance—we had three or four men stationed on the outside, who applied to the building sufficient force to cause it to sway back and forth as from the effects of a windstorm. With the first tremor of the structure, the gun on the pegs began to creep toward the right, or its heavier end—very gradually, but perceptible to the twenty-odd pairs of eyes there glued upon it—until finally, the muzzle end slipped entirely from the peg and fell free, the effect of which was to cause the butt of the gun to come in sharp contact with the ceiling overhead; the jar of the impact caused the hammer to fall as though the trigger had been pulled, the cap exploded and at the very instant of the explosion, all eyes observed that the gun was pointed exactly at the head of the boy lying on the near side of the bed.

Notwithstanding this, however, Ed Andrews, who was chief engineer of the whole performance, then had the gun placed in the exact position in which it was when the cap exploded, and found, by measuring, that the muzzle of the gun was almost five feet from the boy's head. Then, having a boy who was just the height of Margaret Havens, and who was also right-handed, as we proved her to be—stand up in the door of her room, as the state claimed she had done—and point the empty gun at the head of the boy as he lay in bed, we showed by measuring, that if the shot had been fired from that position, the muzzle of the gun would have been a distance not to exceed twelve inches away, which would have caused powder burns upon the victim, as we showed in evidence; and that at a distance of four or five feet, powder burns would not be likely.

Although we had gone through this performance on the day before, to the extent of placing the other gun on the pegs, capped and half-cocked, and shaking the building, and had seen the experiment work to perfection upon three different trials; yet the fact that the gun from which the shot had been fired, having been unused for several months and might for that reason, or because of it, like its mate before being filed, would not pull off from half-cock, and so fail to act as we hoped—I confess that one of the tensest moments of my life was that between the time the gun began to crawl and the explosion of that cap. For I thought and now believe, that certainly the liberty, and probably the life, of Margaret Havens, hinged on that test. And I further believe that the verdict of not guilty, later returned by the jury, after considerable more testimony had been taken pro and con, when we returned from the view, was in fact made up in the minds of a majority of that jury, the very instant the cap exploded; albeit there was a minority that held out for conviction of murder in the first degree, for a day or two, but finally came over to the majority.

A few weeks after the trial, I saw Judge Bennett at his home in Weston. He referred to the Havens case as being in many respects the most remarkable of the many he had tried or seen tried, either while on the bench or at the bar. He said, "I have wondered if I permitted you fellows to go a little far in re-enacting the scene in the presence of the jury. But in thinking it over, the only element of doubt in my mind is as to the substitute for the windstorm; I resolved that doubt in your favor at the time, because, as you could not command the wind at the time, I thought it fair to permit you to develop your theory, by substituting a force which would reasonably have the same effect upon the building as a strong wind, shown by the evidence to have been blowing at or about the time the gun was discharged."

He then added: "I certainly must compliment you fellows—"

"Don't say 'you fellows,' Judge," said I. "Ed Andrews was the 'author and finisher,' and to him is due 99.4 per cent of your compliment. The rest of us were merely 'also rans.' "

Andrew J. Horan, one of my associates in the defense of this case, is living and in active practice of the law at Summersville. Ed Andrews and John D. Alderson have both been deceased for twenty years or more; as also Theodore B. Horan, George H. Morrison, and Judge Bennett.

XLII

FIRST CAMP ON ELK; AL JENNINGS
IN WEST VIRGINIA

MY FIRST experience in camping on Elk River
was in the spring of 1878. Lawrence Fitzhugh,
Jim Follansbee, Will Fry and myself had bought an
old johnboat from Alex Smith, who lived on upper
Kanawha Street. This boat had been a splendid one in
its day, having been built by Henry Payne, a young
colored man, who was one of the prime boatbuilders of
that day and generation. Alex had used the johnboat
for two or three years, and finally it had sprung a leak
and sunk and had withstood freshets of a whole winter
season without receiving any attention. Each of the
four of us had dug up twenty-five cents, aggregating
a whole dollar, which was the purchase price demanded
by Alex. We hauled it out on the bank and put it in
floatable shape, but were never able to make much of
a boat out of it. It was, however, fit to run a trotline
by constant bailing, and we used it for that purpose, with
indifferent success, for some weeks. There were no oars
with the boat when we purchased it, so we went down to
Henry Payne's, who lived with his mother, Aunt Felicia, in the basement part of the old Virginia Row,
which was a long, story and a half, narrow brick building, on the river bank, and extending most of the way
from Capitol Street up to the lot opposite the Hale
House, now Hotel Ruffner—the basement frontage being on the road leading from the end of Capitol Street
down to the ferry—for the purpose of getting a pair of
oars. Henry had some new oars, for which he wanted
a dollar and a half a pair, but that being way beyond
our limit, we purchased a pair of old ones from Aunt
Felicia for fifty cents.

When tired of trotline fishing, we decided to go up Elk for a few miles and establish a camp, where we could spend the time from Friday evening, after school, until Sunday evening or Monday morning school time. Early in May a circus had come to Charleston, and certain of the circus employees, just after the night performance, had undertaken to get gay and put something over on a sturdy and resentful bunch of Charlestonians, with the result that the circus was wrecked, some of the tents demolished, the canvas thereof divided into numerous parcels, and distributed among the victors, and afterwards parceled out in smaller sections to their friends.

We had become the presumably legitimate owners of a section of this canvas, which was ample for a tent for the ordinary fishing camp. We set out on a pilgrimage up Elk River to spy out a proper place to pitch our tent, and hit upon a likely spot on the south side of the river in the Duling Bend, about a hundred yards above the head of Mink Shoals, four miles above Charleston. The old Elk River boom was at that time in full operation, and by paying several visits down to the head of the boom we were able to gather up divers boards and planks which lodged at the head of the boom, which we used in constructing tables, benches, bunks, etc. For four or five weeks before the close of school, the four of us would repair to the camp immediately after school was out on Friday afternoon, carrying with us enough provisions to last during our stay.

On one Friday afternoon we got to camp along about five o'clock and found that two young fellows had preceded us and taken possession—one was Harry Craig, the son of the proprietor of the principal meat market in town, who was indeed a welcome visitor, because of the fact that he had brought with him a "back load" of meat, consisting of steaks, chops and bologna sausage in generous quantities; the other was a young chap by the name of Forney Jennings, a fine little fellow, and a favorite with everyone—who had resided in Charleston but a short time. His father, who was called either Captain or Doctor, I forget which, and three sons, one of them named John, another named Frank and another Ed, had located in Charleston as instructors in music; and the family, with probably one or two outsiders, composed a brass band. I do not remember whether Craig and Jennings had played hookie or not, but they must have done so, if they were attending school at that time, because the four of us had lost no time in getting away after school adjourned, nor in covering the distance between our homes and our camp, and they had been there some time when we arrived. We fished and fooled around the balance of that afternoon, Saturday and part of Sunday, when along about noon Capt. Jennings, the irate father of Forney, descended upon us. He was mad as a wet hen, and proceeded to give the bunch of us a complete tongue lashing, calling us toughs and hoodlums and applying to us vicious other choice epithets, for having tolled his son away without the knowledge or consent of his parents. I remember distinctly that Forney bucked up to the old gentleman and absolved us from all blame or responsibility, by stating that he had come of his own free will and accord, and wholly without our knowledge. This seemed to mollify the old gentleman to the extent that he apologized and I believe even went to the extent of breaking bread with us; after which, however, he immediately departed, taking Forney with him.

The Jennings family left Charleston soon after that event, and about two years later I was in an engineering corps, which ran a railroad survey from Charleston by way of Sissonville, over to Ripley. There we ran across Captain Jennings and his boys, among whom was my old friend Forney. Captain Jennings was then the proprietor of a drug store, and I believe he and the boys conducted a brass band also.

In later years, I heard much of Al Jennings, the out-law and bandit, who was finally run to ground and sent to prison; and who some years later, after having served his term or being pardoned, decided to stage a come-back, rehabilitate himself in the good opinion in which he was once held by the people of Oklahoma, and become their Governor—which he came within an ace of doing. During his campaign for Governor, I chanced to be in Ripley, and ran across my old friend, Holly G. Armstrong. Knowing that this Jennings family had lived at Ripley, I told Holly that I used to know all of them, but never knew one by the name of Al. I stated that the boys whom I remembered were named John, Frank, Ed and Forney. Holly said, "There is a lady coming across the street who can tell you all about them. She is a sister-in-law of John Jennings." Upon being introduced to the lady, I asked her about the matter, and she explained that Al Jennings' full name was Alfonso, and that when he was a boy he had been called "Fonny" or "Forney."

I have often wondered whether my old friend Forney Jennings' early associations were in any wise responsible for his deflection from the straight and narrow, or whether, on the other hand, it was their influence that caused him to ultimately return to the paths of rectitude and virtue—and politics.

After maintaining this camp at Mink Shoals for a couple of months our bunch decided that we were too close home, and that the surroundings were not sufficiently wild and woolly for our venturesome spirits and determined to extend our activities farther up the river. So we struck camp, brought our equipment back home and began preparations for the next exploit. By this time our johnboat would scarcely hold together, so we decided to build a new one. We took the old boat and carefully knocked it apart and just as carefully preserved each piece. By the use of these pieces as a pattern, we were able to reconstruct an exact counterpart of the old craft; and I must say that we did a pretty fair job. The boat was 18 feet long, with two sets of oarlocks, and built of light yellow poplar, excepting the bottom which was of oak.

I believe it was sometime about the middle of July that we started on our trip up Elk. Having found that Jim Follansbee could not accompany us, we got Ben Brown who was glad to take his place. Having but one pair of oars, and it being quite necessary that we have the second pair, we borrowed some splendid new ones from our friend Beech Goshorn.

The first day out brought us to a point just below Jarrett's Ford, at the mouth of the little hollow where the old Taylor & Tibbetts storehouse stood, on the north side of the river where we camped for the night. A short distance below that point, we spied, in passing, a cornfield, where we stopped and made an examination to see if the corn was in roasting-ear. Finding such to be the case, we helped ourselves to a generous supply and proceeded on our way. Thoughtlessly and unfortunately, whoever husked the corn after we got to camp, undertook to make way with the husks by throwing them into the river. Now, it happened that Aunt Vine Hammack and her son, Dick, owned that cornfield, and Dick had some occasion to be out at the river bank and saw the corn husks floating out in the stream. This set him to investigate as to whether or not his cornfield had been violated, and finding that such was the case, he proceeded upstream to find the culprits. Of course he caught us red-handed. I knew Aunt Vine at that time and knew that she had a son by the name of Dick, who was considered something of a bad man, and I took it for granted that this was he, and for my part, was no little uneasy as to what might be the outcome. Greatly to my relief, however, Dick chided us very mildly, and after rebuking us for not having come and asked for the corn, told us if we wanted any more to go down and help ourselves.

Within the next day or two we reached the head of Queen Shoal, at which place we decided to make our permanent camp, especially as my old friend, Harvey Samples, had a general store on a large houseboat, which was moored just above the mouth of Queen Shoal Creek. A short distance above this boat we pitched our camp on the little narrow bottom along the edge of the river. It was no trouble to catch fish in those days; and while the river was clear, we provided ourselves amply with camp meat, simply with hook and line. In a few days, however, it began to rain and soon there was a log tide in the river.

When the water began to recede, we put out a trotline and caught catfish and turtles galore. It was while baiting this trotline one day that I saw the wonderful Queen Eddy Pike, which, according to tradition, had swallowed a Newfoundland dog that was in the act of swimming the river at that point. Lawrence Fitzhugh and I both saw it at the same time, and thought at first it was the shadow of the boat—until it swam off—and each vowed that it was as large as a cross-tie, and that we saw dog hair in its teeth—but as Lawrence is dead and I have no living witness, I am going to modify somewhat that statement, and say that it looked to me at the time and under the circumstances to be almost as large as a small cross-tie; and that what we thought to be dog hair may have been the tail of a partly swallowed fish.

We caught an enormous soft-shelled turtle on the trotline, with which I had quite an experience. I was acting cook that day and thought I would vary the menu by having, instead of fish, a nice fresh fried turtle; which they say is beef, and pork, and mutton, and veal, and turkey, and chicken, in composite. After the turtle was fried to a nice brown turn, I announced that the meal was ready; every fellow promptly gigged his favorite piece and put it on his plate and proceeded to carve—but it would not carve. The ordinary table knife, the extraordinary carving knife or the super butcher knife, made no more impression on that turtle than it would on sole leather; and we had to skirmish around and find odds and ends on which to make our meal. We then decided that we would have turtle soup the next day, and thereafter again fry and serve the turtle. We had turtle soup all right, but it was nothing to brag of; and the second frying to a nice brown turn made the meat no more susceptible to the knife than at the first. As a last resort, we were compelled to use the turtle for catfish bait, and if my recollection serves me, it was even too tough to tempt the catfish.

And then came the flood; a rise of ten or twelve feet in the river, which forced us to move our tent on higher ground; and then set in a rain which kept up at short intervals, for four or five days, during which time we ran completely out of camp meat; no fish, no turtle, no anything, except bread and bacon. Ben Brown and I each had a shotgun and we had killed a few squirrels from time to time ever since we had been out. When the famine came, however, the rain kept us from hunting. Finally, one day, in desperation Ben and I started out to kill some squirrels between showers. We traversed the woods for a mile or so back of the camp, but saw never a squirrel. Suddenly, however, we roused from his lair, a vicious wild hog—a razorback shoat of about 40 pounds avoirdupois—which raised its bristles and showed no sign of retreat. I confess that I was not entirely sure that this was a wild hog, but as our larder was entirely empty, and as this hog acted as, and seemed to want to make us believe he was—a genuine wild hog, we both decided to take him at his word and deal with him accordingly. So we cut down on him and bore him triumphantly into camp. Harvey Samples was there at camp when we came in with the trophy of our chase, and asked us where we got that shoat. We told him that from his actions he was evidently a wild hog, and that we had taken him at his word and slain him as such. Harvey laughed, made a slight examination of the pig, and remarked that he believed it belonged to some of the Kentucky Mullenses, who had shortly before that time moved into that section. Some little time later, one of the "Kentucky Mullenses" showed up and inquired about his pig. Samples saw him coming and came up to the camp to be present at the interview. When he first mentioned the pig, Harvey said, "Yes, I guess these boys did kill your pig, thinking it was mine. You know I have some shoats running out and I told them if they found one they could kill it; and it seems that they killed one of yours by mistake. Let's find out what the thing will weigh." We took it down to his store and found it weighed about forty pounds. Harvey said pork was worth three and a half or four cents on foot—we settled with Mullens by paying him a dollar and a half.

And so Harvey Samples made four life-long friends. The last time I saw him before his death, which occurred at a ripe old age, some eight or ten years ago, he asked me, with a twinkle in his eye, if I remembered the time he kept me out of jail for hog stealing.

As the rain and high water continued, my three companions voted to strike camp and return home; but for my part I decided to go over to Tige Johnson's camp at the mouth of Donager, on Big Sycamore, and put in the rest of my summer vacation. So when they turned back, I trudged over to this camp, about ten miles away. On reaching my objective about noon, I found everybody much agitated over the fact that a four-year-old child of Milt Jeffries, who lived near Cedar Rock, about a mile below Johnson's on Big Sycamore, had early that morning been bitten by a copperhead. All the neighbors had congregated and all the known snakebite remedies, except whiskey—consisting of split chicks, turpentine, etc.—had been applied, and Milt, the father, had been dispatched to Clendenin, about fourteen miles away, for the whiskey as the real antidote. He had started out on foot, expecting to find a horse on his way, and should have made the trip either horseback or afoot, in eight or nine hours. That time elapsed from the time he started, and all hands were wondering why he had not returned. Nightfall came and still he failed to show up. In the meantime the snakebite had yielded to the treatment applied, and the child seemed to be in pretty good shape. Along about nine o'clock, those of us assembled heard up on the mountain side, half a mile away, the voice of Milt Jeffries, lustily singing that grand old hymn, "How Firm a Foundation Ye Saints in the Lord," and in due time Milton appeared, drunk as a biled owl with about two teaspoonfuls of whiskey in a quart bottle; and with the explanation, "Hic, I dropped the bottle and the cork came out, and I had a hard time saving what little (hic) bit is left." I do not know what became of the two teaspoonfuls, but that the boy was up and running around the next morning.

(A short time after the above appeared in the *Wild Life Magazine*, March, 1931, I received from some friend, the newspaper clipping which follows. W.E. R.B.)

LIFE OF AL JENNINGS, BANDIT, IN WEST VIRGINIA IS RECALLED

Train Robber and Highwayman Who Attracted Wide Attention
by His Exploits Once Resided in Ripley and Also in
Charleston; Attended State University

Al Jennings, who capitalized on notoriety acquired as a train bandit and highwayman by becoming a lecturer and evangelist, lived at Ripley for four years about 50 years ago, and for several months resided in Charleston with his brothers.

Jennings' life in Ripley, where he operated a drug store with his father and three brothers, was recalled last week by W. L. Morrison, of 2 Elmwood Place, in connection with Jennings' latest bid for publicity. Jennings announced from Mexico several weeks ago that he had been using an airplane in prospecting for gold.

The Jennings family, consisting of Mr. Jennings and four sons, John, Frank, Ed, and Al, and one daughter about 14 years of age, lived at Ripley for several years, Mr. Morrison said. The family was musically inclined and above the average in intelligence. The men were of fine physique, iron nerve and a taste for excitement and were interesting and entertaining.

"The drug business appealed to the Jennings family so they opened a small store on the main street of the town about 1880. During their careers as druggists every male member of the family was arrested at one time or another. I remember very distinctly of being present when Al, who at that time was called "Fonny," a nickname for his real name of Alfonso, appeared before the late Judge R. F. Fleming to answer to an indictment. He appeared to greatly enjoy the publicity he was obtaining and the attention he was attracting. At that time Al was a handsome young man about 19 years of age. His heavy crop of auburn hair was combed out in all directions much like the bobbed-haired girls of today. He was without his coat when he appeared before the jurists but he wore a vest of very prounounced hues. Pockets of the vest bulged with papers and toilet articles.

Attended State University

When he was not selling drugs or whiskey, Al was reading law in the office of the late Judge V. S. Armstrong. Later he went to West Virginia University for a year and the college catalogue gives his residence as Appleton City, Mo. I believe that the Jennings family originally came from Missouri.

"West Virginia apparently was entirely too tame for the restless spirits of the Jennings boys and about 1884 they left Ripley and after sojourning in Charleston for a time moved on to Indian territory, now Oklahoma. In the west all of them became cowboys, practicing law on the side. It was not long, however, until they commanded front page newspaper space in papers in all parts of the country when they engaged in a rifle battle with another outfit of cowboys in which it was alleged that some of the opposing faction were killed and that Al was wounded.

All of the brothers were arrested by marshals and for a time were confined in one of the military forts in the territory. They got out of this trouble soon and for a time devoted themselves most assiduously to the practice of law and soon had charge of most of the important cases entered in the territory. It was said that the adroitness and versatility of the boys usually enabled them to win their suits regardless of the merits of the case.

Houston Opposed Them

Usually opposing them in these suits was Temple Houston, son of General Sam Houston who was at one time president of the Republic of Texas. A bitterness developed. Houston and Frank Jennings met in a border saloon and engaged in an argument concerning a law suit in which they had been opposing counsel. Jennings was beaten to the draw and thus was brought to a close what probably would have been one of the most brilliant lawyers of that great territory.

Soon after this, Mr. Morrison continued, Al blossomed out as the leader of a successful band of train robbers. Eventually he was captured and was sentenced to a long term in a prison at Columbus, Ohio. Even in prison he commanded front page space several times because of his action. He eventually obtained his release and for a time kept himself before the public by writing a series of magazine articles.

I think the public should take a charitable view of Al's escapades for I don't believe that anyone who knew him personally believes, that, in the true sense, he was the desperado that he was pictured. It was rather his love for publicity and excitement that led him into many of his spectacular stunts.

When I was a boy I asked Al one time when he was home from the university concerning his opinion of the school. He was very courteous, so much so that I still remember it, but he did not have a high opinion of the university. His talk to me was more like that of a father, than of one on the threshold of a career as an outlaw.

XLIII

"ROCK OIL," "RHEUMATIZ," AND ENGINEERING ON SYCAMORE

IN THE confusion and excitement of relating that story about Milt Jeffries' boy getting bitten by the copperhead, I overlooked one feature of the incident which concerns one of the various snakebite remedies, which was brought on the ground by a neighbor. Old man Clark Jarrett, who at that time lived at the forks of Big Sycamore, about two miles above Donager, was on hand with a round black bottle which would hold something less than half a pint. I was curious to know the contents of the bottle and in reply to my inquiry, he said it contained "Rock Oil." He took out the cork and I smelled of and examined the contents. It smelled like lamp oil and putting my finger deep down in the bottle I found, on drawing it out, a heavy black liquid, something of the consistency of black-strap molasses. Jarrett stated that a year or two after the war, a fellow had come through that country selling this Rock Oil for medicinal purposes, guaranteeing that it would cure all the ills that flesh is heir to, even including housemaid's knee—and especially "rheumatiz," and that he had bought this bottle at the price of fifty cents. He said he had tried it for "rheumatiz" and various other ailments, but finding that it wasn't worth a continental for any other purpose, he just concluded it must be good for snakebite and had accordingly saved it for all those years—the small amount unused and which had not evaporated—and brought it along. I finally learned that some enterprising chap who lived up around Burning Springs in Wirt County, where, in 1860, oil was first produced in West Virginia, had bottled up a lot of crude oil and sold it far and wide throughout the state as Rock Oil, a newly discovered panacea for various ailments.

A few days after I arrived at Johnson's camp, my father visited the place to see how the stave job was progressing. A large tract of land owned by him and Henry S. Walker, extended from Big Sycamore over on to Little Sycamore and embraced a good portion of the drainage of the latter stream. He and Mr. Walker had contracted with George C. Acree to cut and transport to the river and to raft and run out to Charleston, the poplar timber on the land owned by them; the drainage of Little Sycamore, being reputed far and wide as producing the finest body of poplar timber "that ever growed out of the ground." At that time Acree had established a log-camp near the head of Little Sycamore and had his cutters in the woods felling trees. I accompanied my father across the dividing ridge between Big Sycamore and Little Sycamore, by way of a rough and narrow zig-zag path leading from Cedar Rock across to Little Sycamore, a distance of about one mile. We found Acree over at the camp which he had newly installed, and I learned that he was building a commissary and boarding house, down at the mouth of Little Sycamore, and was preparing to build a tramroad from the mouth of the creek up to and beyond his camp; of which more later on.

On returning to Johnson's camp that afternoon, my father remarked upon the very poor path crossing the hill between the two camps, and asked me if I couldn't improve the grade and recalled to me the fact that I had seen an instrument commonly called a quadrant, used for the graduation of roads, etc., and suggested that I try my hand at making an instrument of that kind and run a grade line across the hill on five degrees, which he thought would be about correct.

I thought my father had left me a pretty big assignment, but set about nevertheless to devise some sort of

a contrivance which might enable me to perform the
task. At school I had simply finished Ray's Higher
Arithmetic and Evans Elementary Geometry; and there
or elsewhere had learned that there are 360 degrees in
a circle and that the circumference was 3.1416 times
the diameter; and on this basis I started to work to devise, erect and construct a quadrant, or a feefus, dinkus
or gadget which might serve the purpose of a quadrant
in locating a five degree path across that hill. I got
hold of a nice pine board, part of a goods box, and borrowed from somebody a pair of carpenter's compasses
and a tape line. I decided on shaping that board in the
form of a semicircle, the arc of which would be 18
inches in order that each inch around the rim would
represent 10 degrees; and dividing 18 by 3.1416 I
found the radius of the circle to be approximately 5.73
inches. Having established the halfway places on the
arc and on the diameter, I drew a line connecting these
two points, and then measuring one-half inch on the
arc, on either side of that line, I had my five degrees
established both "gwine and comin'." I left about an
inch of board above the semicircle, with a smooth top
surface along which to sight, and bored a half-inch
auger hole in that part of the board immediately above
the point marked for the center. I then made a Jacob-
staff, with a plug extending from the top at right
angles, which would fit into the auger hole in the board
snugly enough to hold the machine intact, unless turned
by the hand. Then by means of a Minie ball suspended
by a linen thread fastened to a tack in the exact center
of the circle—I had a machine with which to measure
vertical angles as accurately as the best ever made. A
boy of my own age, by the name of T. I. Cline, who was
a son of Preacher Cline, who lived on the headwaters of
Big Sycamore, was my rodman. The rod consisted of a
cane or staff a little longer than the Jacob-staff. When
the "instrument was set up, the rod was placed along-

side the Jacob-staff and the point representing the height
of the instrument was marked on the rod by tying around
it a red flannel string so that it would be visible through
the brush. Of course, this process had to be repeated at
each setting up of the instrument. The grade line was
duly run across the hill and properly staked; and the
five degrees fitted the ground almost perfectly. A few
days thereafter, Tige Johnson had a couple of men dig
out, according to the grade stakes, a horse and footpath
about two feet wide across the hill. It has been more
than fifty years since I last saw that path; but was reminded of it about two years ago by the following incident, which is the only excuse for all this detail about
its construction:

A few years after George Acree's timber job on Little
Sycamore was completed, Floyd Holcomb bought that
portion of the land on which Acree's camp was situated.
He cleared out quite an extensive farm and operated a
store at that place for a great number of years. About
two years ago I was talking to Floyd about things in
general pertaining to that neighborhood, and asked him
if they still used that path leading from the Cedar
Rock on Big Sycamore over to Little Sycamore. He
said, "Yes, and do you know that for years and years that
was the best graded piece of road in Clay County?—and
just as good as any grade they have got now. Do you
know how that road got graded that way?"

"Well," I said, "enlighten me."

"Well, sir," he said, "it was Bufflers that done it!
I have heard my granddaddy say that when his daddy
first come into that country, that path was there on exactly the same grade just like it is now; and that the
Bufflers had made it in crossing back and forth from
Big Sycamore to Little Sycamore. He said that Bufflers
was the curiousest animals in the world—that when
they start uphill or downhill, they travel on a perfect
grade and don't vary not nary particle. Don't make no

difference whether they are going straight up or straight down or quarterin'." And so it is with many of our favorite legends.

I was talking to Henry B. Davenport the other day about an oil well he had drilled on Floyd Holcomb's place over on Little Sycamore, and Henry told me this story: When he was having this well drilled, he had occasion to be at Floyd Holcomb's a good many times and on one occasion he found floating around in the pond, which his oil drillers had made to hold water for drilling purposes not far from Floyd's house, a bee gum and a lot of drowned bees thereabout. He called Floyd's attention to the matter, suggesting that somebody had evidently stolen one of his bee gums; and Floyd replied that such had been the case, but seemed to be very little concerned about it. Davenport asked him if he had any idea who had stolen his bee gum, to which Floyd replied he knew just who it was. Davenport asked if he intended to have the fellow arrested and punished, and Floyd declared he had no such intention; that he did not intend to say a word about it; and that he knew exactly how to handle the situation; that the fellow who had stolen his bees was one of his very best customers there at the store, and that he would not think of doing anything which might forfeit either his friendship or his trade, but that he would simply charge the fellow a little extra for every article he bought out of the store; for instance if he bought a pair of shoes he would add fifty cents to the price; if a sack of flour, he would add ten or fifteen cents, and so on until he had fully compensated himself for the value of the bee gum. Davenport said that four or five years later he chanced to be at Floyd's house, and inquired as to whether or not he had ever gotten paid for his bee gum. Floyd said, "Why Henry, that very fellow that stole that bee gum left here not over twenty minutes ago; he bought a pair of shoes that was selling for $4.25; I charged him $5.00

for them shoes and he went away thinking he had got a good bargain. Talking about getting paid for my bee gum, why, sir, I have already got seven or eight times the price of that bee gum, and am still going strong."

Soon after this path was completed and Acree's camp fully established, I moved across the hill and took up hunting quarters over there. Squirrels and pheasants were plentiful around in that neighborhood, which made it, of course, a very attractive place for a boy with a shotgun. While out hunting one day a short distance above the camp, near the mouth of a small hollow that comes in on the right, now called Tom's Hollow, I was almost an eyewitness to a tragedy which made a lasting impression upon me: A young chap by the name of Tom Mitchell, one of the cutters employed by Acree, was chopping down a rather small white poplar tree, about twenty inches in diameter, which grew near the edge of the creek bank on rough ground on the surface of which grew numerous roots from surrounding trees. In those days they felled trees altogether with axes, never using a saw, and in order to take advantage of the ground, Mitchell had to chop this tree rather "high on the stump" and have it fall squarely across the creek. When the tree started to fall, Mitchell retreated from the stump a few steps, to be out of the way of all danger, but suddenly observed that the top of the tree had lodged on some birch trees across the creek, which caused the tree to slide back over the stump, exactly in his direction. He started to step out of danger, but in so doing caught his foot in a root and fell flat on the ground where the butt of the tree caught him first on his head, crushing it almost into pulp, and then rebounding and resting upon his breast. I was only a short distance down the creek and heard his "buddy," whose name I have forgotten, call out for help. I reached the place as soon as possible, and his companion and I made an effort to get the body out from under the butt of the tree; this, however, we never succeeded in doing until two or three other men had reached the spot, and the tree was lifted off of the dead man's body. From that time to the present, I believe, that place is known as Tom's Hollow.

We took the body down to Acree's camp, and later some of his friends and relatives came in and asked that it be conveyed to and buried in the Harrison Pierson Graveyard up near Yankee Dam. At that time there was merely a footpath leading from the camp down to the mouth of Little Sycamore, much of it passing through dense laurel thickets. The body was placed on an improvised stretcher and carried by four men, and for three-fourths of the way it was necessary for axemen to go ahead and chop out the laurel to permit the stretcher to get through. I remember that it took half a day to make the awful trip of four miles from Acree's camp down to the mouth of the creek. The body was then placed in a canoe and taken up the river to the Pierson Graveyard.

At that time Acree was building a boarding house and commissary at the mouth of Little Sycamore, in the little bottom on the lower side; and was beginning the work of manufacturing wooden rails for the tramroad. These rails were manufactured by means of a whipsaw, and the first whipsaw pit was but a short distance up Little Sycamore Creek from the mouth, and was operated by Major John McKinney as pit sawyer, and Milt Jeffries or "Doc" Cart, top sawyer. The rails were usually of oak, hickory, beech, maple and sugar. They were about five inches by three and a half or four, according to my recollection, and every one of the rails used in that tramroad, which eventually was six or seven miles long, was so manufactured. In the stiff curves, in order to prevent the truck wheels from wearing the wood, the rails were stripped with thin iron plates slightly wider and somewhat thicker than the ordinary barrel hoop.

And so it is that Little Sycamore bears the proud distinction of having the first railroad of any kind, ever built in Clay County; albeit the motive power was furnished, not by the iron horse, but by the flesh—and—blood, long-eared, shave-tail, hybrid species of the genus equus.

XLIV

LOGGING ON ELK; BLUE PIKE AND CATFISH

A FEW days after the July number of *Wild Life* appeared, a friend of mine whose name will not be disclosed—out of consideration for his family and church connections—stopped me on the street and asked me if there was or had ever been an instrument for manufacturing lumber, called a whipsaw, as mentioned in the last preceding installment of these annals. On being asked what he meant, he said he was 65 years old and that he had heard the expression "whipsaw" or "whipsawed" all his life; but had always heard it in connection with playing faro-bank and never dreamed that there was a woodworking machine by that name. Said he had been whipsawed many times, and had never known that there was more than one process.

I told him he ought to be ashamed of himself for being so totally ignorant concerning things which everybody should know and so erudite concerning those things nobody should know. He agreed with me and we parted friends.

Having always found more sport in fishing and fooling around the river than in hunting, and as there was no fishing at Acree's camp on the head of Little Sycamore, I soon moved my headquarters to the camp down at the mouth of the creek, where fishing was of the finest and game almost as plentiful. Acree's commissary and boarding house combined the boarding house being in charge of John Stoffel and his wife was far enough along toward completion to afford cooking, eating and sleeping quarters, though of a primitive sort. While not aware that any of my ancestors, near or remote, ever had Indian blood in their veins, I am frank to confess—or boast as the case may be—that the primitive quality in things pertaining to the great outdoors, carries to me a very strong appeal—in fact an exhilaration and a thrill which man—or machine-made or unmade things, can never awaken.

I caught bass and gigged red-horse and suckers in the daytime, and with bank poles at night caught catfish until the keen edge wore off and the sport began to pall—and then came the thrill of my life, up to that time:

A short distance below where Little Sycamore Creek empties into Elk, there is a good-sized bayou formed by a long peninsular bar extending for something like 200 or 300 feet down the river from the creek's mouth; and between this bar and the river bank is a large pool, deep and still, forming a splendid harbor for river craft of every sort. While the tramroad was being built up the creek, George Acree had caused to be cut along the river hillsides and for some little distance up the creek, the poplar timber suitable for saw logs, and had the same hauled and rafted ready for the next "log tide." One of these log rafts was moored in the bayou above described, and one day, when I happened to be near this raft, I saw in the crystal clear water, a huge blue pike, not over ten feet from the upper end of the raft in the shallowest part of the pool. There were two or three gigs at the camp, a hundred yards away, and I ran back and grabbed one of them and told Mel Cart, who was working on the building, to get another and follow me. On returning to the river we saw the pike just where I had left him, but when we stepped on the raft, which was necessary for us to do, and before we got in striking distance, he swam lazily downstream and disappeared under the raft. After walking noiselessly up and down the raft in the vain hope of getting a glimpse of him, we abandoned the hunt, and Mel went back to work. But my blood was up, and I put into instant action a plan and process to get the monster fish. I had among my possessions a ball of staging, which, being of double strength, made a fairly good pike line about 25 or 30 feet long. I tore up an old broom and took and doubled the wire therefrom, making a leader about 6 feet long, and to this attached a fair-sized pike hook; found a chunk of light, dry, yellow poplar wood, something smaller than a gallon jug, out of which I fashioned a "cork," which I attached to the line about eight feet from the hook, by means of a nail driven in either end. On the river bank near the raft, I found about ten feet of the top end that had been cut from a white oak sapling, the larger portion having been used for "strapping" in rafting the logs. This made a rather clumsy fishing pole, about an inch and a half at one end and a little less than half an inch at the other; but as it was comparatively light and very springy, with the combined qualities of strength and durability, it seemed to serve the purpose fairly well.

A few days previously I had seen a fine, large horny-head, in a hole about two hundred yards up the creek, and had noted at the time what a fine pike bait he would be. Taking a minnow hook and water pail, I went up and caught the gentleman, finding him to be eight or nine inches long, and soon had him securely baited on the pike hook. With a hatchet, I hewed the blunt end and fixed the same securely between the bulge of two logs in the raft beneath the water level and about three feet from the strapping, so as to give it the proper pitch, and then, secured the pole, by means of a tenpenny nail driven through the pole and into the strapping; thus making it impossible to dislodge the pole by a downward or sidewise pull, but easy to accomplish by lifting it upward. Having so "set" my pole, down toward the lower end of the raft where the water was deepest, I threw out my bait, line and cork and sat down to await results. By this time it was late afternoon and I

sat there till suppertime and paid several visits between supper and bedtime; but nothing happened; and
it was not until the middle of the next forenoon, when
I strolled down to the raft in a halfhearted sort of way,
that I failed to see the cork floating in its accustomed
place, and on closer inspection, found that the line had
been pulled under the raft almost directly beneath the
pole. Knowing that the horny-head could not have done
this thing, I felt in my bones that the pike was on. Stepping softly on the raft, I crossed over and gently raised
and dislodged the pole; but even this slight motion was
all that was needed to start the fuss, and in an instant
that pike came out from under the raft and headed
downstream with such a "rulge" as it were, that for
the moment it seemed, I must choose either to let go
of the pole or go into the river; but was fortunately
saved from this alternative by the resistance to the rush
offered by that blessed "cork." And then the fight began. By giving him the "spring of the pole" and following him slowly down the raft, I succeeded in getting him
checked and turned upstream, and then we had it up
and down that raft a dozen times before he showed any
signs of weakening. Finally, however, after a battle of
half an hour's duration, he surrendered, and let me
lead him up to the side of the raft without a struggle.
I had heard of a pike, presumably this one, infesting
that bayou—which was five or six feet long and would
weigh from 50 to 60 pounds, and as I gazed down on
this one alongside of the raft and apparently at my
mercy, I decided that he fully measured up to every
inch and ounce of his reputation; and it was then my
nerves got short-circuited and my knees began to wobble.
My first excited thought was to pull him up on the side
of the raft over the ends of the log and over the strapping. But seeing that this would not do, I thought of
leading him around to the bank for a landing place;
but as the bank was four or five feet high and almost

perpendicular, this plan was discarded, and having neither gaffhook, gig nor weapon of any kind or character, it was up to me either to call for help which was so easily available, or devise some scheme to get the pike on that raft where I could handle him by my lonesome, as I fondly believed. Not wishing to share the glory of the achievement with any one, if possible to avoid it, I led him to the lower end of the raft and around where I might pull him aboard over the smooth bulging side of the end log. Wrapping the staging several times around my hand up to its junction with the wire leader, and also taking a turn or two of the leader, I finally succeeded in yanking Mr. Pike out of the water over the side of the log and high and dry on the raft.

I had thought the battle with that fish in the water was and would be the greatest of my piscatorial career, but when compared with what ensued, when he found himself out of the water and on the raft, that scrap was in comparison, diluted Mission Orange to genuine mountain dew "Moonshine." You have read of Kipling's Fuzzy Wuzzy on the rush—that Injy Rubber Idjit on a spree—if you will keep him in mind and imagine and couple him with an almost two-yard strip of animated whalebone in all its flexibility of action and in perpetual motion, slippery as a greased pig and vicious as a copperhead—you may have a slight conception of what I had to stack up against, as that pike flipped and flopped, "rampsed" and cavorted on that raft, first on top of the logs, then in the trough between—now on its tail, now on its head, now on one side and then the other—but always on the rush. I grabbed him around the body with both hands, and he slipped through like an eel; I sat down on him and he threw me off like a springboard; I tried to lie down on him, and he was gone before I could straighten out; several times I kicked at his head, with the result that the pike side-stepped each time, and I went sprawling on the raft. I bethought myself of the Barlow knife in my pocket, and opening it made a stab at his throat; the blow fell short however, but made a slight gash about four inches long down his side, and the knife slipped from my hand and fell between the logs and into the river. The pike bled profusely from this wound which was inflicted early in the fight, and soon I was smeared with blood from head to foot. Of course, I had sense enough not to put my hand about his mouth, because of those terrible teeth which he occasionally exhibited—sufficient with which to bite off a man's leg, much less a boy's hand—but finally I found an opportunity to thrust my hand up through the gills and crook the middle finger into his throat; but no sooner this, than the pike gave a mighty lurch, his head a mighty shake, dislodging my grip and throwing out my hand with such force that the saw-tooth edges of the gills tore and lacerated the skin on the back of my hand and fingers as though I had engaged in a bare-handed boxing bout with a brier patch; and with this lurch and a leap that cleared the strapping, the pike left the raft and gained the water, and as he did so, the line at a point five or six feet above the cork became fouled on the nail I had driven near the butt of the pole, snapped like a sewing thread, and my pike was gone off down toward Horse-Tail, the cork bobbing behind him as he went.

Just at the close of the last act of the bloody performance, Mel Cart appeared at the top of the bank, having heard some of the fuss on the raft and thinking his help might possibly be needed. About all he had seen was the pike as it left the raft, and together he and I watched it swim away with the cork, down to the head of Horse-Tail shoal, where the visible part of the procession disappeared. Mel, who had taken in the situation at a glance, said, "Wait a minute," and was off up to the camp, from which he returned in a jiffy, with two

gigs. We hastened to a canoe tied a short distance below the raft, and set out for Horse-Tail shoal in search
of the victor of the battle of the bayou, and to avenge
my ignominious defeat; hoping and expecting that the
cork would prove a beacon to our pathway and lead us
to the quarry. However, in that little deep plout just
below the head of the shoal, among some logs and snags,
we found the cork submerged and held under a limb, the
line having been broken at the nail that had been nearest
the leader, and the pike nowhere to be found, although
we spent more than an hour patrolling the river for a
mile below.

I told Mel that the pike was securely hooked in the
stomach and could not possibly dislodge the hook and
was dragging six feet of wire leader and two feet of
double staging, the strands of which would soon sep-
arate and become frayed from constant motion through
the water, and be a white streamer, which would disclose his whereabouts; so we decided to give over the
chase for the time being and go after him that night
with a pitch pine torch. There was a goodly supply of
pitch pine at the camp, which the loggers had brought in
from time to time, as they happened on it out in the
woods, for making torches for nocturnal travel.

The most approved method for providing a pitch pine
light for gigging from a canoe, is to make a strong
wire basket about the size of an ordinary water bucket,
and attach it to the end of an iron bar seven or eight
feet long, which is then securely fastened to the bow
of the canoe, so as to hold the basket at the proper angle
five or six feet ahead of the canoe. Not having such
outfit nor the means to make one, we adopted a common substitute, consisting of a platform made of boards,
and fitted on the canoe at the low bulge, the ends of the
boards extending two or three inches over either side
of the canoe; covering the platform with a two or three
inch layer of sand to protect it from the heat, and building our fire of pitch pine fagots thereon.

Ballard Goad, who was working on the job with Mel, acted as steersman for us that night when we set out in quest of the pike, and Mel and I took our stations in the bow and handled the gigs. We searched carefully all the deep water from the raft down to and through both Upper and Lower Dry Knob shoals, and around the bend to Jack Hanshaws, without finding any trace of our pike. On our return to a point a short distance below Horse-Tail, we had just crossed the river diagonally to a point half a canoe length above where a large log lay in shallow water near the north bank, when Mel told Ballard who was steering with a socket pole, to "prod that chunk laying by that log." Ballard, who was too far back from the light to be able to see more than the outline of the "chunk," prodded it lightly with his pole. Whereupon that chunk suddenly became animated, and tore out of there like a mad mustang, followed by the white streamer made by the frayed staging. We "followed the flag" and overtook it and the pike up near the foot of Horse-Tail shoal where Mel, who got the first shot at him, sunk his gig into the back of the fish, which, giving a mighty contortion of his body, threw the gig 10 feet in the air and 15 feet from Mel's hand; but a moment later we had crowded the crippled fish out in shallow water, where I struck him just back of the head on the under side, both points of the gig penetrating the hollow of the body. While he broke away again from even this fatal stroke and limped off to deep water, it was an easy matter to follow and dispatch him, and land him safely in the canoe.

On returning to camp we measured the pike carefully and found him to be so many inches in length—something near five feet, I do not remember the inches exactly.

The next morning some question was raised as to the weight of the fish. There were several men around the place and each took a guess. These guesses ranged from

40 to 60 pounds, as I remember. Mel Cart guessed 40 pounds and Ballard Goad said 45, and then Mel and Ballard made a bet as to which had made the better guess—the wager being each fellow's interest in a cross-cut saw which they owned jointly. No scales had as yet been provided for the embryo commissary, so Ballard struck out across the creek, for some steelyards belonging to his father, Uncle Alex Goad, who lived on the river bank at the upper side of the creek, where John L. Dickinson's fishing camp now stands, only to find that the same had been borrowed the day before by Jerry or Martin Goad, Ballard's brothers, each of whom lived a mile or more back on the mountain.

But Ballard Preston Goad, as I afterward became more fully aware, was one of the most ingenious and resourceful chaps it was ever my good fortune to know; and he did not propose to be denied in this instance by the mere absence of standard weighing apparatus. So, following a more illustrious but no whit more efficient—in his line—example of making a way where there was none ready-made, Ballard at once set about to improvise a contraption for ascertaining the weight of that fish.

Taking a scantling five or six feet long, he found the mean point between the two ends, at which they would balance, and at that point drove a large nail bent in the shape of a staple, through which he ran a small rope, which in turn he looped over a nail driven in the top of the casing of the front door of the commissary building, after having driven a tenpenny nail half its length into each end of the scantling. The beam being thus provided, suspended and balanced, Ballard found a keg which was just about half full of eight-penny nails. "Now, gentlemen," said he, "it is a well-known fact that a keg of nails weighs 100 pounds. There is about half a keg here, or about 50 pounds. But there is to be no guess work here, as I will show you later.

Attaching a small rope to the keg, he set it on the floor of the building under the end of the beam, and to the nail in which he fastened the rope so as to tilt the beam slightly toward the floor. By means of a rope run through its gills, the pike was suspended from the outdoor end of the beam—when it was found that his weight was not sufficient to lift the keg from the floor. Slowly Ballard proceeded to remove the nails from the keg and place them on the floor, until the keg slowly rose, the beam trembled in the balance and stood exactly at right angles with the door casing, as ascertained by an iron square.

The nail keg was again placed on the floor, and Ballard carefully adjusted the nails remaining therein, so that the mass would present, as nearly as possible, a level top surface. When this was done to the satisfaction of all, the distance was measured from the groove at the top of the keg, down to the nails, and this point on the inside of the keg designated by a pencil mark. The nails were then poured out of the keg and the distance measured from the pencil mark to the bottom, which latter, as nearly as we could figure, was 40 per cent of the whole distance.

"Forty pounds exactly! Just my guess," quoth Mel. "Where's my cross-cut saw?"

"Hold on there, young feller! This show is only half over. It now remains for us to weigh this empty keg. It will weigh five or six pounds—the pike lifted the keg with the nails, didn't he?"

Ballard put the empty keg on the floor and attached it to the beam as before, and, remarking, "You know, gentlemen, that a pint of water weighs a pound," procured a two-gallon tin bucket and an ordinary pint tin cup; filling the bucket about half full of water, he swung it from the outer end of the beam, and proceeded to dip the water from the bucket until the beam was exactly horizontal. Then carefully measuring the contents of the bucket with the tin cup, there were found to be almost exactly four cupfuls.

"Four pounds, plus the weight of that bucket, gentlemen. Shall we agree that the bucket will weigh a pound and a half?—that would make the pike weigh 45½ pounds," said Ballard.

"I won't agree nothin'," said Mel, "we wuzn't to have no guess work about this thing. Guessin' that a pint of water weighs a pound, and guessin' that a tin bucket weighs a pound and a half, don't go with me; you've got to git a better scale on it than that, before you git my half of that cross-cut saw. And besides you are talking about 100 pounds of nails and five and one-half pounds of keg, while my understanding is that it takes nails, keg and all to weigh a hundred pounds."

"Not if they were honest hardware dealers who sold them," retorted Ballard.

"Honest wha-a-a-at?" said Mel.

"And besides," said Ballard, "if you'll figure it, you'll find that even if it took nails, keg and all to weigh 100 pounds, I still guessed closer than you did."

"But you are taking too much for granted in your figuring. I want the weight certified before I'm willing to give up my interest in that saw," declared Mel.

And so these two chaps—the best of friends, chewed the rag over the weight of that pike as long as I remained at the camp—and every time they met until Ballard died, some years afterward; in consequence whereof I must always remain in doubt as to the weight of that pike. I have wondered, if so be it that there is a Valhalla for common mortals who have fought and fallen in the ordinary battles of life, Ballard Goad and Mel Cart have ever met and settled the vexed question as to the weight of that—and settled the ownership of that cross-cut saw.

XLV

BALLARD GOAD; DOGS AND COONS; A BLUE PIKE VS. RED-HORSE

BALLARD PRESTON GOAD, whose acquaintance I had made only a few days before he weighed the pike as previously mentioned, proved to be a most interesting chap. His father, Alexander H. Goad—Uncle Alex, as he was known to everybody, lived, as before stated, just across Little Sycamore from the commissary. Uncle Alex had been a widower, and had married, late in life and after his children had grown, a widow, whose maiden name was Joanna Pierson. Ballard owned a farm back on the mountain below Little Sycamore, some half a mile from the river. He was a bachelor and lived alone in a comfortable log cabin built on a flat hillside or cove, near the top of the hill, where he "did his own cookin' and eatin'."

A day or two after the adventure with the pike, Ballard invited me out to stay all night with him, and go coon-hunting—declaring that he had the best coon dog in seven counties. This invitation I was glad to accept, being anxious to have such an experience, with such a dog, more especially; my previous experience in that line of sport having been with dogs, which, though cracked up to be such, were no more fit for coon-hunting than a lap dog.

As we approached the cabin, a dog came bounding to meet us and was all over his master in a jiffy, with all the usual manifestations of canine affection and delight. I received a formal introduction to "Friday," and of course my first question was to learn why the name. "There is a long story connected with that dog, and I'll tell it to you while I am getting supper." And here it is as told by Ballard:

"About three years ago I was setting out on the porch one evening, and a dog came sneakin' and snoopin' around the corner of the house—the sorriest, orneriest, skinniest, starvedest looking dog I ever hope to see—the hair was all off his back where some woman had scalded him; there was a big scab on the side of his head where some boy had peeled him with a rock, and he was limpin' on his left hind leg—he was just about as near no dog at all—and that all shot to pieces—as a dog hater would wish to see. There was a hatchet lying there on the porch, and my first thought was to grab it and sling it at the dog. He didn't see me at first, but when he did get sight of me, he kind of gave back and crouched and looked straight at me and wagged his tail. Well, sir, it was the most apologizin', the most appealingest and beseechingest look I ever got from man or dog—or woman either—so far as that goes. I'll give you my word and honor that he said it—just the same as words could have spoke it—'Mister, for God's sake, don't kill me; don't drive me off—look what I have gone through with— starved and scalded and beat and bruised and kicked and cuffed and crippled up, till I can't go no further— take me in and feed me and give me a chance, and I'll be your friend for life.' Well, sir, somehow or other I couldn't help taking that dog's word for it; and instead of throwing the hatchet at him as I was about to do, I called him up on the porch and took him out in the kitchen and gave him some bread and milk—not too much, in his starved condition; and then I washed him up and tended to his sores and rubbed his leg—it wasn't hurt much—just somebody hit him on that leg with a stick—and later that night I gave him some more bread and milk and next morning I gave him a good stiff feed —and then he began to have more the appearance of a dog. In ten days time you couldn't have told there ever had been anything wrong with him but for the hair being off his back in patches; but he soon came out of that, and here he is now. Come in here, Friday, and speak to the gentleman. Give him a welcome salute—one, two, three!" And Friday looked up at me and barked once, twice and then three times.

"You can see from his size and shape and ears, that he is part hound and part shepherd, but I think he is about half cur—a breed that makes the best all-round hunting dogs. I had him a year before I found out where he come from. A fellow come along one day and recognized him. Said there was an old fellow down in Kanawha County on the waters of Blue Creek, who dug "sang" about half the year and shantied around or holed up under rock cliffs for the other half—who had owned that dog. This man had died about a year before, since which time the dog had never been seen in that locality. Well, whoever owned him, knew how to handle a dog, for when I got him on his feet, I found he was the best trained dog I ever saw—and the aptest to learn. He never leaves the place unless I take him, and while I am gone he looks after the place better than four men and a boy could do it. Nobody can get in this house while he is on guard. He'll let them in the yard, friendly enough, but they must keep away from the house, the stable, the corn crib, hogs and chickens, and every place else where they've got no business. He's the only real coon dog I ever saw and is just as good for squirrels and pheasants—and deer; let me tell you; Upper Birch Run over there heads up against Little Sycamore on one side and the waters of Porters Creek on the other, and there are a couple of low gaps in there about 150 yards apart, that are great crossing places for deer that come down Upper Birch Run and cross Elk River up at Upper Dry Knob Shoal. I used to go out back there with Friday and start deer for fellers placed on stands at these two crossing places. Sometimes the deer would cross at one place and sometimes t'other. If the feller on the stand failed to kill the deer, it would run down Birch

Run and cross at the Dry Knobs, and Friday would follow it to the river and until called off the chase. That occurred several times, until I quit starting with Friday. He's too heavy for a long chase and it was too hard on him. After that I'd make the other fellows and their dogs do the starting, and one day I took the lower stand—the gap next to Little Sycamore, and had Friday there with me—he was trained not to open his mouth until I would holler or shoot—and we heard the dogs coming back of the upper stand and soon heard the fellow up there shoot, and immediately yell, "Lookout! There he comes." But I knew enough about the lay of the ground to know that the deer would not come within gunshot of me, but that he was headed for Birch Run. So I motioned to Friday to cut loose his dogs, expecting him to dash down the hillside to the creek where I knew the deer would run. But, sir, that dog had a durned sight more sense than I did, and instead of that, he took off at right angles to the direction I expected him to, out along the hillside and over the point ridge to the river. I followed as fast as I could and got on top of a cliff on the river point, where I could see Upper Dry Knob Shoal, just in time to see Friday halfway across the shoal wading in the shallow water toward the opposite shore. I supposed the deer had crossed and was gone, and was about to yell for Friday to come back, when I saw that fool dog run up the river bank and hide behind a bunch of willows. In less than half a minute I saw the deer dash out through the shoal, headed for the far shore, and I wondered what had become of Friday. But I didn't have long to wait to find out, for when the old buck had gotten about two-thirds of the way across, old Friday came tearing down the bank and out over the rocks to meet him. The buck thus headed off—knowing the other dogs were coming behind him, had nothing left but to turn upstream and get into deep water where he could wade, but where a dog would be obliged to swim.

"I started off down the steep mountain side, but had only gone a few jumps, when I heard the dogs that had followed the buck down the creek, bust out of the hollow and out through the shoal, and by the time I got to the river, Friday and the three hounds had him bayed there in the river, the dogs all swimmin' and the buck horning them off. I downed him with the first shot and waded out and drug him back to this side of the river. And Friday doing that the one time, wasn't no accident nor pop shot; for another time I had him with me at the upper stand, and pime blank the same thing happened at the lower stand, and Friday cut around the hillside and over the point on the lower side of the creek, comin' in ahead of the deer, just like he did the first time, and done the same thing over again. And that's what makes me say that he's got more sense than half the people I know.

"While that dog don't carry no timepiece, he knows the time of day as well as you can read it from the clock. At 5 o'clock every morning regular, he scratches on my door and keeps a scratchin' till I get up. Then he goes off and hunts up the cow and has her in the stable-lot for me to milk as soon as I get through breakfast. And in plowin' time or harvest, when I am using the horses and they are runnin' out, he brings them up by the time they are needed and never has to be told after the first day.

"He never comes in the house except when I give him a special invitation; sleeps in the little dog house I built for him back in the corner of the woodshed and he won't eat a bite of anything only what I give him in his gourd."

Ballard handed me a scrap of the ham he was preparing for supper and told me to call Friday—who, during the narrative, had left the house—and see if I could get him to take the meat. I did as requested with the result that the dog refused to touch it, either from my hand or on the ground, when I placed it before him. Ballard then produced a large shallow short-handled gourd from behind the kitchen door, and putting in it several chunks of corn bread, scraps of ham—including the piece scorned from my hand—poured in a quart or more of sweet milk, and placed it on a low wooden block out in the yard. Immediately Friday proceeded to dispatch the contents, lapping up the milk as completely as possible before eating either the bread or meat. The meal finished, the dog very deliberately took the gourd handle in his mouth, marched into the kitchen and deposited the gourd in its place behind the door.

"Now," said Ballard, "you asked me awhile ago, why I called him Friday. At the time this dog came to me, I had read about the third time, a book I've got there in the other room by name of Robinson Crusoe—did you ever read it? Oh, you have. Then you know why I called him Friday, without me telling you. This dog has been lots more to me than ever Robinson Crusoe's man Friday was to him—and I know he's got more sense about lots of things. And I have often thought, what I would have been without him—if I had drove that sorry, ornery, half-starved dog away when he come here three years ago, instead of takin' him in and befriending him. Why, I wouldn't trade that dog for the best yoke of oxen in Clay County."

After supper and before the moon rose and we had started off for the coon hunt, Ballard took me into the bedroom and showed me his library, consisting of a rather small but choice, though somewhat queer selection of literary productions; namely, a well-worn copy of Robinson Crusoe, Pollocks Course of Time, sans back or binding and with a few final pages missing— Ivanhoe, The Lady of the Lake, a stray volume of McCaulay's England, a bound volume containing 12 or possibly 24 issues of Godey's Ladies Book of the early 70's, somebody's History of the United States, a complete set of McGuffey's Readers and Spellers, Ray's Higher Arithmetic, Harvey's Grammar, a much torn and battered geography, a stack of Congressional Records, half a bushel of almanacs, and last, but by no means least, Mayo's Guide. I later learned that Ballard, being an omnivorous reader, had devoured each of these books and publications, "from kiver to kiver," over and over again—even including the almanacs, and Congressional Records. On second thought—it may be that the publication last mentioned was at that day and date called the Congressional Globe—at any rate it was the sayings and doings of Congress, by whatsoever name the publication was known at that time.

Although even at that early age I had made up my mind to become a lawyer some day, I am frank to say that I had never heard of Mayo's Guide, but was nevertheless attracted by the appearance of the book and its outer resemblance to books I had seen in lawyer's offices; and Ballard observing the direction of my gaze proudly handed me the book and said, "That's my law. Somebody gave it to pap when he was Justice of the Peace, and he gave it to me." He further informed me that Mayo's Guide was said to contain about all the law there was that amounted to anything, and that there were lots of lawyers who wouldn't use any other book in their practice.

It was then that I confided to Ballard my intention to become a lawyer and asked him to start me off by lending me Mayo's Guide, to read while I was down at the camp, and thus acquire a complete knowledge of the law in my early youth; to which request Ballard readily assented.

Our coon hunt that night was most successful, especially in demonstrating the qualities of Friday as a coon dog. We hadn't gone a quarter of a mile from the house until the dog treed a large coon, which by the aid of our pine torch we were able to "shine," and to shoot out of the tree. We treed two or three others in large trees where we could not locate them—and in fact did not try—as Ballard explained that the pelts were no good at that season of the year, the coons poor and the meat not very good, but that his main object was to show me a real coon dog in action. That he did this was fully evidenced by the fact that Friday did all the dog's part toward bagging three or four coons in two hour's time.

I went back to the camp early next morning, lugging the coon we had killed, fully convinced that Friday was the most wonderful dog in the world, and that Ballard Preston Goad was a peach. And I did not fail to carry Mayo's Guide with me.

Ballard worked at the mouth of the creek only at odd times, and did not return with me that morning; but two or three days later he came while I was at breakfast and demanded sharply, "Billy, where's my law?" Knowing what he meant I got up and found Mayo's Guide, and handing him the book, asked him what the trouble was. He said he had to go up to the mouth of Blue Knob, to try a lawsuit before Squire Shannon at ten o'clock, and urged me to go along. George Acree, who heard the conversation, suggested that we take the canoe and carry along five or six bushels of corn and have it ground at Hiram Lewis' mill at Yankee Dam, which is just across the river from the mouth of Blue Knob Creek. As it was then only about 6 o'clock and we figured that we could take the canoe and cover the seven miles quite easily long before court time, we set forth on our journey. Ballard in the stern of the canoe with paddle and socket-pole and I in the bow to man the oar through the eddies, and a gig, to help push over the shoals. When we had almost reached the foot of Little King Shoal, six miles up, and I had shipped my oar and picked up my gig, to push through the shoal, Ballard, who had just straightened up with the socket-pole in his hand, yelled, "Lordy, lookee, there!" and at the word he suddenly pushed the stern in toward the left bank with such violence, that I was caught off balance and landed kersplash! in the river about 30 feet from the bank. Fortunately the water was only about waist-deep, and as I landed on my feet I saw what had caused the exclamation and the unusual commotion. What first caught my eye was a huge pike, about the size of the one we had killed a few nights before, standing on his tail and about half out of water, not over three or four feet from the water's edge, with a 20-inch red-horse in his mouth, about half swallowed, and evidently trying vainly to complete the job. Our appearance on the scene and the disturbance ensuing, had evidently so interfered with the performance as to cause the pike to so far relax his hold, as to enable the red-horse to wrench himself loose and give a mighty flop which threw him in the air and landed him three or four feet back on the sand bar, where the pike, not to be so easily deprived of his breakfast, immediately followed and was in the act of re- caption, when Ballard, who had jumped out of the canoe with his socket-pole and had reached the scene of the battle just in the nick of time, made a ferocious lunge with his pole, which struck lightly and glanced harmlessly off of the head of the monster and sped on and completely disembowled the ill-fated red-horse. The pike slipped back into the river and was gone, and I floundered out to the scene of action only in time to vainly hurl my gig at him as he sped down the stream, twenty feet away.

We arrived at the mouth of Blue Knob sometime before the appointed hour, after having stopped first on the opposite side of the river to deposit our grist at the watermill, for many years owned and operated by the aforesaid Hiram Lewis.

On the way up the river Ballard had told me something of the nature of the lawsuit to be tried. He said it was an action of unlawful "detainure," brought be-

fore Squire Shannon by a fellow by the name of Cain—
Preacher Cain, as he was called, by reason of being
a local preacher—against a widow by the name of
Charlotte—pronounced Charlotty—Shamblin. He said
Charlotty and a boy she had taken to raise, had cleared
a patch of ground on "company land," on Blue Knob
Creek, and had put in a crop the last spring, and that
Preacher Cain had waited until the crop had "good made
itself," and the boy had died, and then sued her for
possession of land, crop and all. That he was to be Charlotty's lawyer, and didn't know much about the case;
but Charlotty would be on hand and tell him all about
her defense. He further explained that he didn't expect
to get a fee, but that Charlotty was a sister of Joanna
Goad, his stepmother, and for that reason and with no
thought of fee or reward he was going to "fight the
case."

Squire Norval Shannon, the Justice of the Peace, both
litigants, quite a number of witnesses and a goodly
gathering of spectators arrived shortly after we reached
the ground. There was some sort of a building near the
mouth of the creek—a schoolhouse, probably—but the
Squire announced that he would hold court under a large
beech tree nearby. Ballard and his client held a short
conference and when the case was called, he promptly
announced that the defendant was ready and anxious
for a trial—without waiting to hear from the plaintiff.
The plaintiff exhibited some uneasiness, whether on account of Ballard's cocksure manner, or for other cause,
and after a short conference with some of his witnesses
and adherents, moved for a continuance on the ground
of the absence by reason of sickness, of a very important
witness. After much wrangling between Ballard and
the preacher, the case was continued until next Saturday—much to my disappointment, as I was eager to see
the scrap.

As Ballard and I were about to push off our canoe

to cross over to the mill, Squire Shannon asked us to "Set him across," which we were glad to do. On the way over, the Squire said that his daughter, Rebecca—Mrs. Lewis—was a fine cook and he knew she would be glad to give the three of us a good dinner. Although it was then almost 12 o'clock, and we had had no time to get our "name in the pot," Aunt Rebecca gave us a wonderful dinner—one of those regular old-fashioned farm dinners, splendidly prepared and bountifully served, where a fellow will eat three times as much as usual without being conscious of the fact; and for me, an always hungry 16-year-old boy, who had been living on camp grub for two solid months, it was a feast fit for the gods. Three or four men and boys who were "waiting their turn" at the mill, strolled over to the house "to get a drink of water," just as dinner was ready, and of course were invited by Aunt Rebecca to come in and have dinner, and although each in turn said, "No, thank you, mom, I ain't none hungry," each finally, after being pressed, sat down and ate very heartily. I figured that the grists of corn these fellows had brought to be ground would average about a bushel and a half, and with corn worth 50 cents a bushel and the toll of a gallon to a bushel being about 10 cents in value, and the grub eaten by each of them worth at least 50 cents— it was easy to see why the operator of a gristmill always gets rich. I don't know whether Hiram Lewis got rich at that business, but he was for many years a very well-to-do, prominent and influential citizen of his county and state. His two sons, Ben and Clem, little fellows at that time, are now both prominent business men, the former at Sutton and the latter at Charleston; and Aunt Rebecca, who must be between 85 and 90, hale and hearty, still lives at the old home at Yankee Dam.

Waiting our turn we were able to get our grist in the mid-afternoon and return home. On the trip down, Ballard suddenly announced that he had just figured out why Preacher Cain, with all the witnesses he had present, had been so anxious to have the case continued. He said, "You know that your father has been the lawyer for many years, of those Lewisburg people who own the big tract of land on which that clearing was made. Now Preacher Cain saw you up there with me, and found out that you are Col. Byrne's son, and he jumped to the conclusion that you must be there as a witness for Charlotty Shamblin, to prove that she had permission to make the clearing. So you must go back with me next Saturday when the trial comes off."

And that is why I came to be present at the trial which did come off the next Saturday.

XLVI

"PREACHER" CAIN GOES "A-LAWIN'"

ON THE following Saturday, Ballard Goad and I took a short cut over a part of Jack's Bend, going up the river from the mouth of Little Sycamore, about three-quarters of a mile, and up White Hill Hollow on the north side of the river, following around the ridge between the waters of Big Laurel and those of Main Elk, and came off down to Blue Knob at Charlotty Shamblin's home, and she took us down and showed us the premises in controversy. We found the corn, bean and 'tater patch to comprise about an acre of creek bottom land, lying within a horseshoe bend of the creek, a rock cliff jutting out from a low point ridge, extending halfway across from creek to creek at the heel of the shoe, and a substantial log—and—brush fence in two sections of 50 to 60 feet in length, one above and one below the cliff, comprising the other half of the barrier. This little bottom had been heavily timbered with poplar, oak and hemlock trees, which had been cut three or four years previously, as indicated by the stumps, and only the prime saw logs therefrom taken away, leaving on the ground a large part of the tree trunks, as well as the butts and laps or limbs. I was struck with the very ingenious manner in which the builder of this fence had made use of the small and large saplings growing along the fence-row, by slightly hacking the larger ones so they could be bent over upon or along the fence, and held down by piling brush and limbs on their bent-over tops and the smaller saplings bent over without hacking, and treated in the same manner, so that all these saplings could be and were interwoven in and had become a part of the brush fence, and yet all were alive and had their green foliage.

Going down to the place of the trial at the mouth of the creek, we found Squire Shannon, Preacher Cain and quite a large gathering of people. We had scarcely gotten on the ground when Preacher Cain came up, and, introducing himself, greeted me very effusively, saying, among other things, how delighted he was to know the son of his old friend, Col. Ben Byrne, a man for whom he had the highest regard and for whom he had voted and for whose success he had prayed every time he had run for office. He had all the white-eyed piety, sanctimonious seeming, and that peculiar intonation of voice, so common among and affected by a certain class and type of gospel spreaders, which, coupled with the overwhelming unctuousness of his greeting, left me anything but a favorable impression of the gentleman—hence my response to his greeting was not as gracious as it might have been, which may have confirmed him in the belief attributed to him by Ballard, that I was there "to swear agin him."

Preacher Cain was the first to testify upon the trial. He stated that in the fall, winter and spring last past, he and his two boys had cleared and fenced the ground in controversy, consisting of about an acre—maybe a leetle more an' maybe a leetle less—being mighty keerful uv my oath, can't space-efy adzactly—up the creek thar in the horseshoe bend jist below Sister Charlotty Shamblin; that he had gotten the ground ready for the plow, but that just at that time in the spring the rain had set in and as it looked like it would be a long wet spell, he went over on Middle Creek to attend a protracted meetin', 'lowing to plow and plant when he got back— his boys was big enough to help in the clearin' but nary one big enough to plow—and when the meetin' was over he was called to the bedside of Brother So-and-so, who was very sick over on Charley's Fork of Big Sycamore, and he stayed there two days comforting and praying with the brother until he died, and that the folks of the deceased put at him to stay and officiate at the burial service, so that it was three weeks before he got back home, to find that Sister Charlotty had done plowed and planted the ground in corn and beans and 'taters and that the corn was already up. That he had at once gone to see Sister Charlotty, and remonstrated with her about her very reprehensible conduct in thus appropriating his ground, cleared, fenced and put in shape for cultivation by the sweat of his brow, and that of his boys; but that Sister Charlotty was stiff-necked and obdurate about the thing, and that while it was to him a most distressing and painful duty, in justice to himself and those dependent upon him for a livelihood, he was compelled to resort to law to vindicate his rights.

The manner and mannerisms, tone and inflection of the witness, were the same as noted by me in my few minutes conversation with him, and in his testimony he interlarded frequent protestations of his own veracity, integrity and righteousness.

Ballard's cross-examination was brief, so far as the questions were concerned, but made somewhat lengthy by the prolixity of the answers.

Q. Mr. Cain, when did you do the first work on the disputed premises?

A. Well, now, Brother Goad, it would be hard for me to fix the adzact day and date that me and my boys done the first work—I am on oath you know, and I am very particular about my oath—I would not swear a lie fer the land—nor for two such places, for that matter.

Q. Was it before or after cold weather had set in last fall?

A. Well, now, Brother Goad, thar you go agin, tryin' to pin me down to dates, an' me a tellin' you I can't fix adzactly the day an' date. But I believe when we begun, it wuz not very hot an' not very cold—jist moderate.

Q. Was it before Thanksgiving?

A. I am not able to space-efy adzactly, but it runs in my mind that it wuz a leetle before Thanksgivin'— mout a bin a leetle afore an' mout a bin a leetle after. I am on oath, mind you, an' you can't git me to swear no lie; I didn't come here to lie—but I come to tell the truth, the whole truth, an' nothin' but the truth—an' you nor no other man can't git me to swear nothin' else.

Q. Had any clearing been done or any brush fence made there before you and your boys began the clearing last fall?

A. No, sir; I can answer that mighty quick. Not a lick had been hit sence the big timber was cut two or three year before. Me an' the boys cleaned up the ground uv the logs an' butts an' laps uv the big timber left laying on the ground — grubbed or cut down the saplin's an' small stuff — an' built the brush fence ourselves — every log, limb an' brush uv it — We got it all ready fer the crop an' would have put it in last spring, but fer preventin' Provi-dence, like I tole you.

Q. Did you build the brush fence first or did you do the clearing first?

A. Well now, Brother Goad, you've did enough clearin' an' brush fencin' to know that you do it all right along together — part uv the time you are working at one an' part uv the time at t'other — an' that's the way we done it.

"That's all," said Ballard.

Cain's two boys, about 12 and 14 years of age respectively, followed their dad as witnesses and tracked with him in every detail of the cleaning up, the grubbing, hacking, cutting, building of brush fence and getting the ground ready for the plow. The only difference was that they simply answered very briefly, and in the negative or affirmative, according to the desire of the questioner as plainly indicated by the very leading and suggestive questions, as propounded by their father.

But under Ballard's cross-questioning, the boys did

not fare very well. While his manner toward the lads was most kindly and not in the least calculated to embarrass, confound or mislead, he soon had the little fellows in deep water, by questions, mildly and suavely put, as to details concerning which they had not been coached and which had not been covered by their father. Several other witnesses testified that they had seen Preacher Cain and his two boys sometime the fall, winter or spring before, doing some work on the premises in question — grubbin', choppin', packin' bresh an' sich like; one or two had seen him there in the fall, one or two in the winter, and others in the spring; and all these witnesses stated that the place in question was some distance from and out of sight of the traveled path leading up Blue Knob Creek and over the point, and therefore could not say whether the widder Shamblin had done any work on the premises or not — that they had never seed her or Johnny, the boy she had took to raise doing any work there until they begun plowing for the crop. One or two of them had "seed Charlotty an' Johnny a plowin' an' a plantin' late last spring."

At the conclusion of the plaintiff's evidence, the defendant Charlotty was sworn and testified. Charlotty said that about a year and a half before, in the late fall or early winter, and two years or so after the big timber had been cut, she had conceived the idea of cleaning up that little bottom, for a corn, bean and 'tater patch, and that she and Johnny, a lad of 16 or 17, she had raised, had set about to rid the ground of the logs, butts and laps, by rolling or carrying the same out to the steep creek bank, so as to serve as a further barrier against the ingress of cattle and hogs, and with the balance, to construct a log and brush fence from the cliff across the upper and lower ends of the bottom, about 120 feet in all, to the edges of the creek bank, and that after stringing the logs, butts and large limbs as the foundation for the fence, they had hacked all the saplings near by — just hacked them enough to bend them down across

or along and parallel with the logs, but not deep enough
to kill the sapling — so they would live and help keep
up the fence — and upon these logs and bent-over saplings they had piled the smaller limbs of the tree laps,
and so partly constructed the brush fence in question;
and that from time to time and at odd spells up to the
spring before the trial, they had cut or grubbed the saplings and brush in the enclosure and added them to the
fence, so that against the time the ground was ready for
the plow, the brush fence was "horse-high, bull-strong
and pig-tight." That owing to bad weather and other
causes she had not gotten the clearing all done in time
for a crop the first spring after the work was begun, but
had it ready in good time for the next spring. That in
March of that year, she put a small part of the ground
in potatoes and that in May, she put the balance in corn
and beans.

That just before Thanksgiving the year before,
Preacher Cain, who lived across Blue Knob and up a
hollow, about half a mile from where she lived and
about a quarter of a mile from the land in question —
and on the opposite side of the creek — came to her
house to borrow some meal. That she told him she didn't
have "no meal to spare," and that he already owed her
two pecks of meal, for two "borryin's" he had already
made; and he finally told her that he "was starvin'," and
that if she would let him have another peck of meal "to
keep his family from starvin'," him an' his boys would
work in the clearin' down in the bend, to pay for the
meal. That the boy, Johnny, was sick at the time with
a bealed ear and a bone-felon, and not able to work, and
as she was anxious to get the ground in shape for the
next spring planting, as she had missed getting it ready
the first spring — she let the preacher have the meal
and furnished him an axe and mattock with which to
do the work; which tools he carried away with him,
upon the assurance that he would take the meal home
and him and the boys would come right over to the

clearin' and start to work. That she gave him about time to get back and then went out the point just below and around the bend from her house, and to the top of the cliff overlooking the clearing, where she could see what was going on. That "sho'nuff," there he was — him and his two boys, down there choppin' and grub-bin', an' sproutin'. That she stood there a few minutes watchin' them, without being seen, when suddenly she heard their dog barking at the base of the cliff on which she was standing, whereupon the preacher and his boys left off work and come up to the cliff and started to diggin' with the mattock — "fer a ground-hog, I reckon — I couldn't see them down where they wuz — but heerd 'em, an' I know there is a ground-hog hole there under the cliff." That she stood there a few minutes, still without making herself known, and then went home and sent Johnny out to watch them — Johnny was able to "be about," but not able to work — and Johnny told her they were still digging down there when he had to come home fer supper. That the next day the preacher come and told her he had broke the mattock-handle "grubbin'," and she had to hunt up an old handle, "that was warped and crooked and not much good — but bet-ter than no handle"; that she said nothing about the ground-hog and neither did the preacher. That he said the next day wuz Thanksgivin', and that he had to preach somewhere over on Laurel an' had to git wood to last while he was gone — so he couldn't do no more work till he got back — and said he wanted to borry my axe that he had — to git his wood with — an' when I next seed the axe it had a piece broke out of the bit as big as a hickory nut; and it wuz nearly Christmas before he struck another lick in the clearin', and then him and his two boys worked — he said — half a day, cuttin' a few saplin's and packin' a little bresh an' doin' a little sproutin' that I could have done in less than an hour.

Then he put at me to borry some more meal and a piece of hog-meat — I had just butchered a couple of shoats I had fattened on the mast — and fool-like, I let him have the meal and the hog-meat, and he was to go right ahead in the clearin' — and I never seen him again till Aprile, when he starved out agin an' come to me fer more meal an' hog-meat — an' I told him not another bite till he worked out what he had already borryed — and then, him and his two boys did do a little pilferin' around down there in the clearin', gittin' it ready to plow — helpin' Johnny, who was then able to work. And then he wanted some more meal — he had done got some hog-meat, the Lord knows where — but I have my 'spicions — and when I up an' tells him I didn't have no meal to spare — which wuz the truth — an' then he gits mad and I don't see him no more until he sues me fer my possessions — an' he's still got my mattock — he did fetch the axe back, but he had done broke it so it wasn't no count only fer the handle.

Well, me and Johnny finished the clearin' an' the brush fence, an' about the time it was ready to plow, they did set in a wet spell — the preacher told the truth about that — but that was the only truth he did tell — so it was late when me an' Johnny got the corn an' beans planted, an' me an' Johnny hoed the corn first time an' about the time we got it laid by, Johnny took newmoney fever an' died in about ten days; an' then the preacher he tuck it in his head that as Johnny was dead, an' I wouldn't have no witnesses only me — he would lay claim to my possessions — cause he had witnesses who had saw him workin' there, an' I didn't have none, since Johnny was dead, and couldn't prove nothin' only by myself.

This recital of Charlotty's was crisp, snappy and emphatic and delivered in a most convincing manner, and made in response to a very broad question by Ballard calling for a full statement of the facts. When she was through, Ballard did not find it necessary to ask any further questions, but turned the witness over to the preacher for cross-examination.

That he was considerably flabbergasted by the long and well connected statement of his adversary, was clearly evidenced by the first question he propounded:

"Sister Charlotty, you don't know that we wuz diggin' out a ground-hog there at the base of the cliff — moughtn't we have been grubbin' or sproutin'?"

"No; I don't know it wuz a ground-hog — but I do know you wuzn't grubbin' or sproutin' there in that cliff — An' I ain't your sister Charlotty, nuther."

"Well, I'll show different about the grubbin' an' sproutin'," said the preacher.

"Charlotty," said the preacher, for his next question — leaving off the "Sister" — "you say you have your 'spicions how I got the hog-meat you told about — what do you mean by that?"

"Well, ef I must tell it — Sam King had some hogs runnin' on the mast out on the mountain about two mile back of your place, an' one of them come up missin' about that time, an' about a week or so after that, he found the hide in the woods, where you — or somebody — had skinned it — an' you havin' no hogs — that's why I had my 'spicions."

"Well, I'll show different," said the preacher.

After a few more questions, as irrelevant as the two above, and answers about as juicy to the bystanders, to which, each time the preacher responded weakly with his stock phrase, "Well, I'll show different," — the cross-questioner decided he had got enough, and laid off.

Whereupon, Ballard announced to the court that he had no other witness there present, but that up the creek about a mile he had witnesses which he would ask the court to go and examine — that is that the court should have a view of the premises and get the truth from mute and eloquent witnesses that could not lie. Over the strenuous objection of the plaintiff, the court ordered the view, and we all repaired to the disputed premises.

On reaching the ground, Ballard sent some one to

Charlotty's house for an axe, armed with which he went to one of the slightly hacked and bent over saplings described by Charlotty as being part of the brush fence, standing there alive, with green foliage and with brush piled on the bent-over top — and carefully cut out a small block, which took a part of the hack which had been made to bend it; this block he split half in two, so as to show the annulations or growth; smoothed the surface with his pocketknife, and showed Squire Shannon that there were two distinct annulations between the bark and the axe mark in the wood; proving conclusively that the hack had been made for at least two seasons; corresponding exactly with Charlotty's statement as to when the brush fence had been begun, and contradicting the preacher's statement that he had begun building the fence less than one year before. Not satisfied with the one blocking, Ballard blocked two more bent saplings in the lower part of the fence and three in the upper end, and each registered two growths. Ballard also found another sapling in the fence that had been deeply scarred near the top, by a large limb of the laps piled on it, and from it took a block showing that the scar was two growth-years old. He then took us to the base of the cliff where Charlotty had said she thought the preacher and his boys were trying to dig out a ground-hog, and showed that nothing had been cut or grubbed or sprouted anywhere near — but further showed that at one time, somebody had done a lot of digging, with a mattock, the marks of which were plainly visible in the soft shale, in the edge of the hole at the base of the cliff. The view ended, we all returned to the place of the trial, where Ballard announced that the defense rested.

Thereupon Preacher Cain, by way of alleged rebuttal, sought to repeat his own story and to have his witnesses do likewise; but Ballard soon convinced the court by reading something from Mayo's Guide, that in an orderly conducted lawsuit, neither party would be permitted to "thrash over old straw," and after a lot of wrangling, the case was closed and the argument begun. The preacher did not seem very keen about arguing the case, and said he would be willing to submit it without argument. But I could see that Ballard was all keyed up and "spilin'" to make a speech; and he had his way.

The preacher led off in a manner that intrigued me from the very start. I had heard lawyers make court speeches and I had likewise heard ministers of the gospel deliver sermons, but never before had I heard such a conglomeration of the two. Something of its general trend and flavor comes back to me after a lapse of more than half a century:

May it please the court—ah—an' the members of this large an' intelligent—ah—congregation. I appear before you this morning—er—whatever time a day it is, as plaintiff in this action uv lawful detainure — as brother Goad calls it—ah—. I don't know what the law books calls it—ah—but I do know what the Bible says —ah—an' the Bible says thou shalt not covet what is thy neighbors—ah. An' now I want to talk about the evi-dence that has been swore to here in this court—ah— an' before this congregation—ah; an' sister Charlotty —but she don't 'low me to call her sister—ah—so I'll jist call her the widder Shamblin—ah—; the widder Shamblin she says—ah—no, she don't say it nuther, she only 'spicions—ah; she 'spicions me fer stealin' an' killin' an' skinnin' Sam King's hog—ah. An' you know the Bible says—ah—that nobody ever seed the righteous fersaken—ah—nor his seed beggin' bread— ah. An' now my brethun, I ax you—who air the righteous—ah? An' I'll tell you who the righteous air, by tellin' you who the—ah. The Holy Scriptures says that them that serves the Lord—ah—airly an' late—an' go forth an' preach my gospell—ah—to every living creature—ah. An' my brethun what hev I been doin' fer the last seven year—ah—ever since I was converted an' had my sins washed away—ah—by the blood that flowed from Calvary—ah—at the protracted meetin'

over on the Horse Fork uv Laurel—ah—jist seven years
ago this summer—ah. Why, a servin' the Lord airly—
ah—an' a servin' the Lord late—ah—an' a preachin' the
gospell to ever livin' creature—ah—that would turn out
to hear me—ah. An' you know that the Bible further
says to them that goes forth to preach the gospell—ah—
take nothing in thy scrip—ah—that the Lord will provide—ah—; an' that means—ah—that when the
preacher is out preachin'—ah—not only that he needn't
pack his own grub along—ah—but also that he don't
have no need to worry about his wife an' youngins left
at home—ah—while he is out preachin'—ah—all except gittin' wood—ah—an' I most generally gits enough
wood—ah—to last ontil I git back—ah—an' then, as fur
as that's concerned—ah—my woman kin hannel a axe
purty nigh good as I can—ah; an' when I come back
home—ah—I always brings back a load uv provisions
—ah—that my congregation gives me—ah. An' so
may it please the court—ah—you see I don't haveta
borry meal or hog-meat offen sis—offen the widder
Shamblin—ah—an' I don't have to steal none uv Sam
King's hogs—ah—nor nobody elses hogs—ah—fer, as
I told you—ah—the Bible says the Lord will provide—
ah—an' the Bible is the word of God—ah—an' the word
of God don't lie—ah. An' as fer as ground-hogs is
concerned—ah—I like ground-hog—ah—an' I don't
keer who knows it—ah—; an' it ain't no disgrace fer
anybody to eat ground-hog—ah—an' some uv the best
people I know eats ground-hog—ah. An' sometimes I
do go out an' kill me a ground-hog—ah—jist to help
the Lord provide fer me an' my family between spells
uv preachin' the gospell—ah; but as fer me bein' diggin'
fer a ground-hog when the widder Shamblin says she
seen me diggin' with her mattick—ah—I never borryed
her mattick—ah—nor her axe nuther—ah—nor she
can't prove it—ah—I wasn't diggin' fer no ground-hog
—ah—but ef she seed me at all like she says she seed
me—ah—with my own axe an' my own mattick—ah—

me an' my two boys—ah—a clearin' an' a hackin' an' a grubbin' an' a packin' bresh—ah—on my own possessions—ah—which the widder Shamblin coveted and come like a thief in the night—ah—while I was away preachin' the gospell—ah—an' disposed me uv—ah—an' me earnin' my bread by the sweat uv my brow—ah—jist as the Bible tells us to do—ah—that is, I mean to say—ah—ah—ah—I mean when we ain't preachin' the gospell—ah.

An' the Bible further tells us, my brethren—ah—that out of three witnesses—ah—shall the truth be established—ah. An' I have brung not three witnesses—ah—but five or six witnesses—ah—besides me an' my two boys—ah—that many more than the scriptures says a feller needs—ah.

An' the widder Shamblin comes by herself—ah—nobody else come to swear fer her—ah—an' I guess Brother Goad will ax this court—ah—to go agin the scriptures an' say—ah—that the mouth uv one witness kin establish more truth—ah—than the mouth of three or six or eight witnesses—ah. An' he may want to tell you that them pieces he chopped out uv them saplings—ah—speaks fer themselves as he calls it—ah—an' shows that the bresh fence was built a year before it was built—ah—but this court ain't goin' to pay no 'tention to no sich stuff—ah—an' the Bible don't say nothin' about establishin' the truth by the mouth uv no saplin'—ah—nor no three saplin's—ah—nor no six saplin's—ah. Amen!!

I remember only some of the high spots in Ballard's argument in reply to that of the preacher. One point he made was that in his "pleading of the case" preacher Cain had run true to form, "going out after ground-hogs," when he should have been addressing himself to the questions of "who done the clearin' and fencin'," just as Charlotty had said he did, when she hired him to work for her in the clearing and he went off after ground-hogs; and that speaking of hog-meat, concerning which the preacher had shown himself so sensitive by devoting his whole time to that subject, which was not spent in talking about ground-hogs — everybody who had heard his speech, was forced to believe now, if they had any doubts before — that Charlotty's 'spicions about the preacher "skinnin' Sam King's missin' hog," were undoubtedly well founded. He took up the blocks from the saplings, referred to the two years' growth showing indisputably that the hacks were two seasons' old, and that the saplings themselves there in the brush fence showed that they had been hacked and bent over and brush piled on them, when the fence was being built.

His peroration was about as follows:

And now, speaking of "skinnin' " — I propose to do a little "skinnin' " myself. This reverend gentleman thought he saw an opportunity to take advantage of a poor widow woman, and law her out of her rightful possessions and take her crop away from her after she had it all worked and laid by — believing as he did that she had no witnesses other than herself, to swear for her — while he had all these fellers to come and swear they had seen him working on the place; but overlooking the fact that these silent witnesses that cannot lie — these saplings from which these blocks were taken — were standing there then and are standing there today, grim sentinels and watchmen, making an unimpeachable record of the whole transaction as it progressed from day to day and from season unto season; and convicting this reverend gentleman of being of the identical type described in a certain book I have at home called Pollock's Course of Time in portraying the characteristics of the most despicable of all God's creatures — the hypocrite;

> "He was a man
> Who stole the livery of the court of heaven
> To serve the devil in; in virtues guise
> Devoured the widow's house and orphan's bread,
> In holy phrase transacted villianies
> That common sinners durst not meddle with.
> At sacred feasts, he sat among the saints,

And with his guilty hands touched holiest things;
And none of sin lamented more, or sighed
More deeply; or with graver countenance,
Or longer prayer, wept o'er the dying men,
Whose infant children, at the moment, he   ,
Planned how to rob; in sermon style, he bought,
And sold and lied! and salutations made
In scripture terms."

The preacher didn't offer to come to the bat again, and the squire promptly gave his decision in favor of the defendant.

As Ballard and I were going back to the camp, I had him repeat those lines for me, and thought to memorize them for future use when I became a lawyer; but, although I have seen many mean men in my time, I have never been fortunate enough to get one mean enough to deserve it, in a place where I could use that quotation on him.

XLVII

THE STORY OF YANKEE DAM AND THE "SOB" TREE; RAFTING ON THE ELK

A FEW DAYS after the trial at Blue Knob, I went across the creek to see "Uncle Alex" Goad for some purpose, and encountered Ballard at his father's house. On leaving, I made some remark to Ballard concerning a very large service tree that stood in the corner of his father's yard, remarking that it was by far the largest "sarvis bush" I had ever seen. Ordinarily a service is from one to three inches in diameter, but upon measuring the one in question, we found it a little more than eight inches. During the process of measuring, Ballard told me that the tree had stood there ever since he was a small boy, and did not seem to be any larger now than when he first saw it. He said that from his earliest recollection it had been called "The Sob Tree"; and, of course, I promptly asked why it was called the "Sob" tree. A question of that kind always brought ready response from Ballard Preston Goad, and I have thought that at times his quick mind and ready wit often served him to formulate answers hot from the griddle, as ordered—quick service, so to speak—made while you wait.

"Of course," said Ballard, "I can only tell you the story as I have heard it ever since I can remember. This was an old, old place when my daddy moved here when I was a child. The folks that first lived here come from some place in New England, along with other New Englanders that settled up about Blue Knob and Yankee Dam. That's how Yankee Dam got its name — from them Yankees that settled in there and built the dam and the mill. I disremember the name of the people that lived here first, but any way, they had a beautiful daughter — a young girl about 18 years old, and

she had a lover, and her and her lover was engaged to
be married, and before they got married the war with
Mexico broke out and he was drafted — or any way he
went into the army, thinking — and her thinking — he
would be back in a few months and then they'd git married. And for a while she stood up all right, not hearing from him, but when maybe six months had come and
gone and no news from her lover, she used to go out under that Sarvis tree and cry and sob and sob fer her
lover, and she kept that up for several year — maybe two
or three, or four — a cryin' and sobbin' every day under
that tree, until she just natchally grieved herself to
death for her lover. That's how, they tell me, they come
to call it the Sob Tree."

I thought the story a pretty good one and repeated it
on several occasions in after years, long after Ballard
died, when I happened to be about Little Sycamore and
had some one to look at the tree and listen to the tale.
About twenty years ago, I had occasion to look in the
dictionary to find out the proper spelling and pronun-
ciations of the names of trees of that genus — whether
it was spelled with an "a" or an "e" — sarvice or service.
On turning to the word I found "Service-tree" — cor-
ruption of the latin sorbus. Then looking for "sorbus,"
I found "Sorb—the wild service tree."

It is quite clear to me now that some one who spoke
of that tree — whether a New England Yankee, or a
scion of the old Virginia stock, some of whom had
strayed into that section — most likely the latter —
slurred his "rs," so that in saying "Sorb" he pronounced
it "So'b," from which evolution, or devolution — or
what have you — it is easy to get "Sob Tree." And
when you have a Sob Tree, it is an easy matter for a fellow with the creative imagination, such as that possessed by Ballard Goad, to supply the sob-stuff.

Not long after this incident, there came a pretty hard
rain which was soon followed by a "log tide" of five or six
feet in the river, and as there were three log rafts at the

mouth of the creek ready to be run out to Charleston, preparations were made to start them out on the following day. One of these rafts consisted of yellow poplar saw logs, ranging from three and one-half to six feet in diameter, the average of the entire raft being about four feet, which, by the way, it was said, at the time, was the biggest raft — that is, contained the greatest number of cubic feet — by which, instead of board measure, logs were sold in that day — ever to go out of Elk — or rather to start to go out of Elk — qualification to explain itself later on. For the benefit of those — and there are many of this generation — who never saw an Elk River log raft.

The logs are rolled into the river at a point where the water is sufficiently deep to keep them well afloat. Saplings, preferably of white oak, because of its straight grain and toughness — from three to five inches in diameter, are split in two pieces, and used as "strapping," to hold the logs together, side by side, the strapping extending crosswise of the log at each end and secured by a wooden pin tightly driven in an auger hole through the strapping and extending about four inches into the log. When the logs are thus securely rafted together, two oars or sweep stems are provided, made of straight saplings or small trees, usually poplar, from fifteen to twenty feet long, and five to eight inches in diameter at the butt. The butt of the stem is hewed off evenly on one side for two or three feet to accommodate the blade, which consists of a plank — usually "whipsawed" in those days — from 7 to 9 feet long, 8 or 10 inches wide and about two inches thick, which is bolted with wooden pins to the stem, and set at such an angle that when the oar is in place and the small end or handle is about the height of a man's breast, the blade will be wholly submerged in the water and practically parallel with the surface. The two oars are fixed exactly in the middle of the bow log and stern log respectively, by means of "the saddle," which consists of a heavy block of wood securely pinned on the top side of the log, the thickness of the block being regulated to give the fulcrum the proper distance above the water. A round, well-seasoned hickory, dogwood or locust pin, about one and a half inches in diameter is securely fixed in the saddle, standing about six inches high. A slot is bored and chiseled through the oar-stem at the proper balancing point and this slot fitted loosely over the pin in the saddle, so that the oar will seesaw freely up and down, to facilitate the dipping and raising of the blade. To the casual observer, it would seem a very simple matter to manipulate one of these oars, and it would be attended with no danger whatever; but many a riverman has found to his sorrow that an oar on a log raft is just about as tricky as a mule, and has gotten kicked off the raft and into the "tumbling billows," by some unexpected quirk or spasm of the oar-stem in his hands, when the blade has got caught in cross-currents, or struck floating debris or a slightly submerged floating log or tree trunk. In starting out with a raft, the first thing the experienced oarsman, fore and aft, sets about to do, is to "get the feel and balance and sweep of the oar." That is to so accustom himself to the weight of the oar, the dip of the blade and the length of the arc described by the sweep, as to be able to handle it with the greatest facility and alacrity and to cause no lost motion or manpower. And another thing: the oarsman must be quick as an antelope and sure-footed as a Rocky Mountain goat, because, ordinarily, the semicircular path he travels back and forth in manipulating the oar is treacherous in the extreme — sometimes on top or side of a saw log and sometimes in the space between logs, and generally wet and slippery, yet if he should lose his footing, fall down and lose his hold on the oar, he has not only greatly imperiled the safety of the outfit, but he knows full well that under the unwritten maritime law of the raging Elk, he will lose his shirt tail as soon as he gets into port.

An ordinary log raft is usually manned with two men at the bow — oar, called bowsmen, and one at the stern, called the steersman, but on an extra long and heavy raft, it sometimes requires three men on the bow and two on the stern oar. Ballard Goad, tho a comparatively young man, had already won his spurs as the best log raft steersman in Elk River below Clay Court House, and George Acree selected him to steer the big poplar raft. I had never gone out on a log raft, and was eager to avail myself of this opportunity to make the trip on the big one, as helper to Ballard on the steering oar, and we had three men on the bow. On this short trip, I learned something of the qualifications of a steersman, by observing Ballard very closely in his handling of the craft. The steersman is boss of a log raft in motion, and does the thinking for the whole crew, while the bowsmen simply obey orders and do most of the heavy work, excepting that when sharp turns are to be made, the steersman has to work hard and work awfully quick to keep the raft properly headed to avoid rocks and shallows at times, and to keep from grinding against the bank on the outer rim of the curve. The steersman must not only know his river like the farmer knows his cornfield or the teamster his mud road, but he must know the river currents, their "draws" and eddies and swirls, which vary their tricky habits and peculiarities, according to the stage of the water — and he must likewise know exactly how "to git the advantage" of the currents in a way to make them his aid rather than a hindrance in the safe navigation of his craft. In rounding a point, he knows he must "hug the willers," to keep the current from drawing him into the bank on the outside of the curve; but he must not hug them so close as to drag on the bar or strike a submerged and invisible rock; he must know the location of dangerous rocks, the bad "swirls and eddies," lest his raft be caught in one such and "turned end fer end," and yet in avoiding such dangers he must not encounter other menaces just as dangerous. He must be able — not only once, but forty or more times in the forty miles from Little Sycamore to Charleston, to avoid Scylla and yet not run afoul of Charybdis. In the long, straight stretches, of which there were few, Ballard kept the raft as nearly as possible in the middle of the stream, and upon approaching a bend, and well in advance, he would give the order "holder right!" or "holder left!" until the bowsman, with his aid, had thrown the raft over sufficiently to take advantage of the situation — and then sing out "ease." Whereupon the bowsmen would rest on their oar, and Ballard would handle the craft with the stern oar, until he gave a further order. From Little Sycamore to Queen Shoal, a distance of 15 miles, the river traverses the wildest and roughest section of country between Sutton and Charleston, and its serpentine course for that distance is attested by the fact that to follow the road across the mountains, the distance from Little Sycamore to Queen Shoal is only eight miles; the curvature of the course of the river being responsible for the seven miles difference in the distance. In traversing this 15 miles of river, we passed over some of the worst and trickiest shoals on Elk River — Horse-Tail, Upper and Lower Dry Knobs, Big Laurel, Big King and Little Spread, all of which we negotiated without mishap — we even slid down through Twistabout, where so many raftsmen had met disaster that it had become a common saying among river men — "We seen sights in Twistabout" — without a scratch. When we reached the long pool called Queen Eddy, between Little Spread, at the mouth of Porters Creek, and Queen Shoal, we congratulated ourselves that we "were out of the woods," as the remaining shoals, although some of them long ones — Queen itself being the longest on Elk River, yet they were always considered "smooth sailing" as compared with some of those we had already navigated — when, just as we were entering the head of Queen Shoal, and Ballard was "holding her up hard to the right," to avoid some angry breakers which he saw ahead on the left, Bang! We ran afoul of a submerged rock wall right in our pathway, and had gone over it bumpety-bumpety-bump, for about half the length of the raft, before we came to a standstill; and then the raft suddenly changed ends, putting the stern, on which Ballard and I were standing, in the front, with the battered raft pivoting in the middle, on the rock wall. The strapping had broken — or at least cracked to such an extent about the center of the raft, that she was humped up in the back like a tomcat going to war. Some men over at Snyder's Mill, down the shoal a little way, seeing our predicament, got in a canoe and started to come to our rescue. From where they were with the canoe it would have been impossible to reach us in the swift shoal, except by first poling and pulling up by means of the willows and water birches, to a point sufficiently above us, that the current, by a little guidance of the canoe on their part, would bring them over to the raft. This they were in the act of doing, when the raft that had been following in our wake, hove in sight, bearing down rapidly upon us. Unfortunately, when our raft had swung around and finally settled down, the upper end extended out in the channel thirty or forty feet from the wall on which it was hung, and, when the steersman of the oncoming raft discovered us, it was too late for him to change his course so as to avoid striking us, except by turning his raft so abruptly to the left, that it would inevitably have thrown him on the breakers which he could plainly see on that side of the channel — even if he could have missed us at all. But he did not miss us! but bumped into the upper, outside corner of our raft with such force that some of our four- or five-foot logs popped clear of the water and piled up on the logs ahead, with such a grinding crash as I never before heard and such a jar as I never before or since have felt. But fortunately for the five of us on the raft — who had all huddled up on the down river end — the violent impact caused the raft to part in the middle where the strapping had broken, and our section to catapult off downstream with terrific force and velocity — so great indeed was the force, that our section of the raft, already sloping downward so that some of the front logs were entirely submerged, took a dive which would have washed us all overboard, but for the fact that we clung tenaciously to the oar-stem and to each other. By the time we "came up," and got straightened out, we found we had lost all our logs except about half a dozen — on which we were sailing gaily down the river, when the Snyders, in the canoe, followed and rescued us half a mile below. The logs in the other half of the raft were forced by the impact over to the right of the wing-wall and lodged down behind the Snyder milldam; from which place they were later and with great difficulty, on account of their enormous size, rolled and hauled out into the river, and left for succeeding freshets and "log-drives" to carry them into the boom at Charleston. From our rescuers Ballard learned that only a few weeks before, some "Government money" had been spent in deepening the chute in Queen Shoal and constructing a heavy rock wall along the south side, and a short wing-wall about the middle of the river at the head of the shoal for a short distance, sloping outward and downward, so as to direct the water in greater volume into the chute or channel; and that it was this wing-wall that was responsible for our disaster. Beyond paying his respect to a "lot of fool Government men who didn't know nothin' about runnin' a raft or flatboat, tryin' to improve navigation on Elk River," Ballard had little to say about our mishap, although I could see that he was deeply hurt and felt that his reputation as a steersman had sustained a severe jolt. I was glad to afterward hear George Acree say that Ballard was not to blame — that any steersman on the river would have done exactly the same thing.

After being shipwrecked, there was nothing left for the crew to do, except to walk back to Little Sycamore, the distance of eight miles across country.

John Stoffel and his wife, who ran the boarding house at the camp, were the only ones of the outfit who had not gone out on the log rafts, and it was several days before the raftsmen returned; as rivermen were in those days never in a big hurry in tearing themselves away from the bright lights of Kanawha Street. The river had run down very rapidly and about the fourth day after my return, I was sitting in the commissary taking shelter from a hard rain, when I heard somebody "holler" down at the river. I grabbed a coat of some kind and went down to the canoe landing, about two hundred feet away — to find Dr. Richardson, who had recently established a camp up at Big Sycamore, John Stone, and two or three other men in a bateau owned by Stone, which was just rounding in to land. I knew John Stone at the time, but did not know Dr. Richardson. Stone informed me that he was bringing up some goods for Dr. Richardson, and that George Acree had asked him to bring two bags of coffee and some other goods for him, and put it out on the bank at the landing and "holler" to John Stoffel. I told him John Stoffel was not at home — that he had gone up the creek just before it began to rain and had not returned. "Oh, that don't make no difference; I'll just put it off any way," and he began to pull up the edges of the huge tarpaulin with which the merchandise was covered, to find the articles belonging to Acree. I knew that a bag of coffee in those days meant a jute bag containing one hundred pounds of coffee, and therefore asked him not to put the stuff out there in the rain, unless some one of them would help me carry it up to the commissary. He curtly replied that they were in a big hurry — didn't have time to help me take care of the stuff — and he was going to "obey orders, if he broke owners" — and do exactly what George Acree had told him to do — put it out on the bank. I then asked if he couldn't lend me something to cover the goods, to keep them from being ruined; and his blunt reply — "Naw, ain't got nothin' to lend" — meanwhile searching for the stuff under the tarpaulin —stirred in me such a feeling of intense anger, that I burst out crying and started on a dead run for the commissary. I can imagine the astonishment of those men standing in the bateau and in the pelting rain, to see a boy "cut such a shine." It was probably their wonderment that caused a slight delay in the unloading; and what I did was to rush madly into the commissary, grab a squirrel rifle I had a short time previously placed in the corner, loaded and capped, and tear back through the rain and mud, setting the triggers and cocking the gun as I ran—arriving at the landing just as the two men in the bow were in the act of picking up one of the coffee bags, preparatory to setting it out on the bank; whereupon, with a copious intermingling of tears and cuss-words, I let it be understood that the man who stepped out of that bateau with that bag of coffee would get the living gizzards shot out of him. If there ever was a sixteen or seventeen-year-old boy utterly and absolutely bereft of reason from sheer anger, with blood in his eye and murder in his heart, it was I at that moment. The two men who had hold of the bag, quickly let go and straightened up. But John Stone wasn't bluffed a particle. That gentleman was at the time in the stern of the bateau, where he promptly grabbed a gig, and came charging over the cargo headed straight for me, standing there with the cocked gun, pointed toward him. Everybody stood aside until he had almost reached the bow, with gig poised, and where another jump would have brought him to the bank and in gig-reach of where I stood; when, as good luck would have it, Dr. Richardson, who was a 225 pounder, and who was sitting quietly in the bow, jumped up and grabbed

Stone around the shoulders, checking his mad career. Stone was a slender but wiry chap, red-headed, and of that fiery fighting complexion that goes with that kind of hair. He struggled manfully to free himself from the arms of the Doctor, but all to no avail. Then he begged the Doctor to let him go, and then I began to beg the Doctor to let him come. But the Doctor stood pat, and after Stone and I had both quieted down somewhat, the Doctor took things in hand and delivered the Solomonic decree:

"John, I'll take George Acree's stuff up to my camp and take care of it for him until he sends for it."

"All right, Doctor — you are the boss; but I hate—"

"Never mind, John, what you hate; let's get going, boys, and get out of this rain." And so the chapter ended. When the bateau pulled out and I started back to the commissary, I was trembling like an aspen leaf and so weak that I could scarcely walk; and it was two or three days later before my shattered nerves began to behave.

In later years, in thinking over the situation presented by the incident above related, I have often thought of the "high pints" arising for the legal fraternity. Supposing a fatality had resulted, either from John Stone "harpooning" me, or from me shooting John Stone? It might be said that John Stone was in the wrong, because I was not offering to do him any immediate harm at the time he grabbed the gig and started for me, and that he brought on the trouble. On the other hand, it might be said that I was in the wrong and brought on the trouble by coming there with the rifle, and threatening death and destruction to anyone who put the goods out on the bank. It might be said that Stone had shown criminal intent when he struggled with Dr. Richardson to free himself in order that he might assault me with the gig, and then begged the Doctor to let him go for that purpose. It might be said on the other hand that my criminal intent was shown in standing on the bank armed with a cocked gun, and begging the Doctor to let Stone come on, so I might have the pleasure of shooting him. I am going to leave this up to the lawyers to decide; being only too glad that no court was called upon to settle the identical question, more than half a century ago.

Some years later I came to know John Stone very well and he and I became the best of friends. On more than one occasion we have discussed the incident of our early clash, and indulged various surmises as to what would have happened but for the kindly and timely intervention of our good friend, Dr. Richardson.

Dr. Richardson was in the business of buying walnut timber on Elk and its tributaries for several years afterwards, with his headquarters at Clendenin. In the early 80's he married Miss Alice Burton, a stepdaughter of Jim Hayes who was one of the old-time hotel keepers "at the mouth of Sandy." My impression is he came there from about Lexington, Kentucky. I became quite well acquainted with him after the incident above related; but while I lost track of him many years ago, I will always have a warm spot in my heart for him as the man who saved a fool boy from a very serious consequence.

XLVIII

MAJOR A. H. CAMPBELL AND THE "PAPER" RAILROAD; THE "WICKED" TREE PEELER VISITS CHARLESTON

IN THE FALL or winter of 1878-79, there was begun the survey for a railroad to extend from Charleston up Elk River on the south side and out at the headwaters to some eastern connection; and immediately following the location for the first few miles, some little grading was done. Breaking ground for the construction of this railroad was a notable event in Charleston, and attended with great ceremony and circumstance, which was witnessed by a large concourse of people, assembled at the old brewery, which stood on or about the site of the present waterworks, just below Coal Branch. All the celebrities in and about Charleston and vicinity, and several eastern capitalists, who were supposed to finance the proposition, were present at and participated in the event. I remember that some prominent personage, probably the Mayor for the time being, removed the first "shovelful of earth," by the use of a miniature silver spade, made especially for the occasion by Charles P. Fisher, one of the two jewelers of Charleston, bearing an appropriate inscription to commemorate the occasion. The official name of the railroad has slipped my mind, but "The Black-Jack Railroad" was the name by which it was commonly known.

Major Albert H. Campbell, long a resident of Charleston, was chief engineer and took charge of the survey in person. His engineering corps, consisting of about a dozen persons, including the cook, were quartered on a large houseboat, built for the purpose, and navigated by "Tip" Jarrett — Harrison, his proper baptismal name having given place to Tippecanoe and contracted to "Tip," as in the case of his illustrious eponymist.

Tip was a son of Eli Jarrett, long a resident at Jarrett's Ford. Under "Tip's" skillful management, this houseboat was moved upstream from time to time, so as to keep abreast with the surveying party, some of the members of which would leave their work temporarily, to help get the boat over the shoals.

My father, along with several other residents of Charleston, was interested in this railroad, and one of the easterners likewise interested, a gentleman by the name of McCaffrey, who lived somewhere in Pennsylvania, was an old acquaintance and friend of my father. Mr. McCaffrey had two sons, Jim and Will, who were two or three years older than I, and when Major Campbell was making up his corps for the survey, my father was instrumental in having him include the McCaffrey boys as rodmen. In the latter part of the following April (1879), my father received from Mr. McCaffrey, a telegram stating that his wife had died suddenly, and requesting that his sons be immediately notified to come home. My father showed me the telegram, at the same time lamenting that my brother George, who was some five years my senior was not at home, so that he might act as messenger; whereupon I volunteered to go, and suggested that I get some one to go with me, and that we two take the places of the McCaffrey boys on the survey. I was going to school at the time, and was one of the two members scheduled as the first graduating class of the Charleston High School recently theretofore organized by George S. Laidley, and booked to graduate in a few weeks; and my father at first demurred to my proposal, as he did not wish me to leave school; but the matter being urgent and I quite insistent, and as he had no one else in sight for the job, he finally consented, and delegated me to find a companion, which I speedily succeeded in doing, in the person of Nick Fitzhugh. Nick and I left that evening on two of Ed Erwin's livery horses, stayed all night at Stephen Stoffel's at Jarrett's Ford, and the next mid-afternoon found the party a few hundred feet above Middle Creek, where we delivered the telegram to the McCaffrey boys, who took our horses and rode back to Charleston.

It was on Saturday that we joined the party. Nick took the place of front-chainman and I that of back-rodman, and the work proceeded with only a short interruption. On Sunday morning, most of the members of the corps lent a hand to Tip in getting the boat up over Leatherwood Shoal — one of the three longest and steepest shoals on Elk. This was done by means of a hand-lever capstan placed on the head of the boat, and about 1000 feet of one-inch manila rope. The end of this rope was carried forward as far as it would reach and attached to an iron bar driven in the river bed. Two men at the capstan, with one man at the bow and one at the stern, each with a push-pole, to "keep her in the chute" and aid in propelling her forward, were required for this job; and the boat crew ordinarily consisted of Tip Jarrett, Sam Campbell, the Negro cook, and two axemen from the surveying party; but at "off times," all the boys pitched in to help. We moored the boat right at the mouth of Leatherwood on the upper side, and two of the boys started up the creek to find a nice place to do their week's washing — when we heard them yell something about a fish, and one of them came tearing back to the boat to get a gig. Tip Jarrett grabbed the three-pronged gig from the roof of the boat and rushed off up the creek, most of the party tagging along with him; when we reached the riffle just below the first long deep hole, we saw a pike struggling in the shallow, swift water, trying to get farther upstream. Tip promptly harpooned him and threw him out on the bank, and I supposed the show was over; until the two boys who had raised the alarm, cried out excitedly and in one voice, "Aw, that ain't the one we saw — that's a baby; on up in the big hole." Proceeding as directed, we discovered in the lower end of the hole a pike about twice the size of the other — which Tip promptly landed with the gig; whereupon one of the fellows said, "Ah, that ain't the one I saw — that's a baby!" and sure enough, in the deep water near the extreme upper end of the hole, we found the third pike, which was two or three times as large as the larger of the other two. By this time, Major Campbell, who had heard the row, came up and joined us; whereupon Tip handed him the gig and showed him the fish, which was lying quietly in the far side of the pool, snug up against the edge of the cliff, in water about four feet deep, and about gig-handle length away. "Hit him hard, Major," said Tip, "he's a big one"; and the Major let drive, releasing the gig handle as he struck. The first lick was not fatal and we had quite a lot of excitement in keeping the badly wounded pike from leaving the hole and getting back to the river, before the Major gigged him for the third and last time.

These pike weighed seven, thirteen and thirty-two pounds respectively. We had luckily happened on them when they had gone or were going up the creek to spawn, which accounts for finding so many in one place.

There were four Campbells on this party; the Major, Chief Engineer, his son Bert, level rodman, George Campbell, level-man, a Pennsylvanian, and Sam Campbell, the cook; "No three of them related," as some fellow remarked.

I don't know whether the boys had caught or killed any fish before we joined them, but I know that killing those three pike stirred the "little red gods" in every man Jack, and set everybody fish-crazy; and that afternoon we had Tip take the boat across the river to the Triplet Rock, where several of us fished the balance of the day and set our poles overnight. I do not remember anything about the fish we did catch, but as they were plentiful in those days, I presume we caught a good many —but I do remember one we did not catch. George Campbell had a large pike hook which he attached to a piece of trotline, and baited the hook with a big wad of pike entrails — a dainty morsel for a catfish. He got a large heavy pole to which he fixed his line, and stuck the butt end of the pole in a crack in the Triplet Rock. Shortly after we had gone to bed that night, we were startled by a loud splash, and George jumped out of his bunk exclaiming, "There goes my pole," and went outside the boat in his night clothes. "Sure enough it was my pole and it must have sunk, as I couldn't see it anywhere," he reported as he returned.

The next morning he and I went out to look for his lost pole — knowing as I did — or at least thought — that instead of having sunk, it had been carried away by a fish. We scanned the river from side to side, both upstream and down, and then got in the johnboat to make a thorough search. More than a half a mile above the Triplet Rock — almost up at Lick Branch, we found the missing pole, afloat near a small limb protruding from a snag which stuck out of the water. On approaching the pole, we found the line wrapped around this limb, and an enormous mud-cat lying alongside the snag on the bottom of the river. On closer inspection we could see that the fish had not only wrapped the line once or twice around the protruding limb, but he had taken several hitches around a bunch of snags at the bottom of the river and had so wound and woven the line around the snags that he didn't have over six inches left free.

How to land our big mud-cat was a puzzle. We had no trouble in unwinding the line from the protruding limb, but found it impossible to disengage it from the snags at the bottom of the river, after making several attempts to do so; meanwhile our fish was lying there quietly on the bottom, looking on like a disinterested spectator. Despairing of success in that manner, we yelled for some one down at the boat to bring the gig, which we had not foresight to bring along; and Tip

Jarrett, hearing us, grabbed the gig and came running up the bank and up the road, and we met him at the bank with the boat and brought him over to where we had left our fish. Where we had left it — Yes. But where we found it—No! For in the two or three minutes absence, that fish had, as George Campbell, who, when excited, stuttered slightly, expressed it: "G-got tired fooling with us and v-vamoosed."

Two or three days later we had the houseboat up at the foot of Camp Creek Shoal, when, while we were all at supper, Newt Nichols, who lived on the head of Camp Creek, "hollered over" that he had a basket of eggs for us; and I promptly jumped in the johnboat, paddled it over and got Newt and brought him over to the houseboat. Just before we reached the stern of the boat, where I intended to land, Newt suddenly grabbed the gig, which was lying in the johnboat, and slammed it into a big fish of some kind, which, after some trouble he succeeded in landing. The folks at supper hearing the commotion, rushed out to see what was going on, just as Newt was lifting the fish into the johnboat; when George Campbell exploded — "m-my m-mud-cat, b-by gum! Look at the t-trotline." Sure enough, this 35-pound mud-cat had a piece of George Campbell's trotline in his mouth, and his pike hook firmly fixed in his gullet, as we later found.

Newt Nichols insisted we take all or the greater part of the mud-cat, as he had killed it with our equipment, and for the further reason "that it was in George Campbell's mark"; but, assuring him that we already had more fish than we knew what to do with, we not only prevailed on him to take the mud-cat, but as well several smaller catfish we had on hand, for his own use and that of his neighbors.

Our survey proceeded without incident worthy of particular note, until we had passed Clay Court House (on the opposite side of the river), passed the mouth of

Big Buffalo, where preacher Steve Weeks lived on the Fitzwater place and the Eagle Bend, where old Uncle Enoch Eagle greeted us with the news that just around the bend was a "master laurel patch that no railroad couldn't get through" — passed the home of Thumbless Jim Frame at the head of Spread Shoal and had reached those large rocks in the edge of the river opposite the mouth of Little Laurel, about seven miles above Clay Court House. Col. Fowler, a rather small man of about 60, and not too robust, was the transitman, using one of heavy W. & L. E. Gurley transits, which was a man-sized load to carry. A few days before we reached the point alluded to there had been "a big tide" in the river, which, in receding, had left a heavy deposit of mud and muck, at the lower end of the rocks mentioned. In "moving up" to the next hub upriver from these rocks, Col. Fowler, with the transit on his shoulder, chose his path over one of the rocks — the lower one — and by some mischance, lost his footing, and took a header over the side of the rock and landed head foremost in this deposit of mud and muck, a fall of some seven or eight feet, and that transit did exactly the same thing. I was at the time standing only a short distance away, as was William R. Reed, of Clay Court House, who had joined the party some time perviously, as an axeman, and we both rushed to his assistance, to find Col. Fowler with his head completely buried and his legs sticking straight up in the air; likewise the head of the transit completely buried and the legs of the tripod spraddled out and pointing upward at an angle of 45 degrees. First rescuing Col. Fowler, and finding that, because of the soft mud with which his head had come in contact, he was not seriously hurt, we and other members of the party, who by that time had reached the scene, turned our attention to the buried transit, expecting to find it a total wreck; but greatly to the surprise of all, found it wholly uninjured barring a generous coating of muck with which it was plastered. On the following day both Col. Fowler and the transit were ready for business; albeit the Colonel complained of a soreness in his neck and shoulders — and then and there proposed to me that if I would carry the transit for him "out and back," and also from point to point on the line, he would teach me to run it. I had always regarded that instrument with a feeling of respect, almost akin to awe; having the notion that it must involve an experience of years, after thorough technical training in engineering, to manipulate such a formidable looking contraption; hence I was only too eager to accept the offer and enter at once upon my course of instruction. In a day or two I was able to set up the instrument, use the vernier glass in setting on zero; taking the back-sight, turning on the front sight, or point ahead, reading and recording the angle turned, and doing all the mechanical work of the veteran transitman. It was so easy and so simple that I was astonished at my own stupidity in imagining it so difficult and complicated.

About the time we had proceeded thus far with the line, our camp provisions were beginning to run pretty low, but as Major Campbell had arrangements at Charleston that a canoe load would be sent up at certain intervals, and as they had always theretofore been forthcoming, and as the next shipment was then about due, we were not much worried. Several days passed, however, the shipment became overdue, and our provisions had almost reached the vanishing point; when Major Campbell decided we must do a little foraging on our own account. Ever since Nick Fitzhugh and I had joined the party, we had had an abundance of fish. But fish for breakfast, fish for dinner, and fish for supper, soon palls on a fellow. We also killed plenty of squirrels and occasionally a duck. But at last we ran almost entirely out of bacon, entirely out of lard and flour, and were very low on everything else except meal and canned tomatoes.

Learning that Crocket Beasley, a farmer living up the river three or four miles, had a surplus of bacon, Bert Campbell and I trudged up to his place one day and returned, each lugging a 20-pound slab of the fine country cured variety; and, whether that was where the expression originated or not, there went up the glad acclaim from our hungry comrades that "we had brought home the bacon."

In a few days we had run the line a little above Turkey Run, but as the river had by that time gotten very low, we did not undertake to get the boat over Turkey Run shoal; but went ahead with the survey as far as Crocket Beasley's orchard, about a mile below the mouth of Big Otter, now Ivydale; there Major Campbell said we would quit until and unless our grub arrived. On returning to the boat and finding that nothing had arrived, Major Campbell, for some reason, had the boat dropped down the river to the head of Whetstone, where we stuck in the head of the shoal and could get no farther. Be it known that a craft can be taken upstream over a shoal, on considerably less water than downstream over the same shoal, as in the one case the water is to an extent damned up ahead of the bow, and will have the tendency to buoy the craft; while in the other case, there being no such resistance, the weight of the boat has the tendency to displace all the water in the shallow channel, and leave none to buoy it up.

We held a council of war that night, and bright and early the next morning, I was dispatched to Charleston in quest of supplies, or the reason why. My instructions were to walk over Spread Bend and down to Clay Court House, and have Uncle Jack Stephenson send up such provisions as might be had at that place, to tide the party over the emergency; and for me to get a horse there and proceed as expeditiously as possible to Charleston, deliver a letter from Major Campbell to my father, explaining the situation, and hasten back with the answer. I found Uncle Jack at Clay Court House, and he at once set about to have some grub "canoed" up to Whetstone; but I found it impossible to get a horse, as every fellow who had one was using him in the plow. So I struck out afoot for Jacob Salisbury's, three miles below, opposite the mouth of Leatherwood, only to find that he had no horse to spare. I tried again at Hiram Lewis' at Yankee Dam and likewise at Harrison Pierson's, a mile below, but without success. Little Sycamore was the next chance, and I trudged on down there, hoping to find George Acree's fine saddle horse available; but on arriving, was dismayed to learn that George and his horse were away from home. Seeing no alternative, I decided to fool away no more time trying to find a horse, but to hike it in to Charleston. Reaching Stephen Stoffel's about 6 o'clock, just in time for a good supper, I ate ravenously and almost immediately "hit the hay," just about as tired a young chap as ever hiked the highway; having covered 38 miles in just about ten hours actual walking time. The next morning I got up so stiff and sore, that it took me until noon to walk the eleven miles into Charleston.

I delivered Major Campbell's letter to my father who on the following morning sent me back with a letter to the Major, informing him that the eastern capitalists had failed to provide the last installment of funds as promised, and that the Major had best quit the work and return to Charleston. I got a splendid saddle horse at Ed Erwin's stable and rode him through to Whetstone against supper time, to find the boat still stuck in the head of the shoal. Major Campbell returned to Charleston on the horse I had ridden, while the balance of the party stuck to the ship. In a day or two, there came a rain which gave sufficient water to allow the boat to proceed downstream. I stayed with the ship until we reached Little Sycamore, where I disembarked, and it proceeded on down the river.

And that was the end of the Black-Jack Railroad.

It was about the first of June when I got off the boat, and I put in the time either at Acree's camp at the head of Little Sycamore or the one at the mouth, until late in the summer. On returning to Charleston I found that it had been my misfortune to miss one of the most thrilling experiences that ever befell a peaceful and God-fearing community.

On a certain May morning in that year (1879) some member of the family of Dr. Wm. P. Hogue, who lived on the north side of Virginia Street, just below the street subsequently opened and now called Dunbar, discovered that one of the elm trees, of which there were several growing in the front yard, had been "peeled" during the night before; that is, the bark near the ground had been severed for about one-third the circumference of the tree, by some process which left in the bark and the sap of the wood at and above the point of severance, the distinct imprint as of the teeth of a large and powerful animal; and the bark and the point of severance had been stripped upward, some strips still hanging loose from the tree and others pulled off and lying on the ground nearby. This very unusual occurrence caused more or less excitement, and scores of people stopped to examine the tree and comment and venture surmises as to the cause. Some one present advanced the idea that a circus having been in town a day or two previously, most likely a wild animal of some sort had escaped from the menagerie and, being pleased with the environment, had established permanent quarters in Charleston on account of its many trees; and that, in his prowling the previous night, he had peeled this tree in order to lick the sap, or for some other reason best known to himself. But the interest and excitement of that morning was as nothing compared with what developed later, when on the following morning an elm tree down on Clendenin Street had been treated in exactly the same manner; on the next morning a third tree up near Bradford Street, and so on for ten days or two weeks, a fresh assault every night on a new tree, in a different quarter from the one last attacked. After the first two or three repetitions, it became absolutely certain in the minds of all, that some animal HAD ESCAPED from he menagerie and that he went on a rampage every night. Every man and boy in town who could muster a "shooting iron" of any sort, or could get hold of an axe, hatchet or other formidable weapon, armed himself early in the evening and patrolled the town completely during the entire night for the first time or two, and afterward in squad relays, in diligent search of the marauder; and this was kept up for about a fortnight, when, as suddenly as they had begun, the depredations ceased; the people breathed a sigh of relief that the "Tree-Peeler" had vamoosed and that there was no further need of vigilance in that behalf. But on the second or third morning after the troops had been disbanded, the trouble broke out afresh, within a stone's throw of the tree first assaulted, and kept up intermittently, every two or three days for a couple of weeks longer, when the Tree-Peeler went completely out of business; the last tree peeled being one on Dickinson Street, in the old Capitol grounds — and has not been again heard of, except in song and story, until this good day.

There was never any positive identification of the Tree-Peeler; but after he had been operating several days, some one seemed to discover that the mark left on the trees did not, on close inspection, show all the indications of having been made bona fide, by the teeth or claws of an animal; but showed some semblance of having been caused by a sharp metallic instrument of some kind; whereupon it was decided that there was a "nigger in the wood pile"; and the next question being to find him, a little band of young fellows consisting of my brother George Byrne, from whom I got the connected story — Tom Jeffries, Jim Laidley, Joe Jones,

Will Goshorn, Jim Mahan and possibly others, undertook that job. For some reason or other — most likely because he was generally up to devilment of some kind—their suspicions fell upon a certain "gentleman of cullah," whom we will call Joe; and they set about to watch Joe's nocturnal movements very closely. Whether due to this surveillance, or by mere coincidence, the activities of the Tree-Peeler were suspended for a few days, and the boys, believing the trouble to be at an end, "called off their dogs"; whereupon the operations of the Tree-Peeler broke out afresh, but not continuously as before; and again the boys took up Joe's trail and again the Tree-Peeler laid off for two or three days. And so it went on for a couple of weeks, when, the novelty of their job of sleuthing the elusive Joseph wore off, and the thing was becoming irksome, the boys decided to resort to another expedient. They did not have sufficient evidence on which to base a charge against Joe that could justify his arrest, consequently they decided to "frame him." Knowing Joe's fondness for ardent spirits, and his proneness to drink to intoxication whenever the opportunity afforded, and likewise his fighting disposition when drunk, they fixed it so and furnished a little money to the end, that Joe and a couple of his pugnacious acquaintances would get together in the back room of a certain saloon, where they could get all the whiskey they could absorb — and simply await results. In an incredibly short time Jack Foley, the policeman stationed out in front of the saloon to be in readiness to take care of the situation sure to arise, was hastily summoned to quell a disturbance in the back room, where he found Joe standing over the prostrate forms of his two companions, one of whom did not "come to" for an hour. Joe was promptly arrested and taken to jail where he was kept in durance vile for a period of 30 days or more. And the Tree-Peeler went out of business completely and forever.

Some of these boys, in shadowing Joe, had observed that in passing through an alley leading to his home, Joe on one or more occasions disappeared momentarily in an old dilapidated stable, the door of which opened on the alley; and after the Tree-Peeler had quit, and while Joe was yet in jail, they investigated this stable, and there found, carefully concealed, an ingeniously contrived dingess or geefus — or what have you — made something in the shape and about the size of a large man's hand, with fingers of half-inch steel, sharply pointed at the ends and slightly crooked downward, and with a handle about a foot long. On experimenting with this implement, it was found that by setting the teeth in the bark near the base of the tree, with the ball of one's foot, and keeping them forcibly pressed in, and at the same time drawing the handle forward by repeated jerks and with considerable force, the bark was gnawed or clawed off exactly as the "Tree-Peeler" had done it, and a few jabs of the claws in the sap where the bark was peeled off, left the tooth or claw prints just as found on the trees that had been peeled.

Why any human being would go to all the trouble and incur all the risks incident to a performance such as the "Tree-Peeler" put on, is beyond comprehension; but that the same was actually perpetrated on the good people of Charleston; and that Curfew was voluntarily observed by every kid in town for more than a month — albeit every boy would valiantly exclaim "Who's afraid of the big bad Tree-Peeler!" is as much a part of the History of Charleston, as that the City has twice been the Capital of the State. I have always envied the Charleston boys who took part in this performance, in which my absence from town prevented me from participating.

XLIX

THE ELK JOINS THE KANAWHA; WHO'S
WHO AND WHY ALONG THE
LOWER VALLEY

IN THE year 1881, two more railroad surveys up Elk River were launched. The first to begin was started at Charleston about mid-summer, and proceeded up on the south side of the river covering the same ground as the "Black-Jack" survey. I do not remember the official title, but it was called the "Doane Road" and the survey got along up to Strange Creek, or Birch River. In October of that year, the Baltimore, Cincinnati & Western Railroad Company began a survey up the north side, beginning at Charleston, and for a time the two projects were going forward at once, and there seemed to be a spirited rivalry as to which company would be the first to get its railroad built. Major A. H. Campbell was Chief Engineer of the Baltimore, Cincinnati & Western, and as I had been on two other surveys made under his supervision, since that of the Black Jack—one from the mouth of Big Sandy, now Clendenin, up that Creek to and up Left Hand and over to Spencer, and over to and down Reedy to Palestine, thence down the Little Kanawha River to Parkersburg; and the other from Charleston up Kanawha Two Mile via Sissonville to Ripley, Jackson County—and had acquired some engineering experience—the Major offered me the position of transitman on the corps, which I was overjoyed to accept.

Capt. Berkeley Ward, of Chatham, Virginia, was Assistant Engineer, in charge of the party; George Washington Gail Ferris, who, a dozen years later, achieved world renown by inventing and installing the "Ferris Wheel" at the World's Fair in Chicago—then fresh from Troy Polytechnic Institute—was leverman; Charlie Mebane, of Thomasville, George, a cousin of George F. Coyle, then recently established in the mercantile business in Charleston, was level-rodman; I operated the transit, and the balance of the party consisted of J. W. Dyer of Charleston, Mark, Polk, Vernon, and Grant Jarrett of Jarrett's Ford, and others, whose names I do not remember, including a Negro cook.

We began the survey at the westerly end of the old Lovell Street suspension bridge, taking our elevation for level readings, from a bench-mark out in the base of the upper stone pier of the bridge, which, as I remember, was 599.63 feet above sea level—tidewater in the James River—as established from the levels run through by the engineers who located the C. & O. Railroad.

We established our first camp on Mink Shoals Creek, just where the present hard road leading up Elk, strikes the creek after crossing the hill. We had two large wall tents used for sleeping quarters, a cook tent, and large fly, which we used for a dining room in mild weather.

It took us the greater part of three days to survey the line and run the levels, to the Conner place where the highway leaves the river and turns over the hill; and we had gotten thus far when we stopped work on Saturday afternoon. On the next day, Sunday morning, Ferris called me away from camp, and confided to me that while he was chock-full of the theory of engineering, he had never had any practical experience in the field, and that in consequence, he had gotten his notebook "all balled up," so he could not make heads or tails of it, and asked me if I could help him straighten it out. While I was wholly lacking in theoretical engineering, I had had considerable experience in running the level, and of course knew how to keep the field notes. We set about to get his notes straightened out, but finding that for some reason it was impossible to do so with any degree of certainty, we decided to go back to our starting point and re-run the four miles of levels. This we proceeded to do, and finished the work about sundown that Sunday afternoon. From that time forward Ferris had no trouble with his field notes.

In about ten days we completed the line up to a point a mile or two below Jarrett's Ford, and had moved our camp to the mouth of the little hollow, just below Jarrett Stoal, near where the old Taylor & Tibbetts storehouse stood. As I recall the names of those living along the line of our survey at the time, beginning with the Conner settlement, there were "Bub Conner, George Conner, Preston Conner, John H. Conner, Virginius Conner, called "Uncle Ginny," and Joel P. Conner, bringing us up to the mouth of Mink-Shoal Creek; then came Charlie Duling, living in the Duling Bend, and next above was Wes Jarvis. I do not remember of any house between Jarvis and the mouth of Cooper's Creek. Less than a mile above Cooper's Creek was the Big Chimney, which towered as a monument to the salt industry which had once flourished at that point. The Big Chimney consisted of a base of massive stone, ten or twelve feet square and six or eight feet high, surmounted by a beautiful red brick cylindrical structure fifty or more feet in height. A few short years ago, alas, some fellow connected with road building, either for the county court of Kanawha County, or the State Road Commission, profanely, impiously and iconoclastically—and, I might add—damnably—instigated by the devil, and without the fear of God before his eyes, wrecked, dismantled and destroyed this priceless monument and landmark, in order that he might have, in the brick and debris, material near at hand, to fill a mudhole in the road. "Imperious Caesar, dead and turned to clay; stopping a hole to keep the wind away!"

Peter Saeffler lived in the bottom at and below the mouth of Little Sandy, and Lewis H. Ewart, afterwards Sheriff of Kanawha County, lived on the point of the hill just above the creek, on the place later owned by Ed Slack. The next house was probably Aunt Vine Hammack's, on the river front, or Stephen Stoffel's, back on the slope of the river hill—whichever came first—just below Jarrett's Ford, and next came the Taylor & Tibbetts storehouse, in which resided for the time being, Sam Samples and his wife and their small son Jesse, who had just returned from a sojourn in the West and had stopped there temporarily on their way back home from the mouth of Dull's Creek.

We camped at Jarrett's Ford for about three weeks. Levi Jarrett, father of Polk and Mark; and Owen Jarrett, father of Vernon and Grant, then lived at Jarrett's Ford, on the opposite side of the river from our camp.

John T. Reynolds lived a short distance above Jarrett's Ford at the mouth of Reynold's Branch, at the upper end of the present town of Elkview; and Ben Melton, the father of John J. Melton, late Sheriff of Kanawha County, lived in the bottom above; "Doc" Cart lived at Buff Lick, a short distance below the mouth of Blue Creek on the south side of the river, and James A. Price—"Uncle Jim"—lived immediately below the mouth of Blue Creek. At that time Col. Charles I. McIlvaine, from Philadelphia, lived in a red bungalow at the mouth of Blue Creek, that he had built, on ground just across the creek from Uncle Jim Price. Colonel McIlvaine was for some two or three years engaged in making "sawed" staves, on Blue Creek, probably the first sawed light barrel staves ever made in the southern part of the state. Colonel McIlvaine was a writer of some note, and, under the pen name of "Tobe Hodge," contributed numerous articles which were published in the leading magazines of that day, one of which was entitled, "The Legend of Polecat Hollow," —and, which, as I distinctly remember, undertook to deal with the life, habits, characteristics, manners and customs of the gentle dwellers of the Elk. He called on us, out on the line one day, when we were near Blue

Creek, and some of our party, among whom being Captain Ward, Ferris, and myself, visited him two or three times at his bungalow, where he entertained us quite royally. "Colonel" Price, son of Uncle Jim—who was a strip of a lad at the time, was Colonel McIlvaine's right-hand man—in everything but work. "Tobe Hodge" was a very interesting character and wrote very readable articles. Some of them, I believe, have been preserved and are to be found in the State Department of Archives and History.

Our next camp move was to Jordan Creek, three miles below Clendenin, where we pitched our tents in the small creek bottom some little distance above where the road crosses. Ben Young lived on the river bank, immediately above the mouth of the creek; and Jesse James lived up Jordan Creek a hundred yards above us. While camped at Jordan Creek, Ferris and I learned that there was to be a dance at the Hale House in Charleston on a certain night, and, being able to get off about 4 o'clock in the afternoon on account of it being too rainy to work, we got a couple of good saddle horses, rode into Charleston in good time for the dance—left about two o'clock in the morning when the dance was over, and were back at camp in ample time for breakfast. I do not recall whether either of us went to sleep at his post the next day, but do know that I was about all in by quitting time. I do not remember who lived first above Ben Young's at Jordan Creek, but "Uncle Jim" Kelly lived about a mile below the mouth of Big Sandy, in a one-story house that is yet standing—one of the very few remaining old landmarks. While "Uncle Jim" Kelly's house was by no means a commodious one, he could "eat and sleep" more people than you would suppose could be accommodated in a house of twice the size; and Kelly's was far famed on land and water as the place where a fellow could get the best "eatin' grub," and the most of it, of any place on Elk River, not excepting the Hale House, the St. Albert, Roy's Tavern, or Sam Dandridge's restaurant in Charleston or Bill Riley's or Jim Hayes' hotel at the mouth of Big Sandy—all famed in that day for their culinary excellence and hospitality. It was while we were at and about the mouth of Big Sandy, that Jim Hayes, the hotel keeper, a widower of about sixty, returned from a trip to Cincinnati, which he had taken by steamboat from Charleston and return, surprising his many friends, by bringing with him his bride, his junior by five years, and her daughter, a very interesting young lady of nineteen, by the name of Alice Burton. It seems the widow Burton, and her daughter, were fellow passengers with Jim Hayes on the steamboat enroute from Cincinnati to Charleston, and becoming acquainted on the trip, the romance began which culminated in a wedding as soon as the boat landed at Charleston. "Dock" Woods and Morrison Copen each conducted a general store at the mouth of Big Sandy, at that time both doing a thriving business, as that point was the center of great activity in the lumber business, especially staves and crossties, on Big Sandy and for several miles up the Elk. Squire Jarrett, a brother of Levi and Owen, before mentioned as living at Jarrett's Ford, lived across the river where the town of Clendenin now stands. The only other person I remember—besides the Jarrett family—living over there at that time, was Burwell Swaar, for many years a Justice of the Peace and prominent citizen of that section.

Our next camp was at Queen Shoal, a short distance below the famous saw and gristmill operated by everybody's "Uncle" Dan Snyder, the power for which was furnished in generous volume by means of a rock wall dam, extending from the head of the shoal almost to the foot, which diverted a large part of the water via the millrace thus constituted, into the fore-bay and thence upon the mill wheel. Several members of the

Snyder and Brawley families lived in the immediate vicinity of the mill. Between the mouth of Big Sandy and the Snyder mill there were one or two residences, one being at Broad Run, about two miles above Big Sandy, but I do not remember their owners' names.

While we were camped at Queen Shoal an incident occurred that tickled Captain Ward immensely. I carried in my kit a copy of the first volume of Tucker's Commentaries, which I read at odd times, and one day a queer looking old fellow, who claimed to have been with the Doane surveying corps, came to our camp and informed us that the Doane railroad had "busted up" somewhere up in Braxton County, and that he was "footing it home," and applied to Captain Ward for a job with us, recommending himself quite highly for any place in which we might desire to use him. Captain Ward expressed some curiosity as to the position he had held with the Doane party and the old chap replied, "Oh just anything they wuz to be done, but my main job was 'geoliger.'" On being informed that we did not need anybody in that line, the "geoliger" departed, and the boys all had a good laugh, and chided Captain Ward for not availing himself of the opportunity to distinguish the party by the addition of a "geoliger"; and then some scoundrel remarked that the corps would then have been the proud possessor of both a "geoliger" and a lawyer among its personnel. And thence forth everybody spoke of me as the lawyer. A few days later, some of this same devilish bunch brought an old codger to the door of the tent in which Captain Ward and I were at work—having told him he would find a lawyer inside—and our visitor, on entering and having sized us both up, and satisfying himself by ocular inspection and comparison, as to which of the two was the lawyer—strode up to the Captain and said: "Mr. Lawyer, I was to see you to fight a case fer me. I'm goin' to sue Jim Jones fer a lie-bill, an' I was startin' to Charleston to

git me a lawyer, an' them fellers out thar told me they
was a lawyer in here, an' fer me to see him, an' save me
a trip to Charleston. You see me an' this feller Jim Jones,
we both live in the same neighborhood back here about
five miles from the river, and Jim—he use to be a purty
good feller an' minded his own business—but lately,
about a couple of months ago, he come to bein' a dis-
turber uv the neighborhood, stickin' his nose into ever
body's business, an' not tendin' to his own—an' gits several fellers around into fights an' furses an' lawsuits—
an' makin' himself a regler neighborhood nuis-ness. An'
nigh on to a month ago—me an' him ain't never had no
trouble up to that time—he loped me fer lettin' my hogs
git into his medder—"medder,"—is what he called it—
briar patch an' sinkfield, I calls it—which I had turnt
the hogs out, soon as I knowed about em bein' in—an'
tried to fix up the fence sose they couldn't git in again—
they wa'nt no fence in the fust place—an' I fixed it lots
better'n it were afore the hogs got in,—an' I tole him so,
an' that they wa'nt no stock law agin hogs runnin' out.
An' they wuz a lot uv fellers gethered up by that time,
an' I shot him purty hard; and then he gits mad an'
thows up Barbary Ross to me—an' I tells him that my
wife's a damn sight purtier woman than Barbary Ross.
An' then he up an' tells me would I be willin' to go
afore a Noterary Republican an' swear that at a certain
time I wuzn't at the schoolhouse up on the ridge; an' I
up an' tells him that I ain't havin' nothing to do with
no Republican uv no kind; and he's keepin' it up—
a-noratin' around what he thowed up to me; an' I want
him sued fer a lie-bill."

Captain Ward was able by a superhuman effort to
keep his face straight during the whole recital, being
afraid, as he afterward said, that he might do something
to cut off the copious flow of words from our visitor.

But when the story was ended, and the Captain could
sufficiently gain his composure, he said, "I'm very sorry

suh; but I am not a lawyah. You are evidently looking
for that gentleman sitting over there,"—pointing to me.

The old chap turned around and fixed on me a most
searching gaze of appraisal; after which he slowly stooped
and picked up a battered haversack which he had deposited on the floor, and remarking, "Well, I guess I'll
be gitten on to Charleston," strode out of the tent and
was gone. Half a dozen of those cusses who sent him in,
eavesdropped the whole performance; and you can bet
I never heard the last of it— and I was "the lawyer" as
long as the party held together. Captain Ward culled
out and never tired of using choice selections from the
old fellow's story, as long as I knew him. But while
Captain Ward enjoyed to the fullest, a good joke on
the other fellow, he let us in on a number of rich ones
on himself. The only one I remember sufficiently to repeat, is substantially as follows:

Captain Ward was born and reared in a rather remote
section of Virginia, and on a creek called Pohick. A few
years back he was engineer in charge of some railroad
construction in Virginia, and while engaged in the work,
an old chap whom the Captain had never seen before,
came up and engaged him in conversation, in the course
of which, he asked the Captain what part of the country
he hailed from. The Captain replied, giving the name
of the county in which he was reared, and added, "On a
creek called Pohick."

"Pohick!" exclaimed the stranger, "My Gawd, who'd
ever a thought a feller raised on Pohick, would have
sense enough to engineer a railroad!"

L

THE CAMP AT THE END OF THE WORLD

THE Elk River, seventy miles above its mouth at Charleston, in that wildly picturesque portion of central West Virginia, makes an abrupt bend in its course, where the waters, now with impetuous rush, now in placid pool, are baffled and turned to the right in a graceful semi-circular sweep of almost a mile, by beetling cliffs rising sheer from the river level, to an elevation of several hundred feet. These cliffs and their huge rocks, which, in the ages, have fallen away and found lodgment in and along the side of the stream, to the pioneer raftsman, as his craft swept into the curve from upriver, gave the distinct impression of having reached an insuperable barrier to his further progress—a cul-de-sac, or the jumping-off place; hence from the earliest history of the country, that locality has been called, and still bears the name—"The End of the World." The beautiful river and the fishing shack nearby at the lower extremity of the curve described, where the curvature reverses and turns the other way with scarce less freakish trend, are the subject of these verses. "To him who in love of nature holds communion with her visible forms," and can both speak and interpret her language —these lines are dedicated:

CAMP AT THE END OF THE WORLD

We are told of the river the streams whereof made glad the City of God
The places of hallowed habitude, ere the foot of man there trod;
The groves that were God's first temples, the valleys and mountains
    and hills,
The precipice steep and the caverns deep, the forests, the rocks and
    the rills—
These made that city fair of which poets sing, that was builded by
    handwork divine,
Far surpassing in grandeur the pretentious piles of mortar, of steel
    and of pine;

And the river which gladdened that celestial home with its waters
  that eddied and purled,
Was the stream that flows by—'neath the mild azure sky—
  By the Camp at The End of the World.

Far, far from the haunts of men remote, on the bank of that river
  sublime,
Surrounded by nature's most beautiful forms—save those that have
  yielded to time—
Is the Camp in the heart of that City of God, where all things com-
  bine to beguile,
The world-weary mind with delights of the kind that cause e'en the
  saddest to smile;
Where the beautiful Elk glides on to'ard the sea, with its liquid and
  rhythmical note,
Attuned to the voice of the myriad choir of songsters of angelic throat;
Where the morning sun smiles on a forest of flowers, their petals with
  dew drops impearled,
Where the sweet eglantine and wild grape e'er entwine,
  The Camp at The End of the World.

There oft comes a time in the life of each one; the man, the youth
  and the child—
When we hear, mid the discordant notes of the throng—and answer,
  the call of the wild.
'Tis Nature's own urging to her to return and be purged of the sham
  and veneer
That like barnacles grow on our souls as we go, through life from
  year unto year;
And we pause and reflect on the vainness of things, the fruits of our
  infinite pains,
Successes or failures, our joys and our woes, our struggles and
  losses and gains;
We pine for a respite from travail and toil—that maelstrom in which
  we are whirled—
And 'tis then the soul yearns and the heart fondly turns
  To the Camp at The End of the World.

And when the silver cord is loosed and the golden bowl is broken;
When the senses shall cease to record aright and passing things leave
  no token;
When the sun shall fade and the moon shall pale and the stars shall
  vanish from sight,
When the lights burn low with a flickering glow, the universe
  shrouded by night;
When the vain things of earth no longer allure—the daughters of
  music brought low—

When former delights have relinquished their charm and the spirit
    turns backward its flow;
When the order shall come to give over the fight, and the flag of
    life's battle is furled,
Let me sleep—let me dream—by the murmuring stream,
    In my Camp at The End of the World.

Made in the USA
Monee, IL
22 May 2023